ROUTLEDGE LIBRARY EDITIONS:
SOVIET SOCIETY

Volume 26

I0084139

WOMAN IN SOVIET RUSSIA

WOMAN IN SOVIET RUSSIA

FANNINA W. HALLE

Routledge
Taylor & Francis Group

LONDON AND NEW YORK

First published in 1933 by Routledge

This edition first published in 2025
by Routledge
4 Park Square, Milton Park, Abingdon, Oxon OX14 4RN

and by Routledge
605 Third Avenue, New York, NY 10158

Routledge is an imprint of the Taylor & Francis Group, an informa business

© 1933

British Library Cataloguing in Publication Data
A catalogue record for this book is available from the British Library

ISBN: 978-1-032-86028-2 (Set)
ISBN: 978-1-032-86058-9 (Volume 26) (hbk)
ISBN: 978-1-032-86063-3 (Volume 26) (pbk)
ISBN: 978-1-003-52110-5 (Volume 26) (ebk)

DOI: 10.4324/9781003521105

Publisher's Note
The publisher has gone to great lengths to ensure the quality of this reprint but points out that some imperfections in the original copies may be apparent.

Disclaimer
The publisher has made every effort to trace copyright holders and would welcome correspondence from those they have been unable to trace.

FANNINA W. HALLE

WOMAN
IN
SOVIET
RUSSIA

LONDON

ROUTLEDGE

Translated from the German Original of 1932 by
MARGARET M. GREEN
First Published in 1933
Reprinted 1934
Cheap Edition 1935

Printed in Great Britain by Butler & Tanner Ltd., Frome and London

CONTENTS

v

CONTENTS

LIST OF ILLUSTRATIONS

vii

LIST OF ILLUSTRATIONS

PREFACE

THERE is no lack of attempts on the part of Western European writers to do justice to the mighty events which have changed the face of Russia in almost every aspect during the past fifteen years, and this not merely in their political and economic significance for the present, but as a chapter in the whole history of the human race. This book is akin to such attempts in its outlook. It does not lay claim to that objectivity which is often arrogated against the writer's better knowledge, and which would be attainable only, if a book could come into existence without an author. Certainly, the facts recounted in the following pages are nowise coloured or distorted by party prejudice, but they are admittedly seen subjectively in the sense that the writer does not regard open-mindedness as equivalent to absence of conviction.

The conviction upon which this book is based is that a creative process on an immense scale is going on in the new Russia, in a certain sense the process of the humanization of many millions. The process of emancipation now going on in Russia differs from all earlier ones in the recorded history of mankind in that it is carried out according to plan and on an unprecedented scale. And however that process may turn out in the course of historical development, one thing has already been attained : the humanization of woman.

A fundamental remoulding and reordering of all human relations is being attempted in the Soviet state on a hitherto undreamt-of scale. And because these also include the relations between man and woman, because in the new history that is being unfolded in the land of the Soviets woman has a special part to play in all fields, because here for the first time the feminist question is conceived as part of the great social question and is being brought near to its solution through the conscious will of the community, therefore the problem of the Russian woman is also the problem of Russia—in so far as we regard it not as a political, economic, or purely cultural question, but as one of human history in the sense indicated above.

Whilst this method of approach is not alien to certain authors of earlier books on the Soviet Union, I have been conscious of a second aim in writing my book, one which my non-Russian predecessors could not set before themselves, however sympathetic their understanding. It was my design to present the universally human problem of the Russian woman not merely as one of a complex of contemporary problems, but as the last link in a chain of evolution which has been going on for centuries and which is Russian in its essence, and purely Russian. From the very beginning it was plain to me that Russia, however much one may be disposed and resolved to judge the latest chapter in her history as a chapter in the history of the human race, can for the present be judged only by Russian standards.

For the statement that the new factors cannot be understood without knowledge of the past is even truer, perhaps, of the Soviet state than of other countries. And the certainty that this is so, that we have here a single line of development, a single great historical process in which people and events bear a peculiarly Russian character, induced me to preface the chapters dealing with the position of women in Soviet Russia by a broad sketch of their past. If it seems too detailed to the reader, I appeal to the several indications in it of a link of the present with the past, as well as to the obvious fact that the Russian woman approaches the manifold tasks that confront her in the present with a spiritual capacity, a spiritual preparedness, which can only be explained historically, and which are wholly favourable to the Revolution.

I may, I think, claim familiar knowledge of the Russian character, the Russian nature, the Russian people, and Russian culture, not only because I was born in Russia and grew up there, but also on the strength of many years of study of ancient Russian art.   Indeed, it was not least my preoccupation with the early relics of the Russian creative spirit which called forth the wish to trace in the present those features of the Russian national character with which I had become familiar in the past, and to turn my attention from the history of Russia as recorded in her works of art to her genius as it was moulding a new humanity and new womankind, for I was firmly convinced that here too I should find the same creative force at work.

   Books have not only their destinies, but also their histories.   If I were to relate the history of this book in full, it would itself fill a whole book.   The collection of the material, to which I have devoted more than half the past two years in various parts of Soviet Russia, was no easy task under the present difficult conditions, in spite of the liberal encouragement and support of countless institutions as well as more or less distinguished men and women, to whom I now express my warmest thanks.   In particular I am indebted to the V.O.K.S. in Moscow, the Society for Cultural Relations with Foreign Countries, which was always and everywhere ready with information and support.

FANNINA HALLE.

Vienna,
   July, 1932.

ABBREVIATIONS AND EXPLANATIONS

Baba	Woman.
Byt	Being, existence, way of life.
G.P.U.	State Political Administration.
Ispolkom . . .	Executive Committee.
Katorga	Forced labour in the Siberian mines.
Kolkhos	Collective farm.
Kolkhosnitsa . .	Woman worker on a collective farm.
Komssomol . . .	Communist Youth Association.
Komssomolets . .	Young Communist (boy).
Komssomolka . .	Young Communist (girl).
Kossynka . . .	Head kerchief.
Likbes	Abolition of illiteracy.
Narkomyust . . .	People's Commissariat of Justice.
Narkompross . .	People's Commissariat of Education.
Narkomsdrav . .	People's Commissariat of Public Health.
Narkomvnudyel . .	People's Commissariat of the Interior.
Nyanya	Children's nurse.
N.E.P.	New Economic Policy.
Okhrmatmlad . .	Protection of Motherhood and Childhood.
Pyatiletka . . .	Five Years' Plan.
Politgramota . . .	Political ABC.
Rabfakovka . . .	Woman student in Workers' Faculty.
Rabkorka . . .	Woman labour correspondent.
R.S.F.S.R. . . .	Russian Socialist Federative Soviet Republic.
S.A.G.S. . . .	Registry Office of Births, Marriages, and Deaths.
Shenotdyel . . .	Women's Section.
Shilploshchady . .	Superficial area of dwelling.
Shilstroityelystvo .	House-building activities.
Syemstvo . . .	Provincial organ of self-government in Tsarist days.
Sovkhos	Nationalized farm.
Sovnarkom . . .	Soviet of People's Commissaries.
Tovarishch . . .	Comrade.
Troyka	The Three, committee of three.
Udarnik	Storm worker (man).
Udarnitsa . . .	Storm worker (woman).
V.U.S.	Higher grade educational institution, University.
Vydvishenka . . .	A woman advanced to a higher post.
V.T.S.I.K. . . .	Executive Committee for the whole Union.
T.S.I.K.. . . .	Central Executive Committee.

. . . And thus spake Nastassya, daughter of Nikulich :
If he is an aged hero, I will strike off his head,
If he is a young hero, I will make him a prisoner.
But should I be overcome with love for the hero,
So be it : I will take the hero for my husband . . .

      —From an ANCIENT RUSSIA BYLINA (heroic epic).

. . . But if a wife refuses . . . to obey, and does not attend
to what her husband . . . tells her . . . it is advisable . . . to
beat her with a whip according to the measure of her guilt ; but
not in the presence of others, rather alone. . . . And do not
strike her straight in the face or on the ear ; be careful how you
strike her with your fist in the region of the heart . . . and do not
use a rod of wood or iron. For he who allows himself to be
carried away to such actions in anger may have much unpleasant-
ness: if, for instance, she loses her hearing or goes blind or breaks a
bone in her hand or foot or elsewhere . . . Keep to a whip . . .
and choose carefully where to strike : a whip is painful and effec-
tive, deterrent and salutary. . . .

      —From the DOMOSTROY (Russian moral code of the six-
           teenth century).

A hen is not a bird, nor a woman a human being.
And who will bring the water ?—The daughter-in-law.
And who will be beaten ?—The daughter-in-law.
And why should she be beaten ?—Because she is the daughter-in-
law.

      —RUSSIAN PROVERB.

Every cook must learn to rule the state.

      —LENIN.

THE LIBERATION OF WOMEN FROM DOMESTIC SLAVERY

". . . instead of making fine phrases, we ought to go to the women and say: We'll peel the potatoes for you and wash the baby's napkins . . ." (*From a speech by a Soviet leader on the socialization of housekeeping.*)

The Woman: Mercy on us! The liberators have come. (*Soviet Cartoon.*)

WOMAN IN SOVIET RUSSIA

WOMEN IN ANCIENT RUSSIA

I. THE PRE-CHRISTIAN ERA

Echoes of the Matriarchate

IN an ancient *bylina*—one of the Russian heroic epics which embody traditions that have come down from the earliest times—the following story is told : Prince Tugarin makes an attack upon the city of Kiev. Prince Vladimir of Kiev sends a messenger to fetch the world-famed hero Ilya Muromets. But Ilya is not at home ; only his young wife, Ssavishna, is to be found ; she says that he will soon come. And then :

> She bids her people saddle a good horse,
> Robes herself in a hero's garment,
> Nor forgets to take a quiver full of hardened arrows,
> A strong bow and a sharp sword,
> And scarcely has she mounted in the saddle
> But she is off and away.
> And so appears in the city of Kiev,
> Before the great Prince, before Vladimir. . . .

And there everyone believes that the hero Ilya Muromets is standing before them. Darkness comes upon Tugarin and he flees amidst curses, whilst in reality Ilya Muromets " neither knew nor dreamed who went to battle in his place against Tugarin ".

Another *bylina* tells how the wife of the hero Dunay Ivanovich boasted that no marksman in Kiev could outdo her. And when she matched herself against her husband, she beat him.

The old *bylinas* sing of similar warlike qualities in other heroines. We have historical evidence of the bravery of

Russian women in the pre-Christian, heathen era in the statements of the Byzantine chroniclers, who record among other things that when, after a fierce battle against the warriors of Prince Ssvyatosslav of Kiev, the Byzantines stripped the enemy dead, they found women among them who had fought bravely in male armour beside their husbands. So, too, records have been preserved, both of the Byzantine Emperor Mauricius and the German Archbishop, St. Boniface, in which the faithfulness of the Slav women is mentioned with admiration and praise : so great is it that after the death of their husbands they sometimes take their own lives.

In this light perhaps the following passage in an ancient Russian *bylina* can better be understood : Vassilissa Nikulishna hears that Prince Vladimir intends to get rid of her husband, to whom she is devoted, in order to marry her. She resists the union and tries to prevent her husband from carrying out the fatal task allotted to him by Prince Vladimir. But her husband only scolds her for her pains ; he pays no attention to her warning and is killed. Vladimir comes to fetch her. But Vassilissa begs permission first to take leave of her beloved. The prince dismisses her, accompanied by two heroes. Then the woman seeks her dead " dearest friend Danila Denissich, bows low before him again and again ", and suddenly announces to the two *bogatyri*, the heroes who accompany her :

> Ye, oh ye, my two *bogatyri*,
> Go and say to Prince Vladimir :
> He shall not leave me lying on the open field,
> In the open field with my dearest friend, Danila Denissich !
> And then Vassilissa brought forth her steel knife,
> And then Vassilissa cut off her white breasts,
> And Vassilissa covered her bright eyes with them.
> And the two *bogatyri* only wept for her. . . .

Many traits in the figure of the ancient Russian woman as mirrored in folk poetry—in the epics and songs—and in the ancient customs, manners, and ceremonies, etc., handed down and surviving till quite recent times, justify the conclusion that, freedom loving as she was, she acted with independence in the choice of a husband, and indeed she seems to have been socially pretty much on an equality with him. The same appears from the ancient Russian Chronicle of Nestor, where we learn that during the games and festivals by the water the women were " abducted " (married) by the men according to previous agreement, or that Rognyeda, the daughter of the Prince of Polotsk, refused to marry Prince Vladimir of Kiev because he was the son of a slave-woman. In the Muscovite Russia of the sixteenth and seventeeth centuries that would have been unthinkable.

One *bylina* contains an allusion to the fact that in pre-Christian Russia women sometimes took the decision into their own hands, without reference to the man, in the matter of choosing a husband ; the poem tells of the *bogatyr* or hero, Dobrynya Nikitich, who meets a horse-woman in the open country and attacks her. But the woman " seized little Dobrynya by his red-gold locks and thrust him in her deep bag ", and, when they reach home, explains to the man that, " if she should be afflicted with love ", she will marry him—which actually happens.

This account contains echoes of the era of mother right, which persisted much longer among the Russians, and in general among the Slavs, than with the other peoples of the European family. In this connection the historian Pokrovskyi (*History of Russian Civilization*) points to the very significant fact that the general Indo-European root *pater*, *Vater*, *père* (Sanskrit *pitar*) is wholly lacking amongst the Slavs, whereas not only is the Indo-European word *Maty* (*Mutter*, *mater*, *mère*) familiar to them, but they actually have a special word to designate the son of a sister. There is also a special name for a mother's brother and a special designation for a wife's mother, who is the kind, benevolent mother-in-law among the Russians.

These and other peculiarities among the Slavs are explained by some scholars, and especially by a Viennese school of historians of civilization, by the theory that the Slavs, in contrast to the Latins and Germans, belong essentially to the type of people who adhere to mother

3

right. But these are problems which call for a certain degree of caution and into which I will not here enter further.

Nevertheless, it is of interest to observe certain facts. For instance, that among the ancient Slavs the degree of consanguinity was determined, not from the father's but the mother's side. The consequence actually is that in the *Russkaya Pravda* (Russian Law), the earliest book of Russian laws, written in the eleventh century, Article I names in the first instance the sister's son of a murdered man in enumerating the relatives concerned in a possible blood feud. So, too, it is not the father but the mother who forms the centre of the family among the ancient Slavs, and in whose hands, in the period preceding the patriarchate, lay the whole household management, the cultivation of the soil, and productive industry, whilst the man went hunting and was seldom to be seen. The fact is often stressed that in ancient Russian law the so-called tutelage of sex played a far smaller part than, for example, among the Germans. This is evidenced chiefly in the fact that women not only appeared independently before the courts but could even take upon themselves ordeal by battle. Their property rights were so far-reaching that all wives could dispose freely of their own property without the consent of their husbands, whilst the husband could not even dispose of his wife's dowry without her consent.

Slav civilization [says the Russian historian of civilization. Shashkov (*History of Russian Women*)] is ushered in by women. And until the time when, especially among the Russians, women were at last thrust aside and enslaved, that primitive civilization bore within itself such good seeds that it would surely have enabled the Slavs to hold their own with Western Europe. In that case matters would hardly have come to the name of a people regarded as synonymous with the love of freedom acquiring the meaning of slave. [At one time it was said that Slav meant slave.]

The first rulers among the Slavs to become famous were women of great knowledge and wisdom : judges, lawgivers, establishers of order and peace. Amongst the

4

Poles it is Vanda, the daughter of the earliest ruler and founder of the city of Cracow, who was equally famed for her wisdom and her beauty. Among the Czechs it is the Amazon leader, Libusha, who created a constitution designed to deprive men of all their rights and set up a feminine state. Before her death she indicated the spot where the city of Prague was to be built, for which she foretold a splendid future and great wealth.

On the threshold of Russian history stands the Princess Olga, an historical figure who ruled in Kiev for almost two decades after the violent death of her husband, Prince Igor (945–73), until the majority of her son Ssvyatosslav. She stood at the head of her army like a male prince, and avenged the death of her husband on the Drevlians in the same manner as that adopted centuries later by the Moscow Tsars, by extirpating the best men in the enemy camp. She went hunting, travelled through the land, levied taxes and tribute everywhere, arrived at Tsargrad Constantinople, where it is said that she was baptized— at any rate she was much inclined towards the Christian religion—promulgated laws, and introduced a new order ; in short : she appears as the popular " great man " of her century. And the " holy " and " wise " Princess Olga survives in the grateful memory of the Russian people as does hardly a single male prince ; the sledges in which she travelled through the land were long preserved in her native city of Pskov.

Doubtless the position of woman in pre-Christian Russian society was favourably influenced by the heathen belief in her magic powers and wisdom, her knowledge of the secrets of nature, her prophetic gifts and ability to cure disease, her sublime mission. But an additional important factor in the many-sided development of Princess Olga's personality may have been her position as a *matyeraya vdova*, a widowed mother, so that besides her princely rank she enjoyed a further peculiar privilege. For widowed mothers, especially if they were the mothers of sons, were accorded absolute authority in the family in ancient Russia in accordance with a custom dating from the earliest Slav period. In general mothers stood high in honour in pre-Christian Russia, which explains the fact that all the heroes and heroines in the ancient Russian *bylinas* were brought up by their mothers. A childless widow was regarded as an " orphan ". In the later Christian period, this reverence for mothers was transferred to the Mother of God, who is nowhere in the world so deeply revered by the people, of whom there are nowhere so many ikons—images—and to whom so many churches have nowhere been dedicated as in Russia.

We learn, too, that other princes' wives of that era— who were, it is true, like the ancient Russian princes, largely of Norman and not Slav descent—received ambassadors and actually negotiated with them. In the treaty concluded between Prince Igor and the Byzantine Emperors Constantine VII and Romanos I in 945, ambassadors of the Russian women are expressly mentioned among the Russian envoys. Not only had the princesses their own cities, but sometimes their own armies which they maintained at their own cost. And other women of less than princely rank often owned their own landed estates, villages, and moneyed wealth, which they managed themselves. Further, Russian women in the earliest period also had the right to plead in person before the courts or to appoint representatives ; in some cases they enjoyed further protection by the courts, occasionally even special privileges. For instance, if anyone wronged a woman the penalty was very much higher than in the case of a man. Some of these rights were retained even in the period of Russian history in which the subjection of women reached its climax. But by far the greater part of the independence and freedom which they enjoyed in the pre-Christian period was lost to them for many centuries.

II. THE CHRISTIAN ERA

The Subjection of Women by Church and State

THE conversion to Greek Orthodox Christianity about the year 1000, which erected a barrier between Eastern and Western Europe in the course of time, especially in what was later Muscovy, and even between the Russians and the latinized Slavs, gave rise to totally new conditions for the Russian people, and affected among other things the position of women. The essential point is first and foremost that this Christian religion came from Byzantium, and that the virgin Russian soil, still in its primitive childhood and but little removed from a state of nature—forest and steppes, north and south—was inundated by a mighty flood of sophisticated urban civilization. It brought with it a dogmatic, ecclesiastical culture which negated life and combated recklessness and exuberant spirits, and its innermost essence and protagonists were not only alien to the Russian character, but were its very opposite, hateful to its spirit. Amongst a youthful people, the youngest in Europe, a people barely stirred to life, still steeped in the powerful cosmic oneness of man and nature, a people drunk with beauty and the joy of life, monasticism, other-worldliness, and asceticism were exalted as the highest ideal. An ecclesiastical literature was transplanted to Russia as if it were a matter of course, one which combated the immorality and licentiousness of the Byzantines, especially of the women of their highest classes, but which was totally out of place here in primitive Russian conditions. The noxious flower of a luxurious world whose ideas and conceptions had gathered in Byzantium for centuries from all parts of the globe, a world full of oriental prejudices against women, her " impure " nature, her sinfulness and vice, was transplanted in its entirety to northern soil. And because that world had nothing in common with the physical and psychical atmosphere of Russia, there arose such a distorted image of woman as the essence of all that is evil and hellish that there was only means of salvation : to flee from her at all costs.

In the earliest Christian centuries, in the period of the so-called *dvoyeveriye* or twofold faith, that is the religious syncretism in which formalist, ecclesiastical conceptions were rather more blended with and adapted to the popular mythological and legendary notions—a state of affairs, moreover, which actually continued into the eighteenth century—the position of women in ancient Russia seems to have undergone little change. A woman was still the *podrushye*, the friend of her husband, and Prince Vladimir Monomachos (at the end of the eleventh century) in his famous *Pouchenye*, a kind of didactic testament, still expressly advises a man to love his wife, although indeed he adds cautiously " without her gaining power over him ". But now family relations were more distinctly defined by Christian law, and heathen polygamy and arbitrary divorces were opposed from above : this favoured the development of the patriarchal form of community, the principal of the kindred, determined by social and economic conditions and particularly firmly rooted in Russia at a later date. It also meant that women's right of choosing a husband freely—at least among the ruling classes—was gradually lost. For records of child marriages appear as early as the twelfth century, doubtless owing to the growing prevalence of oriental customs, and such marriages were of course arranged solely by the parents.

But women came to be subjected more and more to the will of the family, later of their husbands, and about the same time the *terem* makes its appearance on the scene, a most peculiar object, alike in its significance and its architecture : a building in which aristocratic Russians used to conceal their wives from all the world. This institution is closely connected with the tendency to take refuge in the idea of monasticism, which found such favour among the female members of princely families, in consequence of the constantly deteriorating position of women, that Vladimir Monomachos in the above-mentioned book could not refrain from offering his children a piece of good advice : " It is not monasticism that will bring you salvation, but good works." Nevertheless, the contemporary ancient Russian chronicles have nothing else to record of royal ladies, especially childless widows for whom the cloister became almost compulsory, but that they renounced the world, fasted, castigated themselves, or founded cloisters and churches. And it is only these pious deeds—now and then he records

8

marriages and births—that seem worthy of record and imitation to the chronicler, who is a faithful son of the Church. So matters continued in the land of Russia till the Tatar invasion in 1238, though conditions were different among the common people ; but of them we know no details.

In the fifteenth century, when the Tatar yoke was thrown off after nearly 250 years, and a race appeared upon the new scene in Moscow considerably changed and far more deeply imbued, culturally and biologically, with Asiatic Mongol elements, the subjection of Russian women was already in full swing. It is true that Sophia Palaeologos, the wife of Tsar Ivan III, received the Venetian ambassador Contarini in the newly erected Moscow Kremlin in 1476, and honoured him with an audience ; but she was a Byzantine princess by birth, educated in Rome, and that alone seems to have given her a privileged, exclusive position at the Tsar's court. Nor can we draw any conclusion from the fact that the oldest Russian free city republic, Novgorod, which had been spared by the Tatars and consequently clung tenaciously to its traditions, was led in its last despairing struggle against Moscow's appetite for expansion by a widowed mother, the famous Marfa Possadnitsa, Marfa the Regent. By her extraordinarily keen intellect, her brilliant oratorical gifts, her self-sacrifice, and her bold and hardy spirit, she stirred the people and the *boyars* to action again and again, and so came to be the last embodiment of Novgorod's freedom, a figure symbolic of the oldest Russian conception of freedom. But Marfa Possadnitsa was an exception, too, a belated flowering of the spirit of the more or less pure-bred, freedom-loving, pre-Christian Russian women, whose further development was paralysed for long ages.

At the beginning of the sixteenth century the incarceration of women was already an accomplished fact in the Muscovite kingdom. The *terem* served not only as a nunnery, a protection against the allurements of the sinful outside world, it had already come to be an impenetrable fortress, an iron wall shutting out friend and foe, an Asiatic, Islamic harem with a superstructure of Byzantine asceticism.

And now one of the saddest chapters in the history of Russian women begins. Not only were women in general regarded as dissimulating, perfidious, cunning, flatterers, blabbers, as the essence of all that is satanic, but as impure, inferior beings, altogether in the oriental spirit. In church a special place was allotted to them on the left ; they were not permitted to approach the altar, nor might they receive the Holy Sacrament through the principal door—the Tsar's door—but only through one which was opposite the altar on the left. As a bride a woman received an iron wedding ring, whilst the bridegroom's was golden. And when she was married she had to cover her hair and wear a headdress to the day of her death. If she uncovered her hair, though only by accident, it was regarded as a serious sin, as the greatest scandal. And if somebody else uncovered it, he must answer for the crime before the Patriarch's Court.

> The women's lives [writes the Austrian ambassador, Herberstein, one of the first Western Europeans to come to Muscovy about that time] are wretched. For they regard none as honest who so much as walk in the streets. And so the better classes keep their women so secluded that nobody gets a chance to see or speak with them ; nor is the management of the household entrusted to them, but only sewing and spinning. . . . They are seldom allowed to go to church, and still less often to visit friends, unless they are so old that nobody takes any further notice of them or suspects them. . . .

And the nobler the family the greater the severity with which the women were treated. The " Tsarevni ", the Tsar's daughters, hopelessly buried in their *terem*, without the slightest prospect of ever in their whole lives escaping from their slavery and being allowed to love, were the most wretched among women, and it is said of them that they did nothing day and night but pray and bathe their faces with tears.

Not only Herberstein, but other witnesses, testify to the fact that in the sixteenth century the wives and daughters of noble Russians, with the exception of widowed mothers, of whom we know that they enjoyed special privileges, might not be seen even by their brothers and near relatives, much less by strangers. Nevertheless, it happened in rare, exceptional cases, when the master of the house wanted to give his guests the highest testimony of friendship and regard, that the secret of the *terem* was disclosed and the wife, or the married daughter or daughter-in-law, of the host was shown to his male guests, on which occasions a peculiar ceremony was observed, one which strikes us as heathen in character. The Russian emigrant Kotoshikhin describes the ceremony in an account written in Sweden in 1666, but applying equally to the previous century (*Russia in the Reign of Tsar Alexyey Mikhailovich*) :

When at a festival or for some other cause guests assembled in a noble house and the banquet began, the host gave orders that his wife should appear before the guests. The wife then presented herself in the room where the banquet was being held and stood in the " wide space "—in the foremost corner—whilst the guests remained standing near the door. The hostess then greeted the guests according to the " minor usage ", that is, she only bowed to the waist, whereas the guests returned the greeting according to the " major usage ", that is, they bowed to the earth. Then the host also greeted his guests according to the " major usage " and expressed the wish that they should kiss his wife. But the guests asked him to kiss the lady first. The host yielded to their request and kissed his wife first. Then all the guests bowed to the earth before the hostess one after another, stepped up to her, kissed her, and bowed to the earth as they retreated. The hostess thanked each separately according to the " minor usage ". And then she offered each in turn a goblet of wine whilst the host again bowed to the earth before each separate guest, however many there might be, and begged them to drink the wine. But the guests begged the host to taste the wine first. The host ordered his wife to drink first, himself drank after her, and then both together poured out wine for each guest ; each drank the wine, bowing to the earth, and bowed again to the earth when he returned the goblet.

After thus entertaining the guests the wife returned with a

bow into her own apartments to her female guests, the wives of her husband's guests. Unmarried women were not admitted to this ceremony ; they were never presented to strange men.

Foreign contemporary accounts add to this description that the wife only appeared to entertain the guests if the latter specially asked it of their host ; that she was kissed on both cheeks, but not on the mouth ; that the women came to such receptions in rich, festive garments, and changed the outer robe several times during the ceremony ; that they did not appear till after the banquet, and then were attended by other married or widowed women, probably of somewhat lower rank ; and lastly that before they offered their guests a goblet of wine or vodka they sipped it themselves.

> This custom [says the Russian historian of civilization, Sabyelin (*Domestic Customs of the Russian Tsarinas in the Sixteenth and Seventeenth Centuries*)], which provides additional confirmation of all the reports of the incarceration of Russian women and the division of ancient Russian society in two halves —a masculine and a feminine half—also proves that the married woman, the mistress of the household, was accorded a high position in the circle of family friends, and that the privilege of seeing her and being entertained by her marked the climax of hospitality. So, too, we find in this custom an expression of the universal, characteristically Russian manner of honouring a woman, for bowing to the earth is the oldest and supreme form of homage to an individual.

These last words indicate the fact that we have here a custom dating from the earliest times, presumably a pre-Christian custom, still retained in Christian times, like other heathen customs, in spite of the altered position of women.

About the middle of the sixteenth century, at the time of the Tsar Ivan the Terrible, who may be regarded in a certain sense as the final outcome, culturally and politically, of his age, the *Domostroy* or Domestic Ordinance was drawn up in his immediate entourage ; it was a code of manners and morals by the Pope Sylvester, and in many respects it sums up all the attainments of the past in the moral and spiritual field. In this Domestic Ordinance, which, however, should rather be called a Monastic Ordinance, for it interdicts all that is of the world, and especially of the flesh, and fills the day and even half the night with prayer—in this Ordinance woman is already reduced to a mere object, degraded to a possession of the " domestic and family abbot ", whose part it is only to command, whilst she must obey under all circumstances :

> . . . If a wife refuses to obey, and pays no attention to what her husband . . . tells . . . her . . . it is advisable . . . to beat her with a whip according to the measure of her guilt ; but not in the presence of others, rather alone. . . . And do not strike her straight in the face or on the ear, be careful how you strike her with your fist in the region of the heart . . . and do not use a rod of wood or iron. For he who allows himself to be carried away to such actions by anger may have much unpleasantness ; if, for instance, she loses her hearing or goes blind or breaks a bone in her hand or foot or elsewhere . . . Keep to the whip . . . and choose carefully where to strike : the whip is painful and effective, deterrent and salutary. . . .
>
> . . . But if her fault is very serious, the matter not so simple, and her disobedience beyond all bounds, then strip off her shift, seize her hands, and give her a sound beating—nicely and courteously, so as to eschew all anger. . . .
>
> . . . A woman must consult her husband on all occasions about everything. . . . If she receives an invitation or summons anybody to visit her, it must only be if her husband permits it. . . . But she must talk with her guests of nothing but embroidery and household matters . . . and the way in which good wives should live and conduct their households, and instruct the children and servants, and how they should obey their husbands and seek their counsel upon everything. . . . And if she knows of nothing edifying, she must seek word of it courteously. . . . With good women like this one can pass the time : not for the sake of eating and drinking, but for good converse. . . .

The same methods are recommended in the " education " of children ; the slightest motion of independence is ruthlessly suppressed with brutal violence, and in small things and great the one and only ideal is held up of the autocratic father, the eldest of the kindred, the patriarch, to whom all members of the clan must submit slavishly.

> Russian slavery [says Sabyelin, in this connection] was never complete slavery. At bottom it was a childish state. . . . And if in actual fact a humiliating form attached to this childish state, that was only an expression of the simple native conception of the kindred, which greatly overestimated paternal authority, and in consequence all other authority. . . .
>
> And if we admit that these were the moral forces that were active in our society before Peter the Great, we thereby automatically answer the question what the position of women was in that society. For if people had not yet even conceived the idea of the value of personality, how could the notion of women's independence even arise ? For this reason women were for the most part regarded as minors, as children who must be kept in tutelage. . . .

The women confined in the *terem*, deprived of any possibility of education or intellectual activity, spent part of their time in embroidery, and raised the craft of embroidering with pearls and gold on precious brocades —the so-called " needle-painting "—used principally for ecclesiastical purposes, to such a high artistic standard that in many respects it is worthy of comparison with the painted ikons, the images of saints ; but part of their time was spent in feasting and drinking and they missed no chance of enjoying carnal pleasures. The consequence of this comfortable, overfed existence was that they were very fat. But we have proof that the men liked it in the fact that the Russian ideal of *krassavitsa*, beauty, in those days, and till much later among the common people, was the stout, corpulent woman, and always " white " or fair-skinned, of whom it is written : " May God in his goodness send stoutness, beauty will come of itself."

Adam Olearius, a German traveller in the seventeenth century, describes the outward appearance of Russian women as follows : " The womenfolk are of medium height, as a rule well built, with delicate features and limbs, but in the cities they all paint, and so coarsely and noticeably that it looks as if somebody had rubbed a handful of flour over their faces and painted the cheeks red with a brush. . . ."

He also says : " As the children of great lords and merchants have few household duties or none, they show little concern for them when they marry, and only sit sewing and embroidering beautiful handkerchiefs with gold and silver on white taffeta. . . ."

As for the Russian men, according to Olearius they are—

> as a rule big, fat, stout people . . . with a great opinion of long beards and fat bellies, and those who have such are held in respect among them above the rest. . . . They attach great importance to bathing. So that in all cities and villages there are a number of public and private baths, where they are often to be found. . . .
>
> And since the women paint themselves openly, it is the custom for a bridegroom when his marriage approaches to send a pot of paint among other presents.

But although presents were exchanged, the bride and bridegroom did not see one another before the wedding. The parents on both sides concluded the contract, the " sale and purchase ", between themselves ; the bride was regarded as a commodity, but she must be spotless, virgin, otherwise she was exposed to the utmost humiliation and insult. And

> since the bridegroom does not set eyes on the bride [writes Olearius] until he receives her in the marriage chamber, it sometimes happens that he is deceived, that instead of a lovely bride he has a misshapen or sickly one, or indeed receives in place of the daughter some friend of hers or even a maidservant ; there are such instances among persons of high rank. It is therefore no wonder that they often live a cat and dog life and that wife-beating is so common in Russia.

In contrast to the wife the husband was, of course, entirely free and sought illicit " love " even when he was married, and, in addition to all this, the bride's father would hand him a " new whip " before the wedding as a symbol of authority ; it was called *durak* (fool, idiot)

15

and was intended solely for his wife, and it was often hung up over the bridal bed.

The wife was chastised with this *durak* for any and every cause, however slight, a proceeding which was seriously held to serve a high moral purpose and was called " teaching the wife ". Of men who did not teach their wives in this manner it was said that " they did not build their house nor trouble about their souls and would come to a bad end—in this world and the next—and that their house would fall to ruin."

Women who were accustomed to such treatment had no conception of anything different and thought that they only existed to be beaten. Hence the anecdote told by Herberstein and other Western European travellers in various forms of the Russian woman who marries a German or Italian and, when he does not beat her, goes on asking him why he shows her no marks of his love until he is roused to give her such a drubbing—without observing the rules prudently recommended in *Domostroy* —that in the end she dies of it.

Olearius, indeed, disputes the statement

> that a Russian woman would assume that her husband's heart was full of love to her if he strikes and beats her much, and otherwise a lack of love and favour, as many historians declare, founding their statement on the Russian chronicle *Petrei Petreus* and certainly on Herberstein. . . . That was not my experience [he says] and I cannot suppose it. . . .

But Russian proverbs which probably date from about the same time, the fifteenth and sixteenth centuries, when it was still said in Germany that a woman, an ass, and a nut-tree only existed to be beaten—proverbs which bore witness for centuries to the position of women—present in their laconic pertinence the same hopeless picture : The husband does not strike, consequently he does not love. Those whom we love, we torment. I love her as my own soul and shake her like a pear-tree. Beat your wife, it improves the cabbage soup. To be alone is a misfortune, to be with a woman—a double misfortune. A hen is not a bird, nor is a woman a human being. Woman is a cooking-pot, strike her, she won't break. Beat your fur and you make it warmer, beat a woman and you make her wiser. A woman is like a cooking-pot : whatever you put in it boils. Twice in your life you love your wife : when she enters your house and when you bear her out of the house, etc.

According to ancient Russian custom it was the duty of the master of the house to " provide " for all the inmates, bondsmen and servants, as well as for his own children, that is, he had to marry the girls and young men. This custom the estate owners maintained until the abolition of serfdom ; among the Cossacks it was the Ataman who presented the bride to his men like a father, and a number of great lords—Grand Dukes and Tsars —did the same in their immediate entourage.

In ancient Russia the right to choose a bride himself belonged to the Tsar alone who, like the Byzantine Emperors and Central Asian Khans, looked for a bride among all the maidens of the land. Thus a special ukase was issued to all *boyars*, estate owners, and so-called children of *boyars* both in the city of Moscow and in the provinces, ordering the authorities to judge the " virgin daughters " as brides for the Tsar, and anyone who possessed such a " virgin daughter " was required, " without hesitating for a single hour ", to send her to the nearest town and, after inspection there—in which, as Sabyelin supposes, a standard stature was required, following the example of Byzantium—to Moscow. In this way sometimes no less than 2,000 brides of all classes assembled in Moscow and the Tsar's bride was chosen from among them by a process of narrowing selection ; often she was a girl of quite simple birth.

For centuries marriage in church was regarded as a privilege of the upper classes. Even as late as the eighteenth century the common people married without ecclesiastical ceremonies so long as the " double faith " survived and the struggle against bigamy, which was still widespread in Siberia, continued ; they married " without a pope ", with heathen customs " around a green willow ".

In mediæval Russia, unlike Western Europe, the " virgin-knot " never existed, nor were there ever witch trials nor public burning at the stake. But as late as the eighteenth century women were often confined in nunneries for magic practices, and likewise put to death. (The last public execution of a witch, a poor peasant girl, Anna Maria Schwegemann of Kempten, was in Germany in 1725, and the last public death at the stake in Europe was in 1807 in Spain.) But in place of the virgin-knot there was the *terem*, in which on the one hand espionage by the ferociously jealous men flourished, whilst on the other hand all kinds of women—nuns, fortune-tellers, pilgrims, pedlars—found their way in through the mediation of the numerous maidservants. Among them was a particular type of woman whose trade it was to bring young women and strange men together by various crafty means.

Thus foreigners who lived in Russia at the time state that Russian women were not inaccessible even to strangers—although Christians who did not belong to the Orthodox Church were reckoned among non-Christians and regarded with a certain horror. In such cases a special moral code actually grew up among the women : if a woman sins with a stranger, it was said, it is pardonable, for the child that may be born will be christened ; but if a man sins with a strange woman, the child will not be christened and so, because it may increase the numbers of those of " unchristened faith ", the sin is all the greater.

The men, however, did not subscribe to this theory and avenged any unfaithfulness in their wives most cruelly. Sometimes wives avenged themselves on the men by secret calumny and libel which—whatever their source —were always believed. It even occurred that women killed their husbands. Wives who murdered their husbands were punished by the law with inhuman cruelty, buried alive, tortured to death. But if a husband murdered his wife in jealousy or as a punishment for some misdemeanour, there was no law to punish him.

Foreigners who came to Russia from the mediæval

18

feudal West and—in spite of their romantic and chivalrous upbringing, which was unknown in Russia—were doubtless well accustomed to much that was rude and coarse, not only among the mercenary soldiery, were particularly repelled by the barbarous manners, the ceaseless swearing and cursing, and especially the rough and unblushing addiction of Russians of all classes to " the lusts of the flesh and debauchery ".

They are led into such wantonness by the plentiful leisure that they enjoy [writes Olearius], for you see them every day standing about and loitering in the market and the castle. And especially drunkenness, to which they are more addicted than any nation in the world. . . . The sin of drunkenness is so common in all classes, priestly and secular, high and low, male and female, young and old, that if you see them now and again lying in the roads and rolling in the mud, you take no notice, for it is a daily occurrence. . . .

Nor were matters otherwise in the fifteenth and sixteenth centuries, and even in the seventeenth, in the religious houses, which were occupied by men and women together : on all sides coarse excesses and drunkenness prevailed. And this continued until, about the middle of the seventeenth century, a reaction set in and a new wave of asceticism, native this time, arose and went so far as utter negation of sex and marriage and swelled to a vast sectarian movement which shook all Russia to the depths ; and this movement produced a number of outstanding women leaders. Chief among them was the *boyar* lady, Morosova, a charitable widow closely connected with the Court. She was the most zealous follower of the protopope, Avvakum, who led the obstinate struggle of the Raskol schism, the dying ecclesiastical dogma of ancient Russia, against the Patriarch Nikon, the Russian religious reformer and pioneer of a new age, who counted the Tsar among his disciples. The fanatical *boyar* lady, Morosova, whom nothing would induce to abandon the Byzantine law which had already reached a state of petrifaction in Russia and was barely recognizable, was imprisoned and tortured, the martyr and heroine of an idea, though an idea no longer tenable. She died as the wives of the pre-Christian Russians died on the battlefield at the side of their husbands—exciting the admiration even of their enemies—and as Russian women again died heroically barely 200 years later in the revolutionary movement fighting against the domination of the Tsars.

It was no longer possible to delay the dawn of a new age.

THE DAWN OF A NEW AGE

THE EXTERNAL REFORMS OF PETER THE GREAT
AND CATHERINE II

JUST as a woman stands at the threshold of the earliest period of Russian history, Olga, Princess of Kiev, so this first chapter of Russia's history, in which the idea of Muscovite Byzantinism reached its climax, triumphed on all sides, and then collapsed within itself, was concluded by a woman. But this time it was not a widowed mother, but the Tsarevna, the Tsar's daughter, Ssofya, the sister of Peter the Great, some years older than he was, an ambitious, intriguing woman who had grown up in the *terem* and was a true child of the pharisaical atmosphere that prevailed there. She was given to excesses and equal to anything, however shameful, but outwardly she appeared as an advocate of fasting, prayer, and asceticism, addicted to none but pious deeds. And as her brother Peter was still too young to assume the reins of government, her path led to the throne instead of the nunnery, for she stopped at nothing and followed in the footsteps of many an imperial predecessor in Byzantium, an indirect descendant and the last of their kind.

And now on a single occasion during the four centuries of its existence the *terem* celebrated a belated victory. But only for a short time. Only until the young Tsar Peter, who was to have been supplanted by his sister, grew up and seized the reins of government with a firm hand in 1689, sweeping away the Tsaritsa Ssofya together with the *terem* and everything connected with it.

Peter the Great, who proved to be a great reformer in the matter of Russian womanhood as well as in other things, took the first step towards the liberation of women from slavery in his edict of 1704. Parents and relatives

21

were forbidden to force a daughter to marry. The betrothal was to take place six weeks before the marriage, and after that the bride and bridegroom were to be allowed to meet without hindrance. If during this period they were not attracted to one another, they were free to abandon the marriage. Parents and guardians were required to take an oath that the young people had not been forced into marriage, and estate owners were required to take a similar oath in respect of their serfs. This decree abolished compulsory marriage in Russia, at least in theory ; but it chiefly affected the well-to-do classes. The innovation made no difference to the women of the common people ; they were abandoned to the arbitrary will of their overlord so long as serfdom persisted, just as much as they were to that of their husbands until the October Revolution of 1917. We have proof enough of that in the sad, heartrending folk-songs and poems which nearly always lament the " bitter lot " of a woman who must give herself to one whom she does not love.

Nevertheless, a new era dawned with Peter the Great : a new page in Russian history and also in the history of Russian womanhood was turned. Russia, with her double, Eurasian aspect consequent on her geographical position, had long had her face turned towards the East ; she now turned to the famous " window looking out upon Europe ", and the colossal organism, now stirring slowly, was violently wrenched into two unequal parts.

Russians who travelled abroad, and there saw women self-assured, free, conscious of their strength and their æsthetic and moral worth to society, were struck dumb with amazement. The accounts that they give are full of astonishment at what they have seen and experienced. And their families at home learned with no small wonder of the " extraordinary miracle " that " the womenfolk there are agreeable, well-bred, pleasant, and free ; they even interest themselves in politics and constantly appear at public festivals, a thing which is considered honourable and freely permitted. . . ." (Pekarskyi, *Learning and Literature at the Time of Peter I.*)

Before long " assemblies " were introduced in the Tsar's new capital of St. Petersburg, founded in 1703—feeble imitations of the Versailles evenings, " free gatherings in some house ".   All of a sudden the doors of the *terems* opened wider than ever before.   The women, who had hitherto known only their national dress, were put into whalebone and modern European clothes and appeared in the salons together with their husbands, whose long beards and full coats had been forcibly removed unless they had already discarded them voluntarily.   There, on new, polished parquet floors the minuet was danced in the European fashion and instruction was given in elegant manners under the guidance of Swedish and French prisoners.   But it is obvious that this newfangled fashionable society still belonged at the bottom of its heart to the remote Middle Ages, to the dark corridors of the Moscow Kremlin.   And so, even at a later period, foreign visitors complained that on these evenings people smoked in the presence of ladies, and that the women, stiffly decked out, always held a little aloof from the men and stared at one another, and that the fine gentlemen usually got so immoderately drunk that they had to be carried home by servants who were hardly less drunk.   For, indeed, Tsar Peter had himself decreed that anyone who offended against so-called good manners was to be punished by drinking from the " goblet of the great eagle ", assuredly no small matter. Masked balls were arranged too, and cavalcades with gentlemen and ladies in disguise : fools' festivals, great Councils under the presidency of a Prince-Pope surrounded by totally drunken cardinals, and the like.

Outwardly Western European fashions came more and more to prevail, and although inwardly nothing was changed for the time being, yet woman, hitherto the " satanic creature, the offspring of the devil, a temptress and nothing more ", gradually evolved under foreign influence—only, it is true, among the upper classes—to " the most marvellous of nature's creatures ", of whom the poet Lomonossov actually sings : " Oh, ye heroines of Russia ! "

With Catherine I, the widow of Peter the Great, for the rest a small, insignificant woman, that epoch of women on the throne was ushered in in the Russia of the eighteenth century which an Italian historian has described as a perpetual " tragedy in a house of pleasure ". Under Catherine II French influence on the Russian upper class became marked ; she was a German princess by birth, actively associated with Voltaire, Grimm, Diderot, and other French philosophical Encyclopædists ; she summoned the sculptor Falconet to St. Petersburg and herself wrote plays, satires, fairy-tales, and memoirs. The whole Court lived in the same scandalous manner as that of Louis XIV and Louis XV, with the one difference that here instead of the French ladies who enjoyed great favour there were masculine favourites, chief among whom was Prince Potyomkin, " the Pompadour " of the Tsaritsa Catherine II. And so the vital instincts of the upper-class women, so long suppressed in the captivity of the Moscow *terems*, began, under the patronage of the empress, to find an outlet in wild excesses —marked by brilliance and grace, perhaps, but overstepping all bounds. And although at the same time these women, like Catherine herself, wrote both witty and allusive plays, and displayed a certain degree of culture and some intellectual interests, nevertheless, as a Russian historian of civilization has said of them, they represent " a generation of young girls of high moral character who, when they grew up, turned into courtesans ". But in the middle of the nineteenth century not only women, who in the interval had been fully roused from their ignorance and lethargy, but also the leading intellectuals among the men declared ruthless war upon this type of Russian " young lady ", dating from the time of Catherine II and existing only for men.

In order to " overcome still further the prejudices of past centuries and to give the people a new type of education ", Catherine also introduced educational reforms. But they were only half carried out, for there were not enough educators in Russia. Nevertheless, schools were opened in a few large towns, and in the Ssmolnyi Convent, at a later date the most aristocratic seminary for the daughters of noblemen, four hundred and eighty girls were housed under the direction of a Frenchwoman and taught foreign languages and the fine arts.

In 1783 an Academy was founded in St. Petersburg on the model of the French Académie des Sciences ; subsequently it was attached to the Academy of Learning, and its function was to " establish the rules of orthography and grammar and to promote the study of Russian history ". All the literary men of the period—including Dyershavin and Fonvisin—besides a number of women of the upper classes, joined the Academy and co-operated in its work. The Princess Dashkova was made its President, whereby a woman was accorded a position only accessible to her in the new Russia of to-day, never in Tsarist Russia. It is true, indeed, that Katharina Dashkova was an exceptional woman ; she had been interested in politics from her earliest youth and at the age of eighteen she inspired and carried out the *coup d'état* of 1762 by which the feeble-minded Peter III was deposed and Catherine II placed upon the throne. Like the Empress, she was in lively correspondence with all the European celebrities of her time ; she made the personal acquaintance of Voltaire and Diderot when travelling in Europe, both of whom speak of her with enthusiasm, and Alexander Herzen describes her as " a Russian feminine personality in whom we are conscious of the sparkling, still somewhat unbalanced forces which were already bursting forth, rescued by Peter from the stagnation of Moscow ". But Princess Dashkova stood practically alone in her age and society, and so, after the death of Catherine II, when storm clouds gathered once more around the Russian throne, she was obliged to retire into exile, to a remote village, whence she was later rescued by her friends.

Like the reforms of Peter the Great, the " enlightened absolutism " which marked the time of Catherine II, with all its Western cultural influences and administrative innovations, only touched the surface of the Russian society of the day without penetrating deeper into the organism. The common people were wholly unaffected by it all. Nay, more : the process of reducing the peasantry, hitherto relatively free to move at will, to a state of bondage, a process which began at the end of the sixteenth century and assumed the form of serfdom under Peter the Great, was finally completed during the reign of Catherine II. The farm servants were made over body and soul to the *barin*, the estate owner, the last traces of individuality were wiped out, and the miserable family life of the peasant was gradually subjected to the tyranny, the arbitrary power, of the lord. People were married to one another without the smallest consideration whether they were willing or not. The *jus primae noctis* was gradually established, and later cases frequently occurred in which masters made the serf girls whom they had violated strip naked and set the dogs upon them. . . . And so there was probably no outrage, no treatment however shameful, to which these serf girls and peasant women had not to submit. All the barbarism, all the fits of sadism and tyranny on the part of the men— invariably aggravated by immoderate drinking—which hitherto the mass of Russian women had suffered were now transferred to these poor creatures.

In the first half of the nineteenth century it actually happened often that serfs were sold without land. And it was not uncommon at that time for advertisements to appear in the papers like this : " For sale : a maidservant, about thirty years old, a young brown mare. Inspection at the house of the Government Secretary." It must be stated at once, indeed, that there were also exceptional cases in which serfs, if they had distinguished themselves by special talents, devotion, faithfulness, or other quali- ties, were either freed altogether by their masters or else taken into the house and counted as members of the family ; sometimes, in fact, their deeds won them im- mortality. There is a famous case of this kind known to Russian literature : the *nyanya* or nurse of the poet Pushkin, Arina Rodionovna, played the same part in the poet's life as Goethe's mother in his ; she had a genius for telling fairy-tales and singing songs and had an unusually imaginative and wide command of language, and she it was who first initiated her charge into the spirit and beauty of the Russian language and had a certain share in determining his poetical development. The poet was devoted to her to the end of his life and dedicated a number of poems to his " little old dove ", " his friend in hard times ".

But let us resume. In the reign of Alexander I (1801–25), which " opened with the Messianic idea and ended with Arakcheyev's knout " and in which the Universities of St. Petersburg, Charkov, and Kasan were founded—whilst Moscow University, already in existence, was a foundation of the Tsaritsa Yelisaveta Petrovna, the daughter of Peter the Great—the position of Russian women continued to be governed on the lines laid down by the Tsar's grandmother, Catherine II. True, French novels formed part of the mental nourishment of the so-called educated Russian woman even then, but she had hardly been stirred to a sense of her own personality, and the great French Revolution, which at first only bewildered Russia, did not exercise its influence upon men's minds and souls till much later. If we read Tolstoy's *War and Peace*, a novel of the times of the Napoleonic wars, we are astonished how the women there depicted—the sisters Karagin, Vera Rostova, Ellen Besukhova—who speak French only and exist solely for their husbands and children, go blindly on their way and how little they are affected by the events around them. The same is true of Gogol's ladies, " simple and agreeable ", and " agreeable in every respect ", as also of the colourless, empty feminine character which the poet Griboyedov has presented in his classical comedy, *Woe to the Man of Intellect.* In actual life only the celebrated Durova, who was wounded as a cavalry-woman among the soldiers in the battle of Borodino against Napoleon, recalls the masculine bravery of the Russian heroines of pre-Christian times. For the rest, the Napoleonic wars robbed a large number of women of their husbands and of the prospect of marriage. In the effort to give a new meaning to their lives, these poor creatures wandered about like lost souls and turned to all kinds of mystic and pietist doctrines, frequently to Catholicism. It was not till the next generation, when the influences of the great French Revolution began to make themselves felt, that a new type of woman appeared, the type of nineteenth-century Russian woman. And she it was who proved a link in the chain of development which the Middle Ages had interrupted from the pre-Christian Russian woman to the modern woman of modern Russia.

First in the train of these women comes that favourite character in Russian literature, the beautiful, passionate, and courageous Tatyana Larina of Pushkin (in *Yevgenyi Onyegin*), the first who dares to confess her love to a man and thereby grows in a sense above his stature ; and soon afterwards we come across them in real life too.

For hardly had Nicholas I ascended the throne when the clash of opposing elements began. The first sign of protest discernible at a distance was the revolt, on December 14th, 1825, of a brave band of officers and intellectuals, influenced chiefly by the French Revolution, who had joined together after the " patriotic war " of 1812, and whose undertaking was condemned to failure from the outset for practical reasons of organization ; Pokrovskyi calls it " the first and last attempt at a middle-class revolution in Russia ". Colonel Pestel, one of the leaders of the Decembrists, wrote to Tsar Nicholas before his execution : " Your Majesty, I was led by the love of our people to commit a crime against you. I could not belong to society, because I have never desired anything for myself. I belong to the whole community and am ready at any moment to shed the last drop of my blood for the good of mankind and for love of it." His comrades were of the same mind and four of them died with him. All the rest of the " secret society " was sent to Siberia, but the men did not go out to the darkness and the wilderness alone. Almost all of those who were condemned to forced labour in the horrible mines in the primitive conditions of the Siberia of those days were accompanied voluntarily by their wives, a few by their sisters and mothers. . . .

Did these Decembrist women share their husbands' convictions ? Records published at a later date, especially the Memoirs of Princess M. Volkonskaya who at the age of eighteen—she was twenty years younger than her husband—sacrificed a life of brilliance and wealth without a moment's shrinking, show that many of these women understood and shared their husbands' ideals and knew of their plans, so that they too served their husbands' cause. Before Princess Volkonskaya was allowed, as " the wife of a political offender ", to travel in a carriage the 6,000 versts to her husband in Nyerchinsk, she had to renounce in writing all her rights, even her personal family life, and she left her child behind with relatives, for she was not allowed to take it with her ; deeply moving is the simple account she gives of her first meeting with her husband who, like all his comrades, was chained hand and foot on the day of his arrival in Siberia :

> . . . Ssergei rushed to meet me. The clatter of his chains staggered me : I did not know that he was fettered. The sight of those chains so stirred and affected me that I fell on my knees and kissed his chains first, and himself afterwards. . . . I only saw him twice a week [she continues]. In the early days of our exile I thought it would certainly be over in five years. Later I told myself that it would be ten years. Still later—fifteen. But after twenty-five years, I stopped expecting. . . . I prayed God for one thing only : that he would let my children (she had given birth to two children in exile) get away from Siberia. . . .

The coronation manifesto of Alexander II (1855) restored their freedom to the exiles—after thirty years : they were allowed to return home. But as many had died or been killed in the meantime, their number had been reduced from 121 to about 31 men.

It would be vain to seek in the eighteenth century for parallel cases—for women like Yushnevskaya, Fonvisin, Muravyova, Davydova, Naryshkina, Rosen, Yentaltseva, Pol, the three Bestushev sisters, Torsson's mother and sister—many of whom spent their whole lives with the

exiles beyond the icy Altai Mountains, in Chita and
Nyerchinsk. These were wholly of the nineteenth
century ; like their husbands, they were the children of
the great French Revolution and the Napoleonic tempest,
and they already anticipate the generation of protesting
Russian women who succeeded them. And so the poet
Nyekrassov erected a magnificent memorial forty years
later to the two " exiled princesses ", Volkonskaya and
Trubetskaya, in his lyrical epic *Russian Women*. And
Vera Figner in the Moscow " Museum of the *Politkatorshan* " (abbreviation for " political offenders condemned
to hard labour ") has dedicated these words to the
portraits of the Decembrist women exhibited there :
" Spiritual beauty is a kind of beauty which remains
living through long ages, and the captivating personality
of the women of the second quarter of the last century
still shines for us in the imperishable glory of past times.
Their deprivations, losses, and moral sufferings unite
them in a sisterhood with the women of later revolutionary generations."

In the sombre epoch of Nicholas I (1825–55) Russian
despotism—" absolute monarchy mitigated by murder ",
to quote the Marquis de Custine—reached its climax.
All mental vitality was frozen and petrified, and people
hardly dared breathe. And yet it was precisely in these
years that great Russian literature and journalism arose
out of a submerged, burning indignation which welled
up in a mighty stream carrying all that was creative with
it : the activities of Herzen, Granovskyi, Turgenyev,
Pushkin, Lermontov, Byelinskyi, Chaadayev, and others
swept on in advance of their age.

As regards women, it was the classical period of
marriages that were unhappy because they were unequal,
and of " misundertood wives " : girls of delicate refine-
ment and high birth, the so-called " muslin misses ",
educated in the aristocratic Ssmolnyi Institute, suffered
under husbands who were rough and cruel and often
brutish. And so literature (especially the works of
Pissyemskyi) is shaken by a deep groan, a barely suppressed cry of agony, on behalf of Russian women who

felt themselves humiliated and wounded in their marriages, and many future champions of feminism, including Nyekrassov, whose whole work is overshadowed by
the vision of his mother bowed down by sorrow, sprang
from these tragedies of family life. That was why the
banner of woman's liberty which George Sand raised
about that time was greeted in Russia perhaps with more
joy and enthusiasm than anywhere else. All that was of
worth in Russian literature and intellectual life looked to
George Sand as a prophetess and followed her teaching
and her ideas. Except Byron, there is hardly a single
foreign writer who has exercised so strong and lasting
an influence upon Russian literature and the minds
of Russian women as this champion of women's emancipation.

The seed fell upon fruitful soil. On all sides there was
an eager desire for education, for an escape from the
existing cramping limitations, which a few pre-eminently
gifted women—Stassova (the sister of the celebrated
historian of art), Likhachova, and others—tried to satisfy
by studying hard alone. " My youth was without a
care, without any serious purpose or any other aim but
pleasure," writes Stassova, and characterizes thereby the
whole life of middle- and upper-class women in the
'thirties and 'forties of the past century. The Tsaritsa
Marya Alexandrovna and the influential inspector of the
Grammar Schools of St. Petersburg showed great sympathy with the educational aspirations of women. And
education, hitherto the monopoly of birth and wealth,
was made accessible to all girls, without distinction of
rank, by the establishment of " Marya Grammar
Schools ".

If, now, we glance at the rising Russian literature of
the 'fifties and at the female characters which it depicts
with loving devotion, we find a very different picture, and
yet, as we note with interest, always the same : a woman
of strong character, insufficiently equipped for the
struggle of life, seeks an answer to the miserable question
of escape from her satiated, selfish existence, and would
like to perform some selfless, liberating deed. With that

object she usually turns to a man who, though he is
talented, eloquent, and her superior in knowledge, is her
inferior in strength of will and incapable of social or
other service : a " superfluous person ".   Such are both
Olga and Oblomov in Goncharov's books, as well as
Turgenyev's women.   And it is a remarkable if not
characteristic trait that Russian men are so seldom equal
in energy to their vigorous mates that realist writers are
sometimes reduced to giving their women characters as
husbands purely imaginary, fantastic conspirators or
foreign busybodies, instead of native Russians (for instance, the Bulgarian Inssarov in Turgenyev's *On the
Eve*, and the German Scholz in Goncharov's *Oblomov*).

But already the time was at hand—at the end of the
'fifties—when a universal tremor, an awakening from
centuries of sleep, the first great Russian awakening,
passed tempestuously over the land.   It was not in vain
that all the best minds, all the representatives of progressive thought in Russia, had been demanding reforms for
decades.   It was not in vain that Alexander Herzen's
Bell had rung the alarm from " another shore ".   Defeat
in the Crimean War finally revealed the utter rottenness
of the prevailing political and economic system and made
plain how out of date it was.   Not only all sections of
society, but even the Government, at last realized how
untenable was a social order based upon serfdom which
blocked the path of all free economic development, all
development of the country's productive forces ; and the
Government began to yield.   The oppressive hand of
the censorship was lightened, so that the press could give
voice to opinions on burning questions.   A number of
judicial reforms were discussed.   Later they were actually
carried out, and especially the question of abolishing
serfdom was seriously considered.   A new generation
arose of " rationalists ", publicists, and moralists—Chernyshevskyi, Dobrolyubov, Pissarev, Pomyalovskyi, and
others—who put up a brave and resolute fight for a
fundamentally new philosophy of life, a new social order,
new ideals.   An intellectual revival set in, an eager craving for culture and knowledge, and this swept along all

sections of the population, even in the remotest provinces. On all sides public libraries, reading circles, Sunday classes, and societies of people trying to educate themselves sprang up. A breath of freedom swept through the universities.

The Slavophils' discovery of the Russian national character, which was to provide the foundation for the social structure, brought lower-class women to the fore, who had hitherto been seriously neglected. Turgenyev is one of the first to make a serf woman the subject of study, in his *Papers of a Sportsman*; besides several others he depicts the tragic figure of the waiting woman whose master has her hair cut off and sends her away to the village because she has dared to fall in love with a man. But instead of calling for struggle and protest, Turgenyev appeals for gentleness and forgiveness. Ssaltykov-Shchedrin is much more strongly opposed to the system of serfdom. His story of Mavrushka, the wife of the serf Pavel, is deeply moving. Originally free, she marries Pavel, whom she loves, and so becomes herself a serf. Yet her mistress does not think her humble enough. Strife breaks out. But Mavrushka remains firm and proclaims a hunger-strike. It is an unequal fight, however, and in the end Mavrushka hangs herself.

Ostrovskyi, the creator of the Russian theatre, took up the cause of women of the trading class and wrote his drama *The Tempest*. Pissyemskyi's moving piece *The Bitter Lot* again concerns the wretched life of the peasant woman, and Pomyalovskyi, who throws a light upon the life of the small officials in his *Lower Middle-Class Happiness* and there lets fall the expression " muslin miss " with a touch of scorn, finds women of fine character even among the daughters of this narrow class, women who, like most in Russia at this period, were consumed with longing for " a different life ". The priest's daughter, too, now takes her place in the ranks, and shortly afterwards the prostitute makes her first appearance in Russian literature, in the works of Dosto-yevskyi. From all manner of obscure corners the

" injured and insulted " were dragged forth to the light of day : the whole of life assumed a new aspect.

But the forerunner of the next generation of writers, who concerned themselves exclusively with types from the masses of the people, was the poet of *Russian Women*, whom we have already mentioned, and of *The Mother*, Nyekrassov, whose poems, springing from the suffering lives of the peasant women, are one ceaseless, tormented cry for the abolition of slavery and for reforms, a flaming accusation of the existing order.

Here is one of these accusing poems : the melodious *On the Road*. The poet is travelling by mail-coach, and the driver tells him about his wife, who was brought up in her master's house. There she acquired not only aristocratic manners, but also aristocratic habits, and when one day the whim of her *barin*, the master, determined that she should become the wife of an obscure peasant, two lives were involved in a chain of miseries.

Or the typical portrait of a toiling peasant woman : Darya is the wife of the peasant Prov. Her life is filled with hard work and constant anxiety about the children. And yet she is a strong, handsome woman, " bearing on her brow the mark of the capable and strong." Like so many in the Russian land settlements " Darya's expression is serious and tranquil, her movements vigorous, and her gait and glance show her to be every inch a queen." At work, the poet goes on to depict her, when she stands with loosened hair, sickle in hand " in the midst of the tall corn ", she is always patient and bears hunger and cold with equanimity, and when she reaps each sweep of the arm brings down a whole sheaf of corn. Even when they bury her husband, Darya does not neglect her work. It is hard for a woman to lose her husband, the father of her children, and moreover her comrade in labour. But she has hardly dried her tears when the young widow hastens to the forest—in mid-winter—to cut wood. When she gets there she gives herself up during the heavy toil to memories of her life with her husband, sheds bitter tears and laments, and sinks in her weariness almost into a state of unconsciousness. She dreams that she has been working for a long time without her husband and is troubled and uncertain whether she can manage the labour of house and farm alone. . . . But during this waking dream the poor peasant woman Darya freezes to death—a symbol of the " bitter lot " of many such Daryas, of the lot of the Russian serf woman.

THE LIBERATION OF THE PEASANTS AND THE EMANCIPATION OF WOMEN

> Three hideous portions to woman Fate gave :
> The one : to a slave to be mated,
> The second : the mother to be of a slave,
> The third : to a slave subjugated.
> And each of these burdens has heavily lain
> On women of Russia's domain.
>   —NYEKRASSOV (*translated by* JULIET SOSKICE).

ON February 19th, 1861, the abolition of serfdom was proclaimed in the famous Manifesto of Tsar Alexander II, and thereby the " aristocratic " period of Russian history reached its end and passed away. The event was an important turning-point in the history of Russian woman likewise.

In the immediately preceding years the feminist question had entered upon the practical phase following that of discussion in literature which, more than anything else, had championed and served the cause of women, had helped to awaken their social and intellectual interests, to enlarge the sphere of their domestic activities, and demanded their admission to all branches of education and work—here we need only mention the names of Byelinskyi, Herzen, Pissarev, Dobrolyubov, Chernyshevskyi, Mikhailov, and Shashkov.

At the time of the Crimean War, in the mid-'fifties, there were already 148 secondary schools for women in Russia with 168,000 pupils. A number of freedom-loving women authors raised their voices, and among them at the end of the 'fifties the name of Marko-Vovchok emerges, who described the sufferings of the serfs and made a great stir. From 1859 onwards a special women's

journal appeared, *Rassvyet* (Daybreak), and in the autumn
of the same year came the longed-for opening of the doors
of the University of St. Petersburg to women who aspired
to study : Korssini was the first woman to attend lectures
in the Faculty of Law, and others followed her example
till by 1860 there were several dozens of them. The
same process was repeated in Charkov. Three years'
teachers' courses were opened for 250 women students
who had attended a girls' grammar school or a recognized
institution.

A vigorous fight was put up for the admission of women
to the study of medicine, which the Government resisted
because it regarded this as the culminating point of the
women's movement, exercising a revolutionary influence
upon the youth of Russia. But in 1861 this stronghold,
too, was captured, and Nadyeshda Ssusslova—curiously
enough, a peasant's daughter—made her appearance as
the first woman medical student in Russia in the lecture
halls of the Medical Academy in St. Petersburg. But
she, together with two other women who joined her—
Bokova and Koshevarova-Rudnyova—were not long
tolerated there, and in 1863 the three had to emigrate
to Zurich where, among a total of four women students,
two Russians had studied medicine as early as the beginning of the 'forties ; here they completed their studies
with brilliant success in 1867–8. Their example soon
gathered a following and hosts of Russian women
students now made their way to Switzerland, only stimulated the more in their efforts by the opposition of the
Russian authorities to women students of medicine.
Thus in the summer half of 1873 there were 96 Russians
among 110 women students at Zurich University, mainly
intending doctors. True, the Russian women students
were recalled home in the same year by a ukase of the
Russian Government, which in the meantime had re-
verted to unconcealed reaction, on the pretext that these
women were living an immoral life abroad and becoming
infected by socialist ideas. Those who might refuse to
obey were threatened with the refusal of admission both
to later examinations and to employment. A large pro-

portion of these students—who first pushed open the doors of the universities to women in Germany and France as well as in Switzerland—returned thereupon to Russia.

On their return home these medical students found the Medical Academy for Women available to them for the continuation of their studies ; it had been established in the meantime, in 1872, as a concession to their demands. But it and the other women's universities only survived for a decade, during which time it produced 750 women doctors who did admirable work later.

Froebel courses and the first kindergartens were started in St. Petersburg in 1871, thanks to the authoress Tsebrikova, and afterwards the " Bestushev courses " which were of special importance to the Russian women's movement because they developed later into " women's university courses " (departments of history and philology, and mathematics and physics) which were a centre of education to hundreds of women. In Moscow, too, university courses for women were shortly started. And now the women thronged to the new educational centres from all parts of the country like a stream of lava after a volcanic eruption, as if driven by some subterranean elemental force. At last the tension was relieved, the forced passivity thrown off, and the liberated energies of the Russian woman, naturally vigorous in action and eager for action, swept onwards unchecked. All previous, traditional ideas were cast away, everybody thronged to the university, everybody panted for independence, freedom, and public activities. Even those who had conjured up these spirits were amazed, and Kornilova, a celebrated revolutionary who lived through these years, writes that the marked exterior of the Russian bluestocking, the woman student, the woman Nihilist of the 'sixties and 'seventies, with hair cut short even in those days, with a cigarette in the corner of her mouth and the inevitable spectacles, always standing out from the multitude, " sometimes had such a provocative effect upon those about her that in the early days it required no small measure of courage and sincere devotion to avow openly one's repudiation of the old social order."

37

Whence came this flood of womanhood forcing its way so tempestuously into life ? What connection of cause and effect was there between the emancipation of the peasants and of women ?

The liberation of twenty million peasants, no longer to be delayed, brought with it tremendous social convulsions ; their forced labour had enabled their masters to pile up vast fortunes. The defeat at Ssevastopol was not least among the causes undermining the authority of the Tsar, the Little Father, and the superstructure which protected him, the belief that State and Church were inseparable. This revolutionary change affected the family likewise, and its patriarchal form began to break up about the same time. From all sides rose tidal waves of spiritual and intellectual life. Ideas of liberty, which first penetrated to Russia in the works of George Sand, now received a new stimulus through St. Simonism which came from France and there proved but short-lived ; and this wave of thought was received with enthusiasm amongst the leaders of the Russian intelligentsia, with Chernyshevskyi at their head.

In some respects these champions of the liberation of Russian women, whose rights they invariably advocated as their own cause, went even farther than the French Utopians, because they were greatly influenced by the doctrines of the Socialists and Communists and by the revolutionary ideas of the 'thirties and 'forties. At this period people read and debated much, and a vigorous feminist movement was started, born of passionate protest. The mass of the peasants and the generation of workers, just emerging, stood for the time being pretty much aloof from the movement, as was natural. The discontent of the peasants, deceived in their hopes, who received the " great reform " with a series of revolts, the discontent in many circles among the intelligentsia, and the growing strength of capitalism, which clamoured for a reconstruction of the groundwork of economic and social life—all these laid the foundations of social destruction.

The vast majority of the women who were carried away

by this fermentation within Russian society belonged, with the exception of a handful of daughters of rich land-owners, to the middle classes, the rising bourgeoisie : families belonging to the small nobility who had been half ruined by the abolition of serfdom ; the so-called *rasnochintsy*, those who were not of the nobility but were free from the payment of dues, comprising the lower military ranks, the priesthood, the lower officials, and the liberal professions ; in a few cases they also sprang from the merchant class.

Whereas a certain proportion of the sons in this class could find employment in the State service, the daughters had a hard struggle for their livelihood and had to take up a profession. But the demand for professional services was for the time being very small, an evil which affected not only the women but also the men of the democratic intelligentsia which Pissarev has called the " critically minded proletariat ", and which was destined later to play so large a part in the Russian revolutionary movement. For the very problem of their bare existence, their vital interests, inevitably made this Russian intelligentsia the enemy of ignorance, darkness, and oppression and drove them to enter upon a struggle for greater freedom, for conditions under which they might find a suitable outlet for their abilities, their knowledge, and their readiness to serve. (We find, moreover, in the ranks some examples of the so-called " aristocratic penitents ", those who feel under the obligation to expiate guilt against the people and so act as their protectors against their own class, thereby making atonement. One of the last and greatest representatives of this generation of penitents was Count Leo Tolstoy.)

The majority of the representatives of the Russian intelligentsia had themselves sprung from surroundings where they were in close touch with the masses, especially of the peasants ; many of them actually lived under like conditions and bore the same deprivations as these oppressed classes, and most of them were very open to receive the newly emerging socialist ideas. Moreover, because the intelligentsia frequently identified themselves

39

with the masses, there began about this time that " going among the people ", that selfless service of the people which we shall discuss later, and which marks a sharp dividing line between the genuinely democratic Russian intelligentsia and the more prosperous classes with their liberal point of view. By far the greater number of Russian women students belonged to the *Narodniki*, the revolutionary-minded group who " went among the people "—indeed, we can hardly imagine it otherwise— and who, from 1861 onwards, began to fill not only the universities but also the prisons and fortresses.

But at this point, where the radically freedom-loving wing of the Russian movement for women's emancipation parted company with the liberal wing, the path of the Russian women's movement—which had scored successes as early as the 'sixties and 'seventies that were the object of later struggles in several other countries— divided from that of the Western European feminist movement, which did not begin till the end of the 'nineties. For the Russian women's movement, which was in advance of its time and had practically no doctrine of its own, was purely democratic from the outset, which gave it something of a revolutionary quality. And, although it sprang from economic need, yet it drew its sustenance hardly less from an ideal, mainly social and ethical, source : the urge for knowledge and the opportunity to use one's powers, and the aspiration to serve the people and to be able to help them in their distress.

The practical professions that come in question in this connection are in the first instance those of teacher and doctor. And so there was a time when the term " teacher of the people " in Russia meant a woman who left the city, where any work would be more remunerative, and went of her own free will to some God-forsaken village for a miserable pittance, where she was utterly alone and at the mercy of authorities who were hostile from the outset, there to teach and counsel not only the school-children but their parents too, devoting herself selflessly to the work. Consciously or unconsciously these women played a part in politics through their cultural labours.

40

And the same applies to the country women doctors, nurses, and midwives. These, it is true, were better paid, but their vitality was soon worn out by the constant demands made upon them and the fact that they had to practise medicine in all its branches, since they alone were trained, and that not only among their patients in the village but all over a large district. These thousands of women who devoted themselves to some occupation in the country were in the employ of the *Syemstvos*, the only liberal self-governing bodies in the provinces ; they were readiest to offer the women, whose work they valued highly, an opportunity to carry out cultural labours with greater or less success.

At a later date a large number of women who devoted their whole lives to the revolution followed this path of cultural labour in the country : Ssofya Bardina, Ssofya Löschern von Herzfeld, Olga Natanson, Ssofya Perovskaya, the two Figner sisters, and many more. But it did not by any means satisfy all women, and again and again doubts were expressed, anxious questions posed, until Chernyshevskyi, the acknowledged leader of the younger generation, who paid the price of his revolutionary ideas with lifelong exile and was imprisoned in the Fortress of St. Peter and St. Paul in 1863, answered in his novel *What is to be Done?* the question how the women's question might rationally be translated from theory into practice. From a purely literary point of view the novel is of small importance. But its influence stamped the character of a whole era. Side by side with the revolutionary Rakhmetov, who, like Turgenyev's heroes, is not clearly worked out, stands the principal heroine, his wife Vera Pavlovna, who has escaped from the " dark vault " of family life and attains economic independence and a field for her social activities by the establishment of a Communist Producers' Co-operative Society on a business footing, and so appears as the originator and organizer of one of the first cells of the future Socialist State.

This novel of Chernyshevskyi's raised a tremendous storm. In practical life and in literature a regular campaign was conducted against its teachings, both by angry parents, who felt their acknowledged patriarchal rights endangered and by some husbands, for wives now began to run away in scores. But it was no use, and Vera Pavlovna's dress-making establishment was accepted as a new revelation by women who aspired to exercise their powers; it was exalted to an ideal, imitated by thousands of women all over Russia, and reappeared in the form of co-operatives of shoemakers, bookbinders, and other trades. Everybody now aimed at economic independence, at professional work. And the communes, which were already widespread at that period—homes that offered a shelter to women workers and students who had left their parents or their husbands and lived there together with men students—these so-called St. Petersburg communes of the 'sixties provided a model in almost every detail, as we shall see later, for the residential communes which have been steadily spreading in Bolshevik Russia of recent years.

The material conditions of the inmates varied [so the eyewitness Kornilova, whom we have already quoted once, reports of the life in one of these communes], but all resources were regarded as common property. Mutual help was acknowledged as the supreme rule of the common life. This commune made living very much cheaper and so brought the young people together and strengthened the influence of those among us who were above the average in knowledge and intelligence. It also enabled us to realize our socialist ideas in practice, in our private lives and, whilst we were no better housed, but rather worse, than the factory workers, we were not obliged to distinguish between mine and thine among comrades. The commune meant much, in particular, to women from the provinces. Not infrequently there were some among them who had broken completely with their rich and influential families and arrived absolutely penniless with the object of studying. Of course they all hoped to find work of some kind. But without acquaintances or connections they very seldom succeeded. Many women would have been utterly lost but for the mutual help within the commune, without, in fact, the active support of youthful comrades. Everything conventional and insincere in our mutual relations was absolutely ruled out, not the smallest regard was paid to outward appearances, and we lived among friends as if in the innermost family circle.

As was to be expected, constant attacks were made by the opponents of the communes on the morals prevailing in them; calumnies rained down upon them. Rakhmetov's observation in *What is to be Done?* provided material for such calumnies, for he says : " My clothes —your clothes, my pipe—your pipe, my wife—your wife." But in fact to Chernyshevskyi, and in general to the Nihilists, whose lives were austere and almost ascetic and who regarded women primarily as comrades, love and the erotic instinct were romantic, out-of-date sentimentality. " Away with erotic problems," he exclaimed, very much in the spirit of the watchword given out by a large proportion of the youth of Soviet Russia some sixty years later, though in a different form. " The present-day reader takes no pleasure in them, for his mind is occupied with such questions as how to perfect our administrative and judicial system, with finance and the peasant problem."

For the rest, women who aspired to education and an independent life and met with vigorous opposition from their families were not infrequently obliged to leave their parents' houses secretly, or even by stratagem, by means of so-called *sham marriages* ; that is to say, the girl married someone of like mind by previous agreement, but only to outward appearance, and then the official husband presented his wife with a passport of her own, which was refused to her under Tsarist law until the beginning of the present century unless she had the consent of her parents or husband. In this way the women secured freedom to go their own way. It was in particular women who wanted to study abroad who entered into these " fictitious " marriages, which had become a standing institution among the Russian intelligentsia in the 'sixties and early 'seventies. Many of the revolutionary women who afterwards became famous were obliged to resort to such sham marriages, since otherwise the road to education and social activity would have been closed to them. Ssofya Kovalevskaya contracted a sham marriage in her day; afterwards she made an international name as a mathematician and was professor at Stockholm University—tragically enough she failed to find a home in Western Europe. As happened not infrequently, in her case this sham marriage afterwards developed into a real one, but it was not happy.

Ssinyegub, one of the ablest propagandists of the early 'seventies, has left an interesting account in his memoirs of the way in which these sham marriages came about in his time.

> One day [he writes] when we were living in the commune, Charushin came and told us that he had received a letter from an acquaintance in Vyatka who was a class teacher in the Diocesan School there and had taught some of the older pupils about the service of the people. In this letter, he said, she told him that several pupils who were ready to model their lives on these ideas when they left school were meeting with bitter opposition from their families. One of her best pupils, the daughter of the village priest, was so crushed beneath paternal despotism that she had determined upon flight, but was discovered and subjected once more to her father's authority. All correspondence, and even books, were strictly forbidden to her, and her family were making every endeavour to force her into marriage. . . . Since there was no escape except through a fictitious marriage, so the letter ran, the recipient was asked to find a suitable husband. Without hesitation I offered my services. . . !

And then Ssinyegub, at that time a young student, started on a journey of some thousand versts to secure the longed-for freedom for a totally unknown girl in a remote village, provided by his comrades not only with the better clothes required for the solemn occasion, but also with borrowed presents, to be returned after the wedding. He called upon the girl's parents and was well received by them, and then the girl rushed in in the presence of another local visitor, according to previous arrangement, flung her arms round Ssinyegub's neck, and cried: " At last you have come, Sseryosha ! "

The priest, who ascertained from the papers presented

that Ssinyegub was of noble birth and the son of a rich landowner, joyfully gave his consent to the union. Within a few minutes the whole village knew that the secretly betrothed fiancé of the *batyushka's* daughter had come. The public betrothal was celebrated, rings were exchanged, the young people played the part of lovers, although they had never seen one another before, the trousseau was prepared, the marriage celebrated with festive rejoicings, and the young couple set out straightway for St. Petersburg without the parents having the slightest suspicion. The wife found shelter in one of the many women's communes and devoted herself to study and at the same time to socialist propaganda among the workers.

But Ssinyegub, who meanwhile had fallen in love with Larissa, the beautiful wife that had been entrusted to his care, might not, as a revolutionary, even confess his love to her under the circumstances, and his intercourse with her was simply that of a good comrade. It was not till later that it turned out one day that Larissa, too, had long ceased to be indifferent to her husband, and thus the " fictitious " marriage was changed into a real one. When a few years later Ssinyegub was condemned to nine years' *katorga*, or hard labour in the mines, for socialist propaganda among the workers, Larissa joined him in his exile in Siberia and so set forth upon the thorny path already trodden by so many hundreds of Russian women since the Decembrists' wives, and still to be trodden for many years after her day.

WOMEN IN PRE-REVOLUTIONARY RUSSIA

IN THE REVOLUTIONARY MOVEMENT

" . . . Vigorous movements for freedom have always found an echo in the souls of Russian women of all classes. And when once the Russian woman was roused to defend down-trodden rights she surpassed the men in energy thanks to her steadfast and unwavering fanaticism," writes Amfiteatrov, one of the best authorities on the history of Russian womanhood, who calculates that the women's share in the social struggles and risings of the nation may be gauged at a ratio of one to four (*Women in the Social Movement in Russia*). But even of the 7,000 serfs sent to Siberia by their masters during the reign of Nicholas I more than a third were women.

In the Cossack revolt of 1819, called after Chuguyev, women took the lead. Twenty-nine of these women fighters were scourged with whips after the suppression of the revolt. But not one of them begged for mercy or pardon. In the Ssevastopol revolt of 1830 no less than 375 women were condemned to death. Fearless, carrying their children in their arms or leading them by the hand, they faced the death-dealing cannon. Not only did the women take a leading part in a revolt in the celebrated " peasant military colonies " of Alexander I in the Government of Novgorod, but they came forward as instigators of the revolt whilst it was being prepared. And the stronger the resistance to tyranny and oppression, the larger was the number of women combatants in the ranks of discontent.

The actual revolutionary movement in Russia, for which the ground had been gradually prepared since the Decembrist rising, started, as is well known, at the time of the liberation of the peasants, the abolition of serfdom, which was received with protest both by the deeply disappointed peasants themselves and also by a section of the masters who lost class by it. Immediately afterwards the first revolutionary organizations came into being. And before the end of 1861 the first proclamation in Russia, issued by Chernyshevskyi, appeared : " To the Peasants ", calling upon them to organize themselves for a future revolt. Shortly afterwards the first illegal journal, *The Great Russian*, saw the light of day. Chernyshevskyi, who was also the life and soul of the new journal, was arrested for issuing the proclamation and sent to *katorga*, hard labour in the Siberian mines.

In that same year the student riots began in the universities of St. Petersburg and Moscow, which later became regular occurrences. Their immediate occasion was the decision of the Government, which had meantime adopted a thoroughly reactionary course, to introduce new regulations for the university students, to abolish the students' right of association and assembly, to dissolve their existing associations, and especially to adopt various measures in order to limit the number of the revolutionary students who belonged to the unprivileged, poorer classes. But the students resisted desperately, raised flaming protests, and, by refusing to submit to the new regulations, provoked the Government's retaliation. Hundreds of these young people were imprisoned and exiled and the universities were closed. It is significant that permission for their reopening was later accorded with the reservation that women were no longer to be admitted to the lectures : a proof, no doubt, that those in high places already understood and estimated correctly the part played by the women. A number of popular writers and publicists were arrested besides Chernyshevskyi, together with the students—Mikhailov, Pissarev, and Shelgunov. But neither these measures nor the alienation of otherwise progressive circles under the influence of the Polish insurrection of 1863 succeeded in subduing the agitation among the students : in the years that followed the universities continued to be centres of unrest and revolution, and the word student was still synonymous with revolutionary.

Moreover, the proclamation entitled *Young Russia*, issued about this time by the students, is of interest ; its authors, as Pokrovskyi (*Russian History*) points out, had a prophetic presentiment of the form and aims of the future revolution in Russia, without any acquaintance with the contemporary Communist literature of Western Europe, or even with the *Communist Manifesto* : various demands were enumerated in it the fulfilment of which were among the earliest measures of the Soviet Government—free education in all schools, the *absolute equality of women*, the socialization of the land, the abolition of private trade—that " legalized theft "—and State shops.

By 1874 things had progressed so far that the revolutionary propaganda had a widespread organization at its disposal. Its headquarters were in St. Petersburg, where the group of " *Chaykovtsi* ", named after their leader— a group to which Kropotkin belonged for a time—had been in vigorous activity since 1873, with its motto of " going among the people " and seeking to win support for the socialist idea in the villages. But it was principally due to Bakunin's influence that the originally peaceable propaganda more and more assumed the character of a revolutionary movement and aimed at preparing for an armed rising.

According to the conception of that " unclassed intellectual ", who took part in the revolution of 1848, later addressed his " confession " to Tsar Nicholas I from a Russian prison, and begged Alexander II for a reprieve, and whose doctrines contained a Pan-Slav element to the last, the Russian peasant is a born socialist by nature. Bakunin held that the Russian *mushik*, thanks to his historical past, to the negative attitude of the state authorities, and the still living tradition of the village commune, is the chosen instrument for the abolition of private property in land, for him a self-evident demand of the revolution which has as its final aim the world revolution, " the creation of a new world without laws and therefore free ". In this sense, he claimed, the Russians were also the saviours of mankind. Bakunin held, moreover, that the people needed no instruction, and the sole task of the socialists was to show them the way to free themselves from exploitation and state tyranny. But in order to accomplish that task the true revolutionary must cease to be a stranger to the people, must no longer try to influence them from without, must lose himself in the masses and endeavour to turn isolated outbreaks of discontent, local riots and revolts, into a general rising of the people. The socialist intelligentsia must, therefore, break away from their class privileges, put on the garb of peasant or factory worker, go into the factories and the villages, take up the scythe and the hammer, and live the life of a worker in country or town. " Instruct the people ? " says Bakunin. " That would be very foolish. The people know what they need better than we. On the contrary, we should learn from them and seek to fathom the secret of their lives, their strength —a secret that is, indeed, none too hard to penetrate but remains unfathomable for all those who live in what is called educated society. . . ."

The influence of this teaching on young Russia in the 'seventies was immense. Young men and women left the universities in hundreds, learned a trade, and betook themselves to village or factory in order to prepare for the revolt. Most of those who " went among the people " concealed their origin and gave themselves out as ordinary peasants. The movement spread over all Russia in an astonishingly short time, but soon ended in two monster trials in 1877, known as the " Trial of the Fifty " and the " Trial of the Hundred and Ninety-three " from the number of the accused, who came almost entirely from the ranks of the intelligentsia.

The first of these two great trials, which was a judicial campaign against the " All-Russian Social Revolutionary Organization ", was set in motion in February, 1877. Of the fifty accused almost half were women from the best society who were studying abroad or in Russia and were called the " Moscow Amazons " after the birthplace of the majority. The despairing report laid before the Tsar by Count Pahlen, the Minister of Justice at the time, is an indication of the view taken by the authorities of the

danger to the existing order which these women constituted. The Minister accounts for the success of the
revolutionary propaganda chiefly by the fact that there was
such a surprisingly large number of women among the
conspirators and revolutionaries. " It is solely due to
this participation of the women," he wrote, "that half
Russia is entangled in a network of revolutionary organizations." Of the twenty-three organizations that the
minister cited, five were under the direct control of
women. And Pahlen calculated further that for every
620 men summoned before the courts during a definite
period for revolutionary activities there were 158 women.
The report continued to state that a large number of
those who " went among the people ", as the saying was,
who hired themselves for a daily wage and lived with
the simple country people, belonged to the best families
and—this was doubtless the most serious part of the
whole matter—their relatives, instead of blaming them,
sympathized and praised them.

The brilliant speeches of two of the accused, the
agitator Ssofya Bardina and the workman Alexyeyev—
which were widely distributed later as pamphlets in the
service of the revolutionary propaganda—raised the Trial
of the Fifty to an event of peculiar significance ; in any
case the trial stirred the utmost excitement in Russian
educated circles.

All the accused in the trial belonged to an organization
which had its headquarters abroad and aimed at carrying
out Bakunin's teaching by means of a practical programme
based upon it. In accordance with this programme all
the members were to return home at the same time and
start activities in Moscow, where they were joined by
a few workers. Provided with forged peasants' pass-
ports, they began their activities in the factories, principally in the textile mills, in order to get into direct
touch with the people. If we consider that the working
day in the Russian factories was sixteen hours at that
period, that the workers, men and women, who lived in
poky, dirty barracks, were primitive and dull-witted to
the last degree and quite unprepared for the reception

of socialist teaching, we shall realize what unselfishness and courage were required in order to carry out this programme. In fact the results of a propaganda carried on with superhuman sacrifices were out of all proportion to the privations undergone.

Amongst the numerous women who shrank from none of these things was Bardina, already mentioned, as well as Kaminskaya, Lyubatovich, and Lydia Figner (the sister of the well-known revolutionary, Vera Figner). All four entered a factory with forged papers, but could only work in women's factories at first, as the separation of the sexes was prescribed by law ; and here the conditions were as unfavourable as possible for successful propaganda. Later they managed by a stratagem to secure admittance to the men's buildings, where they read illegal publications aloud, and had the opportunity of distributing pamphlets in factory and public-house and drawing the men into discussion about the political questions of the day. In this way they did, indeed, manage to rouse the interest of the workmen, who had been suspicious at first, but the results of their propaganda were still meagre because the intelligence of the workers was of a low order and their capacity to take in what was said to them still very small.

But even this modest success was enough to make the women, burning with enthusiasm and hardly able to await the victory of their cause, forget the necessary caution, and so the management of the factory in which they took up work at the end of 1874 found occasion by March of the following year to call the attention of the authorities to the interlopers and demand measures to prevent the smuggling of illegal publications into the factories. Lydia Figner and Bardina were obliged to leave the factory and take flight, but were discovered and arrested with the other members of the organization. The subsequent domiciliary searches brought a mass of incriminating material to light, and so the Trial of the Fifty was set on foot, in which a few workers were also involved.

Bardina was at the time in her twenty-second year.

She was the daughter of a District Chief of Police in the Government of Tambov and was one of the medical students who had returned to Russia from Switzerland. A women's Socialist Society, of which she was the moving spirit, affiliated to the Moscow organization at her instigation. And the account given by Vera Figner—herself assuredly a strong personality—shows how forcible her influence must have been, what suggestive power she must have had over those about her. Vera Figner made the acquaintance of Bardina in Zurich, where both were studying medicine, together with a number of other Russian women. Figner was not at that time an adherent of socialist doctrines ; she criticized them and resisted Bardina's persuasive powers. Again and again she argued that the humanitarian labours of a doctor, which she felt to be her vocation, might benefit the people more than revolutionary organization. And it was only Bardina's overwhelming force of conviction that succeeded in refuting Figner's arguments one by one and proving

> that individual efforts are powerless against the overmastering influence of general social conditions . . . that our whole endeavour must be, not to alleviate the sufferings of individuals, to treat single cases, to heal, and to combat the social institutions singly when we realize their evil nature, but that we must combat the exploitation of one human being by another in principle, must combat private property and the right of inheritance, and must not rest until the whole is destroyed. . . .

Her friend, hitherto vacillating, was converted by these arguments.

Bardina's speech before the court certainly does not impress us as the pleading of an accused person ; it is rather a flaming denunciation of the existing order. Bardina never denied that she had carried on propaganda among the workers, and when it was put to her that her activities were directed against the foundations of civilization, against private property, the family, religion, and the state, she replied with a deeply moving paraphrase of the *Communist Manifesto* :

"I have never attacked private property, indeed I dare declare that I am a defender of private property, for I claim that every person has the right to dispose of his own labour and the values created by his labour. . . . And now answer me : Is it I, who confess such a belief, that undermine private property, or is it the manufacturer who pays the worker only for a third of his working day and takes the remaining two thirds for himself without doing anything to earn it ? Is it not rather the speculator who gambles on the Exchange and plunges thousands of families into distress whilst he enriches himself at their cost without himself lifting a finger ? We place the right of the worker to the fruits of his labour above all other rights. . . .

"And as regards the family, I can only ask : Is it not the existing social order which compels wives to leave their families, to enter factories for the sake of a miserable pittance, and there to go to rack and ruin with their children, past hope of saving ? Is it not this social order which destroys the family by forcing women to take to prostitution because of their poverty, and, moreover, represents prostitution as a legal and necessary institution in every well-ordered state, or is it we, because we seek to eradicate this poverty, in which the chief cause of all social abuses is to be found, and consequently the cause also of the ruin of the family ? . . .

"As little am I guilty of undermining the state. . . . Moreover, I do not believe that the state can be undermined by the efforts of individuals. When states fall to destruction it is usually because they bear the seeds of decay within themselves. . . . On the other hand I declare that a state digs its own grave which keeps the people in a condition of spiritual, political, and economic slavery and exposes them to the profoundest poverty, to disease and crime, by intolerably high taxes, by the capitalist exploitation of the workers, and by other abnormal economic and political conditions. . . ."

Bardina's speech before her judges remained the "gospel of the Russian freedom movement" until the crisis at which terrorist methods gained the upper hand ;

she concluded with the words : " Whatever my fate may be, my Lord Judges, I ask no mercy of you and wish for none. Persecute us as much as you will ; I am convinced that so vigorous a movement—clearly the outcome of the spirit of the age—cannot be checked by any measures of suppression. It may, perhaps, be retarded for a time, but it will revive all the stronger, and the process will continue till our ideas triumph finally. . . . Persecute us ! You, my Lords, have the material power at present, but we have the moral power : the power of historical progress, the power of the idea. And ideas cannot be killed with bayonets ! "

Bardina, like the majority of her comrades in the dock, was condemned to hard labour. But in the case of the women the penalty was afterwards changed to exile in Siberia. Bardina escaped from Siberia and returned to Russia in 1881 ; but conditions had changed meantime, she felt that there was no place for her and went abroad, where she shot herself in 1883, unable to get over the memory of her sufferings.

No less tragic was the end of her comrade in the struggle, Betty Kaminskaya, who went mad in exile. A number of influential persons intervened on her behalf, and she was released at last, but it was already too late. On her way to receive treatment Kaminskaya took poison and put an end to her life.

Indicative of the deep and lasting impression made by this trial throughout the country, and especially in the ranks of the youthful students, are the comments of a future member of the *Narodnaya Volya*, a certain Ssalova ; she was a schoolgirl at the time and writes in her autobiography :

> In the dock—side by side with workmen—were students, young girls who had abjured the privileges of their birth and gone to the factories in order to bring light into the realm of darkness. The impression that they made was strong, elevating, and for many of us fraught with consequences of the utmost import. With the school leaving examination just coming, we were all pondering over our future and asking ourselves : " Where shall we turn now ? What shall we do ? " Many of

the boys left the school and set themselves to learn a manual trade. And though they said little about it, we in our small circle saw clearly what their object was. I, too, was resolved to follow in the path of these women in the Trial of the Fifty. I was resolved to work in a village.

Vera Figner writes in the same strain :

The trial aroused sympathy on all sides. The selflessness of these women, who had given up their privileged position for the heavy labour in the factories, the purity of their convictions, and their steadfastness called forth universal admiration. Many of them regarded their activities as a sacred mission. Although it was thus crushed at the outset, yet the party gained in moral authority thereby, nay, it won the halo of heroic martyrdom fighting for its faith !

The trial found a wide echo, too, in contemporary literature. The dying Nyekrassov dedicated some vigorous lines to the heroines of the revolution, and Turgenyev, who followed the proceedings from a distance, afterwards wrote his prose poem *The Threshold* in honour of the Russian women revolutionaries—a work which long continued to inspire young Russian students. It begins with a vision of a vast building, and behind its open door the blackest darkness. . . . But a Russian girl stands on the threshold. She is about to cross the threshold of the revolution. A spirit voice warns her of the dangers and sufferings awaiting her within. But she declares that she is prepared for everything.

" Are you even ready to commit a crime ? "
The girl's head droops : " That, too."
" Do you know that you may lose the faith you now hold and realize that you have been misled and have sacrificed your life for nothing ? "
" That, too, I know. And yet I will enter."
" Fool ! " snarls a voice behind her.
" Saint ! " comes the answer from somewhere.

In the Trial of the Hundred and Ninety-three, among whom were the above-mentioned group of *Chaykovtsi*, thirty-eight women were accused, a fifth, that is, of the total number. The trial did not take place till

55

October, 1877, and most of the accused had by that time been in prison for three or four years. Here, too, the fearless and steady demeanour of the accused won them universal sympathy and respect. Several of them refused to offer any defence or to answer the questions addressed to them. A considerable proportion of these so-called " protestants " were likewise women.

One of the principal accused was Breshkovskaya, " the grandmother of the Russian Revolution ", later well known abroad. She " went among the people " and approved terrorist methods, and later she became a Social Revolutionary. She was a brilliant orator and indefatigable in her energy and although the gendarmes dogged her steps, she travelled all over Russia, disguised as a cook or a peasant women as circumstances required, and recruited members for the " Fighting Organization " created by Gershuni, the founder of the Social Revolutionary Party, upon whom she exercised a great influence.

The Government attached especial importance to Breshkovskaya's revolutionary activities, so that she alone among the women in the Trial of the Hundred and Ninety-three was condemned to four years' *katorga*. But at the end of a year she escaped, was recaptured and sent back to the *katorga* for two and a half years, and returned to European Russia in 1898. There she resumed her revolutionary activities and later transferred them abroad. In 1907, at the age of sixty-two, she returned to Russia in defiance of the law, was denounced and sent again to Siberia, and remained there till the February Revolution in 1917.

Ssofya Perovskaya (1853–81) stands out as one of the strongest and most self-contained characters among the members of the *Chaykovtsi* group. She had occupied a leading position among the revolutionaries for years, and enjoyed their boundless confidence. Whenever occasion arose, she always undertook the most dangerous duties herself, including communication with the imprisoned comrades whom she helped in attempted flight. And because she was naturally tenacious, silent, fearless, and self-possessed, the comrades submitted to her strong will, her experience, and her acknowledged authority in the most important undertakings.

She made the attempt to get in touch with the people earlier than anyone else and travelled in the Government of Tver in order to gain knowledge of the conditions of the peasant population; there she taught the children and lived in the closest contact with the village people. Later she learnt the work of a health visitor and went from place to place—often on foot—to vaccinate the peasant children against smallpox. Both on these journeys and in St. Petersburg, whither she returned from time to time, she came into touch with like-minded people, including the leader Shelyabov, a kindred spirit who was afterwards much her closest friend. Inspired by the idea of forwarding the cause of the revolution, she was unwearying in her schemes. Thus the fact that the *Chaykovtsi* took to propaganda among the people was due to her suggestions and her instigation. She was one of the first, too, who saw the importance of rural agitation, for she was convinced that " no party can work successfully in Russia unless it resolves to get into touch with the peasantry." She was arrested and sent to Siberia, but she escaped on the journey there and returned to St. Petersburg, where she pursued her activities unfalteringly. During the Trial of the Hundred and Ninety-three several of the accused were released on bail and gathered round her in her efforts to revive the organization.

" Nobody would have guessed that the simple woman who drew water from the Neva, wearing a handkerchief over head, a cotton dress, and men's boots, was a general's daughter and a lady of high birth," wrote Kropotkin. How had it come about that this lady underwent such an outer and inner transformation, instead of remaining in society ? The answer is only one variant of the many similar biographies of the Russian revolutionary of the period : the daughter of a former Governor of St. Petersburg, a typical Russian owner of serfs, who not only beat his wife himself but taught his little son to do so,

Ssofya suffered even in childhood under her father's tyranny and hated him, for he ill-treated her as well; she suffered under the oppressive conditions of her home and began very early to rebel against them. Perovskaya had lessons at home. Later she attended the St. Petersburg University courses for women and gradually became acquainted with the whole *Chaykovtsi* circle; she was drawn into the revolutionary movement and, as her father threatened her with punishment, she soon quitted her parents' house for ever in order to carry on a life-and-death struggle against oppression in the widest sense.

And so the assassination of Alexander II, who was murdered on May 1st, 1881, was largely the personal doing of Perovskaya. Not only did she bring the bomb to the spot and prepare the assassination, but she gave the decisive instructions at the last moment. . . . In spite of the urgent appeals of her companions, in spite of all the dangers that threatened her, Perovskaya remained in St. Petersburg after the deed and gave no thought to her own escape. Shelyabov was arrested and it was certain that the death sentence would be pronounced against him and the three other conspirators; since there was no escape, she wished to die with her comrades. She was the first woman in Russia to ascend the scaffold for a political crime, in company with four men. . . .

A few days before her execution Ssofya Perovskaya wrote to her mother, whom she loved more than anyone else in the world:

> . . . I am deeply troubled on your account, my dearest. . . . I do not lament my own fate in the least, but await it with perfect calm: for I always knew that this would happen sooner or later. . . . The only thing that depresses me is your grief, beloved. . . . I need not say how deeply I am attached to you. Ever since my childhood, as you know, you have been and still are the object of my supreme, most fervent love. But I hope that you will take heart and not be angry with me. A reproach from you is the only thing that I should feel cruelly. . . .

And we find one trait in this woman, who seemed compound of will-power and resolution, of an iron determination—a trait which revealed her essentially feminine quality, rare in these women, at the last moment : in this same last farewell letter she ends with a request to her mother : " Buy me a collar and cuffs with buttons, for I should like to tidy my dress for the proceedings. . . ."

About this period the centre of Russian revolutionary activities was the Central Executive Committee, founded in 1879, of the above-mentioned *Narodnaya Volya* (People's Freedom), a definitely terrorist society, which made the *mir*, the village community, the future unit of organization in its programme. Among its twenty-nine members there were some ten women. Besides Perovskaya one of the most striking figures among them was Vera Figner, of whose life we have a record in her memoirs (English abridged edition : *Memoirs of a Revolutionist*), which made a deep impression even in Western Europe. In Russian the book comprises six volumes, including one of poems. From this autobiography we learn that she, unlike Perovskaya, enjoyed a happy, sunny childhood and youth, and was herself not only of a cheerful temperament but an artist of many-sided talent. She was one of the Russian women medical students who refused to return home from Switzerland. After a time she went among the people as a health visitor with her sister, whose acquaintance we have already made, and worked under a Syemstvo for three months. Of this brief period in her life she wrote later : " These three months were a severe trial to me and made an overwhelming impression on me of the people's material distress. But I learned nothing of the people's soul, and as for propaganda, I never had a chance to open my mouth. . . ."

The counterpart to Vera Figner's personal experiences was the general failure of the movement of " going among the people ". In the spring of 1874 it became general, but by the autumn of the following year it was already slackening because a large number of its adherents were arrested and imprisoned and the rest were obliged to escape from the persecution of the authorities by flight from the villages. But what was much worse, and disastrous to the whole movement, was the moral defeat suffered : the exaggerated expectations of the results of the work now gave place to a sense of disappointment. And Vera Figner, who had returned from abroad shortly before, describes it as follows :

> Many had given up all hope ; the programme which had seemed at first so easy to carry out had not produced the expected results. The assurance that we had tackled the problem in the right way and our faith in our own strength were destroyed, and the greater the enthusiasm of those who wanted to carry on propaganda among the people, the bitterer the disappointment. The past was destroyed, and the future still quite obscure. . . .

In this mood many of those who had hitherto " gone among the people " now turned to the terrorist organization, and this new religion of revolutionary action, which Bakunin opposed vigorously, found favour and spread even more rapidly than the movement of " going among the people ". For years the *Narodnaya Volya* kept not Russia alone, but Western Europe too, in perpetual agitation by its deeds of reckless daring, by bomb-throwing and assassination carried out with unexampled contempt of death. But by 1881, the year of the Tsar's murder, this revolutionary group was played out likewise. Most of the members were arrested, and the party lost its influence, partly on that account, but partly because the hopes cherished from the removal of Alexander II were not fulfilled.

Vera Figner, who had been in the revolutionary movement for ten years and for the last four an active member of the terrorist organization, and who had been one of those to sign the death warrant of the Tsar and his councillors, was the only member of the Executive Committee still at liberty. For more than two years after the Tsar's murder she was not discovered, and she carried on her work of agitation in Charkov : in 1884 she fell into the hands of the police, thanks to the treachery of a comrade who later pronounced judgment against himself. As it was not considered desirable to create any more women martyrs, the death sentence was remitted to twenty years solitary confinement in the famous and notorious Schlüsselburg Fortress. It was not till the revolutionary year 1905 that she at last regained her freedom. She left prison with unabated vigour, ready for new exploits, and resumed her work where she had left it off two decades earlier. She lives to-day, eighty years old, in peaceful retirement in the new Moscow, one of the last tragic heroines of a bygone period of struggle.

Side by side with these we find a somewhat different type of Russian revolutionary woman in Vera Sassulich, an assassin who acted on her own initiative. True, she also belonged to revolutionary societies, but her supreme exploit, her assassination of General Trepov, was her own personal undertaking. The revolutionary organization to which she belonged, *Syemlya i Volya* (Land and Liberty), came into being earlier than *Narodnaya Volya*, directly after the failure of the movement of " going among the people ", in 1877, the year of the two monster trials. The society assumed its name in the following year, and had then its own programme, based upon stern discipline and a conspiratorial technique. To this organization fell the task of opposing the reviving reaction and confronting government terrorism against the revolution with revolutionary terrorism. There was enough and to spare to avenge in those days. Thirty-four of the 193 accused in the great trial died in prison, twelve committed suicide, and thirty-three went mad. Amongst the remaining revolutionaries the mood of combative anger grew more intense and reached its climax when Trepov, Chief of Police and Captain of the St. Petersburg Gendarmerie, had a political prisoner flogged who had not saluted him respectfully enough. The affair became known and the revolutionary societies resolved to avenge the crime. People even came from the south and proclaimed their readiness to do away with Trepov.

But Vera Sassulich's shot on January 24, 1878, forestalled them all; overcome at once by indignation and pity, she resolved to take upon herself to avenge the defenceless victim. Fragments have been preserved of her memoirs recalling this assassination; in simple words she describes not only her resolution, but her inner experiences at the time. She discussed every detail with her best friend, Kolenkina, who was later exiled to Siberia (there are records of how they drew lots to decide which of the two should do the deed); she planned how she would go as a petitioner to the Chief of Police and fire the shot from close at hand.

> . . . It seemed to me [she writes] that I was perfectly calm, only I was terribly depressed. Not because I was saying good-bye to a life of freedom; I had long resigned myself to that. My life was no longer life at all, but only a state of transition with which it was well to have done as soon as possible. The thought of the next day weighed upon me indescribably; and of the moment when the Chief of Police would approach me. . . . I did not doubt my actual success; I was convinced that everything would go smoothly, that it would not be in the least difficult or terrible—and yet I was wretched. I had not expected this feeling, but it was not excitement, rather weariness; I even wanted to sleep. But hardly had I fallen asleep when the nightmare sensation returned. . . .

The day dawned. Vera Sassulich put on a new coat and a new hat, took leave of her friend, and set out.

> . . . At the office of the Chief of Police I found about a dozen petitioners assembled. A poorly dressed woman whose eyes were red with tears sat down beside me and begged me to read her petition, and see whether it was properly written. Something was wrong in the wording of the petition. I went with the woman to an officer and asked him to attend to her. My voice was just as usual, nothing betrayed my excitement. I was pleased with myself. The nightmare sensation that had tormented me the evening before had vanished without leaving a trace. Nothing oppressed me unless perhaps anxiety that everything might proceed according to plan. . . .

The adjutant showed her a seat in the front row of petitioners. Shortly afterwards Trepov entered the room with one or two subordinates. " What is your petition ? " " I ask for a certificate of morals."

Trepov scribbled something with a pencil and turned to the woman standing beside Vera Sassulich.

> . . . I held the revolver in my hand already and was pressing the trigger. . . . It would not work. My heart stood still. Once more I pressed—a shot, a cry. . . . Immediately people rushed at me and struck me—how often I had been through it in imagination ! But it was different ; there was a pause. Possibly it only lasted a few seconds, but I was distinctly conscious of it. I threw the revolver away and stood waiting.
>
> Suddenly there was a stir around me. The petitioners had scattered in all directions, the police flung themselves upon me from all sides and seized me. " Where is the revolver ? " " I threw it away, it is on the floor." " The revolver, give us the revolver ! " came shouts from all sides.
>
> All at once some one stood before me : round eyes. From the wide-open mouth issued something more like bellowing than shouting and two rough hands with bent fingers grabbed at my eyes. With all my might I shut my eyes and the hands only scratched my cheeks. . . . A tumult arose, I was thrown down and beaten. It all happened just as I had expected. Only the attack on my eyes was unexpected. But now that I was lying face downwards they were safe. What surprised me wholly was that I felt no pain. . . . It was not till night when I was led to my cell that I was conscious of pain. . . .

Two months later the assassin was publicly tried. The case had excited too much notice to be disposed of in secret. In the court Vera Sassulich admitted briefly and frankly what had instigated her action. " It seemed to me impossible that this affair—the flogging of the political prisoner Bogolyubov—should be passed over without leaving a trace. I waited to see what would come of it. But everybody remained calm and there was nothing to prevent Trepov or any other tyrant from further misdeeds. And so the resolve grew up within me to prove myself, at the cost of my own life, that no one is free to humiliate a human being in such a way and go unpunished. And I could see no other means of calling attention to the affair. . . . Certainly it is terrible to raise one's hand against another human being, but it seemed to me that there was no escaping it. . . ."

Vera Sassulich, an officer's daughter, aged twenty-nine at the time and possessing little womanly charm, was acquitted by the jury, contrary to the Government's expectations. Both in the court, where there were civil servants and representatives of the highest classes of society among the public, and outside where a crowd was assembled, the verdict was received with applause and outbursts of enthusiasm as a triumph of justice. But outside the gates gendarmes were already waiting for Sassulich in order to arrest her again and take her to prison. There was a brief struggle between her friends and the Tsar's servants. She succeeded in escaping and soon afterwards turned up abroad.

And so they pass by us, one after the other, all the women mentioned here and many more unnamed—a generation of heroines, nay whole " dynasties " (the Ssubotin sisters, the Lyubatovich sisters, the Figner sisters, and others), who might be called the great saints of the Russian revolution because of the deep fervour, devotion, and contempt of death with which they fought for an idea without yielding a single inch. There were among the Russian revolutionaries isolated though rare cases of men who were cowed by unbearable conditions and went over to the other camp. But no case is known of such failure among the Russian revolutionary women. The stories of their lives are deeply moving. Their spirit always rose under the influence of criticism, indignation, and protest, and in the midst of struggle. And the greater the tasks set them, the demands made upon them, the greater was their own strength, their power to suffer, their inner readiness. And so they did not suffer in vain. The women who are in the fighting line in Soviet Russia to-day are hewn from the same block as they. Only with this difference : the same super-human powers which then were exhausted by single heroines, passively, in suffering and in order to destroy the past, are now applied by whole troops of active women, " heroines of labour ", this time in order to build up a new life and fight for a new world.

They were all young, these revolutionary women ; some were brilliant, beautiful, gifted with artistic powers, richly endowed by nature in intellect and soul (Vera Figner, Ludmila Volkenstein), womanly to the core and so created for happiness in their personal lives. But in spite of their intense capacity to feel and experience, with them, as with the men revolutionaries, the personal, erotic element, the woman, was always second to the universal, to that love of mankind which threw everything else into the shade. And the resulting marked characteristic of chastity, of purity in the mutual relations of the sexes, which gave its tone to the whole of that and the succeeding generation of Russian intellectuals, as well as the atmosphere of comradeship in Russian student circles which has so often been misunderstood in Western Europe, still prevail in the relations between men and women in Soviet Russia, and is a constant source of bewilderment to foreigners whose attitude towards the problem is wholly different.

Russian revolutionary men and women are first and foremost friends and comrades to one another, who undergo all dangers, sufferings, and privations in the struggle for a common cause, and, if need be, face death together on the scaffold—even when they have found one another (Ssofya Perovskaya and Shelyabov). Not only are their ranks constantly replenished, rather they have been since the 'seventies one unbroken, suffering chain of prisoners, reaching chronologically to the October revolution of 1917 and geographically forming a network of many thousand square miles all over Russia, from Transbaikalia, the Nyerchinsk district (later Ssakhalin was added) right across to the European West— a chain, moreover, of many thousand links, increasing in number ceaselessly.

For more than a decade there has been a little-known " Central Museum of the *Katorga* and *Ssylka* " (hard labour in the Siberian mines and in exile) in Moscow, only accessible to the initiated, representing something different from the revolutionary museums, not a parallel but a supplement; it is unique of its kind. As you walk through its rooms you see step by step revealed the vision of a passion of such vast spiritual and human proportions, of such patient heroism, as can only be compared with the voluntary martyrdom of the early Christians; the immense mass of material has been collected from all sides, carefully and lovingly: portraits, photographs of prisons and localities, plans of the cells in the famous Fortresses of Schlüsselburg and of St. Peter and St. Paul, statistical tables, drawings, farewell letters and other documents, relics, casts, instruments of torture, whole collections of fetters and chains, and the products of patient work. Who does not feel his heart stand still when he reads again and again the tens and hundreds of those executed in these decades, of those who went mad in prison, of those who died of exhaustion, and those who committed suicide? When he reads inside one of the various types of straitjacket—of hard leather or metal—the inscription of one who suffered from it himself: " Ten times worse than flogging . . ." ? Who can look without a shudder even at the wooden models or rough sketches of the clay huts at Yakutsk and elsewhere in the " transfer stations ", the *katorga* and halt prisons, which earned a sad notoriety by their brutality, or at the models of the cells used for solitary confinement in which many of the exiles and the condemned were doomed to spend their whole lives, whether in Siberia or in a fortress?

And one is really overcome with horror when one pauses before the portraits and photographs of the graves of the victims of the *Kara tragedy* of 1889 which made all Russia shudder in its day. Baron Korff, Governor-General of the Amur District, which included the *katorga* division on Kara Sea, was on a tour of inspection; when that exalted gentleman entered her cell the " political " Kovalskaya, who was perpetually on a war footing with the prison authorities and making protests, remained seated, and, when she was ordered to stand up, she answered : " I was forced to come here because I do not recognize your Government, consequently I will not stand up in the presence of its representatives." Orders were immediately given to send the woman to a still more lonely spot, farther north, Verkhnye-Udinsk. Kovalskaya, therefore, who had no inkling of what awaited her, was dragged from her plank bed in the middle of the night, in her sleep, to the horror of her fellow-prisoners ; undressed as she was, she was led away by several warders and military officials under the command of the prison governor, and subsequently transported.

The retort to this inhuman action was a hunger strike on the part of the women who remained behind, in which the men immediately joined. Its effect was further to exacerbate the relations between the convicts and the prison authorities and a fresh and embittered struggle began, until Nadyeshda Ssigida, the mother of two children, who had arrived in the Kara district only a short time before, directly after the death of her husband, boxed the ears of an official whose dismissal the " politicals " demanded, intending to bring the authorities to their senses thereby. But Baron Korff gave orders : " A hundred strokes of the lash and no reprieve." Mrs. Ssigida had fallen ill in the isolation cell where she had been confined immediately after the deed. In spite of the intense excitement among the convicts, in spite of the warning of the prison doctor and his refusal to be present whilst the sentence was carried out, in spite even of the doubts expressed by the prison authorities, the petty Tsar of the Amur District remained inexorable in his resolve. . . .

Ssigida was brought half unconscious to the common women's cell of the " criminals ", in a corner of which were a few of her comrades who had been transferred thither. And after screaming in delirium all night for her mother and children she was released from all sufferings the next morning, a woman barely twenty-six years of age.

A few days later three of her cell companions, who

had procured poison somewhere, followed her : Marya Kovalevskaya, Nadyeshda Ssmirnitskaya, and Marya Kalyushnaya. And their farewell letter, written by Kovalevskaya directly after the removal of Kovalskaya in the name of the two others as well as her own, concludes : " . . . We three women left behind in this prison see no other way of avenging the outrage and indignity suffered by our comrade. The only means of retribution that we have at our disposal is our own death. And so we have resolved to die. . . ." Many others comrades, men and women, in Kara took poison for the same reason. But since the poison proved not very effectual " only " seven persons laid down their lives voluntarily in consequence of the Kara tragedy.

The Museum of *Katorga* and *Ssylka* is administered exclusively by its founders, members of the Society of *Politkatorshan* who constitute a widespread community in the Soviet Union (with 53 branches) and produce in their journal *Katorga i Ssylka* a unique type of literary memoir. The pure and tranquil personalities and the fine heads, with eyes that speak mastery and reflection, to be found among the leaders there, men and women —some of them have undergone no less than twenty years of *katorga*—affect us in the restlessly tense Russia of to-day and of the Five Year Plan like beings from another and timeless world. It is true that this older generation of *Narodniki*, *Narodovoltsi*, terrorists, and Social Revolutionaries, whose rebel activities belong for the most part to a period when there was neither a real proletariat nor Marxism in Russia, are practically repudiated by the latest group of Russian Marxists now at the helm ; their ideas are considered " petty bourgeois " and they are not taken quite seriously ; nevertheless, it is they who with their very bodies, with their sacred fire, laid the foundations of the Russia of to-day. And therefore the young people who come to this museum and are shown round it by their elders, in order that they may learn the history of the Russian revolution, are flesh of their flesh and bone of their bone. And so these young people are the more bound by the words written round the walls : " A new warrior band follows you, ready for struggle and death. . . ."

Another characteristic of the great community of the *Politkatorshan,* one which is most marked in all Russian revolutionaries, is their sense of friendship, comradeship, holding together ; indeed it is the guiding impulse of their lives. A living proof of this supreme sense of community is the " Red Cross ", a unique institution founded in 1881, which endeavoured in every way to mitigate the mental and bodily sufferings of many thousands of revolutionaries—exiles, prisoners, those living abroad—and which—here is the remarkable circumstance—was actively supported by progressive Russian intellectuals who were otherwise out of sympathy with the revolution. It is almost superfluous to observe that the whole work of this organization, which covers the whole area of Russia and has also representatives abroad, is principally in the hands of women. So, too, it was always women who were foremost in assisting an escape. We read, moreover, in the works of Vera Figner how those who were imprisoned for life or for decades struggled through from their profound solitude to a truly heroic comradeship. She says of herself how hard it was for her to leave the Schlüsselburg Fortress, where she spent half her life, because seven men comrades remained behind, and how her eyes, " which had forgotten how to weep " were wet in spite of herself.

Of Ludmila Volkenstein's self-sacrifice and selflessness her comrades have perfect miracles to relate ; she was condemned to death in 1883 for propagandist activities and participation in an attempt on the life of the Governor of Charkov, was afterwards " reprieved ", and spent twelve years together with Vera Figner in the Schlüsselburg Fortress ; later she was transferred to the island of Ssakhalin, and in 1906 was struck by a Tsarist bullet when leading a demonstration of sailors in Vladivostok. When after a year and a half in prison she was allowed to take a walk with Figner, and learned that by no means all the prisoners enjoyed that " privilege ", Volkenstein persuaded her companions in suffering to renounce it until the same right was accorded to all the rest. This voluntary renunciation of the only pleasure known to these women prisoners continued for a full year and a half.

> There could be no humaner being than Volkenstein [says Vera Figner of her in her *Memoirs*]. Her leading characteristic was boundless compassion. " We all need compassion," was her favourite proverb, and so gentle was her soul, so strong her love for all living creatures, that she always stepped aside in order not to crush insects in her path. . . . But if an idea was at stake, a right to be fought for, then her softness and gentleness were united with absolutely unyielding stubbornness. . . .

For twelve whole years this woman was without news of her husband, her children, and her dearly loved mother, whom she had left behind in freedom. . . .

And so it came about as a result of all these characteristics, all this heroism of the Russian women fighting for freedom at the end of the last century, that in Russia woman was actually the soul of the revolution. The example of Sassulich and the Kara tragedy illustrate the pitch of human exaltation to which this renunciation, this sense of oneness with others, could be raised in case of need. But the extent to which it found expression in daily life, and the lofty spiritual level to which these aristocratic women were able to raise their everyday lives under the hardest and most repulsive conditions imaginable—this is revealed in the notes of a number of revolutionary women recently published by the *Politkatorshan*; they spent many years of their lives *In the Women's Katorga*, of which they tell. It is impossible to follow these simple accounts without a feeling of humble reverence, without kneeling in spirit before the surpassing greatness of their humanity.

The introduction is by Vera Figner, who writes from the unexampled wealth of her experience :

> Of all types of imprisonment that which seemed to me the hardest and most annihilating is that in a common cell. In separate confinement there is only the separate will, confronted by the law, the prison authorities, armed with hunger and cold,

with physical and spiritual weapons, in order to break or bend the will of the prisoners. But in the common cell there is in addition the twenty or thirtyfold will of one's companions, which may be very various, weak or strong, vacillating, capricious, and sometimes unmannerly. . . .

It is, I believe, impossible to remain mentally sound during many years of solitary confinement, not to go mad. But to remain mentally sound through many years' confinement in a common cell seems to me to be possible solely with the aid of great self-discipline and re-education. . . .

Through such a stern school of self-discipline and re-education of the personality and deeper spiritual experience some thirty permanent inmates of Central Women's Prison at Maltsev (in the Nyerchinsk *katorga*) passed in the course of many years ; between 1907 and 1912 its gates admitted no less than sixty-two women.

What a living wealth of manifold types, socially, humanly, and racially how varied, is the procession which passes before our eyes in this collection of reminiscences from the gloomiest period of the Russian reaction at the beginning of the century, in the individual portraits of women so lovingly delineated, in those who have depicted themselves. And if we ask how all these women lived, most of whom were very young—there were eighteen still under age, not yet twenty-one, thirty-seven between twenty-one and thirty, and only twelve over thirty—and how they passed the long years behind the prison bars of the *Maltsevka*, this is the answer we receive :

We lived literally in a commune. . . . All the parcels and books and all the money that we received (some got twenty-five roubles a month regularly and others nothing at all) were common property. With the exception of garments, the contents of the parcels were divided equally and there were some among us with skill enough to divide a tiny sweet in three. . . .

However hard one tries to remember, one recalls nothing that would suggest discord among us in consequence of social differences. In this respect our common life illustrates one aspect of the life of the society of the future. . . . This total liberation from everything savouring of the petty bourgeois, this utter

71

negation of all social barriers which hedge in those who live in freedom, favoured the development of an exceptionally pure and close comradeship based upon common intellectual interests and ardent, serious friendship such as can rarely be found in freedom. . . . For this reason we continued to feel long after we had left the Maltsev Prison that we were more closely bound up with the women of Maltsev than with anyone else. . . .

As was common in Russia ever since the middle of the last century and has become so on a gigantic scale in the Soviet Union, so in their small world learning filled the chief part of the lives of these women in the *Maltsevka*, a consuming hunger for knowledge and culture. The most various studies were pursued there, beginning with reading and writing and extending to the most complex philosophical problems.

. . . There were twenty-four women among us in the Nyerchinsk *katorga* who were either half illiterate or had only attended an elementary school. They received instruction in the Russian language, geography, arithmetic, and so on, and many of them left the *katorga* knowing as much as if they had staid at school till they were sixteen. Of course that involved several years of serious, intensive schooling. Instruction was given in groups and individually, and as a number of us had attended a secondary school or an unfinished University course (more than half), each pupil had several teachers. . . .

The political inmates of the *katorga* received a number of books from outside, and so in course of time a valuable little library, systematically collected and comprising some seven or eight hundred volumes, was gradually got together in this remote Siberian prison ; besides good volumes of *belles lettres*, chiefly in French which was the language principally learned by the women, there were a number of learned books, mainly philosophical : Windelband, Haeckel, Kuno Fischer, Avenarius, and Mach, all eagerly studied and discussed. In some cases the women's zeal was so great that two of them who were allowed one day to leave the prison and settle in Siberia were really unhappy, because now they would be without the necessary books to carry on their study of Leibniz's doctrine of monads. It is worth observing that here less attention was paid to the social sciences than to philosophy. Books of the former kind were not admitted by the prison authorities. Some of the prisoners devoted themselves the more eagerly to mathematics, and we hear of fanatics who studied it with such intensity that they even pondered over the problems in their dreams at night.

> . . . The books opened to us a new world of ideas [we read in this compilation of common reminiscences of the women's *katorga*]. . . . Again and again unsolved problems presented themselves to us. . . . Every one of us who now set seriously to work on her own self-development, who began to think, realized that she must first subject her whole mental equipment to a thorough and conscientious examination, and that only then could we establish our philosophy on a firm basis, stone by stone. . . .
> For the whole of the younger generation, all of us, had become revolutionaries because the movement carried us away instinctively and emotionally. . . . Whilst we were free it was only hurriedly that we acquired enough theory for practical purposes, and so with many of us party membership was only due to chance acquaintance, or the influence of friends or our immediate circle. Herein our generation of *katorshanki* was, of course, very different from the earlier individual heroines who had had to develop their revolutionary ideas through great effort and struggle. To our credit, therefore, be it said that we were profoundly conscious of being very inadequately prepared for the pursuit of our aims, and so categorically expressed opinions were considered exceedingly bad form among us and were promptly refuted. In our endeavour to think and probe more deeply in the intellectual and moral field we reviewed in course of time the whole mental artillery of those whose ideas we opposed. . . . Thus we read Nietzsche, Dostoyevskyi, the Bible, the Indian philosophers, Maerterlinck, Pascal, Vladimir Ssolovyov, Leo Tolstoy, and Mereshkovskyi. . . . It was all exceedingly interesting and enabled us to approach things from another point of view, and stimulated our mental activity. Only those were privileged to call themselves convinced socialists and atheists who did not stumble over a single metaphysical difficulty and, be it observed, were capable of applying the principle in their personal lives, with all its consequences. . . .

73

The result was that even the simplest and most natural actions of others were under control, every single step they took :

> You help me in my work, give me your scrap of food, and think what kindness you are conferring on me. . . . Does there not lie concealed here a remnant of lazy and hypocritical philanthropy, the humiliation of a comrade, or even the wish somehow to raise oneself in one's own and other's eyes ? . . . In this way every individual, unselfish deed that was a little out of the ordinary was examined to test its genuineness and purity. . . . And there was no name, no single authority, that escaped this analysis. . . . Doubtless this was the expression of a healthy, youthful, blind zeal, a straightforwardness, a passionate seeking for absolute moral purity. . . . But it produced many dramatic incidents and disappointments ; many thoughtless judgments were pronounced. . . .

As we read these words we involuntarily spin the thread farther and think of the strict moral code at present in force in the Soviet Union, of the many *chistkas*, the relentless party purges which are undertaken from time to time and also spare no one, and this example, too, will show us how deeply some of the characteristics so noticeable to-day are rooted in the Russian nature.

Before concluding this chapter let me mention the very important part played by non-Russian women in the Russian revolution. I will only refer to the Jewesses, who occupy the most prominent position ; in the reign of Nicholas I they were wholly shut out from public education, but from the day when Alexander II's reforms admitted women to education in Russia they were foremost in the ranks of the women students. Amongst the 750 women doctors who passed their examinations at the Women's Medical Institute in St. Petersburg which, it will be remembered, only survived for one decade, there were 169 Jewesses. Later they were doubly enslaved and persecuted : during the reign of Alexander III Jewish women students were forbidden to live in St. Petersburg and had to purchase the right to study by entering their names in the register of prostitutes, for these were granted the right of residence ; and it is all too easy to understand that they rose in such numbers against Tsarism, so that the graves of these victims, as was said, " would line the long road from Paris to St. Petersburg ".

The names of Gessya Helfmann, Ssofya Ginsburg, Olga Natanson, and many more, who come first in the train of Jewish revolutionary women, and in some respects constitute that " leaven which brought about a fermentation in the mass of those Russians who, though generously endowed with talents, were still inert, and, by the blending of both temperaments, hastened the course of the Russian struggle for freedom " (Amfiteatrov), signalize just such tragedies and destinies as those of the first great Russian women revolutionaries. And just as they pointed the way into the future to hundreds of their fellow-countrywomen who came after them, so too it was a Jewess, Cecilia Gurevich—L. Deutsch, one of the first Russian Marxian theorists from Plekhanov's circle, speaks of her as the first Marxian woman—who met him in Russia when he returned from *katorga* at a time when a new phase was already beginning in the history of the Russian revolution.

ON THE EVE OF RED OCTOBER

AFTER the murder of Alexander II, the wholly unprepared Alexander III ascended the throne of Russia— the real heir had already died as a grown man.

If all that was needed had been to inspire the new Tsar with thorough-going terror [Pokrovskyi writes of him in his *Russian History*], that purpose could not have been better achieved. For the poor creature had utterly lost his head : he cried, and agreed on the one hand with those who said Russia must have a constitution, whilst on the other he also concurred with those who declared that with a constitution Russia would be ruined ; he gave the most varied orders to various people, so that his ministers determined to wait for a time till the Tsar came to his senses. But this terror of the Tsar's was of no more use, as it turned out, than the former " benevolence " of Tsar Alexander II at the beginning of his reign.

In 1887 Alexander III scribbled on a report of his

Minister of Education the celebrated words : " No more education ! " And reaction, the most oppressive governmental terror, under the direction of Plehve, who was afterwards murdered, began to celebrate positive orgies, resorting to every possible method, including Jewish pogroms intended to divert the people's attention from what was really going on. The censorship was stricter than ever before. The political questions of the day could only be discussed in the style of Æsop. Siberia was no longer adequate for " political offenders " ; they were sent to Ssakhalin and even more remote regions. Admission to educational institutions was rendered more difficult and restricted to a minimum ; the women's university colleges were closed altogether. But since the women's eagerness for education had by no means abated, a mass exodus of Russian women students abroad set in once again. But there was this difference : whereas formerly they had studied medicine in Switzerland in order to " go among the people " and pave the way for the struggle " for the people with the people's help "— an attempt which failed—they now made their way more and more frequently to Germany where the intellectual leaders of the Western European Labour movement— Liebknecht, Bebel, and Kautsky—were active, and where the young generation of Russians could apply themselves to the study of the political sciences.

For the calm which had supervened was only apparent. Beneath the ashes the fire continued to glow underground, and the Russian political fugitives, gathered for the most part in Switzerland, where they lived in the utmost material and moral privation, literally starving, constituted the first Social Democratic " Group for the Liberation of Labour " in the autumn of 1883 ; with pence laboriously collected they printed in their press revolutionary pamphlets and leaflets to be distributed in Russia illegally. Central figures in this company were the theoretical founder of the Russian Marxist school, Plekhanov, who declared that Russia had entered the ranks of capitalist states, and Vera Sassulich, who was at that time also living in Switzerland and who now fell upon the teaching of

Marx and Engels with characteristic enthusiasm, took up a pen for the first time at the age of forty, and began to write articles which occupied a place of esteem in Russian Marxist literature.

One of the few visitors who came to her from Russia about that time has described the room in which he found her : " The furniture even poorer than in Plekhanov's, the big table covered with exercise books, books, and a quantity of cigarette ends. On the window-sill a spirit-lamp and a coffee-pot from which Vera Ivanovna poured us out strong, black coffee every quarter of an hour. . . ." And Sassulich herself, of whom it was said that at that time she lived exclusively on work and coffee, adds in a letter to L. Deutsch in which she complains about her own life and her loneliness, and laments that one cannot work for the present day but only for an unknown future :

"... Like all decent Russian intellectuals I was able formerly, as you know, to occupy myself forever with doing nothing. . . . Now I hardly cease writing before two o'clock in the morning . . . for months I do not speak a word with a soul . . . I go to Geneva to visit George (Plekhanov) at most once a month . . . there is always something to discuss with him, it always turns out that he has solved some problem. . . . And so my life goes on without human companionship, without reading newspapers or reflecting about myself. . . ."

A whole decade passed. At last news came from home which showed more and more clearly that a Labour movement was springing up there in the form of a mass movement, started by the earliest Russian Social Democrats. And indeed Russia was once again covered with a network of secret societies, and the organizers of the rapidly growing Labour movement were to a large extent those that remained of Bakunin's former followers and of the *Narodovoltsi*, who now declared for Marxism.

This change is perfectly comprehensible, if we remember that the whole movement of the 'seventies, so rich in examples of the utmost self-sacrifice, was mainly the work of the intellectuals, and that the *Narodniki* had not

77

succeeded in bringing about the revolution with the help of the peasants, Bakunin's " born revolutionaries ", whose *mir* or village commune had been regarded as the germ of the future state. Nor had the *Narodovoltsi*, who made terror the chief weapon of revolution, been any more successful. Both entered the lists several decades too early and were unable to stir either the inert masses of the rural population or the working class which was only coming into being. Moreover, the intelligentsia lacked understanding of the significance of the Labour movement : the *Narodniki* regarded the modern industrial workers as hardly different from the peasants, except that they were rather more receptive. And the *Narodnaya Volya* did not even know how to create a mass movement : it chiefly devoted itself to agitation addressed to individuals, and so it vanished from the scene in the mid-'eighties without leaving any trace of its activities among the workers. The same applies, of course, even more to the women workers, although, as we have seen, the leading women revolutionaries had endeavoured to rouse just the women factory workers from their lethargy. Amongst the working women in the pre-Marxian phase of the Russian revolution there are not even individual names worthy of special mention.

It was only due to the advancing industrialization that a change came about, and the above-mentioned penetration of a Russianized form of Marxism achieved by Plekhanov and his school, to which the widely scattered forces of the older revolutionary movement adhered with renewed enthusiasm. United in a " Party of Russian Social Democrats ", they issued their journal *Labour* from 1885 to 1887 and carried on increasingly active propaganda among the workers who, transferred from feudal serfdom to modern labour slavery by the advancing industrialization of the country, learned from these people that abroad there was such a thing as protective legislation and a legal limit to the working day. In this earliest of Russian Social Democratic parties—which, by the way, was founded by a Bulgar—a few women of the intelligentsia played a part, including the Marxist

Cecilia Gurevich, whom we have already mentioned
once, and who distributed illegal literature among the
working women. Other Social Democratic organizations
succeeded it, and though they were quickly broken up,
yet a generation of proletarian, class-conscious, socialist
workers was slowly growing up who carried on the work
already begun, led by the intelligentsia. Individual
names became well known.

And now the triumphal march of Marxism began in
the empire of the Tsar, surely no chance development.
For there are many reasons why Russia, in spite of or
just because of her backwardness, offers the most fertile
soil upon which the seed of socialist theory can bring
forth a rich harvest. The Russian intelligentsia was
better prepared to receive the new teaching than other
countries, since Marx starts from the theses of Hegel,
whose philosophy has always been at home in Russia
and has been a school of dialectics to the Russian mind
for three generations. Likewise the urban workers are
more open to receive socialist teaching than in other
countries, for industrial capitalism, belated by many
decades, skipped the phase of early capitalism in its rise
and, eluding the transition stages, erected a number of
factories of considerable and even immense size in which
masses of workers were drilled into class consciousness,
not only by boundless exploitation, but by being organized
in a collective process of production. And so the few
factories in Russia before the war, which, however, were
of the type characteristic of advanced capitalism, were
already schools of revolution, and the Russian industrial
workers, in spite of their numerical insignificance in a
country of 150 million inhabitants, were thorough-going
representatives of the modern industrial proletariat.

By the beginning of the 'nineties there was no checking
the movement. At this time there was a genuine organization in St. Petersburg with 200 working-class members,
led partly by Social Democrats, partly by *Narodovoltsi*.
And in the organization there were already a number of
working women who soon took a leading part in the
movement and subsequently remained at their posts in

79

the fighting line for decades. One of the earliest of these convinced Social Democrats among the working women was the tailoress Grigoryeva, who was arrested in 1894, was sent to Eastern Siberia for five years, was an active member of the Workers' Committee in Ssaratov in 1901, was arrested again, and was working with the Social Revolutionaries in Odessa in 1905, where she was once more imprisoned. For the rest, Grigoryeva was brought up in the St. Petersburg Orphanage for Illegitimate Children. And it is not without significance for the conditions obtaining there that this Foundling Home was regarded as a breeding ground of revolutionaries, and that there was a group of socialist working women in St. Petersburg consisting exclusively of its former inmates ; some of them were employed in other places, some in the Home itself.

How strong feminine influence already was in this earliest socialist organization may be gathered from Norinskyi's Memoirs, which I quote here from Zederbaum's *Women in the Russian Revolutionary Movement* :

> Our new comrades, the women, breathed fresh life into the movement. The women radiated energy, and at the same time hatred of the enemy, the possessing classes, for all the wrong done to them and their mothers. Many of them, who have united their lives with like-minded working men, are carrying on the struggle to this day. And so they have become the mothers of a new generation of workers, and what is of most importance is that in moments of difficulty they make things easier for their husbands, and in part take upon themselves the burden that hitherto we had to bear alone.

In these words Norinskyi reveals the great significance of women's co-operation to the socialist working men, who gradually accustomed themselves to see in the women true comrades in their lives and partners in the struggle, whereas formerly they had not only to combat the class enemy but also indifference and lack of understanding at home, and consumed some of their energy in domestic strife.

In 1895 we find a " Fighting Association for the Liberation of the Working Class " in St. Petersburg, which counted Lenin among its members. Thanks to the increasing energy devoted to mass organization the Fighting Association was able the next year to start a strike of 30,000 textile workers, in which even workers in the remotest provinces joined and which resulted in a noteworthy practical achievement, a shortening of the working day. The whole generation of younger Marxist intelligentsia belonged to the Fighting Association, which was led by the maturer Social Democrats. There were four women on the Executive Committee, one of whom, Nadyeshda Krupskaya, later became the wife of Lenin and his helpmate in the struggle.

After leaving the grammar school in the middle of the 'eighties, the worst period of the Russian reaction, Krupskaya sought an answer to the old and ever-renewed Russian question : " What is to be done ? " The time was not favourable to the search : after the dissolution and failure of the *Narodnaya Volya*, almost all faith in the success of the revolutionary struggle was lost by large numbers of the intelligentsia. Instead Tolstoy's doctrine of the renunciation of force spread and people reconciled themselves to the theory of " small deeds " which called for a restriction of social activities and adaptation to the existing régime. But when she began to study educational theory, Krupskaya made the acquaintance of various radical groups, began to study Marx seriously, and from 1890–1 taught in the Ssmolensk Workers' College in St. Petersburg, where she carried on Marxist propaganda among the workers. Like a number of similar workers' colleges, the *Ssmolenskaya Shkola* was a reservoir whence emerged the best proletarian workers, the organizing talent of Social Democracy, whence the movement supplemented its forces from time to time.

Lenin, too, was active at the time in the same working-class circle whence came Krupskaya's pupils, and she tells of this period in her *Memoirs* as follows :

By the winter of 1894–5 I had already got to know Vladimir Ilyich fairly intimately. He was occupied with the workers' study-circles beyond the Nevsky Gate. I had already been working for years in that district as a teacher in the Smolensky

Sunday Evening Adult School, and was already fairly well acquainted with local working-class life. . . . The Smolensky School had 600 scholars. . . . The workers displayed unlimited confidence in the " school-mistress ". . . . A consumptive textile-worker wished the teacher a good fiancé because she had taught him to read and write. . . . One worker, a member of a sect, who had spent his whole life seeking God, wrote with satisfaction that only during Lent had he learned . . . that there was no God at all. And how easy things had now become. For there was nothing worse than being a slave of God, as you couldn't do anything about it. But to be the slave of a human being was much easier, as here a fight was possible. . . . Came a one-legged soldier and said : " Mikhail, whom you taught to read and write last year, died at work from exhaustion ; while dying he remembered you, told me to give you his compliments, and wished you a long life." A textile-worker who was a proud defender of the Tsar and priests uttered a warning : " Beware of that dark chap there who's always prowling about." Then an elderly worker argued that he could not possibly give up being a church elder because it is sickening to see how the priests gull the people, and they must be led to see things clearly. But he is not at all attached to the Church and understands quite well about the phases of development.

Workers belonging to our organization . . . did not regard all the women teachers in the same light. They distinguished to what extent the teachers were versed in the work of our circles. If they recognized a school-mistress to be " one of us " they would make themselves known to her by some phrase or other. For instance, in discussing the question of handicraft industry, they might say : " A handicraft worker cannot compete against large-scale production." Or they would intervene with a leading question, such as : " What is the difference between the St. Petersburg worker and the Archangel *mushik* ? " And after that they would give the teacher a meaning look, and nod to her in a particular way."

Not a few of Krupskaya's pupils at that period afterwards occupied a prominent place in the Russian Labour movement and the revolution. She herself was arrested after working for five years in the school and was to be exiled for three years. Her petition was granted to pass her exile in Siberia instead of Ufa, in the Government of Yenissyeysk, in the same village where Lenin was at that time serving his time ; and she now announced her official engagement to him.

Later Lenin issued his *Iskra* (The Spark) in Munich —whither Sassulich moved about this time ; he called her a character of " crystal purity "—and afterwards in London ; Krupskaya followed him abroad and acted as editorial secretary of that party organ till 1903. She worked indefatigably, maintained all manner of complicated, conspiratorial, and vital connections with organizations in Russia, and it is impossible to overestimate her work in elaborating the ideas propagated in *Iskra*. After the conference of 1903, which resulted in the split of the party into Mensheviks and Bolsheviks, Krupskaya remained at her post as secretary of the Bolshevik centre till the October revolution of 1917.

Meanwhile the Russian Labour Movement, and also the significance of women in it, grew from year to year. " The sound instinct of class," says Alexandra Kollontay in her *History of the Women's Labour Movement in Russia*, " impelled the working women to support strikes, and it was not seldom that the women organized and led factory revolts on their own initiative." And in fact working women played an active part in the labour disturbances in the textile mills in Moscow in 1872 and in St. Petersburg in 1874. In the celebrated labour revolt in Oryekhovo-Suyevo, in the textile district of the Government of Vladimir, which wrung from the Government the prohibition of night work for women and children, the leaders were women. In general it is noticeable that the elemental wave of strikes and labour unrest which stirred proletarian Russia again and again in the 'seventies and the first half of the 'eighties was principally in the textile trades, in which cheaper feminine labour had always predominated. And so it is doubtless no exaggeration when women are credited with the lion's share of the economic, and of course also the political, struggles of that period.

In the 'nineties the trade union and revolutionary tactics of the Russian workers developed. The strike of the textile workers in 1896 was the turning-point. But even earlier, in 1895, the history of the Russian Labour movement records a strike, the so-called " revolt of Laferme ", which was the work of women cigarette-makers. The occasion was the announcement that wages, already meagre, were to be reduced. Once again it was the women workers who had the courage to come forward for the first time as an organized body. Not only did they break the factory window-panes and destroy the machinery, but they resisted the police desperately and were only put to flight by the fire brigade who were summoned and turned the hose upon them. It is significant that this strike was a case of the outbreak of mass passion : the organized Social Democrats knew nothing of the whole action, which the women workers had undertaken on their own initiative.

So, too, the historic textile strike of 1896 was due to the initiative of women, who downed tools together with the men and left the mills. An attempt on the part of the masters to impose worse working conditions and reduce wages provoked a strike in 1898 in the Maxwell and Pahl factory, but this was organized.

There was a regular " battle for justice ", as the workers called it later, between them and the police. Fifteen were arbitrarily arrested and, when brought before the court, refused to follow the advice of their defending counsel and petition the Tsar, and four of these were women who played a prominent part, this time also, in the conflict with the police. Many of them, who were beaten till the blood flowed, showed themselves no less courageous and resolute than the men as defendants.

The famous " Obukhov defensive " on the occasion of the strike in Obukhov works, with about 6,000 workers, which took place three years later, was far more serious and cost the lives of a number of victims. For five hours the strikers resisted a vigorous attack of the mounted gendarmerie and the military in collaboration with the police, who used firearms freely. From the neighbouring cardboard-box factory the women workers hurried to their assistance, carrying stones in their skirts which they, together with their children, tore from the pavement to use against the assailants. The sanguinary struggle, news of which spread immediately to all the working-class quarters, lasted till far into the night and gave rise to fears of fresh, serious disturbances, and so the management, at a hint from the authorities, gave in and declared its readiness to make certain concessions.

Amongst the thirty-seven participants in the fight who were arrested there were two working girls of eighteen. One of them was brought up for trial. In spite of her youth the Public Prosecutor demanded a heavy sentence, for the accused had declared in the preliminary examination that she had acted after careful consideration, aware of her responsibility, inspired by sympathy with the workers. She was condemned to three years' imprisonment. The " Obukhov defensive " —also known as the " battle in the Schlüsselburg district "—proved for the first time that in case of need the workers could face not only the police but the military as well, and that a street fight between them and the armed forces of the state need not necessarily end with their defeat. It left traces of long duration among the proletariat of St. Petersburg. In the history of the Russian revolution this battle, in which women played a prominent part, is marked out as leading directly to the struggles of 1905 and 1917.

Although the tempestuous growth of the Labour movement was apparently checked for a time by the war with Japan, it flared up again the more fiercely right at the beginning of 1905 : the dismissal of four workers called forth the strike in the Putilov works in St. Petersburg, which subsequently attained no little fame, and which immediately spread to all the factories and workshops in the city. On January 9th, afterwards known to history as " Bloody Sunday ", Pope Gapon, instigated by a group of workers with whom he was in touch, made this gigantic strike the occasion of a demonstration hitherto unprecedented in Russia. With ikons, images of the saints, and portraits of the Tsar, an immense crowd, a

procession of working men and women—for a number
of wives, mothers, and children of the working men
went too—marched to the Winter Palace in order to
present a petition to the Tsar. The people were received by deadly volleys of rifle fire. . . . Every trace
of faith in the Tsar and his Government was destroyed for ever in those few hours and that very day
the first barricades were erected in St. Petersburg,
in the district of Vassilyi-Ostrov. . . . That morning
one of the many women who, as in all such cases, took
part eagerly in the preparations for the day of the " St.
Petersburg workers' bloody baptism " and came forward
as speakers—Karelina, a working woman—addressed
the following words to her audience : " Mothers and
wives ! Do not dissuade your husbands and brothers
from risking their lives for a just cause. Come with us !
If they attack us or shoot on us, do not weep, do not
lament, be sisters of mercy ! Here are bands with the
Red Cross, fasten them round your sleeves, but not
before they begin to shoot on you." These simple
words roused the women to great enthusiasm, as an eye-
witness testifies, and the answer came as with one voice :
" We will all go with you." More than a thousand lives
were sacrificed by shameless treachery. Among them
were a number of women and children. One of these
women, Berdichevskaya, who fought on the barricades,
was struck by four bullets and died the next day. Before
her death she repeated again and again : " I do not
regret for a moment that I stood on the barricades. . . ."
The massacre of St. Petersburg caused a howl of
indignation throughout the land. A rising wave of
strikes, vast and sinister, flooding all living things, swept
with its menace not only the industrial centres, but even
the smallest towns and settlements. The Government did
all in its power to smother the movement in blood. But
the revolt continued and all that year disturbances broke
out, now here, now there : there was shooting in Riga
and Warsaw, and in Ivanovo-Vosnyessyensk the textile
workers struck. But the climax was the mutiny on the
battle-cruiser *Potyomkin* and the general rising in Odessa.

We are acquainted with these events through Eisenstein's magnificent films. What is much less well known is the predominant part played by a woman, Inna Ssmidovich. She had been a member of the executive committee of the " Fighting Association " since the 'nineties, and before Krupskaya went abroad she had worked as secretary of Lenin's *Iskra*, and organized its secret distribution in Russia.

In 1905 Ssmidovich was in Odessa, where she carried on most dangerous propaganda among the soldiers and sailors, going about as a " soldiers' girl " in the barracks and the quarters and taverns specially allotted for that purpose. Soon she gained a remarkable influence over the soldiers. At the end of 1905, when a mutiny broke out on the steamer *Prut* which agitated all Ssevastopol she made rousing speeches in meetings of thousands of soldiers and sailors. In this way she became known in the city and, when the mutiny had been suppressed, she was obliged to flee from Crimea amidst the greatest dangers.

This woman's presence of mind is illustrated by another flight of hers from the gendarmes in 1902 on one of her visits to Russia with contraband, after she had been arrested in Kiev with copies of *Iskra*. On the way to the court she begged the gendarmes who were guarding her to allow her to go to the closet in the yard of the police-station. Whilst her guard awaited her outside the bolted door she took off her valuable fur and her cap with lightning speed, tied a handkerchief over her head, and left the closet in the cheap jacket which she wore under her " lady's " garb in order to be ready for all eventualities. The transformation was accomplished so swiftly, her appearance was so completely changed, that the gendarmes took her for someone else and let her go unmolested. The trick was only discovered some time later, when no trace of Ssmidovich was to be found.

As we know, the march of history could no longer be checked in Russia. After a general strike in October, 1905—the same month in which, twelve years later,

Russia was finally shaken to its foundations—Tsar Nicholas II, the last and pettiest of the Romanovs on the Russian throne, issued a manifesto in which he gave the people a constitution. True, the concessions contained in it were very slight, but nevertheless they made new methods of struggle possible, opportunities of which the Labour movement was able to make plentiful use thereafter.

The brief survey which I have here attempted of the part played by women in the Russian Labour movement would be incomplete, if I did not touch in a few words upon the feminist movement, which had many points of contact with it. Before 1905, and indeed for some little time afterwards, it still appeared fairly homogeneous. The left-wing feminists showed themselves at this time fairly radical and revolutionary, although their bourgeois attitude was becoming steadily plainer. But as the industrialization of the country proceeded and the influence of socialist ideas became stronger, a cleavage, which had already appeared in the Western European countries, proved inevitable. And so there was soon a proletarian and a bourgeois feminist movement in the land of the Tsars too, and whilst the latter steadily lost influence, the former spread more and more among the masses. The purely feminist demands gave place to those of the proletarian class struggle. In 1907 the first meetings of working women organized by the Social Democratic party were held, with women speakers who not only laid stress on their differences with the bourgeois feminists, but declared that the proletarian women's movement was an integral part of the revolutionary struggle carried on under the socialist banner. Here, too, the demand for the protection of women's labour, for maternity and infant welfare work, and for equal political rights for women, first came up for discussion. The relation of the revolutionary Labour party to the feminist movement was likewise eagerly discussed.

The left-wing bourgeois feminists centred in the

" Women's Political Club " which established four working women's clubs in St. Petersburg. But there was no stopping the secession of the proletarian women from the movement, hitherto more or less homogeneous. And since these clubs, called for the most part " self-education societies ", were very popular, the Social Democratic women managed to open their first club in 1907 under the harmless title of the " Society for Mutual Help among Working Women ". This club was managed by women. And in the winter of 1907–8 a group of women agitators charged by the party with the task of winning the proletarian women for the revolutionary class struggle began active work among its members— some 300 in number—mainly textile women workers, although the membership included a number of men. Chief among these agitators was the future Soviet diplomat, Alexandra Kollontay, who was sent in 1907 as a delegate to the International Conference of Socialist Women in Stuttgart. In so far as police regulations allowed, lectures were arranged, and discussions, meetings, gatherings of the women workers in the associations, and so on. Later, with a fresh wave of reaction, this club was closed. " But its activities," writes Kollontay in her *History of the Women Workers' Movement in Russia*, " clearly left indelible traces : in this club in the Predtyechenskaya the foundations were laid for a revolutionary class propaganda amongst the broad masses of proletarian women in Russia."

In March, 1913, an international Women's Day was celebrated in St. Petersburg at the instigation of the women textile workers, who formed the storm troops of the revolution to the last. In the history of the Russian Labour movement this day, to which *Pravda* devoted enthusiastic articles and even the Duma lengthy speeches, stands as the day upon which the Russian working woman took her place in the international Labour movement. A telegram of greeting to the Women's International gave formal expression to that circumstance.

In the following year the women's day was celebrated

in other towns as well, in Moscow, Ssamara, Ssaratov, etc. In the capital the first issue of the journal *Rabotnitsa* (Working Woman), which still continues to appear, was published on the occasion of the celebration, and the first great procession of the St. Petersburg workers was held—an imposing demonstration followed by a mass meeting at which revolutionary songs were sung and for the first time the red flag waved in the streets of the royal city. Finally the demonstrators were dispersed by the police and many who had taken part in the procession were arrested.

The early years of the world war, which broke out when the Russian workers were in the midst of their revolutionary struggle, paralysed the Labour movement for a time. But secretly it gained new strength from the resentment at the sufferings and privations which the war imposed upon the people of the gigantic empire, and preparations were made for a fresh onslaught. And once again it was the Russian woman, the working woman, who first gave expression to the indignation of the masses. *The international women's day, in February, 1917, was the first great historic day of the Russian revolution* which swept away Tsarism and paved the way for Red October. "Lawyers and journalists belonging to the classes damaged by the revolution," writes Trotski, " wasted a good deal of ink subsequently trying to prove that what happened in February was essentially a petticoat rebellion, backed up afterwards by a soldiers' mutiny." But this same Trotski also writes :

The fact is that the February revolution was begun from below . . . the initiative being taken of their own accord by the most oppressed and downtrodden part of the proletariat—the women textile workers, among them no doubt many soldiers' wives. The overgrown bread-lines had provided the last stimulus. About 90,000 workers, men and women, were on strike that day. The fighting mood expressed itself in demonstrations, meetings, encounters with the police. . . . A mass of women, not all of them workers, flocked to the municipal duma demanding bread. . . . Woman's Day passed successfully, with enthusiasm and without victims.

ON THE EVE OF RED OCTOBER

An eye-witness describes how the women came out on the historic 23rd of February, old style (March 8th) :

The working women, driven to desperation by starvation and war, came along like a hurricane that destroys everything in its path with the violence of an elemental force. This revolutionary march of working women, full of the hatred of centuries of oppression, was the spark that set light to the great flame of the February revolution, that revolution which was to shatter Tsarism.

A week later *Pravda* published an article entitled " The Great Day " :

Long before the war the proletarian International declared March 8th as an international women's festival. A week ago the former Government in Petrograd wanted to prevent the working women from celebrating the festival. That led to conflict, first in the Putilov Works, which transformed a demonstration into a revolution ! *The first day of the revolution— that is the women's day*, the day of the Women Workers' International. All honour to the women ! All honour to the International ! *The women were the first to tread the streets of Petrograd on their day.* In Moscow it was frequently the women who determined the attitude of the military : they entered the barracks and persuaded the soldiers to take the side of the revolution, and the soldiers followed them. All honour to the women !

And in the succeeding " five days which shook the world " the Russian women remained faithful to their historic rôle, to their revolutionary traditions.

They go up to the cordons more boldly than men, take hold of the rifles, beseech, almost command : " Put down your bayonets—join us." The soldiers are excited, ashamed, exchange anxious glances, waver ; some one makes up his mind first, and the bayonets rise guiltily above the shoulders of the advancing crows. The barrier is opened, a joyous and grateful " Hurrah ! " shakes the air. The soldiers are surrounded. Everywhere arguments, reproaches, appeals—the revolution makes another forward step. (Trotski, *History of the Russian Revolution*.)

91

Thus we see the Russian woman marching along the long and thorny road to a new Russia, the road of the revolution, of which I have endeavoured here to give a brief description in its most important stages : inspired by a courage which not seldom put her masculine comrades to shame, confident, contemptuous of death, sometimes as leader and always with head erect, her eyes fixed on the future which beckons her beyond the struggle and its sanguinary sacrifices.

And what is that future like—already become the present in the Russia of to-day ? What has it brought to the Russian woman, how many of her hopes has it fulfilled ?

THE OCTOBER REVOLUTION OF 1917 AND THE LIBERATION OF WOMEN

LENIN AND WORKING WOMEN

. . . In Petrograd, here in Moscow, in cities and industrial centres, and out in the country, proletarian women have stood the test magnificently in the revolution. Without them we should not have won. Or barely won. That is my view. How brave they were, how brave they still are ! Just imagine all the sufferings and privations that they bear. And they hold out because they want to establish the Soviets, because they want freedom, communism. Yes, indeed, our proletarian women are magnificent class warriors. They deserve admiration and love. And, moreover, we must acknowledge that the " Constitutional Democrat " ladies in Petrograd showed themselves much braver in withstanding us than the young lords.

—LENIN.

"EVERY cook must learn to rule the state." With these words of Lenin's, which, paradoxical as they sound, have to-day half come true, a new chapter began in October, 1917, in the history of Russian women, and doubtless not of Russian women alone.

. . . It is impossible to win the masses for politics unless we include the women. . . . We must win the millions of working women in city and village for our cause, for our struggle, and in particular for the communist transformation of society. Without the women there can be no true mass movement [said Lenin in another passage]. The work begun by the Soviet Government can only lead to victory if it is shared not by hundreds but by millions upon millions of women in Russia. . . .

And further :

In the old capitalist society it required a special training to play a part in politics, which explains why women's share in

93

politics even in the most advanced capitalist countries is exceedingly slight. . . . But it is our task to make politics accessible to every working woman. . . . For from the moment when private property and the ownership of land and factories are abolished and the power of the landowners and capitalists is broken, political duties will be perfectly simple to the working masses and within the reach of all.

And so a year later, in November, 1918, the first All-Russian Conference of Proletarian and Peasant Women met in Moscow, with almost 1,200 delegates even then, representatives of nearly a million working women in Soviet Russia.

It was the working women themselves in the main who started the idea of this conference. A special office was opened to make the preparations, and for weeks beforehand there were countless meetings in factories and workshops in Moscow and Petrograd, intended to present the tasks and aims of the conference to the working women. In order to arouse the provinces as well agitators were sent to all parts of the country who, in spite of the many dangers to which they were exposed from the White Guards still lurking everywhere, carried out their task with brilliant success and met with an enthusiastic response everywhere.

In 1918, when the civil war was still raging, when we still had to struggle against hunger, cold, and unprecedented devastations, when it was still necessary to defeat the enemy on countless fronts, at this juncture the first conference of proletarian and peasant women was summoned. Hundreds of working women, from the remotest factories and villages, had come to Moscow with their complaints, grievances, and doubts, with all their cares, great and small. They all wanted to hear from Lenin why peace had not come immediately after the October revolution, why hunger and cold were still rampant throughout the country. The mass of the women, wholly inexperienced, had hardly an inkling at that time how hard and long is the path of socialist construction, how many obstacles must be overcome before the final victory of the proletariat. The working women had had great hopes of this conference. . . . Especially they wanted the question of peace solved. . . . In the concrete they wanted to know when there would be bread and fuel. And likewise questions were even then constantly coming to the fore concerning the arrangement of their purely personal lives, their *byt* : questions of socialization, of the education of children, and of food-values were raised. The party succeeded in organizing a revolutionary storm troop from the masses of women and to direct their activities towards constructive work.

From this moment steady, systematic, and purposive work began among the masses, designed to create the prerequisite conditions of equal rights for working women ; women began to be drawn into the work of socialist construction and trained leaders were called in. . . . The conference was variegated and brilliant,"

so Nyurina, one of the most influential women in public life in the Soviet Union, concludes her report of this first public conference of liberated Russian women in Red Moscow (*Women in the Struggle for the New Society*).

In the resolution on the " functions of working women in Soviet Russia " passed at this first conference of proletarian and peasant women, stress was laid on the point that, since the conditions of their liberation were exactly the same as those required for the liberation of the whole proletariat, the working women had no specific feminist questions to solve distinct from the general problems of the proletariat.

And so it was not necessary to organize special women's societies in the land of the Soviets. " Organization is determined by our ideological attitude. No special unions of communist women. A communist woman belongs in the party as a member, just like the communist man. With the same duties and rights. On that point there can be no difference of opinion. But we must not refuse to realize this : the party must have organs, working groups, commissions, committees, sections, or whatever you like to call them, with the special duty of rousing the mass of the women, to unite them with the party and to keep them permanently under its influence. That means, of course, that we pursue systematic activities among the mass of women. We must train those who have been roused and win

95

them for the proletarian class struggle under the guidance of the Communist party and equip them." These words of Lenin's were now put into practice, and the women soon constituted organs of the kind with their own methods of working.

At the same time vigorous agitation was carried on among the masculine masses in order to enlighten them about the essence and significance of equal rights for women and the share of the women in constructive work. Lenin defined his view, too, upon this task of the practical politician in writing to Clara Zetkin in the following words :

> Very few men, even among proletarians, think how much labour and weariness they could lighten for women, in fact save them altogether, if they would lend a hand in " women's work ". No, that is incompatible with " a man's rights and dignity ", which require that he should enjoy his peace and comfort. A woman's domestic life is one in which she is sacrificed every day amidst a thousand petty details. The ancient right of the man to be lord survives secretly. Objectively his slave takes her revenge. Also secretly. The women's backwardness, their lack of understanding for the men's revolutionary ideals, diminish their joy and resolution in the struggle. They are like tiny parasites which go unnoticed and destroy and gnaw, slowly but surely. I know the lives of the workers, not only from books. Our communist labours among the masses of women, our political work among them, involves a considerable effort to educate the men. We must root out the ancient outlook of the lord and master to the last fibre. In the party and among the masses. That is part of our political task, just as much as the urgently necessary training of a staff of comrades, male and female, thoroughly schooled in theory and practice, to carry on the party's work among the working women. . . .

After the conclusion of the first women's conference special commissions were attached to the Central Executive, as well as to the Provincial and District Committees, for agitation and propaganda among the women with the duty of organizing systematic recruiting efforts, arranging meetings, lectures, and gatherings, and publishing special literature. In this way delegate meetings were constituted in the Soviet Union, of which we shall hear more, and gradually came to be established institutions ; and they were copied to a certain extent even in certain bourgeois countries—Germany, England, Finland, and America—in the years 1924–7. These meetings have fully proved their worth up to the present day as the first phase of education in practical politics for the proletarian and peasant women and the most important link between the party and the masses.

And now the women set to work with intensified, with tremendous activity. " In collaboration with the Communist party and the trade unions, the proletarian dictatorship of course made every effort to overcome the reactionary attitude of men and women and to destroy the foundation of the old, uncommunist psychology. It was a matter of course that men and women should receive equal treatment in legislation. In all fields we find an honest endeavour to put equality of rights into practice. We gave the women their place in social life, in administration, legislation, and government. We opened educational courses and institutes to them in order to make them more competent in their working and social life. We established communal kitchens and public dining-rooms, wash-houses and mending centres, crèches, kindergartens, children's homes, and various types of educational institution. In short we took that item in our programme seriously which demands that the domestic and educational functions of the single household shall be transferred to the community. In this way women are freed from the old household slavery and liberated from dependence on their husbands. According to their talents and tastes they can develop their activities freely in society. The children have better conditions of development than at home. We have the most progressive protective legislation for working women in the world and it is carried out by the agents of the organized workers. We build maternity homes and homes for mothers and babies, and organize courses in the care of infants and young children, exhibitions of maternity and infant welfare, and the like. We make the utmost efforts to mitigate the distress of uncared-for, unemployed women. . . ."

Twelve years have passed since Lenin spoke thus to Clara Zetkin in his study in the Moscow Kremlin, that same Kremlin within whose walls, only 250 years earlier, women had been confined in their *terem*. And it is fifteen years in all since the equal rights of women were proclaimed in Soviet Russia. In the succeeding chapters I will tell of what has been achieved in that decade and a half.

"DAUGHTERS OF THE REVOLUTION"

THE October revolution, which endowed women with equal rights, imposed the same duties upon them as men, of course. And so from the outset we find women at the front, in the Urals and the Caucasus, in Siberia and the Ukraine, wherever there was need to defend the achievements of the revolution. In this way the great army arose of women who fought side by side with the Red Army soldiers for their newly won freedom during years of civil war, rifle in hand, undergoing the severest privations.

Women as nurses in wartime have always been a familiar idea. Noted and notorious, too, were Kerenskyi's "Women's Battalions", to which even Lenin does not deny a certain approbation. But now thousands of women who had received their baptism of fire as *tovarishchi*, comrades (it is characteristic that the Russian language has no special feminine form of this word), on the October barricades came forward as Red Army soldiers and scouts, as engine-drivers of armoured trains, and secretaries of revolutionary tribunals, as Red sisters, members of cavalry regiments, machine-gunners, and even as commanders. And what is wholly new and unprecedented in the history of womanhood—in spite of the heroines on the barricades of the Paris Commune of 1871—is the fact that in all ranks, in all units, they made good heroically, remained at their posts, and knew how to die on the battlefields.

TITLE PAGE OF THE SOVIET RUSSIAN WOMEN'S JOURNAL
RABOTNITSA
with Portrait of Lenin

[*face p.* 98

PETROVA, A WOMAN MEMBER OF THE RED ARMY
Decorated with the Order of the Red Banner

| face p. 99

"DAUGHTERS OF THE REVOLUTION"

Opinions may, of course, differ as to how far the point of view accepted by many of the intelligentsia in Russia and elsewhere about Tolstoy's doctrine of non-violence and toleration of political opponents is compatible with the conception of the class war, the dictatorship of the proletariat, and the necessity of terror. That question, however, we will not examine here. " You can't tackle the revolution with a rosebud "—so I was instructed by an old working woman in Leningrad who had grown grey in the class struggle and had already attained the rank of a " heroine of labour ". Let everyone decide for himself whether she was right or not.

The history of the Russian revolution still reverently cherishes the memory of the countless " daughters of the revolution " who marched forth from their factories, villages, and settlements, no longer as single heroines, but in such vast hosts that during Kornilov's assault no less than 200,000 working women went to the front from Leningrad alone. Thousands of them never returned home.

In a little selection of character studies A. Bogat, at that time a woman cavalry soldier in Budyonny's army, depicts a number of women from the civil war who took part in various capacities in the struggle for the dictatorship of the proletariat and sacrificed their best years for it.

The examples of which Bogat tells with simple fervour in her vivid portrayal are deeply moving and remind us in some respects of the legendary bravery of the pre-Christian Russian women who fought the Byzantines side by side with their husbands, in masculine attire.

Whilst she was still a young girl Pinyikova, a peasant from the Ssamara Government, went to the front, put on a Red Army uniform, took a rifle, and joined the regiment under the name of Ivan Pinyikov. Ivan Pinyikov often astonished his comrades by his courage. He fought in a number of battles and helped to repel not a few attacks. And Ivan was always among the foremost. So it was in the battle near the settlement of Kharykovskyi. It was a long-drawn-out fight and the soldiers were exhausted. The enemy did not spare ammunition; it rained upon the combatants, claiming more and more victims.

But the attack failed again and again. The units began to waver, the combatants lost confidence. . . . In a flash Pinyikova rushed forwards, and, with a cry of : " On, *tovarishchi*, the victory is ours ! " she swept them all along with her. A resounding " Hurrah ! " As one man they all rushed to the attack. . . . The enemy fell back.

As a soldier who had distinguished herself, Pinyikova was sent to be trained as a machine-gunner. When she had completed her training she returned to the front. . . .

More accounts of her heroic deeds—more victories for her regiment. . . .

In a battle against the Cossacks in which she refused to give ground to the last, she was killed at her post. . . .

Another case of a working woman attached to the staff as a scout, who was taken prisoner by the enemy :

She was dragged to the White Guards' staff. The gold on the officers' epaulettes shone in the light of the candles and torches.

" A Red commander ? What unit ? A Bolshevik ? Here, fellows ! Strip him ! Search him ! "

Her clothes were torn off, and—to the amazement of all— beneath the ragged, dusty soldier's coat a woman was concealed. The harsh, masterful voice, the hardened features, all had pointed to a Bolshevik commander.

They began to interrogate her. From which unit had she come, who commanded it, had they ammunition, whence did they expect reinforcements, and so on. She was overwhelmed with questions, but she answered none.

The cross-examination continued for a long time, for they hoped to extract information from her. For three days and nights she was tormented, beaten till she was half-unconscious, and denied food.

Then the staff returned and the cross-examination was resumed. This time with benevolent smiles, persuasion, and promises of liberty. She remained inflexible.

Blows again, and imprisonment. The next day—new tactics : threats to shoot her, blows. Information about the Red troops was required of her. Comrades were shot before her eyes. She believed that her turn, too, was coming. Nevertheless, not a word could be extracted from the tormented woman.

Mad with rage, the White officer commanded that she should

be given seventy-five strokes of the lash. After the twelfth stroke she lost consciousness. . . .

They let her live because it was the first time that the enemy had come across so steadfast a Russian woman. . . .

Later she succeeded in escaping from captivity.

I met *Tovarishch* Plotnikova [Bogat relates in another passage] by chance on the staff of the first cavalry army. I had already heard that she was one of the heroines of the 19th cavalry regiment. But I had imagined her quite different from what she actually was. Rather small of stature, thin, pale, wearing the Order of the Red Banner on her breast, she seemed still half a child. Only her clear eyes burned with resolution and will-power.

She had taken part in a great many attacks. The battle near the Cossack village Yegorlytskaya had impressed itself especially deeply upon her memory.

An assault by strong enemy forces had forced part of the 19th cavalry regiment to retreat. The exhausted soldiers were thrown into disarray. Only Plotnikova did not lose her head. She flew from one end of the front to the other on horseback. Everywhere she fired the men's zeal and inspired enthusiasm. . . .

At a decisive moment she spurred forwards : " Charge ! " and carried the whole troop with her. The enemy was repulsed and the Red Army soldiers carried their severely wounded comrade out of the firing-line.

Bogat quotes a report of the death of four women comrades at the time of the Kolchak offensive from the Siberian paper *The Red Bell* ; in the course of their activities in the counter-espionage service they had been captured by the Whites and were put to death. An eye-witness writes as follows of the death of Comrade Sorina :

When night fell we sat there and waited to know whose turn it would be to-day.

It was nearly always at midnight that they were called out. And so it happened on this occasion. Suddenly resounding steps were heard on the deck of the barque where the prisoners were kept. They approached rapidly. Our hearts stood still, and a single thought shot through our minds : " Who ? Whose turn is it ? " . . .

Out of the darkness came a low, domineering voice :
" Sorina ! Hurry up and come out ! . . ."

But she, the marvellous girl, still half a child, was asleep at the
time. When she woke she began to undress calmly. There
was soon a low sobbing to be heard in the bedroom, and the
eyes of her fellow-prisoners filled with tears. . . .

When she had undressed, all but her underclothes, she handed
her dress to a friend and said : " Give it to my mother. . . ."
Then she put on her cloak and turned to us : " Do not cry,
comrades. I am going to my death, but I know exactly what
for. Long live the power of the Soviets ! You may perhaps
be saved by our *tovarishchi*. But I shall not see them again.
Good-bye ! "

And without tears, without complaint, she went up on deck
with a firm step, turning round as she went and called to us :
" Good-bye ! "

She never returned. Next day one of the guards told us that
before she was put to death in the guardroom Sorina had taken
off her cloak and handed it to the White Guard standing nearest
to her, saying : " Tell my mother and my comrades that the
technicians in the fatigue company violated me and half beat
me to death with a whip. . . ."

There were countless such women, soldiers of the Red
Army, all burning with enthusiasm as only women,
mothers—perhaps only Russian women—can. For the
most part they were quite poor peasants, *byednyachki*, and
maidservants, *batrachki*, the poorest of the poor, who had
suffered especially severely under the twofold oppression
of their doubly hard fate. Never before having emerged
from their ancient inertia and passivity, they were roused
and conscious for the first time of their humanity which
they now felt they must defend at all costs. There are
but few names that have been preserved. But most of
their lives are alike, and in all cases there is an equally
moving scorn of death.

There were, moreover, some non-Russians among these
" unknown women soldiers ". In a compilation entitled
Daughters of the Revolution (Krassnaya Novy, 1923),
dedicated to these heroines, we find an account of a
German woman settler :

The *kulaks* pointed at her : " Here is a communist ! "

They had long been showing their wolfish teeth. Bandits, beasts, inhuman brutes, seized her and dragged her to the icy barn. The cross-examination began : " Where are other communists to be found ? " She said nothing. That night they tortured her. . . . And at dawn the peasant woman Lea Root was put to death. . . .

Lea Root was a member of the Executive Committee for her village (in the district of the Volga Germans) and chairman of the Food Commission.

" Our Rosa Luxemburg met her death as a brave soldier of the revolution," said the German peasants, and mourned for Comrade Root.

During the civil war sixty-three women in the Soviet Union were decorated with the *Order of the Red Banner.* The majority of these women soldiers, who were no longer quite young and who distinguished themselves by their courage, died prematurely as a result of the unaccustomed hardships. In the membership of the association of " Women of the Fighting Ranks " we find only twenty-three *Krassnosnamyonki* (members of the Order of the Red Banner), all in responsible positions.

The President of this Association is the Cossack Panya Vishnyakova who, formerly a working woman, has been a member of the party since 1903 and had been decorated with the Red Banner for special merit in the fight against Denikin. She attended the Marxist courses in Moscow and learned German eagerly " so as to be able to make herself understood better in the world revolution ".

The deputy chairman is *Tovarishch* Bulle, a fair-haired, sensitive, womanly woman, a Lett, formerly occupied in the Political Section, now in the Comintern, wearing the star of the Red Order on her breast. She knows every single one of her fellow-fighters and had kindly and lovable things to tell me of each.

The *Krassnosnamyonka* Petrova, formerly the wife of a miner, about sixty, served in Siberia in the partisan detachment. She had learned to read and write a little earlier, and had given birth to nine children. At the time of the civil war she was nearly fifty, and she tells how maternal feelings in her conflicted with civic feelings, till she made up her mind to join the army in spite of all. They refused to take her, but she succeeded in securing her acceptance. She then carried important documents disguised as a nun and rendered great services in that capacity. In Chita she actually succeeded in making her way into the enemy headquarters. It was for that that she was decorated with the Red Banner.

In the espionage service there were, according to *Tovarishch* Bulle, a number of *Krassnosnamyonki*, as well as in the machine-gun detachments: one of these gunners, Marussya Popova, who had joined the army as a young and illiterate peasant girl, showed a special interest in mechanics. She soon learned to read and write—the Red Army is to-day the largest " polit-school " in the Soviet Union, a school in which instruction is given in all subjects, including agriculture, a cultural influence of prime importance—and by 1930 Popova had completed her course, not only in the faculty of labour but also in the V.U.S., an advanced training course for teachers.

Patrikeyeva, *Krassnosnamyonka* and soldier at the front, took part in the civil war as a Red Sister. She is a delicate, fair-haired creature with an " angelic voice ", yet she disarmed a scout and was rewarded with the Order of the Red Banner. But once, when she was captured by the White Guards, they cut a red star on her forehead. She managed to escape, however, and returned to the front, worked in a factory till 1929, and is studying to-day in the faculty of labour. Her greatest grief is that her forehead has been disfigured.

The *Krassnosnamyonka* Rosalia Ssamoilovna Syem-lyachka enjoys great popularity ; she is a Jewess and has been decorated with two orders : the Order of the Red Banner from the front, and the Lenin Order, the Order of the Red Labour Banner for exceptional services in " the improvement and simplification of the state machinery, the struggle against bureaucracy, maladministration, and irresponsibility in economic organizations ". Besides this Syemlyachka, who has been in the party since 1902, is a member of the Board of the R.K.I., the Labour and Peasant Inspectorship, in which a good many women work.

Without any positive prohibition, there are practically no women in the Red Army to-day—in view of their physique which does not always allow of their " proving themselves men " ; only occasionally are they found in positions of command in the active service ; there are also five in the Reserve and at Headquarters who have passed through the Military Academy. The " Daughters of the Revolution " have already passed into history, for life confronts the women of the Soviet state with fresh tasks.

THE ABOLITION OF ECCLESIASTICAL MARRIAGE

WHEREAS the February revolution of 1917, and the Kerenskyi Government in its eight months of office, made not the slightest change in the rights of the Church and in the position of women and children, we hear from Lenin at the Conference of Proletarian and Peasant Women in 1919 that the Soviet Government, being a government of workers, made radical alterations in legislation as affecting women in the very first months after it seized power.

Of the laws that kept women in a dependent position not one stone remains standing in the Soviet Republic. I mean by that those laws which exploited the weaker, often indeed the humiliating, position of women : the laws, that is, which concerned divorce, illegitimate children, and the right of a woman to support from the father of her child. . . . In the democratic republics we see that equality of rights is, indeed, proclaimed, but at every step—in civil law and the laws concerning women's position in the family and divorce—we find inequality and the degradation of women. And therefore we say : that is a violation of democracy. . . . The Soviet Government has done more than any other country, even the most progressive, to realize the democratic idea by wiping out the last trace of the disabilities hitherto imposed upon women from its legislation. And therefore I repeat that no state whatever and no democratic legislation whatever has done half as much for women as the Soviet Government has achieved in the first months of its existence. . . .

Lenin's decrees of December 19th and 20th, 1917, on
" The Dissolution of Marriage " and " Civil Marriage,
Children, and Registration " replaced the Tsarist marriage law by the Soviet code, which is characterized by its
vigorous repudiation of the hitherto accepted conception
of marriage based upon inequality and indissolubility, a
tie which concedes to the man the headship and the right
to force upon the woman nationality, residence, and name,
and to decide how the children shall be educated. The
decree abolishes ecclesiastical marriage and divorce, and
the only form of marriage recognized as legal is civil
marriage. The bridal pair are free to be married in
church after the civil registration, as their own private
affair. The principle is established of complete equality
between man and wife, of separate property, and the
mutual responsibility of each to support the other. So
also is the liberty to dissolve the marriage at any time at
the wish of one only of the partners ; further—and this
must be stressed as a peculiarly far-reaching innovation—
the different rights of " legitimate " and " illegitimate "
children are abolished and the children of an unregistered
marriage are put on an equality with those of a registered
marriage. A marriage law, therefore, fundamentally
suited to working people, men and women who labour and
follow a profession.

The code of 1918 based upon Lenin's decree " concerning the registration of births, marriages, and deaths, and
the law of marriage, the family, and wardship " is fast
establishing itself in Soviet Russia, in spite of the predominantly peasant population. Civil Registrars' offices
are being gradually introduced, a particular innovation
for Russia, where hitherto there had been none but
ecclesiastical ones. And according to the records of the
Narkomvnudyel, the People's Commissariat of the Interior, 1,383,633 entries were made during the three
months of October, November, and December, 1924,
alone. That means a total of over five million a year.
At the same date the registered marriages without any
religious ceremony were 71 per cent in Moscow. Thus
the " religious sanction " was regarded even then as

superfluous by two-thirds of those entering the marriage state—only in the capital, it is true ; in the country conditions were otherwise.

Although the new form of " registered " marriage was regarded at first as a kind of concession of the new society to the institution of marriage, it soon appeared that already conjugal relations were entering upon a new phase. In particular the institution of marriage, still preserved, had a disastrous effect upon the relations of the sexes in Soviet society in the early years of the revolution. For it was only registered marriage and proved paternity which gave a woman the right to alimony—a right, by the way, which was wholly absent in Tsarist Russia. And since the law only proved effective in cases when the head of the family did not want to support his wife and children or when a husband wanted to desert his pregnant wife, the men got off scot-free in most other cases.

There was a period in Soviet Russia when thousands of deserted wives were constantly on the tramp, seeking the father of their children who was evading his responsibilities. And at the same time it happened not infrequently that women in poor circumstances who had exercised all their arts in order to have a child by a richer man were far better provided for by the " third " that he had to pay them as alimony than by their own earnings. And so it came about that at that time the courts were hardly less taken up with the numerous cases of such " alimony-hunting ", or something similar, than with genuine paternity suits.

But there were a number of other factors responsible for the many abuses of this difficult transition period. Besides the naturally violent protest against former conditions, there was first and foremost the civil war which dragged on for years, following upon the imperialist war, and which assuredly did not exercise an ennobling influence upon manners and morals. Then there were the terrible famine years 1921–2 which produced a positive migration of the peoples amongst the utterly destitute population : whole families, all the inhabitants of a settlement, were forced to leave their homes and go elsewhere in search of a crust of bread. It happened not infrequently that on the road mothers deserted their children and husbands their wives. . . . Other women, again, sold their bodies simply to keep body and soul of themselves and their children together. The number of destitute and neglected children passed all bounds. And the greater the dangers that surrounded them, the more brutalized did the rising generation become, the more primitive and loose sexual relations, the weaker people's sense of responsibility. . . .

What followed—the period of the N.E.P., the new economic policy—confused people's ideas still more. For whereas the preceding years had let loose the brutish instincts of the starving people, now the instincts of those were roused who scraped together the money which but yesterday had been utterly worthless and so enjoyed a degree of prosperity hitherto unknown in Soviet Russia. The demand for women who had fallen on evil days increased from day to day. Restaurants, cafés, and taverns flaunted themselves again, and wine was sold once more. There was nothing to bridle the human instincts which had at least been repressed in the days of war communism by a stern military régime. The number of divorces and abuses of the law increased vastly even in the country. And so that " free love " which has so often been misunderstood, as well as the misunder-standing or misinterpretation of revolutionary forms, began to degenerate into excesses.

THE SOVIET DIPLOMATIST, ALEXANDRA KOLLONTAY
Authoress of *Love in Three Generations*

[*face p.* 109

THE NEW SEXUAL ETHICAL CODE AND THEORY

"FREE LOVE" MISUNDERSTOOD

IN the days of war communism a large proportion of the rising generation declared that sexual relations rested upon a purely physiological basis. Each intimate contact between a man and woman must be regarded as a separate episode, and was scarcely on a higher plane than the act of drinking a glass of water to quench thirst.

After three years the civil war came to an end. But the sexual anarchy which it had done much to promote continued so long that it gave rise to a considerable literature. One of the first books, which was widely read abroad and has led to a great deal of misunderstanding, because it is still quoted, whereas the problems with which it deals have long undergone transformation, is Mrs. A. Kollontay's tale, *Love in Three Generations*.

The " third generation " is the young people of the years immediately following the revolution. Shenya, the heroine, who speaks in the authoress's name, answers the question what is her idea of the relation of the sexes more or less as follows :

" Sexual life is nothing more to me than a physiological pleasure. I change my lovers according to my mood. At the moment I am pregnant, but I do not know who my child's father is, and, moreover, I do not care." And she continues in these words :

You are surprised, perhaps, that I give myself to a man just when he attracts me without waiting to fall in love with him. You must have leisure to fall in love. And I have no time. We live now in an era of such heavy responsibilities. Of course there is not so much to do sometimes. . . . Well, and then you notice that somebody attracts you particularly. But for falling in love, you understand, there is no time ! For you have barely realized it when he is sent to the front or transferred to another town. Or—sometimes you are so busy yourself that you forget the man. And for that reason the hours that you spend together and feel happy are peculiarly precious. . . . And they bind you to nothing. . . .

This story of Kollontay's, which appeared in a collection entitled *The Love of the Worker Bees*, stirred up widespread opposition in Soviet Russia. In Professor Salkind's well-known twelve *Commandments of Sexual Morality* the sixth is : " Love should be monogamous. Permanence is preferable to variability. Shenya's philosophy is a disease, not a class ideal." A novel hitherto untranslated which became famous almost at the same time, this time written by a man, Romanov (*Without Cherry Blossom*) was received with all the more approval ; here the heroine, a young student, describes her first intimate relation with a man as follows :

There is no love between us, only a sexual relation. For amongst us love is despised as belonging to the region of psychology, and only physiology has the right to exist. . . . The girls have relations with their male comrades for a month, or a week, sometimes accidentally for one night only. And anyone who looks for anything more than a physiological experience in love is regarded as ridiculous, pitiful, feeble-minded. . . .

And now this girl meets a young man who attracts her notice. Their first meeting coincides with the awakening of spring. The girl buys herself a bunch of Cherry blossom in the street—the symbol of spring in the north—and, intoxicated by the fragrance of the warm evening and her own youth, she goes to the young man in a mood of exalted expectation. They are alone. . . .

How her springtide longing was realized she tells later in a letter to a friend :

Even when we love, we women are incapable of proceeding straight to the ultimate end. For us the essential always comes

last.   First we must be carried away by the man, by his clever-
ness and talents, his spirit, his tenderness.   And that is why
we long for a union, not so much physiological but rather of a
different kind. . . .

But this student's surroundings are of a character to
disappoint the girl's expectations.   And the lewdness of
the youth's desires and feelings are quite in keeping with
the plainness of his external surroundings.   And so the
girl continues her story :

> Thanks to the darkness there was little to be seen of the bare,
> neglected room.   So that I might have imagined that I had
> found my first happiness in surroundings worthy of the occa-
> sion.   But I longed for human tenderness and human caresses.
> I felt impelled to regard this man not as a stranger but as
> belonging to me. . . .
> I covered my face with my hands and stood there for a time
> motionless.   He seemed undecided.   But then he suddenly
> burst out : " Well, why stop thinking so long, we are only
> wasting time. . . ."
> His words hurt me, and I receded a step.   But he seized my
> hand with determination and annoyance : " Why the devil this
> play-acting ! "
> I resisted and began to struggle out of his embrace. . . .
> But it was too late.
> When we got up he first lit the lamp.
> " Take the light away," I cried in my pain and shrinking fear.
> He looked at me in astonishment, shrugged his shoulders, and
> put it out.   Without coming near me he then began to tidy the
> bed hastily : " Wanyka's bed. . . .   Else he'll guess what's
> been happening at once. . . ."

And in order to avoid meeting the student's comrade,
the girl goes out by the back stairs.   She goes away,
never to return. . . .
To the student this is only an episode to which he does
not give a thought.   He does not even try to conceal
it from the girl : " The end is always the same, whether
with or without cherry blossom," he says to her, whilst
her whole soul yearns for love.   But he has broken that
love with just as little thought or scruple as the flower at
her breast.

Other groups among the rising generation again have tried to find a theoretical and intellectual basis for the nihilism which governed their sexual lives and to exalt the terribly primitive character of their views on sex to a principle.

Man's sexual life is a purely private and personal affair and concerns no one else, these young people declared, in order to prevent any intervention on the part of the state. Another group put forward the view that women were to be regarded merely as a field to be sown and fertilized. And whilst a third in the provinces proceeded to modify the Marxist thesis—though they had probably never heard anything of Freud's teaching—and declared that consciousness is determined not by what is but by sex, the theory was put forward at the same time that proletarian love must resemble the " love of the worker bees . . .". " If," wrote Yarosslavskyi on the subject, " there are even among class-conscious comrades those who call Karl Marx a Philistine because he was faithful to his wife, we cannot be surprised that we should find comrades on the other hand who are of opinion that communist family life must resemble the love of the worker bees."

LENIN INTERVENES : THE " GLASS OF WATER THEORY "

IN order to check the baleful consequences of all these errors before it was too late, Lenin defined his own point of view as early as 1920 and gave his opinion in a conversation with Clara Zetkin :

" Naturally the changed attitude of the young people to sexual questions is ' fundamental ' and appeals to a theory. Some call their attitude ' communist ' and ' revolutionary '. They honestly believe that it is so. I at my age am not impressed. Although I am far from being a sombre ascetic, the so-called ' new sexual life ' of the young people—and sometimes of the old—seems to me to be often enough wholly bourgeois, an extension of the good bourgeois brothel. All that has nothing

whatever to do with free love as we communists understand it. You are doubtless acquainted with the capital
theory that in communist society the satisfaction of the
instincts, of the craving for love, is as simple and un-
important as ' the drinking of a glass of water '. This
' glass of water theory ' has driven some of our young
people crazy, quite crazy. It has been the destruction
of many young men and women. Its supporters declare
that it is Marxist. I have no use for such Marxism,
which deduces all the phenomena and transformations in
the intellectual superstructure of society straight from its
economic basis. Things are not quite so simple. A
certain Friedrich Engels stated that long ago with regard
to historical materialism.

" I consider the famous ' glass of water theory ' to be
utterly un-Marxian, and, moreover, unsocial. It is not
only natural factors that operate in sexual life, but also
those which have become an element in civilization,
whether high or low. Engels in his *Origin of the Family*
pointed out how significant it is that the universal sexual
impulse has been developed and purified into individual
sex love. After all, the relations between the sexes are
not simply an expression of the interplay between social
and economic conditions and a physical craving which is
isolated intellectually by regarding it from the physiological standpoint. It would be rationalism, not
Marxism, to try to trace the transformation of these
relations to the economic foundations of society isolated
and detached from their association with the whole world
of thought. Of course thirst cries out to be quenched.
But will a normal person under normal conditions lie
down in the dirt on the road and drink from a puddle ?
Or even from a glass with a rim greasy from many lips ?
But most important of all is the social aspect. Drinking water really is an individual concern. Love involves
two, and a third, a new life, may come into being. That
implies an interest on the part of society, a duty to the
community.

" As a communist I have not the slightest sympathy
with the ' glass of water theory ', even when it is beau

tifully labelled ' love made free '. Besides, this liberation is neither new nor communist. You will remember that it was preached in literature about the middle of the last century as ' the emancipation of the heart '. As practised by the bourgeois it was revealed as the emancipation of the flesh. It was preached in those days with more talent than now ; as regards practice, I cannot judge. I do not mean to preach asceticism by this criticism. Such a thing would not occur to me. Communism is not meant to introduce asceticism but the joy of life and vital vigour, attained partly through the fulfilment of love. But in my opinion the hypertrophy in sexual matters which we often observe now does not produce the joy of life and vital vigour, it detracts from them. In the revolutionary epoch that is bad, very bad. . . .

" The young people have special need of the joy of life and vital vigour. Healthy sport, gymnastics, swimming, tramping, physical exercises of every kind, many-sided intellectual interests, learning, study, research, and as far as possible in common ! All that will give the young people more than these everlasting lectures and discussions about sexual problems and so-called drinking life to the dregs. Healthy bodies, healthy minds ! Neither monks nor Don Juans, nor yet that half-and-half product, the German Philistine. . . .

" The revolution calls for concentration, the augmentation of our powers. On the part of the masses and of the individual. It cannot tolerate orgiastic conditions such as are normal with D'Annunzio's decadent heroes and heroines. Unbridled sexual life is bourgeois, a phenomenon of decadence. The proletariat is a rising class. It does not need intoxication either as a narcotic or a stimulus. No more the intoxication of sexual excesses than that of alcohol. . . ."

Well ! The erroneous and mistaken attitude of various groups of young people on the sexual problem could hardly be repudiated more unequivocally and bluntly.

But other party leaders also, including some women, interposed in the same complex of problems.

It has become a commonplace that the great mass of our proletarian youth has quite inadequate notions on the question of sexual relations [writes the well-known woman revolutionary, Ssmidovich, one of Lenin's most worthy collaborators, in *Pravda* in 1925]. The young people seem to think that the most primitive view on questions of sex is communist. And that everything which goes beyond the primitive conception which might be suitable for a Hottentot or a still more primitive representative of man at his earliest phase implies something characteristic of the petty bourgeois, a bourgeois attitude towards the sexual problem.

Ssmidovich goes on to give an account of certain points in the new, unwritten " theory of sex ", with the intention of revealing the tragically ridiculous element in them, and sums them up and tabulates them as follows :

1. Every *komssomolets*, member of the Young Communist League, every *rabfakovets*, student in the faculty of labour, and every other greenhorn, can and may follow his sexual impulse without check. For some unknown reason that is regarded as an irrefutable law. Chastity is condemned as characteristic of the petty bourgeois. 2. Every little *komssomolka*, female member of the Young Communist League, every *rabfakovka* or other woman student upon whom falls the choice of this young fellow or that, of the male—whence such African passions have developed among us in the north, I cannot judge—must comply with his wishes, otherwise she is " petty bourgeois " and does not deserve the name of a *komssomolka*, of a *rabfakovka*, a proletarian student. And now comes the third and last part of this strange trilogy : the pale, haggard face of a girl who feels herself a mother—with the touching expression of a pregnant woman. In the waiting-room of the " Commission for the Sanction of Abortion " you may read many such a tale of suffering in a *komssomolts* love affair. . . .

Finally matters reached such a pitch that all these " burning questions "—the problem of love, marriage, and the family, besides that of education and the schools —became the subject of public discussion in all circles and long refused to be laid to rest.

A number of anonymous questionnaires containing a multiplicity of questions were sent to thousands of students in various towns, asking them about their sexual life.

The answers showed this significant fact among others : the love affairs of a large proportion of the students, especially their first embarcation upon love affairs, was principally influenced by the period of war communism, and their sexual life had no connection with love. Many wrote in addition, varying the passage from Kollontay on the same point : " We have no time to play at love, our work allows us no time for that."

The communist young people's paper, *Komssomolskaya Pravda* was perpetually publishing articles columns long and letters and correspondence, all on the same question.

The older generation, who were drawn into the discussion, scholars, experts on sexual hygiene, and party leaders, gave expression at that time to a view similar to Lenin's, which Ssyemashko, the People's Commissary for Public Health, summed up as follows in an open letter addressed to the young generation of students :

> *Tovarishchi*, you have entered the V.U.S. (abbreviation for universities) and technical colleges in order to study. That is now your principal aim in life. And just as all your impulses and ideas are subject to that principal aim, so that not infrequently you have to forgo some pleasure because it is detrimental to your principal aim—study and the intention of training yourselves as conscious collaborators in building up the state anew—so you must subject your activities and your lives to that aim in every field. For the state is still too poor to undertake your support, the education of the children and the support of the parents. Therefore we counsel you : continence !

Side by side with this eager discussion, tending to a restoration to health of the sexual life of the young generation, efforts were made with no less zeal in another, more educational, direction among the men. The goal was a new attitude towards women, who were to be regarded not only as objects of sexual attraction, but primarily as their equals in the new society. At the same time the young women were constantly advised to defend their new position themselves, not to tolerate the sexual nihilism of their comrades, and to win their respect as women and human beings.

DISCUSSION OF THE MARRIAGE LAW

A HUNDRED AND SIXTY MILLIONS DISCUSS THE NEW MARRIAGE LAW

In October, 1925, when the great wave of excited debate on the sex problem had reached its high-water mark, another and even greater wave swept over it.

For the experiences of the seven years which had passed since the adoption of the " Code for Births, Marriages, and Deaths ", the practice of the courts, and the continuous development of the new communal way of life, including its effect on marriage and the family, had shown that the existing marriage law needed emendation on some points. And so, at the second session of the twelfth meeting of the All-Russian Central Executive, the People's Commissariat of Justice brought forward for discussion a draft " Codification of the Laws concerning Marriage, the Family, and Wardship ", which was designed to meet the new needs.

Kurskyi, at that time People's Commissary of Justice, whose duty it was to expound the draft which he introduced at the session of October 17th, 1925, opened with Lenin's words :

" Assuredly laws are not everything and we shall by no means content ourselves with decrees and nothing else. But in the legislative field we have already done everything required of us in order to make women's position equal to men's, and we have a right to be proud of it : the position of women in Soviet Russia is at present such that it may be called ideal even from the point of view of the most advanced states. Nevertheless, we tell ourselves that that is, of course, only the beginning."

Kurskyi then entered upon the question of the fundamental points in which the new code differed from the old, and said :

" In the first place the function and significance of registration is altered.

" Secondly an unregistered marriage is placed on precisely the same footing as a registered one as far as the material consequences are concerned.

" Thirdly the provisions for the protection of the

117

children are strengthened in cases in which the marriage is dissolved either by divorce or by the clear wish of one partner.

" Fourthly certain guarantees are introduced at the contraction of marriage which require some degree of forethought.

" And lastly the provisions as regards the property of the parties are altered."

Contrary to all expectations the new draft called forth vehement criticism within the Executive itself, both among the representatives of the workers and the peasants. Consequently it was resolved to submit the draft, which affected the vital interests of the whole population so deeply, for discussion throughout the land before it was definitely adopted. The object of this discussion was twofold : in the first place it was to throw light on the people's attitude towards the law and the problems involved in it, and on the other hand the discussion was to serve as a means to eradicate by the force of conviction the conservative point of view which still survived here and there, especially amongst the rural population.

The whole country was shaken to its depths by the question. In countless discussion meetings—from gatherings of thousands of workers in the large cities to the tiny debates in the peasant reading-rooms—the separate points of the new draft were thrashed out again and again. The People's Commissariat received reports of more than 6,000 meetings of this kind, but of course the number of debates actually held was much larger.

The point around which the discussion chiefly revolved was the question whether an unregistered, so-called " factual " marriage should be placed in its legal consequences on an equality with one that had been legally registered. The supporters of the new law argued first and foremost that at the time in question there were in the Soviet Union some eight to a hundred thousand couples whose " marriages " nowise differed from officially contracted marriages, either in substance or form, except in the absence of registration ; and that, therefore, the legal protection which the law provides in the case of registered marriages—which is of particular importance to the wife—ought certainly not to be withheld from the partners in these " factual " marriages.

A number of arguments were arrayed against this point of view. In reply to the objection that the new law might encourage dissolute manners it was urged that dissolute manners were just as widespread, if not more so, beneath the hypocritical veil of criminal prosecution in bourgeois countries, countries with conservative and even reactionary legislation, as in the Soviet Union, and that this was no argument against effective protection for women which the new law was designed to ensure.

But the other additional provisions and changes in the new code—the question of divorce, alimony, and women's property—were also fiercely contested. The opposition of the peasants was far more determined than that of the proletariat, especially against the provision of the new law that women's domestic work should be placed on an equal footing with men's work. For at that time the peasant household constituted a much larger economic and patriarchal unit than the urban family, and the conditions as regards property had been so complicated by intermarriage between different farms that it would hardly be possible to determine what were equal shares in the total property—in case of divorce or of one person withdrawing from the common farm.

On this point, indeed, doubts were expressed in the very first public meeting of the Executive. One member, the workman Kartyshev, quoted the following case in order to illustrate his point :

" . . . A village lad, Vanyka, who is barely eighteen and does not even know how to wipe his own nose, marries a staid young woman, and she begins straightway : ' I'd like to cook my own cabbage ; I've no use for a mother-in-law ! Demand your share.'

" But Vanyka cannot be given his share, for he is not yet properly capable of work.

" Thereupon his wife leaves him, and the upshot is that the last mare and the last goose, the last sheep and the last hen, have to be sold in accordance with the law, and the farm is ruined. Such abuses ought to be prevented."

Or on the question of alimony :

" . . . Let us suppose I have a brother, a young man who has fought in Budyonny's army. He is lucky enough to have two wives and each has a child by him. How can it be that another man pays alimony for him ?

" The law would have to state unequivocally that every sparrow is an independent bird and that every man must bear his own responsibilities."

In a public debate on the subject held in the Moscow Polytechnic Museum the Public Prosecutor Krylenko said :

" Our laws on the subject of marriage and the family plough up a strip of almost virgin soil in our former *byt*. Directly after the revolution we set ourselves to abolish ecclesiastical slavery as well as the intervention of unauthorized persons in matrimonial relations. As a means to that end the registration of civil marriage was introduced. But the question already arose which has been specially often raised since ecclesiastical marriage lost its authority : on what do we base the necessity, the importance, or at least the usefulness of the registration of a marriage ?

" Accordingly we are bound to state that very few arguments can be adduced in support of registration. Why, we ask, must the state be told who contracts a marriage with whom ? For the sake of statistics ? No, that is not the most important point. The most important consideration must be regarded solely as the struggle against ecclesiastical marriage and the protection of the interests of the children and the economically weaker partner. In this connection the very first article of the new draft code of laws concerning marriage and the family abolishes the obligation to register a marriage. Registration is retained merely as a formality in order to facilitate the protection of the interests of the partners and their children, and is regarded as a right, not as a duty.

" But if all factual cohabitation, even if it is not registered, counts as a marriage, the outcome is the possibility of polygamy. That possibility does actually exist, and, although it appears extremely undesirable, the Soviet law does not forbid it. To combat such a thing by means of penal measures and prohibition is, of course, impossible. But we define our attitude towards polygamy in the passage which states that the registration of a marriage is inadmissible if even one party is already married.

" The nearer we come to the socialist order the more will marriage be liberated from all kinds of superfluous obligation, including economic obligations, and will be able to be transformed into a perfectly free union between two persons. Until the state can take over the care of the children, however, marriage retains the form of a kind of economic contract, sanctioned by the law. But whilst the state moves in the direction of making marriage a free union, the law undertakes the protection of the weaker party only when that party is not living in several simultaneous marriages. That, of course, does not apply to the children, whose interests the law guards irrespective of the relations of their parents to one another or to third parties."

In the course of the discussion, which became more and more tempestuous, Mrs. Kollontay expressed her views on the subject of alimony. She founded her argument on the view that the question of marriage and the family required different treatment for the workers in town and country, and that, therefore, the new law started from a wrong basis. She said :

" It is true that the law places a woman who cohabits with a man without being registered on an equality with a legally registered wife, but it ignores more casual relations which we must regard as the consequence of the hard conditions in the villages and of poverty in the towns. For that reason it is impossible under any circumstances to bring the matrimonial relations of the sexes within a legal formula—so long as there are workers' barracks, and a housing shortage and so many half-grown children running about without supervision."

Mrs. Kollontay, therefore, proposed to establish a general insurance fund from contributions of the whole working population :

> What seems unattainable by the efforts of individuals [she wrote in her article *A Common Pot or Individual Alimony*] becomes possible perhaps through united efforts. The general insurance fund for the support of children and mothers should be made up of small contributions—for example, a minimum of two roubles a year—which, however, would of course have to be graded. The larger one's income, the larger one's contribution to the insurance fund. In this way we should start with a sum of some 120 million roubles with sixty million adult contributors. Thus it would be possible to take from the fund the cost of children's crèches and homes, and homes for mothers, to grant support to mothers unable to work, and to provide for their children, at least till they were a year old, and later, according to the size of the fund, till they were three or four.

This proposal, which was almost universally rejected, was nevertheless widely debated. In general the discussion brought a flood of letters, largely from working women, as is usually the case in such circumstances in Russia. Here are a few characteristic examples :

> Ratnikova, Baranova, Sakharova, and Ionova, working women (from the factory " Tryokhgornaya Manufaktura ")
>
> *Tovarishch* Kollontay's proposal is not acceptable. If such a tax were introduced, the men would lose all shame and universal licence would be the result. For as soon as a man knows that he need no longer fear the " third ", he will hardly stick to the woman for a week, but leave her to her fate. She will hardly mean more to him than his decoy-whistle, for instance, which he throws away when he has played upon it enough. . . . And if, in addition, he has paid something like half a rouble in tax, then his object will be first and foremost to pay no more and to bring at least fifty women to ruin.
>
> Kollontay says a marriage is legal when it is registered. But who needs the certificate ? If my husband loves me, he will stay with me always without having signed. But if I don't please him, he won't care a brass farthing.
>
> In our opinion the child, if the father has deserted it, must be placed in a Children's Home. There it can be brought up properly and both parents should pay for its maintenance.

The mother should pay too ! It may serve as a lesson to her ! She'll be less wanton ! Everybody inveighs : " The men ! The men ! " But if a woman doesn't want to, she never has a child.

Gavryushina, Rasumnova, Chukayeva, Goncharuk, Shchukina, Sulayeva, Dyetkova, working women (from the factory " Dukat ")

. . . How ought marriage to be constituted now ?

Of the three drafts, that of the People's Commissariat of the Interior, of the People's Commissariat of Justice, and of *Tovarishch* Kollontay, only that of the *Narkomyust*, the People's Commissariat of Justice, is, in our opinion, in the interests of working women.

The draft of the *Narkomvnudyel*, the People's Commissariat of the Interior, only recognizes registered marriage as legal. If, therefore, this draft should become law, there will certainly be " legitimate " and " illegitimate " children again, and then the old police-court designation will crop up again : " lives in an illegal relation ".

We believe that an interval of nine years has nailed the coffin of the old conditions so firmly that expressions of that kind must not be allowed to revive.

But the *Narkomyust's* draft completely abolishes all earlier forms of marriage and places the registered and unregistered marriage on an equal footing before the law. In the matter of alimony it also serves the interests of the woman entirely. According to this draft the father must pay a certain sum for the support of the child that he has deserted.

Tovarishch Kollontay's draft is altogether unsatisfactory. . . . How can anyone speak of a general taxation of all men ? What has it to do with *all* men, when only *one* man is concerned in the begetting of a child ? What affair is it of the community ? The matter is far simpler : " If you are the father, you must pay ! "

Myeshuyeva, Roshuk, Kostrikina, Trutnyova, Kusavyenkova, Nikolayeva, Parshina (of the Faculty of Labour " Pokrovskyi ")

. . . It is high time that we cast off all petty bourgeois prejudices : is it not altogether indifferent whether a woman lives in a registered or unregistered marriage ? If two people live together with the intention of founding a family, that is a marriage.

And if both sign their names, standing with bowed heads

before some quill-driver, that will nowise strengthen the " foundations " of their family life.

In this part of her scheme, Kollontay is right of course. But the second part, in which she discusses alimony, there is room for difference of opinion.

Why should a deserted mother become a burden on society ? Such assistance could only call to mind the " charity " of the " Empress Marie Fund ". If, on the other hand, this " third " only amounted to a *chervonyets* (ten roubles), the mother would not, of course, be able to bring up her children on that. If, however, this " fund " could provide half the child's main-tenance, that would be worth a great deal.

Nevertheless, the best thing is a system of alimony. For if once a man has succeeded in fooling a woman with poetical spells and African passion, and begetting a child with her, then he should pay his " third ". He will take care to avoid a second third. For even one-third is a bitter experience.

The general discussion of the new marriage law lasted a good year : doubtless the first case in which a whole people, a people of 160 millions, made a law for itself, not through elected representatives, but by all expressing their opinion. And when, in December, 1926, the draft was introduced for the second time in the V.T.S.I.K. (All-Russian Central Executive Committee), the debate raged once more before it was finally adopted, and for the last time the various opinions clashed. Jessica Smith, an American, was present at this meeting and recounts (*Woman in Soviet Russia*) :

> . . . the *Vtsik* convened . . . in the great malachite-pillared, crystal-chandaliered and gold-bedecked hall of the Czar's palace in the Kremlin. Among the delegates seated at the long business-like tables . . . were quite a number of women. A solid peasant woman, with a broad gentle face, her head wrapped in a bright " platok " (shawl), her feet in felt boots, walked to her place on the presidium with dignity and no self-consciousness.
>
> Most of the delegates were of real Russian stock, but sprinkled among them were representatives of the autonomous regions' republics that make up the R.S.F.S.R.—Tartars, Bashkirs, Khirghese. . . .

DISCUSSION OF THE MARRIAGE LAW

In introducing the revised draft of the new marriage code, Kurski explained that registration was retained as the preferable form of marriage since it constituted an indisputable proof for the court in case of legal proceedings. "But the time will come," he declared, "I am deeply convinced, when we will equalize de facto marriages in all respects to registered marriages, or eliminate the latter entirely. Registration will then only take statistical record of the fact, inasmuch as it will always be necessary to keep records. . . ."

Kurski then summed up the reports on discussions of the law that had come to him from all over the country. Taking Archangelski Gubernia as typical of the more backward peasant sections, he said that every village of the gubernia had considered the question, and that forty per cent had been opposed to certain sections of it, while the city population had overwhelmingly favoured it. . . .

The debate that followed was as heated as that of the year before. . . . Riazanov, a Communist, attacked the legalization of de facto marriages. "We are told," he said, "that this draft is a step forward in the sense of approaching the ideal Communist Society, where, in general, marriage relations will not be subjected to any obligatory regulations. . . . I make so bold as to say that in these Communist declarations there isn't a single iota of Communism. When we attain a Communist Society, and all state, all pressure, disappears, then we will ask ourselves, comrades, is marriage a private relation between two two-legged animals which interests only themselves, and in which society, freed from any apparatus of force, has no right to meddle? We have all the more right to ask how in the tenth year of the dictatorship of the proletariat is it possible that, in the name of the Sovnarkom, such a petty-bourgeois, anarchistic draft should be submitted to us? . . . We should teach our young Comsomols that marriage is not a personal act, but an act of deep social significance, demanding interference and regulation by Society. They must know that it is a certain form with sanction in the eyes of Society . . . Nothing but 'kasha' (a messy mixture) will come of this law!"

While this statement was greeted with applause, it was ridiculed in subsequent speeches, and one peasant woman was unkind enough to say that serious attention could not be given to the viewpoint of Comrade Riazanov, since his song was sung, and he himself needed neither registered nor de facto marriage. . . .

Then Moirova, a woman delegate :

" Comrades, I must be a very naïve person. When I first read the draft I was indignant that this clause (that a wife is not obliged to follow her husband wherever he goes) should be included in our law in the tenth year of the revolution, when the equality of the sexes has long been established. Was it really necessary to mention this, I thought. Why say that oil is oily ? . . . But it seems I was wrong. It seems there are still people among us who consider that a wife should follow her husband wherever he goes. This, comrades, is too much ! "

During the greater part of the discussion the men got the worst of it for deserting their wives, for running away to escape paying alimenta, for marrying a wife in the summer to get a harvest hand and divorcing her again in the fall—in fact, the whole argument for the new law was to protect the helpless weaker sex.

At last Tovarishch Motish, a big hairy moujhik from Siberia, could restrain himself no longer :

" On all sides the men are being blamed ! " he burst out. " But it is often the woman's fault when the family breaks up. . . . She sees her husband getting a bit old. Some young fellow comes along with his songs and his accordion. She leaves her husband with three or four children, and goes off with the younger one. In general, at the present time, women are doing many bad things. They are always running to the Genobdel, and slandering their husbands. There a whole women's commission gets together, the husband knows nothing of it—and he is disgraced ! "

THE SOVIET RUSSIAN MARRIAGE LAW

THE discussion of the " New Code of Laws on Marriage, the Family, and Wardship " lasted for more than a year. On January 1st, 1927, the law came into force.

If we wish to appreciate the pioneering influence, social and economic, of the new Soviet Russian marriage law, it will be instructive, before discussing its separate provisions, to glance hastily at the dispositions which governed the legal position of women in Tsarist Russia. And by way of preface let it be stated that in pre-revolutionary Russia a wife, as being formally the property of her husband, was entered on his passport. And so tragedies were not infrequent when for any reason the wife needed a passport of her own, especially if she wanted to leave her husband, and was the victim of her husband's arbitrary will. For according to the law his consent was necessary if she were to be granted a passport of her own. A civil marriage, even if contracted abroad according to the laws of the country in question, was not legal in Russia.

The law recognized only ecclesiastical, religious marriage. A man could not marry before he was eighteen and a woman before she was sixteen, nor either after they were eighty. The marriage contract depended on the consent of the parents or guardian. If, however, it was contracted without their consent, then the " guilty party " was liable to imprisonment up to eight months and disinheritance. Further, marriage with Jews, heathens, and heretics was forbidden.

To a Soviet citizen of to-day it seems like some curious relic of the Middle Ages when he reads in the old Russian code of the " rights and duties arising from marriage " :

103. The spouses are required to live together. (1) Hence every act is prohibited which leads to their separation ; (2) in case the husband moves or is transferred or otherwise changes his residence, the wife must follow him.

107. The wife is required to obey her husband as the head of the family, to abide in love of him, in reverence and boundless compliance, and as mistress of the house to show him every complaisance and devotion.

108. The wife's prime duty is submission to her husband's will : but this nowise discharges her from her duty to her parents.

It is true that jurists (Freund, *Civil Law in the Soviet Union*) point out that the husband's predominance arising from these four paragraphs did not in fact amount to a great deal. The designation of the husband as " head of the family " was simply a title corresponding to that of the wife as " mistress of the house ", whilst there was no legal sanction to enforce the wife's duty of obedience, which was mitigated by the husband's duty to live in concord with his wife. The whole should, therefore, be regarded mainly as a relic of the spirit which inspired the moral code of the seventeenth century, the *Domostroy* quoted above.

Like the marriage laws still in force in most bourgeois states, those of old-time Russia, previous to the October revolution of 1917, were mainly designed to bind the wife to her husband, to make her his appendage. These laws were lifeless forms, filled with an ecclesiastical and canonical spirit, and represented in most cases a violation of living needs. Whilst, therefore, the Soviet Russian marriage law of 1918 aimed first and foremost at secularizing marriage, the present Soviet Russian marriage law, built upon the experience of a new, burning, pulsing life, seeks to liberate women and to place them on an absolute equality. Indeed, it was described by its supporters as only a *first attempt*, the first step towards a true solution, capable of later emendation on the basis of further practical experience. Whereas in bourgeois countries, therefore, the rigid form of the law comes first and the cohabitation of the sexes must adapt itself to that, here life creates its own laws and perfects their detail in such manner as a young, healthy, and aspiring culture sees fit.

As in many other spheres, Soviet Russian legislation is confined to quite a few paragraphs essentially reasonable,

> for the purpose [as the preamble to the code states] of *regulating* the legal relations arising from marriage, the family, and wardship on the basis of the new revolutionary *byt* (life), of protecting the interests of the mother, and especially of the children, and placing the spouses on an equal footing in respect to property and the education of the children.

For beyond this task of *regulation* the state claimed to exercise neither police nor moral supervision; it does not trouble itself in any way about the cohabitation or propagation of its citizens, and the principle: " *All relations between the sexes are a matter of private concern,*" is recognized as supreme. Marriage in Soviet Russia is not only secularized but also detached from any connection with the state; it is a purely civil contract. The marriage laws are regarded rather as standards, as directives, than as laws, and it is only in case of dispute that the state, as the final court of appeal, is called in.

According to the law henceforth in force in Soviet Russia a registered marriage is juridically on an absolute equality with a " factual " non-registered one. The only difference is that in case of a divorce, that is a conflict which in any case requires the intervention of the state, the " factual ", non-registered marriage must first be established by the court, whilst the registration of a marriage implies irrefutable proof.

According to Clause 12 the court accepts as proof of a non-registered marriage " the fact of cohabitation, the existence of a joint household, and the acknowledgment to third parties of matrimonial relations in personal letters or other documents, as also mutual material support in accordance with the circumstances, the joint education of the children, and so forth ".

The provisions serve first and foremost to safeguard the wife to whom, as the weaker party, it is intended to grant a considerable measure of protection against exploitation by the husband as housekeeper in the town and farm-servant in the country. The decisive factor, therefore, in determining the existence or non-existence of a marriage is not the form in which the union was entered upon, but its essential nature ; but it is a fundamental principle that *all kinds of lasting cohabitation only are to be regarded as marriage*, not any transient connection.

Since marriage is a private concern, there is no express prohibition of polygamy. But it is clear from Clause 6 that the state favours, and indeed recommends, the principle of monogamy, for it is there laid down that the existence of a registered or a factual non-registered marriage constitutes a barrier to the registration of a second marriage. (This regulation, directed against the customary polygamy, is particularly stressed in the codes of the autonomous republics with Eastern populations, which differ from that of Soviet Russia. For Kirgiz, for instance, a special decree was promulgated making polygamy a punishable offence.) Thus bigamy is not, indeed, punishable in Soviet Russia, but as soon as the

intervention of the state is called for it involves punishment for concealing hindrances to marriage or for making
false statements at the registry office.   Prosecution of this
nature is not infrequent in Soviet Russia.

So, too, adultery is not punishable, for it is the
private concern of the spouses, since the Soviet state
only takes steps against sexual crimes which really involve
a menace to the Soviet legal system and must be regarded
as a danger to the community.   Likewise sexual intercourse between the spouses—so-called faithfulness to the
marriage tie—is a private concern, and such conceptions
as " concubinate ", " illegitimate ", " illicit relations ",
" the guilty party ", " adultery ", and " *in flagranti* " are
unknown.

There are no ceremonies attached to the *registration of
a marriage* in Soviet Russia ; but the parties are at
liberty to invite their friends and relations to be present.
In contrast with the countless formalities that must be
complied with in bourgeois countries before the contraction of a marriage, the conditions in Soviet Russia have
been reduced to the minimum.   In order that a marriage
may be registered it is necessary : (1) that the parties
should have reached the age limit of eighteen ; (2) that
both should be willing (but the presence of both parties
at the registry office is not essential to registration) ; (3)
that a proof of identity should be given ; (4) that each
party should declare in writing that he (or she) is informed
of the other's state of health, especially as regards
venereal diseases and tuberculosis.

A marriage between two persons one of whom is
feeble-minded or mentally unsound cannot be registered
under Soviet Russian law.

The registration of a marriage between relatives in the
direct line of ascent or descent, or between whole or half
brothers and sisters, is prohibited.   There is no bar to
the registration of a marriage between persons in any
other degree of relationship.   On the other hand, as
already stated, the existence of a previous marriage,
whether registered or unregistered, is a bar to the registration of a fresh marriage.

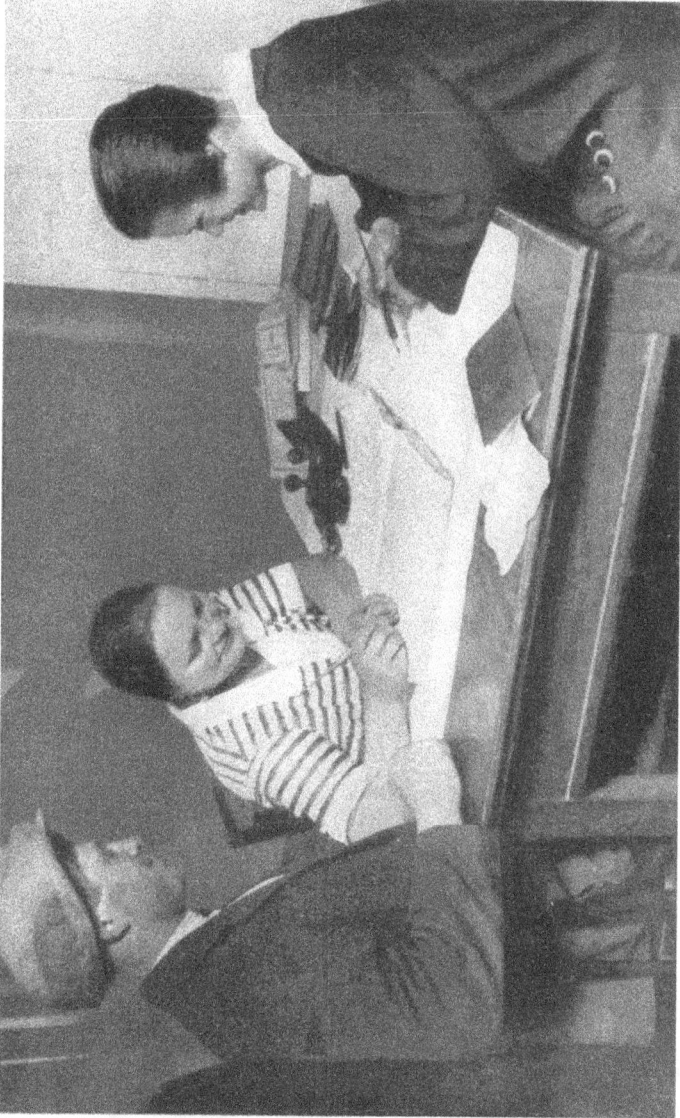

REGISTRATION OF A MARRIAGE IN THE MOSCOW S.A.G.S.
(Registry Office)

[face p. 130

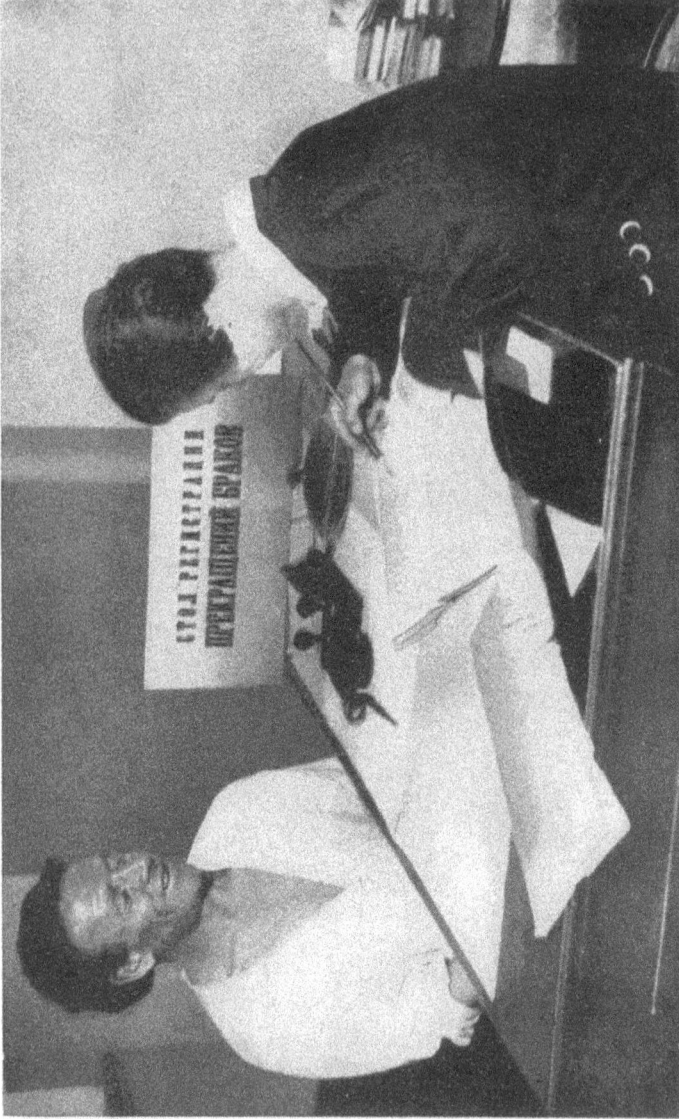

[*face p.* 131

A WORKMAN HAS HIS DIVORCE REGISTERED

Anyone desiring to register a marriage must address himself to the S.A.G.S. (abbreviation for Registry of Births, Marriages, and Deaths) in the place of residence of one of the parties. Thereupon, after examination of the certificate of identity, the parties are required to declare at the " table for the registration of marriages "— " tables for the registration of divorces, births, and deaths " are there too—where a special official (they are generally women) keeps the register, how many previous marriages, registered or unregistered, they have contracted and how many children they have. If one of the parties is prevented by illness from being present, the registration can take place in his (or her) home if desired. Further, the parties are required to state what surname they intend to bear in future, for according to Soviet Russian law the husband can adopt the wife's surname after marriage just as well as the reverse, or, as in most cases, both parties retain their previous surnames.

The parties are then informed of the relevant clauses of the marriage code and are warned of the penal consequences of making false statements, the entry of marriage, which is then made, is read to them, and they sign it together with the registrar. If the parties desire, the registration can be carried out before witnesses. But if a marriage is contracted between two illiterates, then the signature of two witnesses is essential. There is no charge for registering a marriage. If it is desired to have a certificate of marriage, then workers must pay a stamp duty of two roubles and all other persons of ten roubles.

It is worth noting that by Clause 8 the wife is not required to adopt the husband's nationality, but may choose, and that the husband may also acquire the nationality of his wife by means of a simplified procedure. Similarly the question both of the nationality and the surname of the children can be settled by agreement. A principle which once more implies the wife's equal rights.

Clause 9, moreover, allows both spouses the free choice of their occupation. The joint conduct of the household is a matter of mutual agreement. A change of residence by one spouse involves no obligation upon the other. These provisions, too, show how thoroughly the law safeguards the independence of both spouses and seeks to direct marriage along the path of comradeship.

In the matter of the property of the spouses, here, too, Soviet Russian legislation regards marriage as a fellowship in life and labour under conditions of absolute equality between the spouses. It is laid down in principle that property acquired before marriage is not held in common. (Indeed, even the Tsarist marriage law recognized separate property, unlike that of most European states, as also the right of the wife to guardianship, but this was due not so much to its progressive spirit as to the express desire to protect the possessing classes in the feudal state.) On the other hand all property acquired by one or both spouses by their work during marriage is reckoned as joint property. The shares are determined by the courts. What is new is that the housewife's labour, which is nowhere else recognized, is counted as work of equal value. This was intended to check the evil of the abuse of women's labour, which had spread especially among the peasants since 1918 : a man married in the hot harvest season and got rid of the woman again in the autumn without any compensation. But in case of dispute the share that may be claimed is determined by the court. These provisions, too, are applicable both to registered and non-registered marriages. So long as the marriage lasts both spouses are bound to support one another mutually.

In Soviet Russia, in accordance with the logical and consistent structure of the whole marriage code, *the dissolution of marriage* is greatly simplified, whereas in capitalist society it is one of the most difficult problems of modern marriage law. For just as the marriage state is entered by the free agreement of the spouses, so it comes to an end when the agreement to continue together ceases. *It is not the state, therefore, which divorces the parties, but their own free decision.* The state merely takes note of that decision and determines the legal consequences.

There are, therefore, no longer any divorce suits in

Soviet Russia, no causes of divorce are required ; *a marriage may be dissolved at any time either by the mutual desire of both spouses or at the desire of one party only.* The party who desires a divorce is not required to give any further explanation. The divorce, like the marriage, is regarded as a purely private affair, and the so-called principle of guilt is wholly alien to Soviet law. There is, therefore, no guilty party referred to in the formula of divorce, no discussion of intimate details, and no scandals, such as are usual in matrimonial disputes in bourgeois countries. Indeed, the Supreme Court once laid it down that for the court " to concern itself with the conduct of either party in a divorce case would imply an utterly false interpretation of the principles of Soviet law ".

Very simple, too, *is the registration of a divorce* in Soviet Russia—once the spouses have come to an agreement in the matter. The spouses ask for a divorce at the S.A.G.S. and present certificates of identity and marriage. If there was no certificate when the marriage was contracted, then the spouses must either confirm in writing that they are married and state the time and place of the registration of the marriage, or—if it is a question of an unregistered marriage—procure a confirmation of the marriage from the court, which is given on the strength of the above-mentioned proofs. As at the contraction of a marriage, so at its dissolution, each spouse is required to state what name he (or she) means to bear in future. If no agreement is reached on the question, then each party receives the name borne before the marriage. The registrar reads the entry of the divorce to the parties and they sign it—and thereupon the marriage is held to be dissolved.

The registration of a divorce, like that of a marriage, is free of cost. If a certificate of divorce is given, there is a stamp duty of two roubles. Persons in receipt of unemployment benefit or public assistance pay no stamp duty.

Divorce is rather more complicated when it is due to the desire of one party only, that is, when no mutual agreement has been reached. In such cases the S.A.G.S.

communicates the fact of the dissolution in the prescribed form to the other spouse within three days of the registration of the divorce. If the address is unknown, the registry office inserts a notice of the divorce in *Isvestiya*, also within three days, this time, however, at the expense of the party desiring the divorce. The cost of such a notice is about sixteen roubles, but workers and employees, members of the Red Army, and very poor peasants pay a reduced price.

As soon as a marriage is dissolved there is no bar to a new marriage. The so-called period of waiting and mourning is quite unknown in Soviet Russia. And married couples who have been divorced can re-marry one another. There is no law to prescribe how often the Soviet citizen may marry or divorce.

As a woman's economic independence is regarded as normal in Soviet Russia, and the provisions of the law are mainly adapted to the conditions of independent, working women, it is only the indigent party incapable of work, or the indigent party capable of work but unemployed, who has a claim to support from the other party, whether that party is the husband or wife. But such support is no longer for life, as was provided in the Soviet Russian marriage law of 1918 ; Clause 15 limits its duration : for a party who is incapable of work to one year, for an unemployed party to six months, calculated from the date of the divorce. The amount of support to which the divorced party has a claim may not exceed that of regular unemployment benefit.

In case of a divorce, moreover, the question must be decided which of the parties undertakes the education and support of the children. If agreement is reached, it is recorded in the register of divorces and a copy of the entry is handed to each party. In case of dispute, or if the agreement is not observed and appeal is made to the court, judgment is given solely in the interests of the children. In practice the custom has established itself to leave the children with the mother till they are eight years old. Sometimes it happens that the child is left neither with the father nor the mother, but is placed in a

Children's Home. Both parents are then required to contribute to the child's support, each according to his or her means.

Still more of an innovation, perhaps, than all that has yet been recorded of Soviet Russian marriage and family laws is the attitude of the law in the question of illegitimate birth. In Tsarist Russia an illegitimate child was related neither to its father nor its mother till 1902. Thenceforward it was regarded, as is the case in the majority of European and American states, including England, Germany, and France, as related to its mother only, but not to its father ; indeed, the section dealing with " illegitimate children " is one of the cruellest in the bourgeois family code, and might rather be called the law of children's wrongs than children's rights. From the very first Soviet Russian law made birth, blood relationship, the sole basis of legal relationship, and nowise legal marriage, and so abolished the conception of the " illegitimate child " altogether.

It is a fundamental principle that a man is under the obligation to provide equally for all his offspring, so that there is no longer a " double law " for children in Soviet Russia. Children born out of marriage, as the result of a transient connection, are placed on an absolute equality with those born in marriage, but especially in respect of their claim to support and to inherit from father and mother.

But if a father refuses to recognize his child, then Clause 28 provides—again in order to alleviate the situation of the child born out of marriage—that the unmarried mother may report her pregnancy to the competent S.A.G.S. at most three months before her confinement— in order that the matter may be settled before her lying-in —stating exactly the time of conception and the name and place of residence of the father. Clause 29 provides that the man designated as the father shall be informed by the S.A.G.S. of the communication, and shall be at liberty, within one month, to dispute the truth of the mother's statements before the court. If he omits to do so, then his silence is held to be an acknowledgment of his paternity and he is entered as the father. But he may sue the mother within a year for false information.

If the matter is settled before the court, then the parties, both the mother and the putative father, are required to speak the absolute truth on pain of punishment for perjury.

If the father pleads *exceptio plurium*, that is that the mother had simultaneous relations with several men, and if the true paternity cannot be ascertained, then, according to the code of 1918, Solomon's judgment was pronounced, i.e. that all the possible fathers must share the costs of the lying-in and the support of the child. But out of consideration for the child, which might suffer morally later in such conditions of " collective paternity ", the present marriage law recognizes only one father, and that the one best able to pay among all those in question. The Ukraine family code provides in such cases for the joint liability of several men for alimony.

We want to build our lives on a communist basis and devote our whole leisure to the development of our intellectual powers. Then we shall have, besides " palaces of labour ", a bright " palace of motherhood ".

—Vera Lebedyova.

Motherhood is a social function of woman.
Children are the flowers of life.

Soviet Russian Mottoes.

NOWHERE in the world do you see so many pregnant women as in Moscow, in Soviet Russia, in the whole Soviet Union, nowhere are there so many children. The annual increase of the population is estimated at three and a half million: before long a sixth of the earth will be mainly peopled by those who first saw the light in the land of the revolution. If we are to grasp the fact, with all its implications, that this increase is not simply the result of the natural fertility of a people still young and vigorous, but is the first example and model of a population policy systematically carried out, we must bear in mind, firstly the measures adopted by the state and society in the Soviet Union in order to influence the birth-rate, and secondly the legal provisions for the protection of mothers and children.

BIRTH RESTRICTION AND THE SURPLUS OF BIRTHS

LET me begin with a statement : the increase in population shown in Russian birth statistics is equally in accordance—probably for the first time in the history of the human race—with the joint will of the community and the

will of each individual, and is not the result of the blind
sway of natural instinct. The propaganda in favour of
birth control, which is not only allowed by the state but
actually encouraged, and the legal *sanction of abortion*,
represent a broadly conceived rationalization of the
reproductive instinct found to-day only in Soviet Russia,
the first and only country to develop it. All other states
which claim to exercise any influence in this matter
regard it as their function to combat by all available
means the interruption of unwished-for pregnancies, the
restriction of natural fertility, and consequently propaganda for birth restriction ; in short, to force the
increase of the population, if need be, by penal measures.
The experience gathered in connection with Soviet
Russian legislation, which has culminated in an annual
birth-rate of three and a half million and which has
adopted the opposite method, is therefore, like other
Bolshevik experiments, of world-wide historic significance.

Thanks to its novelty and perhaps occasionally to its
excessive boldness, the Soviet state's attitude towards the
restriction of the birth-rate, whether by the prevention
of conception or by artificial abortion, has been often
enough discussed abroad, so that it is pretty well superfluous to reopen the question here. It is known that
propaganda for prevention—in addition to the Birth
Control Centres which are known in other countries
besides the Soviet Union and where information and
advice are given on all questions of preventive intercourse—is conducted by means of numerous lectures,
films, and the distribution of explanatory pamphlets,
which may be bought in the streets of Soviet Russian
towns for a few copeks.

What is less well known, because it is less accessible to
the public, is the activity of the " Laboratory for Preventives ". It has been in existence for about seven
years, is attached to the Moscow Institute for the Protection of Mothers and Infants, and is the only establishment of its kind in the world ; under the direction of
some twenty doctors, it conducts scientific research into
all questions of preventive intercourse and measures to

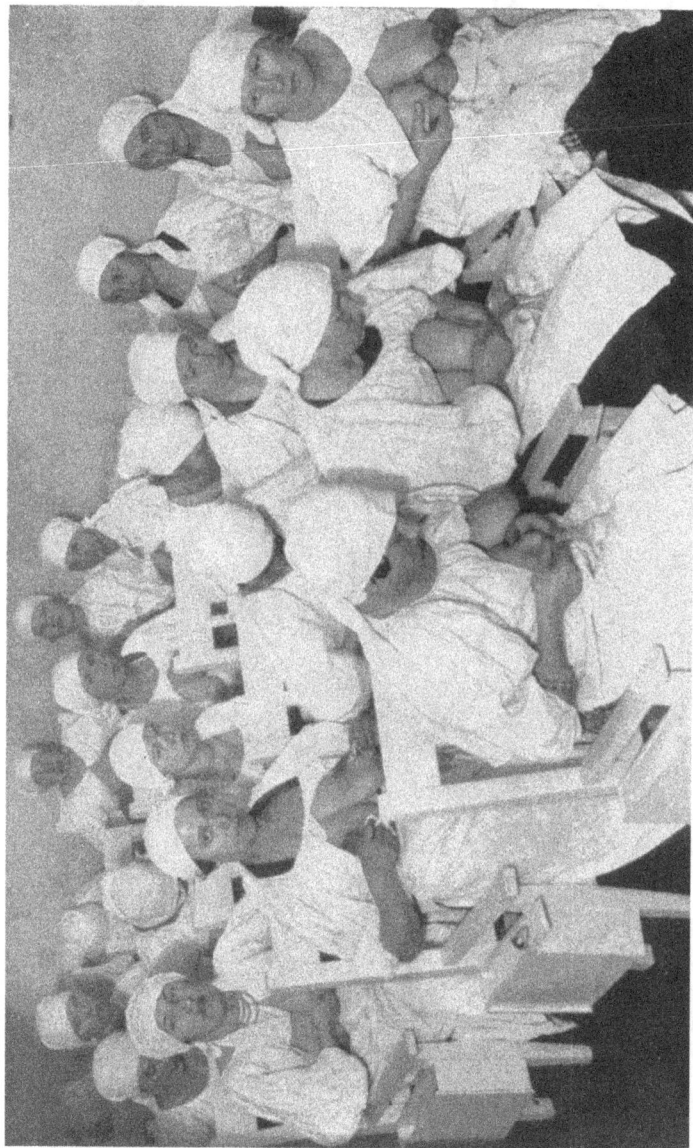

IN THE MOTHERS' MILK CENTRE

[face p. 138

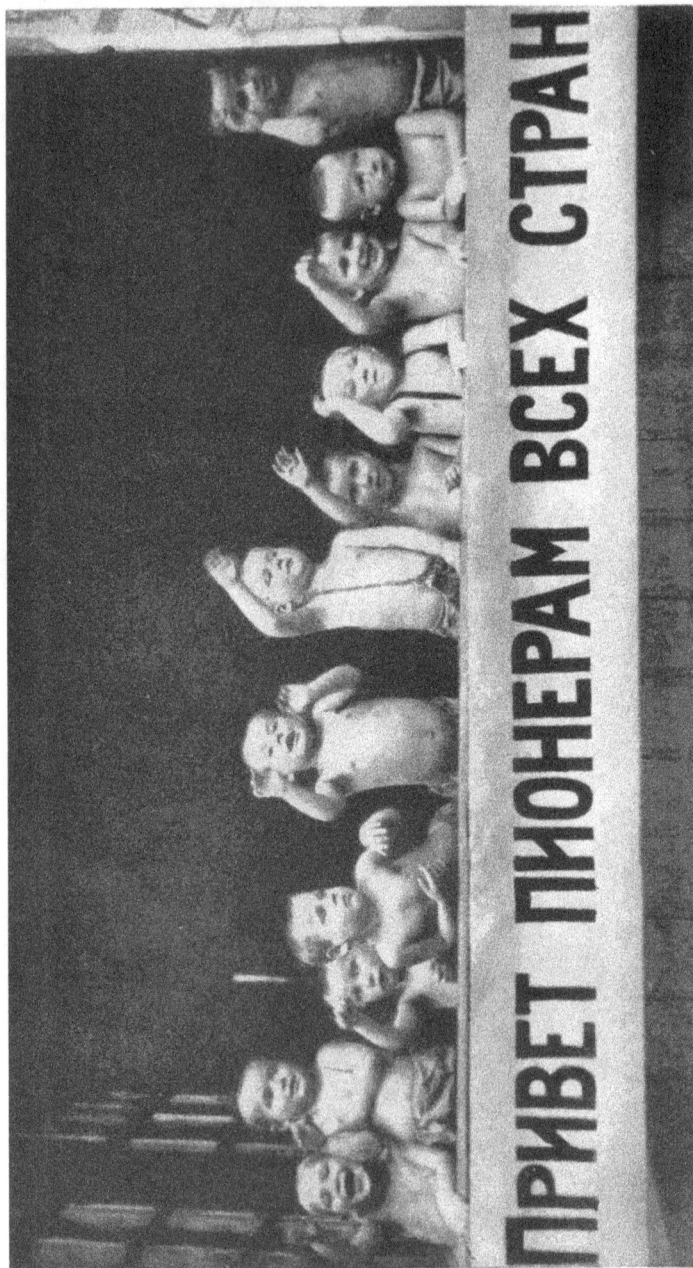

ПРИВЕТ ПИОНЕРАМ ВСЕХ СТРАН

GREETINGS TO THE PIONEERS IN ALL COUNTRIES

[face p. 139

check conception. Up to the present time experiments have been tried in this laboratory with various preparations. Several years ago a small factory for the manufacture of preventives was established, and its monthly sales have increased from 250 roubles in 1927 to 70,000 roubles in 1930. For the time being preventives are short in the Soviet Union, the demand for them considerably exceeds the supply. In order to redress the evil the laboratory intends to put a new remedy on the market shortly which is now undergoing the final process of experiment. These experiments appear to show that the so-called " biolaktin " which is made from butter-milk and which is suitable, on account of its cheapness, for a popular remedy, is perfectly harmless and is preferable in practice to all other means of preventing conception.

This widely organized propaganda for preventive intercourse, which has spread to the villages, is expressly intended to make abortion superfluous and to promote the acceptance of the motto : *Prevention, not abortion.* For in spite of everything that people abroad think they can deduce from the spirit of Soviet Russian legislation, official Russia is convinced of the harmfulness of artificial abortion—*to allow abortion is not the same as to encourage it*—and is seriously concerned with the endeavour to minimize its dangers. But it is realized also that threats of penalties and the legal prohibition of abortion, such as exists in all bourgeois countries, is least of all likely to achieve its purpose. It was decided, therefore, in November, 1920, after the Draconic Tsarist penalties for abortion had been abolished immediately after the October revolution, to adopt the much-abused measure of legalizing abortion. It was the first legal recognition of woman's right, demanded by the feminist movement, to possess her own body, and ought doubtless to be designated as one of the great achievements of Soviet Russia's constructive will.

The legalization of abortion created a state of affairs which resulted in practice in something like this : every woman is at liberty to undergo abortion on condition that the operation is performed with a licence in a public hospital. In order to obtain a licence for abortion the woman must apply to a commission established for that purpose, the *Abortus-Troyka*. The *Troyka* consists of a doctor and two women, one representing the Commissariat of Public Health and one a delegate of the District Soviet (the social element). As a rule a member of the Social Juridical Advisory Commission is co-opted. A fee is charged for the operation—except in special cases—which is graded according to income, but there is a free *abortarium* in Moscow for women with the lowest scale of pay ; the licence is granted for reasons of health and eugenic (because the mother is too young), social, and economic considerations, and is refused only in exceptional cases, especially if the institutions established for the purpose are overcrowded. The principle is laid down that abortion is not performed for a woman in her first pregnancy, that artificial abortion may not be performed for the same woman more than twice in one year, and that the three months' limit may not be passed. Then every case is examined with a view to ascertaining how urgent it is. For the rest, it is held that births are not determined by abortion, but by social conditions. Consequently the relevant circumstances are mainly social or economic, the still lamentable housing conditions and standard of living, the poverty of single mothers, and the like. In the towns it is mostly girls between eighteen and twenty, in the country women from thirty to forty with three or more children (numerous children are the most frequent social cause in the villages) who undergo the operation.

Little as is done to place difficulties in the way of a woman who wishes to have unwished-for issue removed, yet the commissions try to prevent irresponsible abortion by moral persuasion and active assistance. An unwritten law of the new Soviet Republic—and not merely a medical regulation—requires every woman *to carry at least the first child till the time of delivery*, and it is pointed out that from the medical point of view pregnancy is desirable for a healthy woman. In other cases efforts are made to remove the obstacles to the child's being carried till the time of delivery by giving relief, finding accommodation, and so on.

That the technique of abortion in the above-mentioned *abortaria* has been brought to a pitch of perfection hardly attained in any other country, thanks to the doctors' high degree of specialization, is proved both by the very few deaths following on abortion and by the number of foreign doctors who study methods of abortion in these unique institutions. Moreover, another kindred institution has recently been established in Moscow, which likewise has no parallel in Western Europe : the clinic for " incomplete abortion " opened in November, 1931, designed to take eighty patients who are sent from maternity homes and the Rescue Society and are given regular treatment as long as necessary.

It is worth while to visit a Soviet Russian *abortarium*. When I went to see a small one near me in Moscow, the first thing that astonished me was the number of women whom I saw there : and in two rooms, none too large, there were about sixty patients. The Abortion Commission usually continues its meetings far into the night, and yet they can only get through all the work that there is to do with the utmost effort. There is a special rush, I am told, in the spring months and after great popular festivals. Plainly the thirteen existing *abortaria* are not enough for Moscow and its neighbourhood.

In each of these *abortaria* there is a clinical section and an operating theatre. The women who are sent to such an institute by the itinerant dispensaries, after a medical examination and by order of the competent authority, remain after the operation for a period varying from three to five days in order to recover, and then, if nothing arises to prevent it, they return to their work in ten days, the legally prescribed term of leave for abortion.

Passing through the room where the examinations are conducted, and through the laboratory and the room where the shower-baths are taken, which now take the place of ordinary baths in Russia—it is all simple and unpretentious, but hygienically beyond criticism—I was led into the operating theatre, after I had been made to

141

put on a white coat in an ante-room, although I had not
asked it. The doctors occupied there (including four
women) and the assistants wore rubber gloves and
sterilized clothes, and the instruments were taken out of
a pot of boiling water. The scene was the same as in any
Western European operating theatre that is not luxurious,
and there was just the same smell of lysol and other
medicaments.

They were just placing two patients on two operating
tables side by side and the operation was carried out by
two women doctors with the help of their colleagues and
one man doctor. The use of any anæsthetic is extremely
rare—only in the case of particularly nervous women.
One woman lay quite quietly and chatted with the doctor.
The other moaned barely audibly from time to time.
The whole proceeding, which reminds one involuntarily
of pulling out teeth, was over in hardly more than five
minutes. The women were immediately bundled up on
wheeled couches, and one of them, who was wheeled past
me rather pale but smiling pleasantly, spoke jestingly to
me as she went. Fresh instruments were brought, the
doctors washed, and the next patients had their turn.
Each of these gynæcologists performed some ten operations for abortion in a day. In 1930 there were 175,000
in Moscow (55,000 in one *abortarium* alone).

Those who had been operated on in the past two
days were lying in an airy, faultlessly neat room, where
the women are placed in clean beds side by side as soon
as the operation is over ; some were reading, others were
talking eagerly with their neighbours. One of them,
with whom I got into conversation—the others listened
with interest—told me that this was the fourth time she
had undergone the operation, and was full of the praise
of the woman surgeon : " They ought to have none but
women everywhere. They do it much more painlessly,
much more gently and delicately, than the men. Out
with the men from the gynæcological clinics ! " There
are some, so one of the woman doctors in this institute
told me, who have undergone the operation fifteen times.
But the average is seven times, and with some women two

or three times a year. She, too, explained such fre-quency by the lack of preventive remedies.

The experience of twelve years of legalization of artificial abortion is overwhelmingly in favour of the method adopted by the Soviet Union. This legislation has at any rate removed the veil of secrecy which formerly covered abortion and the dangers of ignorant performance of the operation have been reduced to the minimum. " Years of scientific work," we are assured by Dr. Genss, the director of the department for abortion of the Moscow Institute for the Protection of Mothers and Infants, " have proved that abortion performed in a hospital is practically never fatal. There is one death among 25,000 abortions. In Western Europe an average of one to two per cent die. In Germany, where about a million abortions are performed annually, at least 10,000 women die every year from artificial abortion. In the Soviet Union it would be 30,000 a year, if abortion were not legalized. But if that is the case—and there is no doubt of it—then 300,000 women have been saved in Soviet Russia in the last ten years, during which a hundred thousand have come to grief in Germany. All comment is superfluous. . . ."

Since abortion was legalized the number of illegal operations for abortion, which are still severely punished, has of course fallen rapidly in Soviet Russia. To-day it is the general opinion of the doctors that there are probably no cases of criminal abortion in Russia : the law has, therefore, achieved its purpose.

The fears principally of foreign specialists, who raised the spectre of a reduced birth-rate, nay of the gradual depopulation of Soviet Russia in consequence of an " epidemic of abortion ", have, as we know, nowise been justified. The surplus births in the Soviet Russia amount to thirty-seven per thousand of the population (in all civilized Western European states the figure is under twenty). Thus there can really be no question of a menace of depopulation or even of any considerable effect of legalized abortion. Nor was there any epidemic of abortion in Russia, or at any rate only for a brief period; in Moscow, for instance, there were twenty-seven abortions to every hundred births in 1924, whilst the number in Berlin is estimated at fifty-four. Legislators in other countries ought, therefore, to bear in mind, side by side with the statistics of population, the fact which Dr. Genss states in these words : " In the Soviet Union, in spite of legalization, there are relatively fewest abortions : we are *the country in which abortion is least practised.*"

But this fact, which mocks all prophecies, still calls for elucidation and explanation. What is the reason why Soviet Russian women make, indeed, frequent use of their legal right to abortion, but not so frequent that the increase in population is in the smallest degree endangered thereby ?

We cannot overestimate the importance of the above-mentioned propaganda which represents the bearing of children not only as a social function—to that we shall have occasion to return—but also as the duty of women as citizens. Yet even more important, no doubt, is the healthy instinct of procreation in the women of a healthy people. For the reasons already cited that ideal condition has already been realized here in a certain sense, where only *children who are desired*, " welcome guests at the table of life," are brought into the world, children who do not owe their existence to " a stroke of ill-luck in the technique of prevention which cannot be subsequently corrected " or a " lapse ". A Russian woman who wishes to relinquish her social function of maternity and is unwilling to fulfil her civic duty need bring no children into the world. But for the most part she does it, and does it without the compulsion to bring to birth which is still sacrosanct in Western Europe, because it is her *will* to have children, if only in respect for her own healthy instincts. Besides, the Russians are crazy about children, and the love of children in this people which is still—in spite of technical developments, mechanization, and Americanization—in close touch with nature and in a sense still in its own childhood, is an aspect of its character illustrated by many touching instances.

The history of the *problem of adoption* is a proof that even Lenin's legislation was powerless against this love. For at first revolutionary legislation was hostile to adoption. Under the Soviet code of 1918 the adoption of one's own illegitimate children or of other people's was forbidden, for fear of the abuse of child labour and of an unjustifiable extension of the number of heirs in the country. But life proved stronger than the law. The institution of *priymachestvo*, the taking of children, which was indistinguishable from adoption in practice, persisted ; and when after the civil war and the hunger years 1920–1 the number of destitute children rose to alarming proportions, the legislature could not and would not continue deaf to the demand of the masses for the legalization of adoption. Indeed, the concession went so far that in the second version of the marriage law the clauses dealing with this question were put in force immediately. True, a number of safeguards were introduced : the preamble stresses the fact that adoption is allowed only in so far as it benefits the child, not the foster-parents ; a certain difference of age is necessary ; persons who have attained their majority cannot be adopted ; children over ten must themselves consent to the adoption, and Clause 27 allows any third party to appeal for the cancellation of the adoption in the child's interest.

In spite of this, and in spite of bad housing conditions which surpass all conception, and the still far from satisfactory standard of living of the people, the custom of " family protection " has gained much ground in Soviet Russia since 1927, and orphans as well as the foundlings, whose numbers are diminishing and of whom I shall have more to say, almost all remain as adopted children in the families where they are boarded out from the Children's Homes till they are four years old. Very often—as I was told in the Leningrad Institute for the Protection of Mothers and Infants—when a boy is adopted, a girl is taken as well, and vice versa. For here, too, as always and everywhere in the new Russia, there is no lack of enthusiasm and social emulation, and I was told of a case in which a communist proletarian couple had taken three children at once : " Since it is our duty to help the state." When these children are handed over to their foster-parents they are given linen and a basket cradle or bed, and are seen regularly by the visiting nurse in the house of the foster-parents. Further, children placed in the care of parents not their own must be brought twice a month to the Infant Welfare Centre.

So far the experience of this form of adoption is overwhelmingly favourable. The little ones do better in family surroundings than in the best institution, and the practice has recently arisen of paying to destitute parents whose children were to be sent to a Home a sum equivalent to the cost of their upbringing (parents' protection). The authorities do not like to give foster-children to families where there are already small children. On the other hand, it has proved the more satisfactory when they are placed in a home where the children are already more or less grown-up. The above-mentioned Leningrad Institute placed 300 children in the one year 1920 by means of adoption and family protection.

But the fact that the birth-rate is steadily rising, in spite of birth-control propaganda, the legalization of abortion, and the low standard of living, is due to the magnificent maternity and infant welfare work in the Soviet Union, even more than to this characteristically Russian love of children and the moral suasion exercised upon the population, which is assuredly not negligible. We will now look more closely at this welfare work, which may justly be regarded as one of the principal assets of the Soviet régime.

THE PROTECTION OF MOTHERHOOD AND CHILDHOOD

FIRST a brief glance for purposes of comparison at the provisions for the protection of motherhood and childhood in pre-revolutionary Russia.

It is impossible to speak at all of any protection of motherhood, of any legal recognition of motherhood as a service rendered by women, before 1912 in Russia. It was not till then that, under pressure from the increasingly vigorous Labour movement, insurance funds were established to which the factory women paid contributions to the amount of one or two per cent of their wages and were enabled in return to enjoy two weeks' leave before and four weeks after their confinement. No other women, who were not engaged in industry—in particular the great mass of peasant and rural working women—enjoyed any legal protection whatever until the October revolution of 1917.

We must admit that this sin of omission on the part of the Tsarist Government, which was backward in every respect, appears less flagrant when we remember that to this day the United States of America knows nothing of the legal protection of motherhood, and that even in progressive Switzerland there was no insurance for childbirth until the turning of the century, although unpaid leave of absence for childbirth has been established since 1878. Accordingly the legal protection of motherhood in Western European countries is still markedly inferior to that of the Soviet Union, which allows eight weeks' leave of absence with full pay before and eight after the confinement, whereas the legal period of leave in Germany, Austria, and Poland is six weeks, in England, Belgium, Denmark, and Italy only four weeks after the confinement.

But what was worse in the Russia of former days was the provision for assistance at childbirth. According to the available statistics only five mothers in every hundred enjoyed the services of a doctor or midwife. Until the revolution the number of maternity clinics in the Russian cities was utterly inadequate, and it was one of the accepted facts of Russian life that the peasant woman in the country gave birth to her child without any attendance whatever, in the stables.

The state troubled as little about the child's life as the mother's welfare. The few institutions for the protection of infancy were due to the private initiative of charitable societies or of doctors. The first institute, copied from a French model, the so-called " Drop of Milk " (*Goutte de Lait*), was established in Kiev in 1893 ;

in 1901 St. Petersburg and Odessa followed suit. In the provinces the *Syemstvos* set up isolated crèches and maternity homes. The first Infant Welfare Centre was opened in Kiev in 1906 ; in 1911 there were Advisory Centres of this kind in Moscow, but their total number in all Russia was six till the Bolshevik revolution, whilst in the succeeding three years alone it rose to 193. Moreover, there were in the revolutionary year 1905 only a few hundred primitive crèches in the country throughout Russia, and at most fifty Welfare Centres in the towns. No wonder that these conditions were reflected in the figures of infant mortality, which were incomparably higher in Tsarist Russia to the end than in any other country in Europe and were in some cases measurable with those of the most backward Asiatic countries. As late as 1910 two million children—more than a third of the total number of babies—died annually in Russia before they were a year old. (In the last two years infant mortality in the Soviet Union has been reduced by more than half.) A considerable proportion were, of course, illegitimate children and foundlings, who numbered almost 50,000 in Tsarist Russia. In the Moscow Foundling Hospital alone 20,000 foundlings were received annually, were given to nurse by the " guardian " Home to ignorant peasants, and died in large numbers for want of any medical and sanitary supervision. Indeed, the manufacture of angels was one of the most prosperous trades in old-time Russia, and we may deduce that infant mortality was enormous even in the few homes that there were from the fact that in the St. Petersburg Foundling Hospital in the years 1900–9 of almost 90,000 children 43 per cent died. But there were districts where child and infant mortality was no less than 90 per cent.

In spite of the difficult conditions in the country districts, which it has yet to master, the Soviet Government proceeded two months after its victory to build up a system of protection of motherhood and infancy, and in the Decree of December 28th, 1917, the thesis with which we are already familiar was proclaimed : " The procreation of children is a social function of women."

Thenceforth this became the guiding conception, the spirit inspiring all enactments designed to solve the problem of "mother and child", and under Lenin's generous-minded and sympathetic encouragement, it was developed to a well-thought-out, consistent system. And as at the first, so throughout the years, this problem constitutes one of the most important parts in the forward programme not only of the Public Health Authorities, but of all the economic and social organizations in the Soviet Union.

Directly after the revolution the few welfare institutions taken over from the Tsarist era were attached to the People's Commissariat of Social Welfare, at that time under the direction of A. Kollontay ; at her instigation the organization of an Institute for the Protection of Mothers and Children, unknown in the Russia of former days, was set in motion. Two years later matters had progressed so far that the protection of mothers and children had become a weighty affair of state. And in November, 1919, when Vera Lebedyova—a doctor and professor of medicine, who was subsequently for a decade at the head of this widespread welfare work, on behalf of which she performed admirable service—came forward at the first All-Russian Conference of Working Women and discussed the principle of motherhood as a social service performed by women, she said in the course of her speech : " When a woman gives life to a child, she performs work every bit as important as that of the engineer who constructs roads—for the child she bears may later become a civil engineer and build roads. The state needs children, and therefore it must make provision for them. Do not, therefore, suppose that when the state takes thought for mothers in childbirth and for the newly born child, and when it combats infant mortality, it performs a charitable action. Oh no ; in so doing the state takes thought for itself too and pays only a very small part of its debt to you. For the risk to life and health which you undergo for its sake cannot be paid for with money. . . . The task which we have now set ourselves is principally to train the mother as a citizen and to set the working mother free from the care of her child. For hitherto it has been said that motherhood is a heavy cross and a child a scourge of God. All that is to be changed now. . . ."

In addition to this general consideration there was another more pressing and practical which gave the decisive impulse to vigorous action. If women were to take their place in the process of production, to be drawn into the work of building up the new society, it was necessary to enable them to follow an occupation by transferring the care of the children to the state. And so from the very beginning prominence was given, side by side with Lenin's watchword: " Free the women from domestic slavery," to the demand that they should be partially or wholly liberated from the cares of looking after and educating their children. At the present time, when people are devoting all imaginable energies to carrying out the Five Years' Plan, so that none must lie idle, the success of the vast scheme depends ultimately upon the support and co-operation of the women, so that the question is more urgent than ever.

In outline the broadly planned system of protection of motherhood and childhood emerged immediately after the assumption of power by the Soviets. By 1918 there were already hundreds of institutions for maternal and infant welfare which, closely associated with curative and prophylactic establishments, sought to influence the life of the Soviet child from the moment of conception, in part indirectly through the mother, in part directly. And the fact that the wide ramifications of the state *Okhrmatmlad* (abbreviation for Protection of Motherhood and Childhood) have been made an integral part of the public life of the Soviet Union, a part without which we cannot imagine it, is a significant indication of the place allotted to it in the reconstruction now being attempted. *The protection of motherhood and childhood is the path to the new socialist " byt "*—such is the official motto, and therewith a new era dawns in the life of the working woman, especially of the peasant woman.

The whole immense organization for the protection of

motherhood and of the rising generation in the Soviet state, since it was transferred from the People's Commissariat of Public Assistance to that of Public Health, has been placed under the control of the Moscow State Scientific Institute for the Protection of Mothers and Infants. There is a similar Institute in Leningrad, with a woman doctor, Professor Mendyeleva, at the head. In these two institutions all questions concerning the physiology and pathology of women and children are made the subject of scientific research by specialists, children's doctors ; directions for the feeding, care, and clothing of children are worked out for the whole Soviet Union, and provision is made for the training of proper assistants, midwives, and teachers.

The institutions for the benefit of pregnant women and those in childbirth are partly prophylactic, partly advisory. Their efficacy is due to the legal provisions for the protection of motherhood, provisions which go far beyond all welfare arrangements in any other countries. I have already mentioned the eight weeks' leave of absence to which every woman has a right before and after her confinement, and which is reduced to twice six weeks in the case of a constantly diminishing group of women employees. At the present time blood tests are taken of pregnant women before and after their work in order to investigate the effect of labour on the expectant mother scientifically and to deduce practical conclusions from the result, especially in the matter of the legal provisions for leave of absence.

Every insured woman and the wife of every insured workman receives a baby's outfit from the state and an allowance to enable her to suckle her child. There are a number of other laws which provide for an all-embracing protection of pregnant women, and special authorities to ensure that they are carried out—a Commission for the Protection of Labour in the Factories, inspectors of labour, and representatives of labour. A pregnant woman must be put to the lighter kinds of labour in the factory, and may not be dismissed or transferred to another town without the consent of the inspector of labour. Night labour is forbidden to pregnant women and to nursing mothers, whose work, moreover, begins an hour later. For nursing mothers in addition pauses are prescribed on the average every three hours for them to suckle their babies, and factories with more than fifty women workers are required to provide a special room for the purpose. Further laws which restrict the factory labour of adolescent women and forbid child labour altogether show a far-sighted appreciation of the service rendered by women in motherhood and are calculated to ensure healthy offspring.

Assistance at childbirth, too, which is free on principle and, like the whole medical service in the Soviet Union, is predominantly prophylactic in character, has been developed to an imposing structure. In all the sections of Moscow, Leningrad, and the provinces there are numerous medical advisory centres where expectant mothers and women in general are not only examined and advised free on gynæcological questions, but are instructed by addresses, leaflets, pamphlets, and lectures —in short, are carefully prepared in every way for the task of motherhood. Of course there is great congestion at these centres. The interval of waiting is often occupied with lectures within the comprehension of all on sanitary, hygienic, and other matters, and with questions and answers, and there is evidence of a steadily increasing interest on the part of the audience. The walls of these and all other waiting- and ante-rooms are decorated with pictures, statistical tables, and posters which explain the facts about venereal diseases and tuberculosis by ocular means.

At certain intervals a pregnant woman is told to come for further examination. At the end of the seventh month the doctor gives her a certificate of her condition which she must hand in at her place of employment, and then she enters automatically upon her legal leave of absence. During her pregnancy and within a year of her delivery no woman in the Soviet Union may be dismissed from her work.

The number of *maternity homes* is steadily increasing,

as well as the *homes for mothers and children*, almost unknown in Western Europe, in which solitary, uncared-for mothers may spend two months before and two months after their confinement, that is to say their whole leave of absence. In these homes, which people try to make homelike and cosy by adorning the rooms with flowers—so popular in the Soviet Union—and other modest decorations, you generally find a number of motherless children whom the women suckle and care for besides their own children. Here, even more than in the *Mothers' Milk Centres*, we have the practical realization of the motto according to which *every Soviet Russian woman must be a mother not only to her own child, but to all children of the workers and peasants*. In addition to the light work which the women have to perform in these homes they receive instruction in reading and writing as well as in the most important " civilized customs ", and every mother who afterwards quits one of these homes is fully conscious that she has both found help and a sure refuge for her child and has herself undergone a course of schooling. That makes her feel freer, more independent, and surer, so that she is incomparably better prepared for the new life before her. Many of the mothers are employed as children's nurses in these homes, and usually carry out their duties in a spirit of real love.

The system of " advisory centres " is most generously and fully developed in the Soviet Union ; in the industrial centres it already embraces a full 100 per cent of the infants and young children up to the age of three or four. The number was estimated at 3,000 in 1931, whereas a year earlier it was barely 2,000. They are the nucleus of the welfare organization, and their activities are considered the more important because, but for the propaganda which they carry on, some of the women would remain ignorant of their legal rights and could make no use of them. These organizations are able to bring every single mother, but in particular every solitary mother, within the range of their advisory and welfare activities after her confinement. Most of the advisory

centres have " milk kitchens " attached to them. In
addition an exhibition is placed at their disposal from
time to time, representing in visual form the most important points concerning midwifery, the care of children,
and the protection of mothers and infants.

The system of advisory centres has been organized on
the broadest basis and is firmly rooted in the mass of the
people. All the factories in the Union, and every administrative, industrial, or trading institution, elect an
appropriate number of female and male delegates to the
various cultural bodies in the district, and these have
charge of the advisory organization, as well as the schools,
crèches, and maternity homes. The delegates work
together with the representatives of their district Soviet.
The nucleus of their activities as regards the care of
mothers and infants is the advisory centre, to which
are attached all other institutions of the kind under the
control of the district authorities, knit together as a single
whole. Together with the medical staffs of the advisory
centres, the total delegates form a " Commission for the
Betterment of Labour and the Standard of Living ".

The female delegates whose function it is " to combat
the abandonment of infants " keep watch over all pregnant
women who are likely to be obliged to bring up their
children alone, and take care that they are placed in good
time in one of the homes for solitary mothers. And so
the total number of abandoned children in the educational institutions of the whole Union in 1927 was only
about 8,000—to-day it is doubtless much smaller—which
must, indeed, be attributed primarily to the abolition of
the distinction between legitimate and illegitimate birth
through legislation, but also to the educational work of
the delegates. Of course the mortality in these homes
is very low as compared with former times (in Moscow
in 1927 it was only 5·2 per cent), which may be partly
due to the fact that the children are no longer exposed
to the chances of the angel-making industry in the
villages, but are generally put out to nurse with the
families of town workers where, as we have seen, they
usually remain as adopted sons or daughters.

One word more about the advisory centres, some of which are itinerant: for the villages, *sovkhosi*, and *kolkhosi*. These itinerant advisory centres remain in one place at most two months and adapt their activities to the local conditions. For the rest, the activities of the advisory centres include, besides the giving of medical and hygienic information, consultation on social and juridical questions. The main function of these " social and juridical consultation centres ", which are everywhere attached to the advisory centres and are conducted by legal experts, usually women, is to combat the destitution of mothers and children, to discover paternity, to grant legal assistance in alimony proceedings, and to provide work or support for the mother as well as milk for the baby. In the advisory centre Soviet laws are explained, documents prepared, appeals lodged, and verbal or written information given.

A morning spent in a " social and juridical office " in the *Okhrmatmlad* in Moscow conveys a wealth of information on the subject of the protection of mothers and children in Soviet Russia. In a plain room which, however, is beyond criticism in the matter of hygiene, and to which one is admitted only after one has taken off one's upper garment and put on a white coat, two or three women as a rule sit at a table of medium size in front of which several easy chairs are placed. One is the actual consultant (a lawyer), another a nurse, and the third a delegate of the District Commission for the Betterment of Labour and the Standard of Living, who represents the social element. If a woman comes for the first time for a consultation a long interrogatory is filled up, but others are questioned closely without it, since the clientèle is always the same and confined to a particular district.

The ante-room where the women were waiting for admission was fairly crowded. " Fecundity is so great nowadays," one of the women officials on duty said to me, " that it is scarcely possible to attend properly to all the women's wishes." They all came along in turn. I will pick a few cases from my notes at random :

An undergrown, poorly dressed, care-worn mother, herself half a child, appeared with her child on her arm, accompanied by her mother. She was no more than seventeen, a worker in a chemical factory. Divorced from her husband, who was a drunkard, after eight months of married life. But the housing shortage obliged them to go on living in the same room, and whenever she suckled the child he tried to strangle her and threatened to " do the brat in " so as not to have to pay for its support. The child was three months old.

" Why did you not undergo the operation for abortion ? What were you thinking of ? "

" It was too late when I went . . ."

This young mother's mother, a thoroughly well-fed, typical member of the former petty bourgeois, obviously an artful body—she wore a red kerchief on her head, designed to proclaim her sympathy with the new régime —constantly interrupted in a shrill voice whenever her daughter opened her mouth : " Think of her social position ! " But in fact she cared for nothing but to get rid of the daughter who was living with her, together with her child and divorced husband, as soon as possible ; failing that she threatened to kill the child.

The young mother seemed desperate ; she wrung her hands and was furious about the child too. . . .

The consultant tried to soothe her : " Believe me, we will do all we can for you. Else I would not have undertaken this work. We will certainly get you away from your husband ; the child shall be admitted to a crèche, and we will see to it that its father pays the alimony. You can be sure of that. Either we will provide a *nyanya* (nurse) or you will be sent to a home with your child. But you mustn't listen to your mother. She's altogether too quarrelsome. And you mustn't beat your child. How could anyone hurt such a little creature ? We'll help you, don't you worry. You shall even get work in another factory that is less unhealthy for you. Do please calm yourself and don't on any account beat your child any more. . . ."

Another case :

156

PROTECTION OF MOTHERHOOD

A mother with a child on her arm. She had come for the first time. Was twenty-five. A member of the trade union, but for the time being only a " housewife ". After two years of marriage she had been four months divorced from her husband by mutual consent, and he was now working in a *kolkhos*. He earned a hundred and fifty roubles a month and paid thirty roubles a month for the child, which was almost a year old.

" I have only come about a room. . . ." For five people were living in the kitchen where she had formerly lived with her husband and child. She received an assurance that provision should be made for her. . . .

A young, pale, fair-haired woman with a weary, sad expression entered with her child at her breast. She was already known at the centre, a regular client, and the consultant who, in spite of her own youth, looked after each one of these unhappy women like an affectionate mother, received her with the words :

" It wrings my heart just to see you. How is your child now ? Still no answer ? Go yourself and find your husband in the Trust ; I will give you a note."

" I can't go on like this ; I'm at the end of my tether."

" Then I will see about getting you into the home for uncared-for mothers. We can easily find you work, and get the child into a crèche. But a room—that is difficult."

" If I hadn't the child I would go as a domestic servant directly. There are places enough. But nobody will take you with a child."

The conversation proceeded as if the pair were good friends. The child was four months old and screamed unceasingly. The mother, who, by the way, was still unable to read and write, looked tenderly at it and gave it the breast.

" A fractious child."

" How can it be otherwise when you nurse it yourself and are in a state of agitation all the time ? . . ."

Two young mothers pushed forwards. Both with babies, and lived in the night shelter. One had a bad cold and was quite hoarse :

" I've come about the milk. It's not quite enough,

and is getting less and less. . . ." The child's father, who was in the army, was on the Volga at the time. In Moscow he had lived in the barracks. She, too, wanted a room. She was employed in a factory as a sorter. The consulting nurse, who came in at this point and caught sight of the woman, greeted the child with : " Oh, you bonny pet—dear heart ! "

The second woman was a prostitute who had had a child by accident. The child was dirty, quite naked, and looked pitiful. They fetched napkins and put on a little vest, and the nurse retired with the child. . . .

A former domestic servant came in. " He " lived in the same house. " I went with him "—and here was the child. She, too, had been admitted to the night shelter and wanted work. " That is quite easy now ; but the child . . ."

The woman was semi-illiterate and very ignorant ; she told her story : " The father pays twenty roubles a month for the child now, and it is three months old. I ' went with him ' for three months, and now I always go to look for him at the office. He's living with another woman now in her room, but I don't know what to do." " Next time you go to fetch the money from him, try to have witnesses there, then we can sue him. Don't take the money when you are alone with him. We are giving you sound advice. . . ."

Finally, universal rejoicing : a mother with her child who was not only provided with work and a crèche but had even been found a place in a co-operative dwelling. She had just come from the daily lecture on the rights of mothers and children under Soviet Russian law, and was taking part in the social competition for mothers : that meant following rules exactly about the child's sleep, its breast-feeding, and its outings. To-day she had come because she wanted to thank the *tovarishchi* and inspect the exhibition for mothers and children more thoroughly. We left the building together.

On the way we stopped before a blackboard announcing an endless series of lantern lectures for mothers. Every day and at every hour the mothers can receive instruction from doctors and nurses about everything which concerns them as wives and mothers and their children in the matter of hygiene, medicine, social institutions, and legal rights. The invitation to these lectures is differently expressed each time and always in a way calculated to arouse the maximum of interest.

In the exhibition I was struck by a new poster. A plump-cheeked, bonny-looking baby begging his mother : " Look carefully at the exhibition and find out how to manage me properly." There were countless posters like that, more or less artistically executed : " Nothing can take the place of a mother's milk and a mother's love " ; " There is no such thing as bad mother's milk " ; " If the parents are unable to provide for their children's upbringing, then the state must undertake it " ; " The creation of favourable conditions for its mothers is the pledge of every country's future " ; " The cow is no more meant to feed a child than a woman to suckle a calf " ; and so on.

The People's Commissariat of Public Health is perpetually issuing posters of this kind, besides books of maxims, pamphlets, and leaflets, all designed for the one purpose of teaching the mothers in every way how they may bring up healthy children and keep themselves in good health, and these publications are distributed from the appropriate centres all over the Soviet Union, where, like all printed matter, they are sold like hot cakes amongst this greatest of all reading publics in the world.

In the exhibition itself, which embraced several thousand items—posters, photographs, diagrams, casts, tables, plates, anatomical preparations, and articles necessary for the care of children, etc.—I found everything as before. The women who came to see it, and who sometimes appeared with their husbands, were conducted round in groups. From wall to wall, from glass-case to glass-case, they were shown the exact phases of development through which the embryo passes in the womb until it is born into the world as a child. One item of special interest in the exhibition of the Moscow *Okhrmatmlad* is a collection of good reproductions of various old German,

Italian, and Dutch masters whose Madonnas are letting the Child drink from a horn, which is shown as something exceedingly injurious. Equally interesting sometimes are the entries made by those who visit the exhibition ; here, as in every exhibition and museum in the Soviet Union, they are invited to criticize and record their impressions and perhaps their wishes in a book specially provided for the purpose. I opened it at the last page and read : " Undoubtedly the exhibition is very good and useful. The women guides' explanations are also very good and clear. I shall make my wife come straight away to-morrow. The exhibition is of the greatest interest both for me and for her. I have learned many truths here for the first time. Factory worker N.N."

Whilst the advisory centres in the industrial towns get through their immense work as here described with the help of the sections, to which a number of women factory workers belong as delegates, conditions in the country are different and, of course, simpler. There, too, the women—peasants and agricultural workers—organize Commissions for the protection of mothers and babies, but the most important feature of their welfare work here are as a rule the *yassli*, crèches, babies' homes, which have developed remarkably in the villages, so that the *summer crèche*, a type found nowhere but in the Soviet Union, has sprung up. Their importance to working women, whom they relieve of the duty of minding their children and set free for employment, is the same as in the industrial centres, and Lenin, who described them as germ cells of communist society, advocated in his time a generously planned development of the network of crèches in the Soviet state. He claimed that in all factories where women were employed crèches should be established with trained medical and nursing staffs. To-day, therefore, there are everywhere in the industrial centres *factory crèches* and *district crèches*, and in the country in all *kolkhosi* and *sovkhosi* the above-mentioned summer and seasonal crèches, besides two additional types latterly : *evening crèches* at the working women's clubs and *night crèches* for the children of mothers on night-work.

PROTECTION OF MOTHERHOOD

A few figures will show the increase in the number of crèches in the Soviet Union : from 1928 to 1931 the network of children's crèches in the industrial districts has increased from 33,374 to about 130,000, and with the help of the *kolkhos* women one and a half million summer crèches were organized in 1931, as compared with 135,000 in 1928. In 1932 the number was doubled. This growth alone may be taken as proof that since the revolution the children's crèches have become an essential part of every factory and workshop, and of all *sovkhosi* and *kolkhosi*, and that Lenin estimated their importance rightly at the outset. It is impossible to imagine any industrial establishment, any undertaking, any *kolkhos*, any tractor station, any collective undertaking, in the new Russia without such a crèche. And just as the various children's institutions are also training schools for the mothers, so the future Soviet citizens are accustomed early in them to activity, self-reliance, and hygiene, so that the foundation is laid for a communist education, education as a human being who will be able later to take his place whole-heartedly as part of the community.

In addition to this general function of the children's crèches, the *summer crèches*, which are opened in the villages during the harvest for a period of three months only, have a special function. In Russia, as everywhere else, infant mortality used formerly to rise with the coming of the beautiful summer weather. In Russia this was due to a special cause : in summer the peasant women had to work in the fields and, because they were wholly occupied with the harvest, they left their children, not excepting little babies, in the house without supervision or care. But now the children spend the day in the summer crèches during the harvest ; there are about three million of these, as already stated, and their purpose has been explained to the country people in countless meetings.

The statement, therefore, that the organization of the summer crèches has revolutionized the whole of village life sounds credible enough. Nor is it by any means the only revolution in the *byt*, the mentality and manner

of life, of the village population, especially in the collectivized agricultural undertakings. For instance, the
kolkhos woman need no longer work in the fields up to
the last moment before her confinement and seriously
endanger her child's and her own health in order to earn
her bread.

The storm-wind of a new era is sweeping over the
Russian villages ; it does not always blow from behind,
but is sometimes a strong head-wind, this harbinger of
a new way of life, and it blows strongest from the crèches.
The resolution of the Sixteenth Congress of the Communist Party in Soviet Russia declares :

> In the matter of crèches, kindergartens, schools, and curative
> institutions we must carry on mass education on the subject of
> *byt* on the basis of the independent socialist activities of the
> *kolkhos* women, so that we may proceed without delay to provide
> for the care of the *kolkhos* women's children during the harvest
> and lighten their labours.

These words voice anxiety for the success of the Five
Years' Plan and at the same time the realization that
the great Plan stands or falls with the bread problem and
so depends ultimately upon the co-operation of millions
of Russian women in the *sovkhosi* and *kolkhosi*. To try
to realize the Five Years' Plan without them would be
to reckon without one's host—however accurately the
figures may otherwise be calculated.

For the present everything is being done to attach
women in the country and also in the industrial centres
to a system which has at least brought them a highly
developed scheme of protection for mothers and children.
The welfare institutions, which no country has hitherto
equalled, are to be further elaborated in the near future.
For instance, there is a plan to establish special children's
rooms at the stations where children can stay under the
care of doctors and nurses attached to the nearest crèche
during the time of waiting, which often lasts for several
days. The first of these reception-rooms, with warm
shower-baths, bath-tubs, and children's lavatories, have
been opened quite recently in the Moscow stations. It

NADYESHDA KONSTANTINOVNA KRUPSKAYA
Lenin's Widow

[face p. 163

is said that the arrangement of itinerant nurseries on the Volga boats, where there is much room for improvement in the sanitary equipment, is under consideration.

But a much more far-reaching project, which is approaching realization within the framework of the cultural Five Years' Plan, is the introduction of *state responsibility for the maintenance of children*. From the summer of 1932 the feeding of most, if not all, children in the Soviet Union till they are three or four will be undertaken by the state and proclaimed to be the duty of the Public Health service. With a view to this socialization of children's feeding it is intended to establish feeding stations attached to the milk kitchens in each separate advisory centre for women and children. Before the end of 1932 there are to be a thousand such centres in all parts of the Soviet state, including one for 40,000 children in the Moscow Institute for the Protection of Mothers and Infants. In drawing up the scheme special attention is paid to industrial centres. The feeding centres are to serve whole districts and to provide the local crèches, nurseries, and kindergartens. If this generously conceived and novel plan is realized, of which hardly a doubt remains, there will be nothing more of importance to do in the way of child welfare in Soviet Russia within measurable time : the socialization not only of child protection but of the whole of child life would have reached its final stage.

Till then the struggle proceeds on behalf of the children, against the neglect of mother and child. I have already said that it is all done in order that at the first awakening of consciousness the child shall feel himself in the midst of a community and as a member of it, but the fact cannot be too often repeated and emphasized. From the crèche he proceeds to the *ploshchadka*, the infants' nursery, then to the nursery school, and after that to the kindergarten, where he remains till he reaches school age (seven). And here his education in communal work begins at once, special importance being attached to accustoming him to productive work. Toys are preferred with which several pupils can play at once,

163

and the tools that they are given must be genuine and serviceable. Thus it is a matter of course for the four-year-old Soviet citizen to know how to use a hammer and saw and to do practical work with them suited to his strength.

To sum up : foreign opinion—and some people in Soviet Russia—may still have doubts of the success of these plans. But it cannot be denied that there is a determination to protect mothers and children in a degree hitherto unattained in any other country. And one thing more is certain : beneath the Red banner of the Soviets, cared for by the state and society, a generation of new men and women are growing up who are utterly different, even now as children, from their contemporaries on the other side of the Russian frontier.

In the block of dwellings belonging to the Building Co-operative where I lodged with good friends in Moscow, I could not get over the astonishment which I felt whenever I crossed the courtyard, but especially in winter, at the comically active figures, wrapped from head to foot in fur or some other warm covering, which were romping as merry as crickets on the soft, white carpet of snow spread before them, however bitter the cold.

The grandmothers, who are usually less busy, and some mothers, elder sisters, and nurses—occasionally you see a man among them—who fill all the parks and boulevards and benches in Moscow with their own babies or their charges, also keep an eye on the older children at a little distance.

And then when " our " six-year-old Garrik, my special friend, breaks off in the middle of a pitched battle against the counter-revolutionaries or leaves a meeting of the Children's Committee at midday, and arrives with the thermometer thirty below freezing (" Daddy's always shivering ! Whatever does he think ? That I shall be frozen ? Really, I didn't expect a Daddy like that. And he calls himself a man ; he can't ever have romped when he was little "), hot and flushed and with shining

eyes, to satisfy his hunger with Mummy's dinner, and
when I just catch him and ask how he is getting on, there
is always a lot to tell.

On January 22nd, for instance, the day of Lenin's
death, which Garrik remembers perfectly, although it
was before his appearance in the world, I am told exactly
how it all happened : " And then suddenly a long, long
siren sounded in all the factories. . . . Everybody
stopped work at once. . . . And a long siren sounded
from the workshops. . . . The houses shook, and
people even stood still in the streets. . . . At that
moment Lenin died, who was a leader, the first leader
of the ' levorution ' that came after the Tsar. . . . The
Tsar, he wasn't a good man. . . . And then all the post-
men hurried along the streets with telegrams in their hands :
' *Tovarishch* Lenin is dead. . . .' All the trams stopped,
and the trains in the middle of their journeys, and in
the Kremlin suddenly a great, big cannon went off :
bu-bu-bu . . ."

" Look here, Nina Borissovna," he suddenly interrupted himself, " you want me to go abroad with you,
but I won't go abroad ; aren't I a Red ? " . . .

Another time he came marching up with angrily flushed
cheeks. " Why, whatever has happened ? " Something incredible. The eight-year-old Lyuba, who can
hardly write, had " fallen in love " and written a note to
eight-year-old Pavlik : " My sweetheart, my pet, my
treasure, my jewel . . ." " To fall in love ! Anything
so petty bourgeois ! Why, the days of Tsar Nicholas are
past ! " The question was debated excitedly and Lyuba
was punished by being made to stay away from the playground for three days.

And the overcrowded Volga steamboat on which I
spent a week in the summer of 1931 coming from Nishnyi
Novgorod teemed with children of all ages and expectant
mothers. In that short time two new Soviet citizens
actually first saw the light on the steamer. They were
landed with their mothers at the next stopping-place of
any size and taken to a maternity home. Lyalya and
Gena, aged five and eight, my little friends in Stalingrad

where I disembarked, were very much amused when I told them of the babies who were brought ashore right out of the Volga.

Gena had just been appointed a Pioneer at school (the preliminary stage for being a *komssomol*, up to the age of fourteen), and she told me that she was a member of the *Ssankommissiya*, the Sanitation Commission ; that is, she had to supervise the cleanliness of the classroom and of her little schoolfellows' hands, and, if anyone was hurt, to see that there were iodine, bandages, and wadding.

If Gena promises anything which she means to fulfil at all costs, then she gives her " Lenin word ". When I asked her she explained the difference between this Lenin word and an ordinary word of honour : " For instance, a little girl among us gave her word of honour and broke it later on. But if she had given her Lenin word, that couldn't have happened." Gena also taught me a number of pretty new Russian Pioneer poems and children's songs :

LENIN, GRANDPAPA ILYICH

Ilyich, loving Grandpapa—
Little children such as we
Yet may know what our books be ;
We can read and learn full well
All that they about thee tell.
People's battle-leader thou,
Heark to little children now,
One and all we take this vow :
We'll be warriors, stout of heart,
In thy work we'll take a part,
Ilyich, loving Grandpapa.

MARCH OF THE LENINTSI (LENIN BOYS)

Will you be of the Lenintsi ?
　Hear the rules, then, everyone !
Try to serve the whole community,
　Show the others how it's done.

Will you be of the Lenintsi ?
　Work well while you are at school.
You've a job ? Then put your heart in't,
　Not slack obedience to a rule.

You already read books quickly?
Teach the others in all haste,
Set to work to-day with vigour,
Let no instant go to waste.

Will you be of the Lenintsi?
Note the motto: " Be prepared!"
For yourselves return the answer:
" To fight we always are prepared!"

Altogether, grown-up people can already learn a good deal from the Soviet Russian children. Mrs. Nadyeshda Krupskaya, who received me in Moscow, told me how one day in Oryekhovo-Suyevo (a textile village, formerly utterly derelict and neglected) when she was inspecting a kindergarten she wanted to glance at the lavatory and was rebuked by the children stationed at the door: " Why, mother, don't you know the rules? You have to take off your coat before you come in here." The story made me think involuntarily how few grown-up people in the big cities of Tsarist Russia had any idea of the simplest sanitary rules. . . .

LOVE, MARRIAGE, AND THE FAMILY

. . . And as I watched her retreating figure, huddled with cold . . . I wanted to cry out: "Come back, stay with me, I will warm you and not abandon you to anyone!" But I knew that that was a petty bourgeois idea . . . that she might interpret it as love, and I was silent. . . .

—N. Bogdanov.

YESTERDAY AND TO-DAY

THERE is no country in the world—that we can assert without hesitation—in which youth plays so great and leading a part as in the land of the Soviets. In this an old tradition is finding expression. For even in Tsarist Russia, as we saw, youth came forward as the protagonist of new ideas, and the conceptions of "student", "intelligentsia", and "revolutionary", were regarded as almost identical.

So, too, we have seen from the lives and the writings of Russian revolutionary men and women that sex questions constituted no problem in their mutual relations, and that they themselves were in the first instance friends, comrades, sharers of a faith, and fellows in the fight. That is the source of the total lack of constraint in their behaviour to one another and partly, perhaps, of their unexampled devotion to a cause, an idea; a devotion which might suggest mass sublimation to the psychoanalyst.

The younger generation in Russia is an exceedingly sensitive barometer of the state of the country, and in their vacillations you may invariably read all periodical changes of mood. The defeat in the Japanese war and the reaction which spread in Russia after the shipwreck of the revolution in 1905 caused profound disappointment in the ranks of youth. The young people turned away

from politics and for a time personal interests predominated. The new prophets who came forward at that
moment had it all their own way, therefore. This
explains the great success of the novel *Ssanin* which was
famous in its day even beyond the frontiers of Russia,
with its novel-sounding pseudo-revolutionary doctrine of
sexual freedom which seemed for a time to cast a spell
upon everybody. In it the old, strict idea was thrust
aside, and Russian youth followed the new gospel of
unrestricted sexual freedom with the same ardour which
distinguishes it at all times. Sexual took the place of
political nihilism with young people, most of whom sprang
from the bourgeois middle class. The Tsarist authorities, to whom this diversion was not unwelcome, watched
things take their course for a time without intervening.
It was only when Artsybashev's novel was confiscated
abroad and the members of the " Ssanin Club " began too
openly to sink into the condition of an erotic sect—a
phenomenon, by the way, which appears from time to
time in Russian history—that the police in St. Petersburg
adopted measures to check the new pestilence.

The Ssanin movement, however, only constituted a
brief intermezzo and the tide soon receded, making way
for a fresh revolutionary wave, supported henceforth less
by the bourgeois intelligentsia — which retained the
leadership till the October revolution—than by the vast
mass of workers, whose importance had increased immensely meanwhile and who now took the struggle for
political power into their own firm control.

Once more the younger generation was thoroughly
freed from erotic preoccupations, and once more
Chernyshevskyi's words sound in our ears : " Away with
erotic problems. . . . The present-day reader takes no
pleasure in them." Words which preceded those of
Shenya in Kollontay's story by a good fifty years : " You
must have leisure to fall in love. And I have no time."

So matters continued till the world war which, in
Russia as in all countries, involved a sexual catastrophe.
The sexes were separated, the Russian villages deprived
of men, and alike in town and country new relations

between men and women evolved. Everywhere behind the front the shortage of men produced a slackening of morals, of the marriage and family code. The conception of conjugal faithfulness underwent transformation, and love affairs with prisoners flourished more than anywhere else in the vast realm of the Tsar, where a whole " army behind barbed wire " awaited the day of deliverance.

It is true that such love affairs—the outcome of a general demoralization—were rampant enough in other countries too. But in Russia there was a special additional cause : i.e. the fact that the attitude of Russian women to foreigners has always been peculiar and quite different from the great, sometimes excessive, respect of Russian men for what is foreign. Whereas this relation of Russian men to Western Europeans may be accounted for as something purely intellectual, a consciousness of cultural immaturity, in the case of the women the chief motive is emotional, erotic. In addition to the fascination of something alien, which may be a powerful motive in other cases as well, there is the fact that Russian women, with their much more sensitive femininity, feel the lack of a certain tenderness, a more refined form of sex relation, far more than other women in their intercourse with their husbands, who are much more primitive in love—among the masses often brutal and even coarse. Instinctively they look for this, and actually find it sometimes, in the foreigners who cross their paths. Thus Western Europeans who lived in Russia in the sixteenth and seventeenth centuries point out that, although the Russian women were shut up in the *terem* and regarded non-Orthodox Christians as heathens, yet they were not inaccessible to foreigners. And the fact that, as already observed, the women devised a special moral rule for such cases proves that these occurrences were not rare. We shall see later that a similar question arose in modern Russia.

It is not surprising, therefore, that millions of German and Austrian soldiers who were condemned to undergo the privations of war captivity for years in Russia during the world war were at least not wholly deprived of love. For the moral standards of the wives of Russian soldiers in the villages, who were always enrolled for a period of years, had always been a proverb ; and whilst they were respected by their neighbours for the ability with which they performed all the masculine labour in house and farm, they were on the other hand regarded as outcasts, since they were not always particular about keeping their marriage vows.

And now in the war, when the number of soldiers' wives swelled enormously and of the men in the villages only children, the aged, and the feeble remained behind, the prisoners frequently took the place of the Russian husbands :

> However fond I am of my husband [says the *ssoldatka* Anissya, who is living with an Austrian prisoner, in the novel *Virinyeya* by Lydia Sseyfullina, a book which is known abroad], however bitter the tears I shed when he went, all the same I " amuse " myself in his absence. . . . I expect he'll kill me when he comes back, and he'll be right, I know. Still, I don't mean to waste my youth. Women in former days, they say, waited for their husbands for decades even without sinning. But we're too weak for that. . . . Hot young blood—what is there to be said. . . . He must know that himself. . . . I'm sure he hasn't got along without a *baba*, a woman. He'll pick up a nasty disease yet. And if we hadn't enough diseased men like that already. That's the way it is. And even if he beats me or actually maims me, we shall live together afterwards all the same. And even if he kills me in his rage, he'll be sorry afterwards. For I'm a good worker and strong. . . .

Whilst the world war threw all previous moral ideas into confusion, demoralization assumed undreamt-of proportions in Russia in the civil war which followed the October revolution in 1917. For that war was waged, so to speak, within the family. Added to all the brutality which had been sufficiently promoted in good truth by the imperialist war, there came now the hatred of kindred, but in particular the deeply rooted hatred between classes fighting a life-and-death struggle. And so the methods adopted both by Whites and Reds were even more inhuman and cruel than those directed against foreigners. The unchained instincts of the combatants were still more uncontrolled and their sex appetites—in face of the perpetual danger of death—not seldom found outlet in positively brutish forms. And so the constantly recurring rape of the wives of adversaries was among the recognized weapons of war.

The women soldiers of the Red Army in the Bolshevik camp and in the ranks of the soldiery, fighting heroically on every front and in every capacity, up to the rank of commander, enjoyed the protection and the utmost respect of their male comrades. Nevertheless, their position was not always easy for them as women.

The gifted Soviet Russian journalist Larissa Reissner, who died early, and who took a leading part in the civil war on various fronts, has left in her notebook a remark about the inner development of one of these young women Red Army soldiers whom she met in a South Russian mine after the civil war. During a confidential talk between the women this girl told her that after passing her childhood and youth amidst privation she had enlisted in a partisan company in a state of fervent enthusiasm in order to fight for freedom. All the men guarded her with the utmost care :

> . . . And so she blossomed out in the war and grew like a slender, white tree, with her ash-coloured hair. She had her newspapers, her scouting expeditions, her own uniform, her own rifle, the horse that she had captured in battle, her place in the squadron, her first wound—everything in short which the great year 1918 could give her to make up for her joyless past, for an attic without a window, for the deduction of two roubles from her wage of two roubles because of broken cups, for her sixteen-year-old breast squeezed in the dark and her little possessions flung outside on to the steps by her jealous mistress. . . .
>
> But one day—it was the eve of an offensive—the commander of her unit sent for her : " If you are really for the revolution, Ssasha," he said, " then, if you please . . ." and, without waiting for an answer he ravished Ssasha on the floor. . . .
>
> It was not her lost virginity, which she had sacrificed to a man whom she did not love, that the young woman lamented, but the fact that she had to lie to those who were nearest to her. . . .
> Thus she paid her tribute to the cruel war-time. . . .

But there were women who regarded this " readiness
for sexual sacrifice " as one of their military duties and
thought no more about it.   I heard about this type of
women soldier in Leningrad from a fair-haired, blue-
eyed, outwardly attractive and clever woman, formerly a
textile worker and also a fighter in the civil war, now, like
her husband, occupying a high administrative position.
During the few hours that I spent in her office she received quite a dozen men working under her and gave
orders and instructions to each.   When she had finished
her story she added simply and frankly : " I was one of
these women too ; in those days it was a matter of course.
And there was no time to reflect. . . ."

The same perfectly conscious readiness to sacrifice
themselves prevailed also behind the front with some
women, peasants who contributed " green " help as
partisans in the rear—" green women ".   Dasha, in
F. Gladkov's novel *Cement* is one of these " revolutionary soldiers ".   When her husband, a workman,
leaves her in order to fight in the Red ranks against the
Whites, she undergoes the transformation from a " housewife " to a class-conscious proletarian woman under the
influence of the civil war and for love of her husband and
child, for whom she wants to keep the home going.   She
plays a part in the civil war behind the front by carrying
news to the insurgents who retire to the mountains before
the counter-revolutionary troops.   Her fellow-revolu-
tionaries visit her secretly in order to gain news of the
state of feeling in the town and leave her again equally
unobserved :

> . . . And then for the first time in her life, quite freely and
> without being unfaithful to Glyeb (her husband) in her heart,
> she knew other men.   And when she thought it over she felt no
> remorse, as if that, too, was part of the dangerous work before
> the eyes of the enemy spies and in the hail of their bullets.   So
> many old fellows with dim eyes clung to her and did not want
> to return to the mountains.   " I can't leave you, Dashka ! " they
> cried from a full heart.   " I don't want to go on living like a wild
> beast in the forest. . . .   Love me for the sake of this last hour.
> If you help, all the terrors will have no terror for me. . . ."

And it is true, there were moments when she shrank. But that was just where the sacrifice came in. And why should this sacrifice be more than her whole life? But that moment gave the man strength and courage. . . .

After three years the civil war came to an end. How matters stood in the ranks of youth in the critical transition period we have already seen in part. The misinterpreted " freedom of love ", the terrible famine years 1920–1, and the succeeding epoch of the N.E.P. were anything but promotive of gentler manners. The prevailing conditions in the relations between the sexes were altogether chaotic at that time. The younger generation seemed to have lost their bearings entirely. And then the leaders of the revolution and the state stepped in, representing the " conscience of the country " ; to them, judging by their sound old revolutionary traditions, the erotic problem seemed of very little consequence at a time when Russia was tossing in revolutionary fever.

Lenin spoke with pungent irony in a talk with Clara Zetkin about the reading and discussion circles which had become popular in post-war Germany where the chief subject of debate was the sexual problem. He expressed suspicion of those who " kept their gaze fixed upon the sex question like an Indian saint upon his navel ". Especially of the Youth Movement he said that it suffered from a " modern " attitude towards the sex problem and an exaggerated concern with it. He spoke with all his brilliant conviction on the question whether the revolutionary movement had no more urgent tasks than to give the masses clear ideas about sexual matters. At the same time Lenin declared emphatically that he himself was by no means a " sombre ascetic ", that communism had nothing to do with asceticism, and that to his mind young people needed the joy of life and vital vigour.

Little was known abroad of this protest of the older Bolsheviks, some of whom, indeed, went much farther than Lenin and preached almost ascetic ideals. All the more eagerly was the myth of " the socialization of women in the Soviet Union " elaborated, and to this very day it haunts some people's minds, especially where there is a question of anti-Soviet propaganda. But meanwhile the floodtide of sexual preoccupation has finally ebbed and the rising generation in Soviet Russia, the advance guard of the revolution, is faced at the moment with such serious and responsible tasks that sex problems seem unreal to them. Thus sex life in Russia has entered once more upon a non-erotic phase, a process which may be more thorough and wide-spread than ever before. The unquestioning character of the relations between men and women, which was such a distinguishing feature of a small circle of forerunners of the revolution, has now become typical of the Russian masses. And the power that has wrought the change is called, this time : the Five Years' Plan.

WHAT, then, are the relations between the sexes at the present time, in the fourth, final year of the *Pyatiletka*, in the light of which even all individual and spiritual processes must be regarded in Soviet Russia to-day ? And especially : how is it with the younger generation, those who are chiefly building up the new Russia and are in the front line of the economic and cultural struggle ? How is the altered attitude towards life reflected in their minds ?

It is altogether characteristic of these young people, who have been born into the new social order, that they know no yesterday and accept and experience all the new institutions and customs as a matter of course. They cannot grasp that this yesterday should have been so utterly different from to-day, they cannot imagine what life is like beyond the frontiers of Soviet Russia. Certain conceptions, including virtue and sin, are wholly unknown to them. The young people are healthy, gay, wholly occupied with this world, rejoicing in their work and in what lies before them. No task, however hard, but strikes them as play, as amusement. They know nothing of problems, of complications, all the world lies open before them, simple, clear ; in a word, " the sea is only up to their knees."

But I must emphasize at once the fact that the *Komssomol*, in which almost the whole of Soviet Russian youth is organized, is still not altogether a homogeneous mass, for there are at least two sections. That which greatly predominates is the children of industrial and agricultural workers who enjoy all privileges in the educational institutions, universities, and factories, are always to the fore, and are burdened with neither prejudices nor tradition, and these grow into the new life. Among them, too, there are differences between town and country. But the mechanization of labour and the penetration of the new developments into the life of the countryside is blurring the line of demarcation more and more. The other section consists of children of those who were formerly more or less middle-class, intelligentsia, now part of the proletariat. In age they belong, it is true, wholly to the new generation, but since they come from surroundings in which the ideas of the past still predominate, these young people still frequently show relics of the past in their mental habits, and although they, too, are dominated by the new conditions and ideas, yet their attitude towards them is critical, hesitant. But these, like all other contradictions, are diminishing from day to day, and it is probably allowable to speak of the younger generation now as the one decisive and controlling factor in view of its importance to the present period of reconstruction.

And so it is safe to say that at the moment the sexual problem plays no great part in the lives of the younger generation : because they are thinking of other things, have no leisure for it, and have immeasurably more important matters to attend to. The period of iconoclasm, of destroying the past, the destructive epoch, was finally done with about half a decade ago. And hand in hand with the rebuilding of the people's life, which demands the utmost effort, the exertion of all available energies, a process of return to health in the mutual relation of the sexes is going on that is giving rise to a new system of sex morality. True, its outcome cannot yet be gauged, but its fundamental characteristics can already be grasped.

Of course the extremes have not disappeared alto-gether. Not so very long ago people used to say : " Have you a wife from the *Komssomol* ? " and the answer was : " No, I have one of my own." As recently as June 23rd, 1928, *Pravda* commented on several communications that had reached it both about cases of abuse of the new family code, within the letter of the law but criminal from the social point of view, and about attempts to regulate the relations of the sexes on the basis of a morality deriving from the *Domostroy* ; it wrote : " Public opinion in the party cannot tolerate that anybody should excuse his licentiousness with the plea that the party is not a monastic order." But at the same time it stressed the need of reminding the too zealous guardians of family law that " the Bolshevik party must not be identified with the Roman Catholic Church." The consequence was that the paper had to fight on two fronts : against the " Mohammedans " and the " Catholics ".

To-day it is noticeable how little room is left for the sex question in the public life of Soviet Russia. Everything smutty, degenerate, lascivious, disintegrating, everything that speculates on the sensuality of the public in theatre, cinema, and kiosk, all the pornography from which it is impossible to escape in Western Europe and of which there was but little to be seen in Russia even in former days, fails to find an outlet either in literature, in the press, or on the stage. The air is agreeably wholesome, really pure. You are conscious of the same thing at festivities, in the clubs, and at all social gatherings. It is as if the enthusiasm of the struggle had overcome sex. How often I have heard boys and girls say : " We are so accustomed to our social activities that we should be dull without them. For the present we are not much concerned with personal matters. . . ." Moreover, hardly any new literature is coming out on sex problems, and in *belles lettres* the emotion of love and psychical self-contemplation is thrust aside by communal emotions and the con-templation of the Five Years' Plan. Even the instruction of the masses in sex questions, to which so much zeal was devoted till quite recently, has been restricted to a necessary minimum. Whilst, therefore, it is not so very long ago that " physiology ousted psychology ", the former has now been replaced by sociology. " Sociological dimorphism has proved stronger than biological " ; so the Moscow expert in social hygiene, Professor Batkis, described the state of affairs in a private conversation.

And just as life itself at the present time—in view of the dangers which threaten on all sides and the permanent state of siege in which the Soviet Union is placed—is serious, hard, penurious and calls for stern military self-discipline which affects young people with especial suggestive force, so the relations between the sexes in the *Komssomol* are not only natural and comradely, but for the most part sober and objective. Love or any kind of sexual romanticism is regarded with deep disfavour as a bourgeois invention. Young people in Soviet Russia fear nothing more than the reproach of petty bourgeois sentimentality in love, and this fear finds expression for the most part in the denial of love altogether. An inquiry undertaken among the students of Odessa in 1927 is very instructive on this subject ; the question whether there is such a thing as love was answered by most of the men and women students of about twenty in this or some similar way : " I cannot answer your question whether there is such a thing as love. You know quite well that there is no such thing as what people used to understand by love." " I shall not answer your question about love because I simply don't understand what love is." " I do not recognize love and regard it merely as a habit."

All " cherry blossom ", all gallantry, coquetry, all love-making, flirting, and courting, likewise the preliminary state of betrothal and the type of " little woman " are taboo. Feelings, like life itself, have been rationalized, mechanized, and regulated according to plan ; in the eager struggle for the building up of a new life they have been thrust into the background. And because all young people, but especially young Russians, incline to exaggeration, some wags are considering a new Five Years' Plan of having children, and the hero in Y. Olesha's play *The Conspiracy of the Emotions* utters the cry : " We need no love, no mysticism ! Give us a factory to make bed-rooms ! Twenty thousand sexual acts per day ! "

As proof how seriously people are concerned with the cleansing of sex morality and in general of sex relations, especially among the young people, we may take the attitude of Soviet Russian public opinion towards certain phenomena which would be regarded everywhere else as quite harmless. For instance, the social evenings arranged by some *komssomoltsi* at home or in their clubs are often a source of offence. Questionnaires were sent round and a large proportion of the young people who took part in these evening entertainments themselves objected to the spreading " abuses ".

To a non-Russian, indeed, it might be difficult to see what abuses were in question. For though at times manners are pretty free in " Red Corners " of the Youth Clubs decorated with portraits of Lenin and Stalin, yet these " orgies " are nothing to the American evenings devoted to kissing and cuddling. What is most disturbing is the girls' habit of drinking, which many of them seem to think is part of sex equality. But it is plain from the official propaganda directed against them how seriously this and other excesses, including even modern dances, are being combated. For instance, we find a doctor giving vent to his feelings as follows, and clearly unaware that you cannot dance a Charlston to a polka tune : " I was present at an evening dance in a factory school, and I must say that I could not watch the disorderly proceedings for long. What made me most indignant was that when the musicians began to play a simple ' innocent ' dance, everyone present started yelling and clapping their hands and refused to dance to such music."

The authorities have recently proposed to call in special Tribunals of Youth, such as exist, by the way, in the party in the form of " Comrades' Tribunals ", against actual offences against the proletarian sex code, and particularly against sexual profligacy.

The materialization, militarization, mechanization, and standardization of life, the sporting spirit which has been introduced with all the range of its opportunities of excitement into the competition of social life, the ambition to beat records which is perpetually being stimulated and outstrips all measure—all these have produced a new type of young woman in Soviet Russia, masculine in her outward appearance. You know a *komssomolka* at once by her semi-military dress and carriage, by the simplicity with which she does her hair, by her jovial and unceremonious manner, her firm tread, her self-assured demeanour, her tense expression, and her sometimes not very choice speech larded with the current catchwords. Again and again you hear : " That is petty bourgeois ideology " ; " I'm not one of Turgenyev's misses " ; " That is ethical, that is unethical " ; " an undesirable element " ; " You're simply going to bits " ; etc., etc.

Powder and paint are despised. A *komssomolka* does not much care to please as a woman or in any way to emphasize her sex. Smoking is placed on a level with drinking alcohol and the young people are advised to refrain from it. And if on any occasion you see the girls in trousers and uniform, shouldering their rifles and marching in masses to the rhythm of a triumphant melody, they are hardly distinguishable from the boys, so that you understand the words of the poet Ssvyetlov : " Within every *rabfakovka* our Joan of Arc lies concealed."

If occasion arises, the girls use their fists just like the boys. One winter evening when I sat with a friend after the theatre till after two o'clock, her seventeen-year-old sister, a *komssomolka*, returned from a committee meeting just as I was preparing to go ; she was heated, her coat was unbuttoned, and her fists clenched. In reply to the question how it came that the meeting had lasted so long she told us : When the meeting on the other side of the Neva was over the last tram home had gone. With two other comrades she decided to walk all the long way home. On the way the three were attacked by several young men in the middle of the night. But instead of calling for help or running away, as anyone would have done in former days, the girls fought the youths and continued the struggle till the enemy took flight. That was what had made her so late. Such is the soldierly training that girls receive in the *Komssomol*.

When I tell this girl, Kapa, and her friends how middle-class girls spend their time for the most part even to-day in Western Europe—although things have improved here, too, since the world war—and what fills their heads, they open their eyes wide and what I tell them seems incomprehensible.

Co-education, which is carried out in the new Russia not only in pedagogy as a principle but in all departments of life, produces a natural and healthy atmosphere all along the line. The girls are afraid of nothing, even in their inmost thoughts, they know no false shame, no obscure recesses, no backstairs. All artificial barriers between the sexes have been overthrown and people discuss everything quite freely. Children are told the facts of life quite young, no secrecy surrounds sex questions, and nevertheless, or just because of that, the girls retain a certain chastity, an " inner immunity ". Girls and boys clap one another on the shoulder, but familiarities are not tolerated. " What's the good of cuddling ? " asked Kapa, quite astonished ; she seems unable to distinguish between sensual impressions and sense impressions and receives both like rain and snow, like a landscape. Young people even talk freely about everything with their own mothers. And I myself had the following experience in the house of a friendly acquaintance where I was invited to dinner : When another guest said to her that she still looked so young that it was hardly possible to believe that she had daughters of fourteen and fifteen, she turned to the girls and said jokingly : " But you'll soon see to it that I am a grandmother." The younger replied : " You really will soon be a grandmother, for it's bad for a woman not to bring her first child to birth."

In the brilliantly written novel *The Drunken Sun* Gladkov gives a lifelike description of a seventeen-year-old *komssomolka* who is recuperating from her strenuous labours in a sanatorium in the Russian Riviera. Like so many young people in Russia, upon whose physical endurance the Five Years' Plan makes almost super-human demands, she is overworked. In this milieu of a Rest Home for working people, nowhere to be found except in Russia, Marussya makes an acquaintance which might be the one great experience in her life, a real love tragedy, if the scene had been laid in the French instead of the Russian Riviera. But this is what happens here : the man, a high political functionary, takes flight back to his work after a few days, and Marussya writes to the Pioneer party of which she is brigadier :

Young 'uns ! It's just hell, I want you so badly. I can hardly wait for the time when I shall get away from this beastly chaos. I'll never come back to this lunatic asylum all my life. There's a lot of party members and Young Communists here. I share a room with a comrade with a great past : she joined the party five years before I was born. You can see how good she is and how she understands people when I tell you that she could be admitted at once to the League of Young Communists. She has rather sad eyes ; that's because of exile. She has suffered a lot for the workers and peasants. And all the time she has a laughing mouth, like our Pioneers. Besides that there's a good Young Communist, Yasha Masin, with whom I have made friends. He's got 150 per cent brains. Only he's very unbalanced and uncertain in his temper, prob-ably because he's so dreadfully overtired. His illness is called : psychosthenia gravis. That's an excuse for him. His head and shoulders twitch. It's sad to see such suffering ; it hurts you. But never mind—it will get all right. One ought to sacrifice oneself in order to cure such irreplaceable poor workers. It's on them that the success of our socialist construction de-pends. Be considerate to the comrades who teach you and always keep in close touch with them. I won't write about the rest, else this letter will turn into a whole novel. But most of the comrades are worth a lot, like Chaikina, for instance, a partisan of women's rights who regards all the men who have fought shoulder to shoulder with us as enemies, not comrades. She's always wagging her tongue, but she's certainly quite wrong. Then there's a responsible official, Comrade Akatuyev—I simply can't describe him. There's such force in him and he's such a great organizer that he ought to be at the centre—a People's Commissary or in the Central Executive of the party. But he has one weakness. He's frightfully overtired and would like to recuperate among the young people. How can we help him? He thinks that if I laugh and run about like a mad creature, I can restore his youth. I would be glad to, but is it in my power? There are bad elements here, too : odious hooligans—also Young Communists. It's a disgrace that such fellows are tolerated in the organization. But I'm not afraid of them and a little time ago I punched one of them in the mug.

Young 'uns, the country here is glorious. If I could—I'd never go away. And the sea ? It's alive, young 'uns. It's like the sky, except that it's on earth. The stars burn in it and the clouds float. In a storm it's open and understandable, but when it is a still mirror it's incomprehensible. But it's always singing and sighing. And when it rages you feel as if there were immense crowds demonstrating with banners and music and songs and din. It's impossible to describe the sea, young 'uns. Can you describe the revolution ?

Now I must stop. I've scribbled enough. Soon I shall drag myself back to you and we shall dance our old dances again. I'm getting cured here all I can. . . . They even torment me with the Charcot douche. . . . I actually bellow like a cow when they do it.

Again, that's enough ! I send you all a kiss and a hug and love you so much that nobody could more. Be prepared ! I'm always prepared !

Yours,
With communist greetings,
MARUSSYA.

Such words as Gladkov's heroine writes here are being written and spoken in thousands every day in Russia at the present time. They are half party catchwords and half the expression of a genuine enthusiasm for work and an overpowering affirmation of life.

At the time when these lines were written Lydia Sseyfullina's play *The Companions* was having its first night in a Moscow theatre. The central figures are, on the one hand, a literary man who is tormented by the problem how to reconcile his art, which for him is something lofty and inviolable, with the demands made upon him by the grey monotony of his daily professional life and the general average ; on the other hand, the girl student Masha whom he loves, the authoress Volynaya's seventeen-year-old daughter, a *komssomolka* who is employed in a rubber

183

factory. Masha—a presentation of the new woman
hitherto unequalled in Soviet Russian literature in its
telling truthfulness—is in love in her own way with the
poet Nikolay Shevelyov, who is fifteen years her senior
and has a wife and child. Masha and Nikolay resolve to
take a room together shortly. The following scene is
between her and him in Masha's room in her mother's
presence, who is there alone busy with a manuscript when
Nikolay enters :

Nikolay : Good morning. Where is Masha ?
Volynaya : She's washing. Sit down, if you like, otherwise,
go. She'll turn us out anyway.
Nikolay : Not me, perhaps.
Volynaya : I'm not so sure of that. I don't know my
daughter well, but I do know her a little. (She crosses some-
thing out in her manuscript and whispers) : " A dialogue on the
burdens of old age " . . . No.
Nikolay : You're writing here ?
Volynaya : Why not here too ? I write everywhere when the
mood comes on me. In any street, at home, wherever it occurs
to me—without a pause.
Nikolay : You can tell that from the rhymes. . . . You're
afraid of being left behind ?
Volynaya : Yes, I'm afraid.
Nikolay : Anxious lest you should lose touch with the times ?
Volynaya : Yes. But never mind that. I don't want
to . . .
Nikolay : Because it's a strain. And you like to take life
easily.

(Enter Masha)

Masha : And quite right too ! Of all one's ancestors, my
mother's one that one has a respect for, almost a young ancestor.
Live and prosper, mother, I give you leave.
Volnaya : Thank you.
Nikolay (lovingly) : How do you do, little Masha.
Masha : How do you do, how do you do. I've no time. I
must talk to you, mother.
Nikolay : And not to me ? At once and undisturbed ?
Masha : I thought it over last night : either you're the right
man or the whole thing is nonsense.
Nikolay : Let us talk it over alone.

184

Masha : Either we understand one another or I must put you right out of my head. . . .

Nikolay : And out of your heart ?

Masha : Oh, well, out of my heart, my soul, the devil knows what it all means ! In short, off you go and that's enough !

Nikolay : That's not the way to talk to me. And for you, too, it's easily said but hard to do.

Masha : Easy or not—what's the good of talking about it if it must be. But you've gone pretty far ! Nearly strangled your wife. Incurably petty bourgeois !

Nikolay : Natalya Vassilyevna, I must speak to Masha alone.

Masha : Not a bit of it ! (Volynaya motions them away with her hand and writes.) All this leads nowhere. This talking quite upsets me, and it's already destroyed my sleep.

Nikolay : And you don't think of me ?

Masha : Oh, yes, I do, probably too much. It is in your interest to leave your wife without explanations. You're all mouldy, going to the dogs, not working. . . . Disgusting !

Nikolay : I've got a son, I cling to my child.

Masha : Cling to him, who's to prevent you ? But why must you always have him with you ?

Nikolay : Because I'm his father.

Masha : His father—that's of no account. A detail, only essential at the time of conception.

Nikolay I ? A detail ? My son whom I love—he's my offspring and is—the continuation of myself.

Masha : Well, I don't dispute that ; a continuation, that is essential. Some diseased or feeble-minded begetter—no thank you !

Nikolay : Do realize at last that she'll prevent my seeing my son. But I want to help bring him up.

Masha : Why should she prevent you ? You're swamped in the most hopelessly petty bourgeois ideas. Old—primeval opinions! Settle that between yourselves. I was only seven years old when the revolution came. I can't live in the old way.

Volynaya : That's just the trouble, that you belong to two generations.

Nikolay (furious) : And isn't it an evil custom from time immemorial for the mother to stir up trouble ? I suppose she's got a better match in view for her daughter ?

Volynaya : It's true, I'm not a very virtuous woman, but I'm not a procuress and mother-in-law. (Exit.)

Masha : But now have done, Nikolay. It's enough to make anyone hysterical. Always shouting, always jawing uselessly—what is it all about ?

Nikolay : Masha, I love you. That's the great misfortune of my life. I see how soberly you think—you're positively obtuse. But I can't give you up. Oh, my darling disaster ! (He embraces her passionately and kisses her wildly.) Oh, those radiant eyes, that young brow !

Masha : Stop, let me go. . . . Oh . . .

Nikolay : You kiss me too. More warmly, more passionately ! Don't you understand ? My sweet love !

Masha : Let me go ! I've no time. (Throws her arms round his neck and clings fast.) Shame on you, you stupid. . . . Darling . . . Dearest . . . (She kisses him.)

Nikolay : You do love me after all ? Your mother persuades you that I am too old. But you—are mine ? Do you love me ?

Masha : Well, well—fifteen years more to carry about with you—it's no joke. It makes anyone stop and think.

Nikolay : But you do love me ? You won't leave me ? We'll never part ?

Masha : How do you mean—never ?

Nikolay : Never in this life. I can't do without you ! I'll break away from everything—I'll forget my wife and son. And we'll never part.

Masha : Anything is possible. One doesn't talk of what is to come. Are we riveted together ?

Nikolay : Again ? Be quiet ! Kiss me and be quiet.

Masha : Let me go ! (She frees herself vigorously.) When we kiss one another I seem to lose consciousness. It makes me giddy ; do you understand that ? I've let boys kiss me before you, but that was different.

Nikolay : Love !

Masha : Sh ! That's enough. That leads nowhere. It's time for me to go to the factory, to real labour, to the works' conference. You need a clear head for that.

Nikolay : Masha ! We must stay together to-day. I have never been so depressed.

Masha : Are you deaf ? What ? I've told you a dozen times that I've no time to-day.

Nikolay : But I must be with you more often now. Help me to take my resolve. . . .

Masha : You're beginning that again. I've had enough of those phrases and no time for morbid emotions. Tatyanka is leaving her room on the first of February. If you wish we'll move into it on my first free day in February. That's all.

Nikolay : All ?

Masha : What more then ? To the priest, maybe ? We wont go to the S.A.G.S. either. And you'll come to the factory. You must get to know life, if you want to write about it.

Nikolay : And if—my wife kills me ?

Masha : Don't talk nonsense ! She's neither mad nor sick. The fool has driven away my mammy. Where's the old lady all this time ? (Exit.)

Nikolay : Oh, blessed obtuseness ! (He runs his hands through his hair, clenches his teeth, shakes his head, and goes.)

Masha (behind the scenes) : You see, he's going. Come, come, I want you. (She drags her mother in by the hand.) Now for something to eat. The tea's cold, it's yesterday's.

Volynaya : I'll warm it up, if you like.

Masha : If you're not too lazy, do.

Volynaya : Of course one can drink it cold.

Masha : There, am I not right that you—are my mother ? Exactly like me. Disgusting, to make such a fuss about eating. (They both sit down.) Listen, you'll be astonished.

Volynaya : I've been thoroughly astonished for a long time. I can't be more so.

Masha : I want your advice. What shall I do about this man ?

Volynaya : Well, really. . . . So I'm exactly like you. I don't know, little girl.

Masha : Have something. That's for you and this for me. And now tell me, mother, did it ever torment you, this thing that they call . . . love ?

Volynaya : You see, little one, I'm—what they call a light woman. . . . Of course only on that one point. But, good God . . . (She rises.)

Masha : There is no God.

Volynaya : Nobody knows that for certain . . .

Masha : Stop your petty bourgeois talk. You'll forfeit my respect.

Volynaya : No, you can esteem me in spite of it. My frivolity is only on the surface. I had several men—lovers, husbands, or whatever you like to call them. . . . And I forgot them all easily.

Masha : My father, too ?

Volynaya (looks at Masha in consternation, but composes

187

herself when she meets her clear gaze) : As a man I forgot him soon, too, but he was splendid and distinguished as a personality. They came one after another rather casually with me, the men. I was attracted to some by nothing but a spiritual need : now and then you feel afraid of loneliness without love ; to others I was goaded by desire. . . . But you don't understand that yet.

Masha : I'm not one of Turgenyev's misses either.

Volynaya : I'm sure you've not read Turgenyev.

Masha : I can't remember ; perhaps.

Volynaya : It isn't the manners of the " muslin miss " that will save you from sin, but a healthy philosophy of life and emancipated motherhood. Oh, yes, I've had to do with men who pleased me, but I couldn't get used to them for good and all. And now I'm not demoralized because my great love is for creative work, poetry.

Masha : Mother, I'm melancholy. You see, I've fallen in love like an idiot, but when I talk to him it's as if I spoke Tatar and he French. Each only guesses what the other's talking about. Oh, the intelligentsia, how they torture you to death !

Nikolay's wife, Alexandra Pavlovna, the representative in the play of the women a generation earlier, comes to Masha in her room in order to induce her to renounce her husband. She fires at the girl who means to rob her of her husband, but she misses. Masha seizes the weapon and revives the woman, who has collapsed utterly.

Masha : Pull yourself together. Here's some water. (Alexandra Pavlovna sinks into a chair, burying her face in her hands. Excited voices behind the scenes : A shot ! Somebody shot ? What has happened ? Masha opens the door and calls into the passage) : My pistol went off accidentally. No, nobody's wounded.

Alexandra Pavlovna (raises her head, her voice heavy with grief) : I'm sorry I did not shoot you. That would have been a solution, though a terrible one.

Masha : Most terrible for me. . . . To die ? . . . horrible . . . horrible. . . . And why ? You, you . . . Anything so mean ! To shoot me, to destroy my young life ! (She spreads out her arms and cries helplessly like a child.)

Alexandra Pavlovna : A child. . . . Why, you might be my daughter. . . . Your young life . . . You have a young life. . . . And I ? This man is my all. I'm worn out. At one moment he's going to leave me and the next he's not going to leave me. I'm at the end of my tether. May God forbid that you should ever love with your whole heart! And I want . . . (She flings herself at her feet and embraces her legs.) Give him back to me! Drive him away from you! . . . Go away! You have . . . oh, you have still your whole life.

Masha : Don't torment me! Please get up. I don't want anything. Just now I don't want anything. No love! (She helps her to rise and forces her into a chair) : Just now I can only hear the good news : I am alive! My legs move, my eyes see. I had almost lost them altogether . . . altogether. . . . But I'm not terrorized. No! I'm dreadfully sorry for you, but I won't lie to you. I will examine my own mind carefully. And if Nikolay is as dear to me as he was . . . as it seemed . . . In fact, if he is necessary to my life, I will not renounce him . . . No! . . . But I'll never be so love-sick as that. To commit a crime, to murder a human being who is not an enemy, not a traitor, but a comrade! Never! And my life is not a trifle. It should be as precious to every comrade as to me myself. No, I'd never act like that under any circumstances. . . .

A dialogue follows in the rubber factory where Masha works between her and Comrade Ssokolov, of the same age as herself, of whom she was fond before she got to know Nikolay :

Masha : I'm late. No time. The meeting's just going to begin. For shame, Ssokolov, what's this fuss about again? Do leave me in peace at last.

Ssokolov : What do you mean—fuss?

Masha : I can't help seeing that you're making more and more of a fool of yourself about me. You sent a note to me during work. That isn't allowed. It's a scandal, Ssokolov.

Ssokolov : A man isn't made of stone, Masha. I admit it was a mistake. It won't happen again, never! But you're so much to me. You seem to be created for me.

Masha : I wasn't created for you and I wasn't created at all. You're always thinking how we kissed one another that time. But I've forgotten all about it. I only want to be your friend.

Ssokolov : Why?

Masha : Just because there's someone else.

Ssokolov : Very well! And I'll chop off the other fellow's legs.

Masha : That's a petty bourgeois attitude. Joking apart— we're going to take a room together the day after to-morrow.

Ssokolov : So that's how it is. Well, if that's how it is, then . . . (Suddenly furious.) Who . . . who is it ?

Masha : What's that to you ? Are you mad ?

Ssokolov : I ask you who it is. Will you tell me or not ?

Masha : No. Another time. When you talk again like a human being, else . . .

Ssokolov : Why, I'm not a brute. But it's curious how it knocks you over. You mustn't tell, I'm going . . .

Masha : It's Shevelyov, the poet, the same whom you . . .

Ssokolov : Hi-i-im ? Why, he's over thirty. An old man.

Masha : To me he's young. And it's all the same to you. You don't even look at him and already you say : an old man. He's a very handsome man, just the man for me. He may not be thirty yet. A young man.

Ssokolov : Is that what they call young to-day, when at nineteen you're often not only a man but a father ? But that doesn't matter much. The main point is that it is a mistake . . .

Masha : What ?

Ssokolov : Yes, that it's a mistake on your part. And I'm sorry for us both, myself and you. How could you think of such a thing ? He was born long before you. He's quite worn out. I don't mean his body, nor his age. There are people who preserve their bodily fitness. But his nerves ! With nerves like that can you build up even your own life within your own four walls, to say nothing of the social life ? I'm sorry for you, little one. You've let yourself in for a bad time.

Masha : You dare to come to me with your beastly pity ! I'll choose for myself what I need, without father, without mother, without the good old God. And I'm accountable to no one beside myself. I'm not so easily knocked out. Your pity ? Such an idiot ! Get along, my boy, and cry about yourself, because I don't love you. But not for pity of me.

Ssokolov : That won't be in such a hurry. No—no. I'll find another girl all right. Don't forget to come to the conference of galosh-makers at seven o'clock. Some day you'll forget even that, you with your love affairs.

Masha : What do you say ? You blackguard ! Have I ever missed a meeting ?

The play ends characteristically with Masha turning away from Nikolay who, as belonging to the intelligentsia, is alien to her personality.

THE NEW WOMAN AS WOMAN

Now that we have heard the last word about the new woman of Soviet Russia, growing up and entering upon the battle of life under wholly different conditions, we can no longer evade the question : does this new woman feel more satisfied, happier in her personal life, than the women of other times and places ? That question is naturally difficult to answer, for Masha is still too young and, if we observe her more closely, is rather the woman of to-morrow than to-day, so that we must wait till she is maturer. Of the mass of her fellows, either of the same age or a little older, we can only say, therefore, for the present : although all the valves are wide open and external obstacles cleared away, everything is still in flux so that we must nowise regard developments as complete, and in many respects contrary tendencies clash here more than elsewhere.

I have already indicated the origin of these contrary tendencies. But let me touch upon the problem once more. It culminates principally in the attitude of Russian men and Russian women towards the sex question, which diverge more than in other countries. For love is the central inner experience with the majority of Russian women, as with women the world over ; because, with all their external masculinity, they are inwardly thoroughly womanly, very emotionally disposed. And in spite of all the objectivity which is taking possession of Russian youth, it is just here that the great discrepancy between the sexes appears. Whereas the majority of male students in the above-mentioned Odessa questionnaire absolutely refused to acknowledge love as a reality, 50 per cent of the women students do at least admit that their sexual life was aroused by inner forces, by love and passion. It is often asserted, and can hardly be denied, that in their lives the Russian women are more active, stronger, more energetic and purposeful than their men-folk, who are frequently somewhat womanish and vacillating—that the " weaker sex " is superior to the " stronger ". And that may perhaps be explained by

the fact that, whereas the social and ethical element predominates in the life of Russian men, with Russian
women, as women, the individual, personal, and æsthetic
element is stronger. A Russian æsthete of the domestic,
drawing-room type is inconceivable, because he pre-
supposes an ancient tradition ; thus the Russian
" Futurist " group, which the world war swept away,
consisted of so many walking grotesques ; its membership
included the proletarian poet W. Mayakovskyi, who
afterwards committed suicide, and was still making the
streets of Moscow unsafe in 1913 in large check trousers
and a yellow jacket. It is certainly impossible to dispute
the vigorous, healthy sensuousness of Russian men, but
love, the subtler and more spiritual form of sex life, is
practically a sealed book to them, and it is probably for
that reason that they have little power of rousing and
moulding the inner life of women, which is alien to their
nature. Russians are really unimaginative in love. And
it is partly for that reason, and not only because of the
frequently quoted foreign silk stockings, that foreigners
have such a good chance with Russian womanhood.

The consequence is that we hear more and more of
the laments of the specialists' foreign wives living beyond
the frontiers of Soviet Russia ; just as in the world war,
they see themselves deserted. And what is most disastrous and drives matters to breaking-point is the fact
that Russian women are also feeling themselves deserted
by their husbands in some ways, just as in the war : the
hard, bitter struggle carried on to-day on the economic
front and on all fronts in the Soviet Union is a life-and-
death struggle, and grips each single individual in its
stranglehold. Moreover, we must not forget that for
eighteen years Russian manhood has been under severe
fire, exerting all its strength, with nerves tense. For in
addition to the excessive measure of bodily and mental
sufferings endured during the imperialist war, the revolution, the civil war, and the famine years—sufferings in
the bearing of which the Russian people are in any case
incomparably stronger than any other—there have been
latterly the immense demands of the Five Years' Plan,

besides the constant fear of a war of intervention. Super-human labours which, as has been demonstrated, have markedly diminished the sexual vigour of Russian man-hood. The men, who, like the women, always aged early in Russia, are said by the doctors to be for the most part incapable of love by the middle of their forties.

Until recently there was no general day of rest on account of the continuous week, no week-end, no outings ; and even now it is hardly possible, because of the bad housing conditions, to be alone in one's own home or for two people to enjoy a real leisure hour together. Although she denies it in principle, the Russian woman, like every woman, wants to be wooed in some form ; that is true even of the woman of to-day, who partly lives in the future, but still has some contact with the past, if only a faint contact. She, too, wants consideration, tenderness, love, and unconsciously she has in her heart an unspoken longing for romance. But her world is stripped of magic ; the personal element, men, love, occupy but small space—for lack of time and opportunity ; they are almost non-existent, and there is but " little bed ". And so millions of women still unawakened in their emotional life, thirsting for something to relieve the tension of their inner energies, transform all their force, capacity for enthusiasm, readiness for self-sacrifice, and passion, and the stored-up fire of their unexercised femininity into technical dimensions, figures, and super-latives, and joyfully and unselfishly sacrifice them on the altar of the *Pyatiletka*. Later on we shall see that real miracles are being performed, and that just as women were formerly in the front ranks of the revolution, so now they are the leading spirits in the modern Russian epic of labour, the new creation of myths.

It is true, however : once a year there are several weeks' holiday, which are generally passed on that entrancing coast which begins near Batum at the south-eastern corner of the Black Sea and stretches almost continuously to the western coast of the Crimea. Gladkov, in the novel already cited, *The Drunken Sun*, has given an unequalled description of the azure murmur of that sea, the transparent, golden sky arching over it, and the air heavy with the fragrance of water-plants and shell-fish —a place where people rest and "almost die of joy". For, as Knickerbocker says, the sunshine there is not subject to the Five Years' Plan, and so all theoretical opinions about love are forgotten for three or four weeks. Here, in the Red Riviera, people put on their best clothes and drop current catchwords. Here they take paint and powder out of their trunks and the feelings which lie fallow for the other eleven months out of the recesses of their hearts. Here they sun themselves and flirt the live-long day on the shore and bathe in the moonlight of a sub-tropical night. Here their mood is lyrical, they commit follies, and enter upon the feverish war of sex. It is a war between the elemental sensual desire of man —" sexual emotion that is not yet love ", and the many-shaded love of woman, the posy of flowers that bloom the whole year round in secret. But hardly has the struggle begun when it is time for it to be postponed till the next summer holidays.

It is rather too little for the full-blooded type of woman, to which the Russians certainly belong. And so, after all, perhaps it is not so strange as appears at first sight that Professor Nyemilov's book, *The Biological Tragedy of Woman*, could appear in the very country where there is supposed no longer to be any possibility of social and economic tragedy for women. The Marxists greeted this disheartening theory with vehement denial : " The sex question," declares the sex specialist, Professor Salkind, " has never been regarded as a purely biological question." Nevertheless, Nyemilov's book soon ran through five editions in Soviet Russia, where woman does really feel her biological tragedy less than elsewhere, because it is mitigated as far as possible by means of preventives, the legalization of abortion, and the whole legal code.

Nyemilov also received a number of letters in which not only women but men also argued about the questions that he had raised. Some of these letters he published in a supplement to the last Russian edition of the book. None of the women denied that there was a biological

194

tragedy. But many referred to the fact that they found their greatest satisfaction in giving themselves to a man and in motherhood. " There is a tragedy, but it is not so terrible," writes one of Nyemilov's correspondents. " To make someone happy whom we love, even at the cost of great suffering, is rapture to many women." Another writes :

> I quite agree with you that a woman's life is a tragedy, and a terrible tragedy, especially the act of giving birth. But besides the pain and suffering which continue through our whole lives, there are moments in which we are ready to sacrifice even life for the sake of such a thing as a child. You, as men, cannot conceive the joy that motherhood brings. Whether it is only instinct, or whatever you like to call it, so it is. The highest joy that a woman can ever experience is first motherhood. I am still a virgin, but I say frankly : I want to have a child !

But besides this general problem the peculiarly Russian women's problem comes up for discussion. Nyemilov's correspondents complain most that they suffer from the discrepancy between the masculine and feminine attitude towards love, the lack of restraint and the frivolity of men in face of the sexual act. " They might pull themselves together a little, the men, and not squander their ' love ' with such criminal levity," is the constantly recurring refrain of these letters. But one note rises above all the rest : " It is not from the ' biological tragedy ' that we suffer, but from the men's *khamstvo* "—a term which combines in Russian the pleasing conceptions of coarseness, truculence, bestiality, and brutality, in a word, the climax of all that is uncultured. In many cases this statement doubtless penetrates to the core of the problem, so that we may perhaps say : at the moment the tragedy of Russian womanhood seems to be psychological rather than biological.

Whereas Western Europe in general is suffering, perhaps, from an over-cultivation, an excessive differentiation, of sex life, resulting in phenomena which hardly exist in Russia (for instance psychopathia sexualis is almost unknown in Russia and I had to explain the notion of rape combined with murder, for which the Russian language has no word, to several people's judges in Moscow), love with the Russians is far too often degraded to soulless sexual intercourse, a mere satisfaction of desire, without any more elevated personal demand. The men appear to feel quite contented in this state, the women less so. It turns out that Soviet Russian women have every right except the right to be women in a higher sense. Hardly have they come to flower when they are regarded as faded and done with. For in the eyes of their husbands the somewhat primitive measure for the age limit is not the intensity of mutual spiritual interpenetration, not love, which may even increase and grow deeper with the years, but primarily the bare fact of purely sexual attraction and fitness.

It would be a very good thing for Russian women if one new item were to be included in the coming cultural Five Years' Plan : the cultural elevation of the mutual relations of the sexes. As a guiding motto N. Bogdanov's words from his famous novel, *The First Lass*, might be taken : " . . . and my chief wish is that the boys should behave more discreetly and thoughtfully towards the girls, and the girls towards themselves—also."

MARRIAGE AND THE FAMILY IN THEIR NEW FORMS

PEOPLE marry very early in Soviet Russia. Since the prerequisite of marriage is not property, but the working capacity of both spouses, the law makes early marriage easy. The whole is an affair of no special significance : " I like you, there is going to be a room free, let us move into it," the boys say in such cases. Or else : " Let's join forces, let's go to Moscow together." And that settles it. There is no such conception as betrothed couple, no engagement, and even in former days it was not usual among acquaintances to address one another as " Miss " (only the name and patronymic).

If a couple want to register, they go to the S.A.G.S. The registrars are generally very busy and you have to wait in a queue. Whilst you are waiting you can look at the posters on the walls :

MARRIAGE IN ITS NEW FORM

FUTURE WIFE AND MOTHER!

Before you register, do not forget to consult a woman doctor (a gynæcologist):
About the hygiene of sex,
About preventives,
About the future child,
Medical advice obtainable here.

TO THOSE WHO ARE MARRYING AND DIVORCING!
Apply to the Sexual Advisory Centre.

At the S.A.G.S. you come across the greatest variety of couples, from eighteen years upwards, and from the young worker from his bench, the " aristocrat " of to-day, to the semi-derelict " former bourgeois ". In so far as it is possible in an overcrowded office, there is a certain ceremonial and festive air. Those who want to register are wearing their best clothes, have just shaved and brushed their hair, and look clean and gay. Once when I went to one of these S.A.G.S. rooms in Moscow to look on, there was a couple of whom the man gave his age as fifty-one and the woman as thirty-six ; he was seated, she standing ; the woman registrar asked : " And whose family name do you wish to bear henceforth ? " Whereupon the man, who seemed in that milieu like an anachronism, an exhibit from a museum, answered without even glancing at his wife : " My name, of course." But most women retain their maiden names even after marriage so that you never know who is married to whom, which saves a great deal of gossip and needless talk. Another, a young couple, was registered. The man, who was dressed all in leather, and belonged, there-fore, to the ruling section of the population, answered the few customary questions and could not tell for certain whether he was twenty-four or twenty-five. At this the woman registrar showed him his papers and said : " You're twenty-five this very day." The " bride " was at the telephone all the time, which can be used without special leave by the public in Soviet Russian offices, and by the time she had finished her conversation she was registered, married, and provided with a certificate.

197

Nevertheless, more and more couples omit to register nowadays. " Why should I let them make a mess of my passport ? " was the answer of a young barrister, formerly a printer, to my question whether she had been married in the S.A.G.S. And a pregnant domestic help at my friends' who was advised to register asked : " Why ? " " So that later on, if the man deserts you, you can get alimony." To which she replied : " If he's that sort, that he has to be forced to pay for his child, I won't accept anything from him anyway."

It was Sunday when I last paid a visit to one of the larger, centrally situated S.A.G.S.'s in Moscow. The registry office for marriages was overcrowded. Some of the couples had to wait in the hall and on the stairs. I went into the adjoining registry office for divorces, which also contains a " table for the registration of births and deaths."

In the registry for divorces, where there are no posters to be seen, it was much emptier. Only a few careworn women with anxious faces were sitting there in their everyday clothes, having obviously just come from work. I entered into conversation with one of them. She burst out at once : " You see what a lot of divorces there are everywhere now. But it's only because marrying is made so easy. And that's why there are so many neglected children." Afterwards I learned that she was twenty-eight, formerly a domestic help, married eleven years, had three children, and had noticed latterly that her husband, a porter, twenty-nine years old, was " going " with another woman. When she accused him of it, he said : " Then why don't you give me hot suppers any more ? " " Where should I get a hot meal when you come home from a walk at three o'clock in the morning?" " 'You're always amusing yourself, Sseryosha,' I says to him, ' I'm going to amuse myself too. Why should you be the only one ? ' That's what comes of freedom ! "

So they went together to the S.A.G.S. to have their marriage cancelled. He was required to pay sixty roubles a month for the three children (his whole wage was eighty roubles) and to support the wife for six months.

" ' I'll took after the children,' I says to him," the wife went on to tell me, " ' and you must provide their food.' ' I don't agree to that.' ' All right,' says I, ' then we'll take it into court now.' I'm going to hand in the summons to-day and I shan't wink at his tricks any longer. No ! And I'll never register again ! Marriage used at least to be legal. . . ." I replied : " But so it is now." " Not a bit of it," she retorted and went on : " When I came to register my divorce a day or two ago a couple turned up also to register a divorce. He was fifty-one and she forty-nine. Six children, including some who had been married ever so long. . . . What do you say to that ? Isn't it a crazy world ? "

Meanwhile loud cries penetrated to the divorce registry from the marriage registry. What was the matter ? I opened the door and saw the young woman registrar with a flushed face exclaiming to the assembled couples : " Citizens, I won't register more than two more couples at most. The rest can go home and come again to-morrow. I'm only human myself ! I'm at the end of my tether. It's five o'clock already and this is the third day that I've worked overtime for which I get nothing. Must everyone get married all at once ? I can't stand it any longer. More to-day than any other day. Dreadful ! As if they'd all gone crazy. Is this some special day, then ? Of course, now I understand : it's Sunday. An old custom to marry on Sunday. But there is no Sunday with us now, you just remember that. Only three more couples at most. . . ."

But nearly a dozen couples were waiting in the room. And not one of them made a move to go. I am afraid the poor girl will have to work overtime to-day too, and probably till her next free day (the six-day week).

With all the facilities that the new Russian marriage law has brought, change of partners is nowise more frequent in Soviet Russia than in other countries. The same is true of promiscuity.

It is true that we cannot ascertain statistically how many married people avail themselves of the easy possibilities of divorce in the Soviet Union, because both divorce and marriage are frequently only factual and are not registered. Nevertheless, two things are certain : the great epidemic of divorces which followed the period of war and revolution in Russia as in all other states never assumed such proportions here as it did until recently in the United States. And further, the period of reconstruction, the gradual return of people's lives to more regular ways, have decidedly checked the zeal for divorce. Finally, the daily increasing independence and self-reliance of women appears to have done away to a large extent with grounds of conflict.

But apart from that a process is going on in Soviet Russia which may be described as the *rehabilitation of monogamy*. It will be remembered that Soviet legislation, without expressly laying stress on the principle of monogamy, adheres to it, and likewise pays regard, equally silently, to the ethical significance of marriage by refusing to recognize transient unions as marriages. But what is more important is the circumstance that this practical adherence to the principle of monogamy has proved to be something organic. The attitude of Soviet Russian youth to this question appears from the results of various plebiscites, in which three-quarters of the young people declared for the absolute maintenance of monogamy. Various diaries and sets of household regulations reveal the point of view in the Youth Communes, the germ cells of the new *byt* (way of life) and of Soviet ethics. The Communes expressly condemn all fortuitous or transient relations and pronounce that permanent, monogamous marriage alone is allowable and right, " based upon the common ideas and mental concord of two people who love one another." For the rest, it is the custom in the Communes that conjugal disputes which threaten to lead to a dissolution of a marriage shall be discussed publicly by the members, and that those who incur suspicion of being too fond of change shall be called to account and censured.

But it is not monogamous marriage in the old sense which is reviving here after the vagaries of the revolutionary period ; rather development is proceeding according to a law of its own, based upon a new moral outlook and moulding it in turn. Thus Soviet Russia is the only country in the world in which monogamy is not a law existing merely on paper, but rather a living form crystallizing anew, whereas everywhere else it forms a rigid framework which life is perpetually threatening to burst. What has outlived itself in capitalist countries and stands for a conclusion, is in Soviet Russia a starting-point, the beginning of a new development. Thus Soviet Russia provides experimental proof that monogamy is something which regulates itself automatically according to the principles of social ethics and natural science, that it must be regarded as a law implanted in the mind of civilized man, like that which forbids him to commit murder. " Our racial experience seems to show that monogamy is better fitted to the needs of most human beings than any other form of relationship between the sexes. I feel sure it will predominate in marriage by virtue of its own inherent merits—if given a chance," says Lindsey, one of the wisest of those who have given thought to the subject of marriage in recent years.

For that reason, but especially in consequence of the strongly monogamous feelings prevailing among Russian women, the fact that divorce has been made easy legally has no more led to a destruction of the principle of monogamous marriage that the " revolution in morals " has led to a permanent rise in the prevalence of promiscuous sexual intercourse. At the same time it is not surprising that the proclamation of the new divorce laws caused far more agitation and alarm in the Russian villages than in the towns, which were already more or less industrialized. " Why does the Soviet Government allow our husbands to desert their wives ? " asked the *babas* in shocked tones.

But the women were most carefully instructed about their rights by the appropriate women's associations (every village Soviet must include at least one woman as the representative of the interests of the rest), and it was not long before they began to exercise their rights, not least in the matter of divorce. It is worth noting that the request for a divorce immediately after the revolution came for the most part from the wife, but does so even now in 60 per cent of the cases.

Although Soviet law knows nothing of causes of divorce and makes no inquiries why two spouses abandon their life in common, yet it is interesting to observe that the purely subjective and personal reasons for divorce in the Soviet Union are in a large measure political. That was especially the case in the early years of the revolution, when a divergent point of view on the part of two spouses about the changed conditions made life in common impossible. By now the Soviet state is so far inured to politics that differences of opinion rarely assume so harsh and crude a form. Cases have, indeed, been observed in which two spouses, whose attitude towards the new way of life was at first quite different, both afterwards developed along such lines that they were able to rescind the divorce which had already been registered and come together again.

Thus it often happened, and still sometimes happens, that the husband, who is employed in some works, feels himself a member of the great, new community, and does social work, parts from his wife, who is wholly taken up with the cares of her household, her cooking, and her children. The woman, who has hitherto been a " housewife ", is thus often obliged not only to maintain herself but reorganize her whole life, and after a few years of paid employment the former husband and wife realize all at once that they are not so very far apart. And countless instances show that it is not always the men who progress in advance of their wives, but that at least equally often, and probably oftener, the women outstrip their husbands' mental development.

Kovalyov (*The Historical Development of Women's Life, of Marriage and the Family*) tells of typical conflicts which lead to a dissolution of marriage in the Russia of to-day :

> There are hundreds of thousands of individuals from the masses of the people, from the midst of the oppressed classes, to whom the revolution has opened up a way to step out into the general political arena, to receive cultural polish, and to

become active members of the immense and mighty creative work that is going on in the country. It is incomparably easier and quicker for a man to enter upon that way than for a woman. . . . Hence the countless conflicts that result : the husband a " responsible worker " who merges himself in the general political life, and the wife who has remained on the pre-revolutionary level of uncultured ignorance, of illiteracy, and of interests which do not extend beyond market prices, her kitchen, and the care of her children.

We have another variant of the same conflict when the husband, put out by domestic muddle because his wife is otherwise occupied, comes under the influence of a " doll " belonging to the class of former officials, officers, traders, and landowners, and a connection of that kind offers him a comfortable home after his day's work.

These are only two forms of family conflict typical of the transition period, one, as may be seen, caused by the slavish confinement of the wife to the domestic hearth, the other by her endeavour to take her place in cultural and social life or to make herself economically independent.

The fact that the number of divorces in Soviet Russia has greatly diminished in comparison with what it has been, and is doubtless diminishing still further, is due in no small degree to the fact that, in spite of temporary excesses which form the counterpart of the misinter-pretation of the " freedom of love ", the ethical content of marriage was never wholly lost. Moreover, in spite of the unavoidable hardship involved in the Five Years' Plan, the sense of responsibility in contracting a marriage has increased and a reduction in the number of divorces is observable. Under these circumstances it is no exag-geration to speak of a general stabilization of marriage in Soviet Russia. It must be remembered further that the post-war crisis in marriage, which is known likewise in the rest of Europe and in America, is much nearer to a solution in the land of the Soviets than elsewhere. For whilst in other countries the problem gave rise to various suggestions, raising discussion successively of experimental marriage, triple marriage, and companionate marriage, in Soviet Russia we have already a new form of marriage which is gradually maturing.

Like all the other prevailing conditions of life in Soviet Russia, the new form of marriage is something unique, based upon the equal rights of the sexes which are not only legally established but realized in practice in every detail. And thanks to this equality of rights, Soviet Russian marriage may justly be regarded as the realization of Lindsey's ideal of companionate marriage, which the American marriage reformer defines as " legal marriage, with legalized birth control, and with the right to divorce by mutual consent for childless couples ". We know that Soviet Russian legislation goes further in the matter of divorce, for which it requires neither mutual consent nor the absence of children. On the other hand, it is only in Soviet Russia that it is possible to speak of actually existing companionate marriages on a wide scale, although Lindsey tries to represent it simply as a " already an established social fact in this country ". Only here do we find large masses of married couples who can be described as companions in the truest sense of the word. In spite of all concessions to the spirit of the times, there is no country with an ecclesiastical and patriarchal marriage tradition where conditions have been even approximately attained that make such a fellowship between husband and wife in common struggles and a common life possible, and, under certain circumstances, even necessary. There are of course isolated cases already in bourgeois countries of married couples united by similar interests and common endeavour ; but in Russia—and that is just where the great difference lies —these exceptions are the rule.

On my last trip down the Volga I noticed two young people on the steamer. A pretty, fair-haired, girlish-looking woman of the *komssomolka* type, and a young man, also very fair, with a fine head on which he wore the little embroidered Tatar cap which is now so popular in Soviet Russia. I guessed that he was a student of the Workers' Faculty. Each time as I walked along the deck I saw the pair either engaged in some scholarly debate or deep in a fat book. Sometimes, too, they played chess together, which in Soviet Russia is regarded

not as an amusement, but as a serious affair, promotive
of intellectual health, and included, like everything else,
in the Five Years' Plan. But afterwards, if these young
people got up, they walked about hand in hand like two
good children.

I could not make up my mind whether they were a
married couple or two students preparing for an examination. When I made their acquaintance I found to
my astonishment that they had been married for years,
that theirs was an ideal marriage, but they were principally interested in their common study, botany, for both
were scientific agriculturalists. It is significant that they
for their part were both astonished at my astonishment.
In the circle in which they lived in Leningrad, they said,
all marriages were like that, for that kind of common
life simply was the new Soviet Russian form of marriage.

Such comradeship is, of course, only possible where
the wife not only enjoys equal rights but is economically
independent. But it is precisely this economic independence that the majority of Russian women have
achieved in a double sense. First, as the ability to
maintain themselves without the help of a man, and likewise as independence of domestic economy, growing
liberation from the cares of housekeeping and the education of children, which are not, for the most part, regarded
as a woman's real life work. Here, too, a fundamental
change is taking place, to which we shall recur when
we come to discuss the new manner of life.

Clara Zetkin pointed out to Lenin that you had only
to scratch a communist and the Philistine showed through,
as appeared from the fact that a man thought he was
lowering himself if he gave a helping hand in the house ;
but in Soviet Russian marriage things have improved
considerably in this respect. More and more husbands
are to be seen in the cities of the Soviet Union pushing
perambulators beside their wives or carrying babies in
their arms (and that not from gallantry, as is the case in
Paris.) More and more husbands do the housework
when their wives are in employment. And if both
husband and wife are at home together, they share the

housework between them. Some couples have drawn up a regular time-table of the day's work. One evening when I was invited to the house of a specialist in public hygiene with a reputation beyond the frontiers of Russia, he apologized for getting his wife to pour out the tea for me, a guest ; but he was not dexterous enough. Another time a high woman official took me from her office in a People's Commissariat to her home in her official car. When we got there, we found her husband with the children awaiting us with the supper, which he had been preparing. The husband is a proletarian author, and therefore a home worker, and, like many other husbands in the Soviet Union, he does not think it at all beneath his dignity to do the daily domestic shopping, to get the meals, and look after the children.

Her economic independence, her collective consciousness, and the feeling that she can, if need be, do without the help of a man, acts as a strong stay to the Soviet Russian woman and opens out new possibilities in her life. Listen to the story of the peasant woman, Fedotya : she lived with her husband in a commune. When she was going to have a child and was taken to the hospital, he went directly to live with a *komssomolka*. The wife, who had not the faintest suspicion, returned at the end of a fortnight with twins to which she had given birth, and learned why her husband was not there. A meeting was immediately convened, a " Comrades' Court ", and the *komssomolka* together with the husband were turned out of the commune. But the wife stayed in it with the children, worked, learned, grew spiritually, and was happy. And when after a time the husband, now tired of the *komssomolka*, came to Fedotya and wanted to return to her, his wife, after previous consultation with the general meeting of the commune, gave him the following reply : he must prove himself for a year first, and then his readmission to the commune could be proposed. The year of probation is past, and to-day the reunited husband and wife are regarded as one of the most competent and happiest couples in the commune, and are held up to all the others as an example.

MARRIAGE IN ITS NEW FORM

In this way women who have their own employment, who are self-reliant and conscious of their own strength, realize their full humanity and co-operate actively in the work of reconstruction. Doubtless the process by which women are becoming independent is in full swing beyond the frontiers of the Soviet Union too. But within the union it is proceeding with the compelling force of the march of history and takes its place as part of the whole development. It is more than comprehensible that the transition is nevertheless not proceeding without shocks and conflict even there. The clash between a woman's emotional world—her life as a woman—and her social activities, between the past and the present, is, perhaps, a painful mass problem in the Soviet state more than elsewhere. And therefore it has for long constituted one of the principal themes of Soviet Russian literature, where it is treated in many and various ways. Two well-known examples show how the discord is resolved—once in favour of work for the community and once in favour of love.

Dasha, who is already known to us from Gladkov's novel *Cement*, is a hard, unyielding character. In the absence of her husband she passes through such a long process of development, acquires so much knowledge, so much proletarian class consciousness, and becomes so absorbed in her new social activity, that she is wholly transformed as a woman and mother as well. She sends her child to a home, and when Glyeb (her husband), a good communist who loves her, returns and, deeply moved by the spectacle of the new friend and comrade whom he finds in her, approaches Dasha as a husband with wholly new feelings, she refuses to stay with him. For in the meantime she has outgrown not only herself, but also the form of her earlier conjugal relation; she no longer tolerates jealousy and will not allow even the lightest bond to stand in the way of her new freedom, her new aims, and her work. She leaves her husband and leaves a letter behind for him in which she says: " The time will come when we shall build ourselves new nests. . . . Love remains love, Glyeb, only it demands

207

a new kind of tie. . . . When everything has burnt out and is tranquillized, then we shall consider how the new knot should be tied. . . ."

As an example of the second possible solution I will take Natalya Tarpova, the heroine of the two-volume novel by S. Ssemyonov, which bears her name ; her story alone shows how burning the problem there discussed is in Soviet Russia to-day. The first volume, which appeared several years ago, very soon ran through its first edition, like all books in the Union. In it the question was posed, but not answered. For nearly a year—it was all that time before the second volume appeared—it was a kind of drawing-room game in Soviet Russia to conjecture whether the sense of duty or womanly feeling would triumph in the heroine's soul. It is easy to understand this success, which caused the second volume to go out of print even more rapidly. Natalya Tarpova, twenty-four years of age, the daughter of a skilled worker, is an energetic party communist, the secretary of the *fabkom* (the factory committee) of a large works ; she has passed through a full secondary school course, is clever, gifted, and intelligent, and as a woman " pervaded by that undefinable something which stirs emotion in men at the first glance ". Natalya Tarpova struggles through to freedom and creative work and is always careful to maintain her independence in her relation with men.

> Soon after her liberation from the domestic yoke she had a love affair with a married comrade in the party who left his wife for her sake. Possibly she even loved him, her first mate. But she had never thought about her relation to him from that point of view ; she judged it according to the prevailing opinion. Eight months later Tarpova abandoned the man because he had spoken a few tender, fervent, but jealous words to her, impelled by genuine feeling. Such an attitude she regarded as a bar to her personality, and she left him, firmly resolved to be more cautious in future and to avoid permanent ties. Tarpova adhered to her resolve with sacred zeal and was very well satisfied with herself. More than once she was on the verge of relations, but broke them off again without allowing them to burden her spirit.

But before long Tarpova met an engineer who belonged to the class that was her enemy and who only half shared her views, her faith in Soviet reconstruction. He was the first man who attracted her as a woman; she could hardly resist the feeling, and yet she struggled against it with all her might, because the connection was incompatible with her work and her philosophy of life. This time, therefore, Tarpova was not fighting against the man, but against herself. It was a hard struggle that went on in this woman's soul; she " was ashamed beyond measure of her weakness ", and the struggle was between her sense of duty and an equally strong emotion.

But the author gives the solution in the last sentences of the novel in which he describes how the woman in her triumphs at last in spite of all, how she finds her way to the man and says with closed eyes : " How beautiful it is to be alive. . . ." " And when she opened her eyes again there was nothing left of all that makes life hard and tormenting. There was no more shame and no more fear, no more doubts and no more vacillation, no sorrowful hatred of the rest of the world. . . . ' I have come,' she whispered, and, as if inspired, she took Gabrukh's hand and pressed it ardently to her parted lips . . ."

In spite of Natalya Tarpova, the type of woman who clings to her work, who refuses to leave it and to bind herself to a man, is probably more frequent in Soviet Russia to-day, a type, moreover, that is greatly idealized in literature.

In his novel *On the Road* Platoshkin describes a third type of Russian woman, akin to the last mentioned : two Amazons, Nina and Katya, have passed through a whole theory of free love in order to justify their view that they mean to be wife to no man. Nina and Katya even deny the sentiment of love. In their opinion young men comrades ought not to love, nor the young women comrades give birth to children, for love enslaves (especially the woman); the petty network of interests and obligations involved in a household makes the family a form of serfdom, drags husband and wife into the slime of gossip and strife, and leads to love of ease, the desire for comfort, and the abandonment of social work. What Nina and Katya really want is not so much free love as freedom from love. They hate love as a net spread to enslave them, and try with all the passion of fanaticism to destroy love, to stifle it within themselves. " Love, my friend, is worse than a marriage. If you marry, you can divorce," says Nina. " And how love degenerates people, knocks them over. . . . In less than no time a clever person is turned into a duffer, and there is nothing left of a good social worker." Ruthless war is declared on love.

The protagonists of free love hate the family even more than love. " Once you're married, it's all up with you. Done for. You were a human being, now you've ceased to be one. You dig a pit for yourself, shut and lock it, sit in it with the children and suck your thumb," says Nina.

Whilst this Amazon type represents an extreme in the female youth of Soviet Russia which is, naturally, rare in real life in that absolute form, the majority of women who, with all their Amazon qualities, are warm-hearted and genuinely womanly, compensate their sound mother-instinct in children for their renunciation of love and the family. Far more numerous and vital than the Amazons are the *unmarried mothers*. The number of women who are not willing or not in a position to pass their lives with a man, but are none the less unwilling to renounce the joys of motherhood, is constantly increasing. Un-married motherhood, which is more and more becoming an established institution, may be attributed to a number of causes.

Very often women resolve to bring a child to birth which they are already carrying and which is doomed to be fatherless, obeying necessity and not their own impulse. Whilst the surplus of women is generally large in the Soviet Union, there are districts which suffer acutely from a shortage of men. Certain textile districts, where women were in the majority even in Tsarist Russia, are almost exclusively populated by women to-day. For instance, the former provincial capital, Tver, is known throughout the Union because its population consists to 80 per cent of the women employed in its textile mills, and there are plenty of stories and jokes telling how easily a man, however poorly endowed by nature, may have the most beautiful women there, although he is then described as a " productive machine ". And so it seems to be a real matriarchate which is growing up in this Russian " island of grandmothers ". And various Moscow friends confirmed my impression often enough that this idea has occurred to the Russians too.

The second category of unmarried mothers comprises those who accuse men of irresponsible neglect of their paternal duties, not seldom as the result of plentiful experience. Hopeless as it is for a man in Soviet Russia to try to evade his responsibility for maintenance, yet suits concerned with paternity and maintenance are the most frequent cases in the law courts, together with housing disputes. Again and again one hears of girls who are literally forced by men to undergo an operation for abortion, and the complaint is repeated ceaselessly that as soon as the man has paid the money for the operation he regards the whole affair as over and done with. And when the children are born, then the sources of strife between father and mother multiply more than ever. A few years ago the case of the student Rybak was reported even abroad, who strangled the mother of his child because she wanted to hold him to the payment of the alimony which the court had allowed her.

In these circumstances it is comprehensible that an increasing number of women renounce all claims on the father of their children from the outset and voluntarily take upon themselves all the care of the child, all the undivided suffering, but also the undivided joys. And so it is not infrequent, if you ask who is the father of a child, to receive the surprising answer : " That does not matter ; the child is mine and I support it."

A friend of mine who is a doctor from Baku told me of the case of a woman named Klimova, a hydrotechnical engineer, whom he met when travelling on official business in Kirgiz. One night when he woke from his sleep in the room that had been allotted to him he discovered that in the meanwhile two women had been given the second bed, which could not bear the double weight and was breaking under it. That was how he made her acquaintance. When the women heard that their room-mate was a doctor, Klimova came to him the next day to ask his advice. She had a child that she was suckling, and was now, as a newly qualified engineer, travelling on official business ; on no account did she want to abandon the journey. It was, therefore, important for her to know whether she would lose her milk and whether the child would suffer, if she stopped suckling it for the time being. She was travelling on horseback and carrying the child about with her in a large bag, but she could not keep to the times for suckling it. "And your husband ? " asked the doctor. He was occupied else-where. "And do you realize what the consequences may be ? " Of course. But if the marriage came to grief on that account, then it was not worth more. At any rate, it was more important to make the journey than to remain with her husband.

Of course there are many unmarried mothers who, in true Russian fashion, construct a theory of " absolute demand " and exaggerate it. In Moscow I met a very well-known official who declared frankly that in addition to the three children she already had she wanted nine more—a dozen in all—but that she wished to have each one from a different man. Not only was the man in-different to her but, except for his fertilizing service, superfluous in her life. But the reason why she was determined to have all different fathers was twofold : first, she refused any permanent tie, and secondly she loved children of the most varied types. Certainly this was a purely individual theory, which has hitherto met with but little response even in Soviet Russia and whose pro-tagonist is regarded as an oddity even in Moscow. On the other hand, it is significant that the idea of voluntary unmarried motherhood, which is greatly facilitated and encouraged by the total abolition of the distinction between " legitimate " and " illegitimate " birth—no-where else to be found—has great attractions for some foreign women living in Russia and has a certain contagious power.

All the innovations here indicated, which amount to a complete revolution in marriage, naturally place the *family* on a totally new foundation. Here, too, we must distinguish between phenomena of decay and disintegration on the one hand, and those of an incipient stability on the other. The symptoms which point to a process of disintegration are the same in the Soviet Union as in bourgeois countries, except that here, because the process is more rapid, they are incomparably plainer. In the Soviet Union, as everywhere else, women's employment and their inclusion in the process of production, which, as is well known, has nowhere else assumed such proportions, have had a disintegrating influence upon the family. Further, the family as a separate economic unit is gradually forfeiting its *raison d'être* in consequence of industrialization. More and more functions are being withdrawn from its sphere, functions which formerly provided a firm ethical and economic foundation for it. In the Soviet state, thanks to the deliberately sought socialization of life, all this is taking place in an intensified form.

For all these reasons the old patriarchal form of the family is doomed in Soviet Russia. Doubtless it is also shaken to the foundations in capitalist countries. But whereas legislation in those countries still holds unswervingly to the fiction of the patriarchal family, although it is in full process of disintegration, Russian law has from the outset followed the facts to their logical conclusion. And so the disintegration of the family in the old sense stands as a fact in Soviet Russia, which nothing veils and nobody disputes.

Moreover, the process is spreading not only in the towns but in the country, where before the October revolution the family was incomparably more firmly knit and pretty well untouched by the disintegrating effects of capitalist industrialization. On this point I will cite

213

the eminent Russian sociologist, Professor Wolfson (*Marriage and the Family in their Historical Development*) :

If we set out to trace the essential lines in the variegated network of family relations in the Soviet village, we must first of all point out the important fact that the revolution has brought freedom in contracting and dissolving marriage. This resulted in the liberation of youth from the omnipotent tutelage of the family, and placed the power of choice in marriage, which the patriarchal tradition had regarded as a parental privilege, in the hands of the young people. Moreover, the wife's dependence on her husband, which had resulted from the previous conditions, ceased to be, so that she was freed from a lifelong yoke.

These " new rights " deprived the parents of that power which in the overwhelming majority of cases they had possessed to choose the young people's partners in marriage. And " independent " marriages, which only occurred as isolated instances in pre-revolutionary villages, have now assumed a mass character in the Soviet villages.

Even before the revolution a certain rude, primitive type of flirtation with a character of its own was known in the villages. From time immemorial the peasant lads and girls enjoyed themselves together at all kinds of *vecherinkas*, social evenings, discussions, and so forth. As a rule it was a manner of courting and in many cases this sort of pre-nuptial flirtation ended in a proper marriage.

But if as the result of one these amours a peasant girl found herself with child, it was regarded as the deepest disgrace, not only for herself but for the whole family. The disgrace frequently led to suicide ; the affair was sedulously concealed, and if a child was born, it was put to death or got rid of.

Since the revolution extra-matrimonial relations are a matter of course. Sometimes they lead to abortion carried out in the most primitive, barbaric manner, but sometimes the child is born and an alimony suit follows. Either way, pre-nuptial relations no longer call forth the horror which they encountered before the revolution. A girl who has given birth to a child is nowise stigmatized nowadays.

The crisis in family relations which the revolution has caused in the villages finds expression in the fact that the young peasants have secured the right to make their own choice in marriage and that for an independent and self-reliant peasant woman marriage has changed from lifelong slavery to a tie which can be dissolved at any time.

And yet all these phenomena of dissolution present only one side of the problem. In the Soviet Union the family is not only being broken up but also rebuilt on a higher plane. "Painful as the decay of the family may be," writes Kovalyov, "yet it undeniably represents a considerable step forwards. For that is precisely the dialectic of history, that the very incorporation of women in the economic process which disintegrates the capitalist family promotes the rise of new forms of marriage and the family." The small unit of the patriarchal family is replaced by a new and higher family, which already, in the transition period, we can trace in outline.

But Russian developments have in a certain sense paved the way for this historic change. Even at the end of the nineteenth century there were enlarged family settlements in Russia which may be regarded in some measure as precursors of the present-day village commune. Krassnopyorov gives an account of one such family settlement, comprising several generations, the " Antoshkin Mushiks " in the Ssmolensk Government :

> In the middle of the settlement, which consisted of ten huts, there was a large building with steps outside, the whole family's eating house. At a table spread with a white cloth, around immense tureens of *borshch* (a kind of beetroot soup), five-and-twenty persons sat down to dinner, men, women, and children. All the housework was done by the women. In the summer, whilst all the adults worked in the fields, an old woman stayed to look after the children. Another cooked for the whole settlement, a third lit all the stoves, and so on. The settlement provided all its own necessities, both food and clothing. The division of labour was carried out in every detail. Everybody did his share, and everybody complained that he had to work for the others. (Quoted from Milovidova, *The Women's Question*, etc.)

We see, therefore, that even in pre-revolutionary days the conception of the family among the Russians had outgrown the narrow patriarchal community. Historically the feeling of belonging to a wider community beyond the nearest relatives has been familiar to the Russian consciousness, to Russian humanity, from time immemorial. And presumably the Messianic character which is attributed to the Russian people is closely connected with the fact that more than once it has been granted to them to experience a profound oneness with all mankind, with the whole world in its march through history.

Originally the whole upbringing of children was one of those functions that were to be taken from the family and handed over to the state or society. Abroad people talked almost as much of the " socialization of children " as they did of the " socialization of women ", an arrangement by which the child was to be altogether alienated from its parents and the dissolution of the family accelerated. Plans of this kind were actually considered for a time, but it was precisely the communists who opposed them vigorously. Lenin's widow, Krupskaya, wrote at that time about a proposal to take children from their parents directly after their birth and to place them in socialistically conducted children's homes, later to be developed into " children's cities " :

> Parental feeling cannot be suppressed ; rather it will be turned in a new direction, and will bring more happiness than ever to parents and children. Those working men and women who refuse to give up their children and send them to children's cities are, therefore, right. On the other hand, the education of children in socialist society must be so organized that parents as well as teachers can have a share in it.

At the same time Krupskaya suggested the establishment of children's flats and children's sections in all newly built houses, where the parents could be placed in charge and be trained as educators in their free time.

And so it proved in the Soviet Union likewise that the child is the cement which holds the family together and renders its reconstruction on a higher plane possible. It is true that parental authority was for the most part destroyed. Most Soviet Russian children call their father and mother by their Christian name, and, as a modern poem puts it, " regard their father with a fatherly eye ". The parents' unrestricted power and right of disposal has been done away with, just as the oppression and exploitation of the wife by the husband has been abolished within the family.

To sum up : whereas in capitalist countries ever since the war we have heard only of the breakdown of marriage and the decay of the family, in the land of the Soviets it is at least possible to speak with equal justification of a new form of marriage and the family which is beginning to take shape. Only the patriarchal family, built up upon the economic domination and legally sanctioned authority of the husband, is doomed to die out and has already lost all its vitality. And it is already pretty clear what the new form of marriage and the family, in process of growth, will be like. They will be based upon the full economic, political, and social equality of the sexes. And whereas in Western Europe the matriarchate has actually been contemplated recently as a way of escape from the crisis in marriage and the family, and people have thought that signs are already discernible of such a development in America, in the Soviet Union, the country where women have attained to a position of unprecedented pre-dominance, in which certain individuals have held that conditions are making straight for a gynæcocracy, there are no indications, except the Amazon type and unmarried motherhood, of the possibility that a new matriarchate might arise. Perhaps the evolution of the new woman in Russia may be regarded in some respects as a con-tinuation of the pre-Christian development which I tried to trace in the indications contained in the ancient epics and in the lingering echoes of the matriarchate ; yet this continuation does not present itself as a revival of the matriarchal tradition, but as the final abolition of the domination of one sex by the other in all their mutual relations : in love, marriage, and the family.

TOWARDS THE ABOLITION OF
PROSTITUTION

. . . We must prove our mettle, we working women who have come into the productive process. . . . For now that we have once cast ourselves among the general mass, we must work in the proper spirit. . . . Why, I came off the streets, but not a single workman in the factory has ever made me feel it, and I for my part do not make a secret of it. *Tovarishchi*, admit it frankly, and you will be all the better treated, for people will say : she has suffered much.

> —*From the speech of a member of the First Conference of Former Prostitutes, now Workers, in Moscow on October 31st, 1931.*

PROSTITUTION IN TSARIST RUSSIA

ON July 26th, 1913, that is a good four years before the October revolution, the following words from Lenin's pen appeared in the first issue of *Rabochaya Pravda* :

A short time ago the Fifth International Conference against the Traffic in Women and Children was held in London. There the duchesses, countesses, bishops, clergymen, rabbis and police officers ran riot. What a number of banquets were held, and what magnificent official receptions ! What a number of solemn speeches on the harmfulness and wickedness of prostitution !

But what were the means proposed by the elegant bourgeois delegates to combat it ? Principally two : religion and the police. That, it was said, was the safest and most reliable means of attacking prostitution. An English delegate boasted that he had advocated flogging in Parliament as a punishment for procuring : such is a modern, " civilized " champion against prostitution ! A lady from Canada spoke enthusiastically in favour of the police and female police supervision of fallen women. But when the question of the possibility of higher wages was raised, she expressed the opinion that women workers were not worth higher pay. Then a German pastor stormed against modern materialism, which he said was more and more gaining a hold on the people and encouraging free love. And when the Austrian delegate, Gärtner, attempted to deal with the question from the point of view of the social causes of prostitution—the poverty and wretched circumstances of working-class families, the exploitation of child labour, the intolerable conditions, etc.—he was reduced to silence by hostile exclamations.

What loathesome bourgeois hypocrisy flaunted itself at this aristocratic and bourgeois conference! Acrobats of charity and apologists for the police mocked at poverty and distress and gathered to combat the prostitution which after all is maintained by the aristocracy and bourgeoisie!

Before Lenin, August Bebel, in his celebrated book *Woman and Socialism*, pointed out that in bourgeois society prostitution was an institution similar to the police, the army, the church, and capitalist enterprise. Closely connected with this " social institution ", as we know, is so-called regulation, the shameful system of police supervision of prostitutes by which a woman is, after all, fettered fast and irrevocably to prostitution, treated as a mere commodity. Thanks to the campaign instituted against it by Josephine Butler in England more than half a century ago, the abolitionist movement which afterwards spread to all countries, regulation has, indeed, been formally abolished in certain states—Germany, Czecho-Slovakia, England, Belgium, and Holland—with Scandinavia leading the way. But the abolition was nowhere complete and so was one of those half-measures in which many dangers are innate.

True, preventive measures are adopted in bourgeois countries too : by raising the age of consent, protection for the unmarried mother, and for children and those who are exposed to dangers, by education and instruction, by juvenile welfare work, homes, and Care Committees. Likewise the sexual reform aims of the Association for the Protection of Motherhood have a similar tendency. But none of these minor measures reach the real heart of the problem, which is primarily rooted in social and economic conditions so that assuredly its final solution can be reached only in connection with the one great question of our time—the social question.

If we compare the state of affairs as regards prostitution in capitalist, pre-revolutionary Russia with that of to-day, we see the situation in a clear light. As in all other bourgeois countries, it was principally women's lack of rights and their economic dependence that drove them into prostitution. For instance, the records of the statistical inquiry into prostitution conducted in the Russian Empire on August 1st, 1889, show that 83·5 per cent—that is four-fifths—of the total number of prostitutes under control came from conditions of extreme poverty, and that in the Government of St. Petersburg the proportion was as much as 90 per cent. So, too, the statistics of the first all-Russian census in 1897 show that only 8·4 per cent of the female population were self-supporting ; all the rest were in dependent positions. And whilst the earnings of a woman factory worker in the Moscow district in 1885—according to the startling report of the factory inspector, Professor Yanshul—was on the average 9 roubles a month within twenty categories, and that of a male worker on the average 18½ roubles a month —not even a living wage—(the proportion was the same in the Charkov district at the same time, only there wages were still lower), about 1903 the earnings of a woman factory worker in the far larger factories of St. Petersburg and Moscow fluctuated, according to Pashitnov (*The Situation of the Working Class in Russia*), beween 6 and 8 roubles a month, although the price of foodstuffs had risen about 25 per cent at the beginning of the present century. A questionnaire circulated in Odessa shortly before the world war amongst 26,000 shop assistants, male and female, showed that the monthly average wage for a man was 34 roubles and for a woman 13 roubles, and that a third of the women earned less than 10 roubles a month. The women cigarette makers were the worst paid ; about 1901 even, their monthly wage barely exceeded one or two roubles. Under such hopeless economic conditions it is no wonder that many a woman who was paid for her sex instead of her work fell a victim to prostitution merely to keep body and soul together.

At the same time it may be stated that the factory workers, in spite of their starvation wages, simply because they were growing into an atmosphere of rising class consciousness in the factory, resisted the temptations of the streets far more than the domestic servants who were the most enslaved of all, moving principally in petty bourgeois surroundings and therefore least conscious in their thinking ; fully 65 per cent of the total number of prostitutes, that is two-thirds, came from their ranks.

The percentage of seamstresses among prostitutes was lower than that of domestic servants, but still four and a half times as high as that of factory workers ; for they, too, were exposed to the arbitrary will of the women who employed them. And after what has been said it goes without saying that of all industrial groups it was precisely the cigarette makers, the most miserably paid, from whose ranks by far the largest number of prostitutes came.

In Tsarist Russia, likewise, prostitution was combated by means of a system of police supervision, there, too, known as regulation. The figures show how much more widespread prostitution was in those days than in other bourgeois countries : St. Petersburg alone had 40,000 registered prostitutes before the war, whilst in Vienna, for example, there were 30,000. Regulation first made its appearance in St. Petersburg in 1843, under Tsar Nicholas I ; it consisted of compulsory medical examination once or twice a week, for the most part under horrible conditions, and in the case of a prostitute found to be diseased, isolation. The women under police control had a so-called " yellow certificate " given them in place of their papers of identification, and they were not allowed to move without police permission. Further, they were required to live in the houses set apart for them. There they gradually forgot how to work, and what the result was is shown by a much-quoted statement of Dr. Stürmer, the representative of the Department of Medicine, at the Anti-Syphilis Congress held at St.

Petersburg in 1897 : " In most cases the yellow certificate forms an absolute bar to the admission of a woman to working life."

Professor Yelistratov (*Prostitution in Russia before the Revolution of 1917*) states that police supervision in Russia was grossly imbued with class prejudice, and bore with all its weight upon women of the poorer orders. For according to the regulations only women " of the lower orders, that is . . . from among domestic servants and working women " might be submitted to examination. The same regulations were further stated to apply to " the common people ", so that prostitutes of the " upper classes " and of " good birth ", who were also not few in number, were not annoyed by the police. For the rest, the class character of this system of regulation is stressed by the fact that the conditions for subjection to police supervision were such that no single impecunious woman, whatever her conduct, was really secure against it, for the mere district in which she lived, and her " outward appearance ", were enough to count as grounds of suspicion.

There is ample evidence on the plentiful Russian literature which deals with this subject to show what appalling abuses on the part of the Russian police were made possible and easy under such circumstances. The view is generally expressed there that regulation and the barrack system in pre-revolutionary Russia constituted an organization which bound a woman to prostitution to the end of her life and multiplied many times over the pressure of social conditions, which was in any case intolerable. For according to the rules obtaining in Warsaw a woman could only be set free if she were seriously ill and " produced a certificate signed by at least two doctors ", and then only after the expiration of a year ; according to the custom obtaining in Minsk, only " in case of her death ".

The dissatisfaction with this system of regulation, accumulated in certain circles, was intensified by the abolition movement, which had penetrated to Russia, and especially by two sensational criminal trials of the 'eighties, when the superintendents of police in Kronstadt and Nikolayev were accused of close association with the owners of houses of ill-fame. This dissatisfaction first found public expression at the All-Russian Conference against the Traffic in Women and Children held at St. Petersburg in 1910. The conference also caused a great stir because a deputation of the Moscow workers appeared and its leader, the printer Pavlov, was one of the speakers and said among other things : " We have no hope of getting rid, under the present economic system, of the terrible evil that is called prostitution, and that weighs upon the national organism with its deadly effects. We have no hope of healing the festering wound of prostitution by attending this conference, for it can only be healed by doing away with class differences, only by the workers' own efforts. But for that reason we regard it as our chief duty to reveal the deeper causes of prostitution, which appears to be due to the workers' lack of economic and political rights."

Of course the workers' delegation did not at that time succeed in reaching any agreement with the conference, and they were obliged to absent themselves from the subsequent sessions. The unanimous resolution to appeal to the Government to close the houses of ill-fame immediately had no more success than the bill introduced into the Duma in 1913 by the St. Petersburg Club of the Progressive Women's Party, by which regulation was to be abolished and the houses of ill-fame closed.

THE SOVIET GOVERNMENT'S STRUGGLE AGAINST PROSTITUTION

IT is obvious that a special decree for the abolition of regulation was necessary after the Soviet Government had seized power and had issued a " Declaration of the Rights of the Working and Exploited People " and pro-claimed the abolition of every kind of exploitation of one human being by another.

" The fact that a woman has no work and no one to care for her is the fundamental social cause of prostitution," declared Ssyemashko, at that time People's Commissary of Public Health, proclaiming it as the watchword for Soviet Russia, and thereby pointing out a way to eradicate the evil, and one which soon proved right in practice.

In the early years directly after the October revolution, the years of war communism, of universal compulsory labour which embraced alike all women and all men capable of work, when the conditions were as unfavourable as they could possibly be for the development of prostitution, the demand had sunk to zero and prostitution had practically disappeared in Soviet Russia. Of course the Government's struggle against it had no small share in this achievement : its struggle against those prostitutes who wanted to evade compulsory labour and who, like all other parasitical elements, were sent to concentration camps, and even more, its struggle against the procurers and owners of houses of ill-fame, whose numbers were in any case greatly reduced. Nevertheless, efforts were made from the very first to establish a special organization to combat prostitution.

The first Commission to Combat Prostitution which was attached to the Venereal Section of the People's Commissariat of Public Health in 1919, and the second, which was placed under the People's Commissariat of Social Welfare (also abolished in the spring of 1922), did not accomplish much that was positive.

But meanwhile the civil war was over, and the transition to the N.E.P., the New Economic Policy, provided more favourable soil for prostitution to flourish. And experience showed that the solution of the purely economic question, although women had already been placed upon an equality politically, was far from complete. In spite of the equalization of their wages with men's, the majority of women showed themselves backward and unskilled and were consequently hard hit by the growing unemployment. The prerequisite conditions of prostitution, therefore, were daily spreading—at the same time as the reopening of restaurants and bars, the permission of the sale of alcohol, and the demand for prostitutes which is so closely connected with it. In the People's Commissariat of the Interior, a project for the establishment of a " militia of morals " actually made its appearance, in view of this state of affairs, but was repudiated with indignation by the Soviet press. Clara Zetkin wrote in *Isvestiya* on July 8th, 1922, and also opposed it vigorously, saying among other things :

> . . . We ask whether the proposed militia of morals is one of those measures capable of producing a result that could contribute in the smallest degree to a healthier state. On the basis of the experience of all other countries I dispute it. . . . The statement that, but for the intervention of the police, prostitution and venereal disease would be even more widespread is unfounded and arbitrary. . . . All measures adopted by the *police des mœurs*, however reasonably they are devised and however tactfully and justly carried out, are incapable of striking at the social root of prostitution. . . . For the *police des mœurs* have no power to reduce demand and supply in prostitution ; the most that they can attain is a mere outward transformation of the market. Supply and demand will only cease when the economic and social conditions which give rise to them are done away with. . . .

The foundation of a planned and organized struggle against prostitution was laid in the circular worked out by the Venereal Section of the People's Commissariat of Public Health published in *Isvestiya* on December 16th, 1922 (On the Measures to be adopted in the Struggle against Prostitution), which envisaged a far-reaching struggle against prostitution, both prophylactic and direct.

This circular declared :

> After the October revolution, which changed our political and economic organization from top to bottom, mass prostitution began to disappear. The basic causes for this disappearance are, in addition to the economic liberation of the workers : the total social liberation of women, the new form of marriage, the inclusion of women in all spheres of activity, and widespread propagandist and educational work.
>
> The New Economic Policy has again called forth an increase in prostitution, which had begun to disappear. News reaches us from various parts of the Republic of a revival of all kinds of commercial prostitution, of secret centres of vice, and of pro-

curing. The tide of prostitution, which disintegrates social life, is rising. And at the same time the phenomena which accompany it—venereal diseases—are also increasing.

We call the attention of all organs of the local authorities to the urgent necessity of a really energetic struggle against this evil, and suggest the following measures :

(*a*) To act with especial caution in the dismissal of women when staffs are being reduced—in respect of that group of women who are least provided for and incapable of economic resistance (women who have no near relatives, girls with no place to live, expectant mothers, and women with small children). It is the duty of the Section for the Protection of Labour, the trade unions, and the Women's Sections, to defend the interests of these women first and foremost, remembering that measures thoughtlessly applied in this field may drive the most helpless to prostitution.

(*b*) To establish an organization of productive co-operatives, industrial and agricultural, capable of employing certain groups of workless and untrained women.

(*c*) To improve the trade qualifications among women by reserving a sufficient number of free places in the trade schools.

(*d*) To combat destitution among women by establishing homes for unemployed women and girls.

(*e*) To develop welfare work among neglected and destitute children.

(*f*) To widen the field of propaganda and education in order to enlighten the workers about the nature of prostitution, and to teach them how inadmissible it is and how shameful in a republic of workers, and instruct them of the dangers resulting from it.

All these measures are of a preventive nature and check the development of prostitution. But simultaneously with them it appears necessary to make provision vigorously for combating already existing prostitution :

(1) Stricter administrative supervision of all those places where the workers may be tempted to licentiousness and women to prostitution ; but the former methods of supervision adopted in pre-revolutionary Russia, which in practice meant not the protection but the oppression of women, must be quite definitely repudiated ; such are razzias, the persecution of prostitutes, their compulsory examination, etc. *Under no circumstances must the war against prostitution degenerate into a war against prostitutes.*

(2) Vigorous measures against the agents and abettors of prostitution, the owners of centres of vice, under whatever mask they may appear, and the use of all administrative and judicial powers.

(3) The organization of free treatment for those suffering from venereal disease, accessible to all, preferably by means of the establishment of dispensaries.

In order to co-ordinate activities directed against prostitution and to solve all problems arising from local circumstances, the Provincial Soviets will establish special organizations to combat prostitution.

The Central Soviet for Combating Prostitution attached to the *Narkomsdrav*, the People's Commissariat of Public Health, will constitute the directing body which will co-ordinate the work of the Provincial Soviets.

Many as are the urgent tasks which confront the Provincial Executive Committees, the Provincial Trade Soviets, and the Women's Sections, yet the struggle against the reviving and rapidly spreading evil of prostitution must be included in those urgent tasks.

In a workers' state there is no place for prostitution.

(*Signed*) People's Commissary of Public Health

N. SSYEMASHKO.

With special regard to the passage in the circular which says that the war against prostitution must under no circumstances degenerate into a war against prostitutes, the Central Soviet for Combating Prostitution, established immediately after the issue of the circular, in collaboration with the People's Commissariat of the Interior, issued " Instructions to the Militant Organizations for Combating Prostitution " in January, 1924. The following are characteristic points in the Instructions :

1. The most essential activity of the Militia for Combating Prostitution must be to do away with centres of vice, which must be regarded as the ordinary factors that encourage the far-reaching spread of prostitution.

4. Whilst the militia must perform its duty in searching out centres of vice with the utmost determination and tenacity, yet it must refrain from all acts of oppression towards individual prostitutes when, in case of need, it cites them as witnesses.

5. Remembering that a woman who carries on the trade of a prostitute has only entered into it as the result of unfavourable circumstances, material or otherwise, every worker in the militia must observe all the rules of courtesy in the exercise of his functions and must under no circumstances allow himself to be tempted into rough treatment of the women.

Success was not slow to appear. In the course of a single year, from April, 1924, to April, 1925, 2,228 nests of vice were destroyed in the R.S.F.S.R. alone, according to Professor Bronner (*Prostitution and the Methods of Abolishing it*). Equally efficacious was the work of the venereal dispensaries, that is the organizations established in order to combat venereal diseases, which directed special attention to prostitution as the most important factor in the spread of venereal diseases. The dispensaries have done much valuable work through their sanitary committees, also called Soviets for Social Aid, which are in close touch with the various sections of the population that come to them for advice, and study their sexual life with the utmost care ; they instruct the younger generation in sexual hygiene and conduct thorough statistical and scientific research. They also engage the sympathy of proletarian public opinion and organize anti-prostitution " weeks " and " three days " in the provinces as well as the capital in which popular educational literature is distributed on the social significance of venereal disease and prostitution.

So, too, the frequent dramatic presentation of so-called " Judicial Proceedings concerning a Prostitute " called the attention of the masses to the question. After one of these dramatic presentations, in which the prostitute had infected a workman who came to her house (the prostitute and the workman were publicly reproved and the woman who owned the " house " severely punished), the newspaper *Rabochaya Gaseta* opened a remarkable discussion which produced a number of letters. Some of these were published for days in succession, and on February 25th, 1925, the correspondence was closed with the following article by the Central Soviet :

228

STRUGGLE AGAINST PROSTITUTION

On the Sentence in the " Judicial Proceedings concerning a Prostitute "

On the subject of the " Judicial Proceedings concerning a Prostitute " we have a number of letters from workers who comment excitedly on this unwholesome problem of the age. Three persons are sentenced : a prostitute, a workman, and a procuress. There is unanimous approval of the severe sentence on the procuress. And that is as it should be. We must wage ruthless war on procuring, and our criminal code provides for imprisonment and confiscation of property as its punishment. All our correspondents are concerned about the prostitute and her consumer, the workman. And here there are a number of differences of opinion.

Not one of our correspondents thinks the sentence on the prostitute, Yevdokimova, too mild ; some think it too severe. We are inclined to this opinion. For in spite of our repudiation of prostitution, we are unable to accept the view that it should be punished so long as there is unemployment that we cannot do away with. What we may doubtless make the prostitute responsible for is the transmission of venereal disease. But we can only call her to account to the same extent as we should any man or woman citizen in a similar case. The degree of her guilt will then be gauged according to whether the venereally diseased person was aware that she was contagious to others.

The prostitute Yevdokimova does not strike us as a person who thinks consciously. She was altogether outside the great family of the workers, was not even registered as a member of a trade union, had never attended lectures on venereal diseases, and may have had no inkling that she might be contagious. For these reasons the sentence on Yevdokimova seems to us too severe. It would have been better to have formulated the court's judgment thus : " Yevdokimova is acquitted. She is required to undergo treatment and to submit to the control of the Venereal Dispensary. Further, the substance of Article 155 of the Criminal Code shall be communicated to her and the communication acknowledged in writing, which article provides for the punishment of the transmission of venereal disease, and her attention shall be called to the fact that, in case of another transmission of venereal disease, she will be severely punished, for then she will commit the offence with full knowledge."

But the chief interest centres in the workman, the consumer of prostitutes. The majority think the sentence pronounced against him too mild, but at the same time he has his defenders.

The most striking is the defence of *Tovarishch* Ovod : " It was not necessary," he writes, " to censure the workman publicly who went to a prostitute. So long as there is prostitution, there will inevitably be a demand for it." Yet hardly less significant is *Tovarishch* Grysun's answer : " Demand creates supply ; if there were no people looking out for prostitution, prostitution itself would not exist." But Komssomolets Andrey, guided by a sound proletarian instinct, says : " The worker deserves a severer punishment than Yevdokimova, for she was driven into prostitution by unemployment. But he should have been more class conscious ; he is a worker." Truth is on the side of Grysun and Andrey. For is not prostitution a commodity in the form of the human body ? Like every other commodity, it is put upon the market and seeks buyers. If it finds no buyers, it disappears from the market. *Tovarishch* Ovod does not know this elementary truth.

Again, *Tovarishch* Kurenkov justifies the demand, basing his argument upon the physiological needs of men. But let us tell him that physiological need may occur not only in a man, but also in a woman, and that on the one hand it is time that we abandoned all special moral laws applying to women, whilst on the other we must point out that all the talk about the harmfulness of sexual abstinence is altogether groundless, for medical research has shown that abstinence is not harmful to the organism. There are no special sexual energies in the organism, there is only one single reservoir of energy, and if there is excess there, then, as Komssomolets Andrey rightly stresses, a man must direct his energy along other lines, since we have no time to run after prostitutes : we have more important tasks confronting us.

On the strength of what we have said, then, it must be admitted that the workman, who bought the body of the hungry Yevdokimova, acted with full knowledge, and therefore committed an offence that deserved much severer condemnation than hers. With regard to Yevdokimova and her consumer we must state : it is high time that the parts were exchanged. If everything is allowed to representatives of the " stronger sex " in capitalist society, and if their victims must then pay the price of the evil that the men cause, and if there those are provided with certificates of shame and outlawry whom hunger forces to carry their bodies to market, then among us in Soviet Russia they should be punished and their names entered in a black list who go to market to purchase those bodies. We think, therefore, that it would have been better if in the " Judicial Proceedings concerning the Prostitute Yevdokimova ", instead of publicly censuring the purchaser of her body, sentence had been passed that his name should be written on the notice-board of the factory where he worked. Such a punishment would have had a much more deterrent effect than a judicial sentence.

In a workers' republic there must be no place for prostitution. And prostitution will begin to disappear if, while we struggle to consolidate our economic front, while we struggle to liquidate unemployment, we also enter upon a struggle to impress upon the minds of the workers all the inadequacy, all the shame of purchasing a human body.

The Deputy Chairman of the Central Soviet for Combating Prostitution

(*Signed*) N. BRONNER.

Another open correspondence at about the same date is worth mention : between the " Prostitute Tanya " and the Central Soviet. In this letter the prostitute accuses the Soviet " in the name of many " ; it is true, she says, that it has given out the motto that " the war against prostitution must not assume the form of a war against prostitutes ", but in actual fact it does everything to reduce the earnings of the prostitutes to a minimum upon which it is impossible to live. Because of the difficulty of finding quarters, earnings are dwindling from day to day, and if at last quarters are found the price is so high that nothing is left over of a woman's earnings.

In the " Answer to the Prostitute Tanya " which thereupon appeared in the *Rabochaya Gaseta*, signed by the President of the Central Soviet, the People's Commissary of Public Health, Ssyemashko, we read :

> . . . You beg the Soviet to leave prostitutes in peace, and point out that they neither murder nor rob. But you do not reflect that prostitutions are the chief source of venereal diseases, that heaviest of national calamities, and that that consideration alone makes it urgently necessary to combat the institution. The fact of which you complain, that just because of this fight the prostitutes and their clients find it difficult to secure accommodation, and that the measures adopted by the Soviet have caused the earnings of prostitutes to sink rapidly— this is evidence that the plan adopted is right. . . .

Prostitution is a most severe disease of our social organism. We have inherited it, together with other social diseases, from capitalist society, and we shall cure it together with those social diseases, and probably sooner than the others, after we have consolidated our economic life.

We know that it is not the desire for luxury, but rather bitter poverty and helplessness, which leads the vast majority of women to offer for sale the most precious thing that anyone possesses—their bodies. We know also that the war against prostitution hits the prostitutes themselves indirectly by reducing their earnings. And yet we shall continue the war. The interests of the community require it, to which the interests of individuals as well as groups must be subordinated.

But the Central Soviet for Combating Prostitution extended its activities further ; in its endeavours to prevent prostitution it succeeded in increasing the free places reserved for girls in works and factories and technical schools. Likewise the significant clauses 169a, 170, and 171 which were added to the Criminal Code of the R.S.F.S.R. were due to its initiative.

These clauses, which we will preface by three others in order to complete the picture, read as follows :

155. Anyone who infects another person with a venereal disease shall be liable to imprisonment for a period not exceeding three years.

155a. Anyone who knowingly exposes another person to the risk of venereal infection—whether by means of sexual intercourse or otherwise—shall be liable to imprisonment or hard labour for a period not exceeding six months.

169. Rape, that is sexual intercourse enforced by physical or mental compulsion or the exploitation of the helpless condition of the person in question, shall render the offender liable to imprisonment for a period not less than three years.

If the act of rape leads to the suicide of the person concerned, the penalty shall be increased to a period of not less than five years.

169a. Anyone who forces a woman that is materially dependent on him or in his employment to have sexual intercourse with him shall be subject to the penalty indicated in Article 169.

170. Anyone who exercises physical or mental compulsion, whether from commercial or other personal motives, upon a

woman to practise prostitution, shall be liable to solitary confinement for a period of not less than three years.

171. Procuring, the maintenance of brothels, and the recruit-
ment of women for purposes of prostitution shall render the
offender liable to imprisonment for not less than three years and
to partial or total confiscation of his property.

But if the persons forced to practise prostitution were under
the care of the accused, or subject to his authority, or if they
were under age, then the penalty shall be increased to not less
than five years' imprisonment.

But in course of time the so-called *Prophylactoria* established by the Venereal Dispensaries proved to be one of
the most interesting, the most practically vital, and
successful of institutions in the war against prostitution.

THE *PROPHYLACTORIA*

THE *prophylactoria* are workrooms attached to a home and
a medical department in which venereally diseased, workless, and untrained women, mainly prostitutes, are received,
medically treated, kept at work, and re-educated in a
proletarian spirit. At the end of the treatment the pupils
in these *prophylactoria* are placed in factories, in order to
introduce them into working life.

The first *prophylactorium* met with widespread public
sympathy, since the provision of work is here associated
with the rendering innocuous of venereal disease, an
important service to society (hence the name *prophylactorium*); this one originated in 1923 in a producers'
co-operative for unemployed and untrained women. At
the present day there is no large town in Soviet Russia—
from Ryasany, Kasan, Ssaratov, Tula, Tver, Vyatka,
Taganrog, Leningrad, Baku, and Novo-Ssibirsk to
Vladivostok—but has its own *prophylactorium* with
medical and labour departments.

A few figures published by Professor Bronner, from the
Annual Report from October 1st, 1925, to October 1st,
1926, are instructive for the insight they give into the
activities and organization of the first and largest Moscow
prophylactorium (where sacks and underclothing are made),
where 200 women found work and 150 lodging, with an

average wage of thirty roubles a month—at that time a
two-course dinner cost twenty copeks;

On October 1st, 1925, the *prophylactorium*
  harboured . . . . . 92 women
Additional admissions in the course of the year . 276 „
Of these :
  obtained permanent employment . . 98 „
  were discharged by their own wish . . 48 „
  were discharged for breaking rules . . 21 „
  married . . . . . . 16 „
  returned to their homes . . . 10 „
  were placed in Children's Homes . . 5 „
Number on October 1st, 1926 . . . 170 „

SOCIAL COMPOSITION

From peasant families. . . . 155 women
From workers' families . . . 15 „
Members of trade unions . . . 58 „
Belonging to no trade union . . 112 „
Belonging to no party . . . 164 „
Komssomolkas . . . . . 6 „

LITERACY

Able to read and write . . . 58 women
Half-literate . . . . . 76 „
Wholly illiterate . . . . . 36 „

UNEMPLOYMENT

Up to six months . . . . 52 women
From six months to a year . . 19 „
Over a year . . . . . 54 „
Never worked . . . . . 45 „

FAMILY CIRCUMSTANCES

Unmarried . . . . . 87 women
Married . . . . . . 29 „
Divorced . . . . . 35 „
Widows . . . . . 19 „
With children . . . . 34 „
Without children . . . . 136 „
Suffering from syphilis . . . 88 „
Suffering from gonorrhœa . . . 40 „

AGE

14–16 years old . . . . . 5 women
16–18 „ „ . . . . 12 „
18–25 „ „ . . . . 109 „
25–30 „ „ . . . . 25 „
Over 30 „ „ . . . . 19 „

There were shortly four *prophylactoria* in various districts of Moscow, through which 891 women passed in 1928 ; according to D. I. Lass they were 76 per cent peasants, 21 per cent former working women, and 3 per cent members of other social groups. They included 23 per cent illiterates, 46 per cent semi-literates, and 31 per cent fully able to read and write ; 2 per cent had even attended secondary schools. Of the professional prostitutes 49 per cent had syphilis, 31 per cent gonorrhœa, and 11 per cent both together.

The essential characteristic of these *prophylactoria* is that a spiritual and mental regeneration proceeds side by side with the medical and physiological treatment ; the inmates undergo a total change of heart which is mainly due to the fact that from the first day the women have to maintain themselves by the work of their hands, since these are not charitable institutions ; the inmates must work to pay for their board and lodging. Beginning with easy processes which require no previous training, a working woman gradually gains experience, gets to like her work, improves in receptivity and concentration, grows with her ambitions, and, when her re-education is more or less complete, when there is no further cause to fear a relapse and she can be discharged as cured, she is sent to a factory as a trained worker.

In these new working surroundings, where nothing reminds them of their past, but where they are still under the care of the *prophylactorium* and the protection of the women's organizations, the trade unions, the factory delegates, etc., the women are finally initiated into a new life which fills most of them with enthusiasm and pride. Formerly, whilst there was still unemployment, they actually enjoyed certain privileges : in order to prevent a relapse they were allotted work out of their turn.

It goes without saying that in these *prophylactoria*, as everywhere in the Soviet Union, exemplary educational work is carried on ; efforts are made to do away with actual and political illiteracy, and the women's intellectual interests are awakened in every direction. The women in the *prophylactorium*—the word " prostitute " is taboo, and both the doctor and the other officials in the establishment always address their charges as *Tovarishch*—are divided into groups in which those who can read and write may take part in regular instruction in their free time ; in the case of illiterates instruction is obligatory, and so is medical treatment for all ; the working day is seven hours.

The instruction is divided into two sections—for instance in a large Moscow *prophylactorium* with 200 inmates, which serves as a model for all the rest more or less. In the " individual course section " there are eighteen hours a week in general subjects, three hours each, adapted to the general standard of education : Russian, arithmetic, geography, *politgramota* (political ABC), and physics. The physics lessons are helped by visits to the Polytechnical Museum. The courses are eagerly attended by the women, who are generally " infected " with the prevailing zeal for learning after a short time.

In the other " mass " section they are principally educated on the artistic and emotional side. There is a *dramatic club* with a stage in the style of the " living newspaper ", and periodical performances take place under the direction of actors (voluntary social work). The women often provide the ideas of the plays themselves. There is special *musical teaching*, in which war is waged successfully on banal commonplace music, especially the *zyganochka* so popular in those circles, so that the effect is educational. The *prophylactorium* has its own orchestra of wind instruments. Three or four musical performances are arranged each month, and here the Russian national instrument, the accordion, is the most popular. A special *massovik*, an organizer of choirs, games, dances, and so on, provides good general entertainment. From time to time the *massovik* appears with a *bayanist*. This musician, who is particularly welcome in the *prophylactorium*, plays an instrument which resembles several accordions playing together. Sometimes even men are admitted to the entertainments. After eleven o'clock at night—which is not at all late in

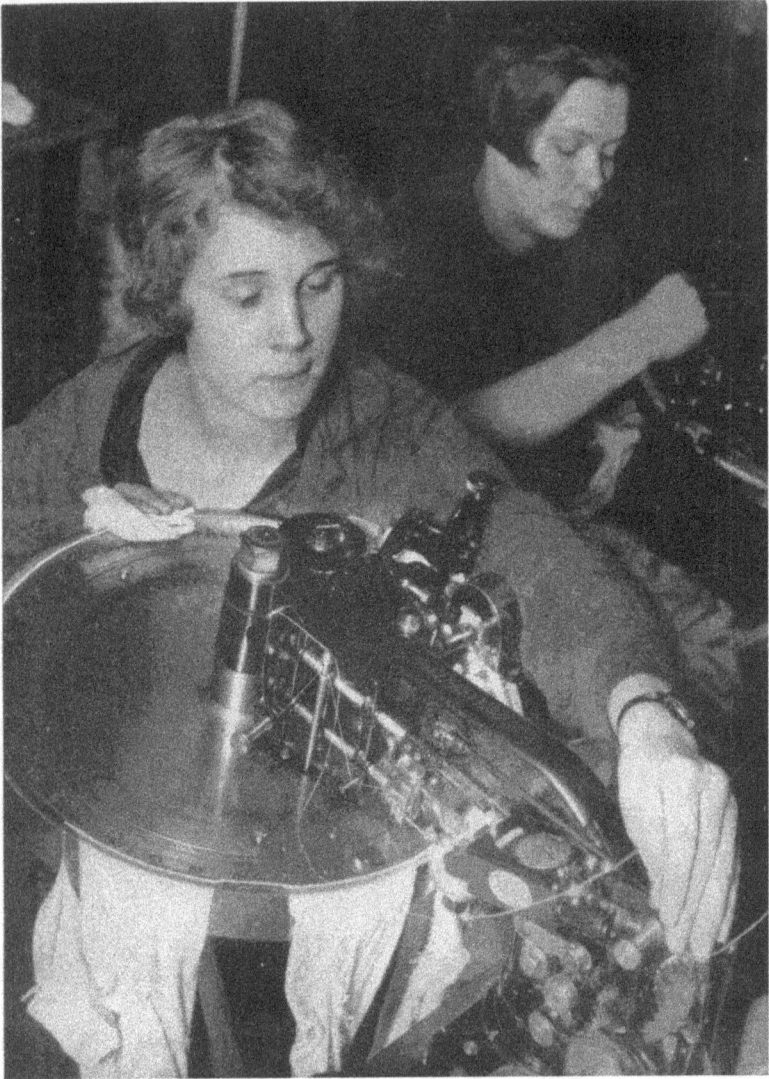

WOMEN WORKERS IN A MOSCOW *PROPHYLACTORIUM*

[*face p.* 237

Moscow—the women are left to their own devices, and keep watch on one another so that the confidence shown in them is not too grossly abused.

Visits to the cinema are also arranged by the mass section ; every day when they go out the women are taken in groups—seventy to eighty each time—to carefully chosen pictures, to which they are admitted free and which are likewise of great educational value, because they divert the women's thoughts and make them think. There is also a *physculture* department in the mass section, that is, sport. There is, of course, here, as in every other Soviet Russian institution, a *Redkollegiya*, an editorial committee which publishes its own wall newspaper under the direction of an expert who feels his pedagogical responsibility. There are further dress making and cutting-out classes in the mass section.

Entry into the *prophylactorium* is voluntary. A special Inquiry Board decides who shall be admitted. Special records are made not only of the state of health but also of the psychical and mental way of life, the " aspect " of each entrant, and according to the result it is decided to which group both of the individual and the mass section she is best suited.

Special case papers (see pp. 262–6), which are filled in carefully and regularly by all the group leaders who come into contact with her, make it possible to trace step by step the whole development of a woman in the *prophylactorium*. And yet more : even her individual tastes and capacities appear in the records, so that her " new aspect " when she is discharged from the institution (generally after the period of a year) can be compared with the old, and the necessary instructions and the measures requisite for her further progress follow automatically.

Thus the principal function of these *prophylactoria* is to change the whole habit of mind and spirit of the women inmates. To that end everything is done—sometimes even by means of artifice—to rouse their interest in reading, in learning and knowledge, and to make them conscious of the great difference between the present and the past. That is particularly difficult because—apart from the minute proportion of " incurables ", who make up about 3 or 4 per cent—these women shrink immediately from all brainwork, and the mere words " address ", " lecture ", or " *likbes* " (liquidation of illiteracy), call forth such intense feelings of repugnance that it is frequently impossible to lure them into the " Red Corner ", the reading corner, if the object is to bring any serious book to their notice.

" But if once you lure them by roundabout means, for instance with Pushkin's story, *The Young Peasant Lady*," the principal of the cultural and educational division of what is now the largest *prophylactorium* in Moscow told me, " then they listen with interest next time even to an extract from one of Stalin's speeches and sometimes even write down what they think about it."

On the blackboards of the central hall of this Moscow *prophylactorium* I saw at the end of 1931 a number of written answers by women who were beginning to read to the question which had been put to them : " Why must we read books, and what do we get from them ? " From these I learned :

> In order to educate oneself, to get more sense into one's head, and to know later on what circle one should join, and how.
>
> *(Name, age 14.)*

Or :

> I want very much to learn something ; I can't sleep at night because of it. I should like to be as well educated as all the others. I should like to understand all questions, so as to be able to answer them in meetings. How can you learn that sort of thing ? I don't want anything else, only to be educated. I should like to know everything. I read books, but I don't understand anything. But I should like to learn to understand everything in books, newspapers, and other writings, and to know about it all. I can't yet, although I listen attentively.
>
> *(Name, age 24.)*

And again :

> I read *The Two Camps* and understood nothing at first. But when I read it a second time I liked it. I read it lying down, and did not hear till afterwards that that is very bad. I read

238

books by artificial light : for when I read and the women are making a noise all round me, I can't make head or tail of it.

(Name, age 26.)

Some of the verbal answers, remarks, and observations of these women, moreover, are no less interesting, and occasionally even amusing. An example :
A woman asked for Tolstoy's *War and Peace*. When she brought it back she was asked : " Did you read it all through ? " " Oh, yes." " And did you understand it all ? " " What is there that I should not understand : as soon as it tells about a princess, she can't be delivered. But folks like us make nothing of it."
The titles of some of the courses given in the winter of 1931–2 show the lines on which the lectures are planned that are given to the inmates of this Moscow *prophylactorium*, which is by no means unique :
1. On Prehistoric Times. 2. On the Descent of Man. 3. What is Petty Bourgeois, etc. ? Similar in tendency are the conducted visits to the Darwin Museum, to the Planetarium, to the Revolutionary Museum before the anniversary of the October revolution, to the Lenin Museum, and so on.
It is also worth noting that of the 200 women in the above-mentioned Moscow *prophylactorium* in the winter of 1931–2 (who pay a small part of what they earn by knitting stockings and making underclothes each month for board and lodging, and can spend the rest on themselves) there were thirty illiterates with whom it was pretty difficult to work, and sixty semi-literates. All the rest, that is the majority, formed a group of the most energetic women, the most eager to learn, and most consciously thoughtful, who either wished to continue their education in various courses or had already begun to do so. Thus seven women were being trained for the public health service, a few wanted to devote themselves to building motor roads, others again wanted to work for the consumers' co-operatives, and one was already studying medicine. All these ambitions are warmly furthered and encouraged by the staffs of the *prophylactoria*. In general

I must emphasize the fact that the understanding and friendly comradeship with which—I may say without exception—the heads of this and similar institutions in Soviet Russia—doctors, principals, etc., down to the militia women on duty there, whose task is in very truth no easy one—approach the inmates is above all praise and deserves our unqualified admiration.

Many of the pupils of the Moscow *prophylactorium* show particular talents, and these, too, are always encouraged : one plays the 'cello well (a trio is arranged specially), another is picked out for the " dramatic college ", and two more are given to writing poetry, of which I will quote an example :

> By the calm moonlight
> In the month of May
> The brothel where I lay
> Was raided and I was taken that night.
> The cold prison once more,
> Witnesses, questions galore ;
> Mean questions and brutal they are
> When a prostitute stands at the bar.
> Five years in a prison cell
> From my young life men stole ;
> They took a heavy toll,
> Those years of unforgotten hell.
> But now it is past like a dream,
> I am that country's daughter now
> Where the people's will is supreme
> And their power with the years will grow.
> The country that is true freedom's home,
> Where to bourgeois tyranny none need bow.
> That country's daughter where this fifteen year
> The workers' songs of triumph you hear.
> No other land, we say,
> Like this is to be found,
> The past is swept away,
> Of it we hear no sound.
> I am the workers' child by right,
> Daughter of peasants and of the Soviet State ;
> Workers of all the world unite,
> The Red Flag shows the way to victory straight.

In this whole educational system—which has hitherto really known nothing of the theory of individual psychology

—a very important part is played by the raising of self-confidence, a result of the newly formed habits and the whole milieu, in creatures who, in bourgeois countries, are saturated with the feeling of their inferiority. By all kinds of special rewards, by the distribution of special honours, in particular cases by festivals designed to spur efforts—in short, by ever-changing means—ambition and zeal and the love of knowledge in the women are so kindled that it becomes necessary positively to check the rush, until the desire to be included and mentioned has turned into genuine interest. Whatever they do, they do with passionate eagerness, whether it is acting or getting up concerts, being photographed, or trying to convert their companions.

And just as all the *prophylactoria* in the Soviet Union are sponsored culturally by other institutions, so each particular *prophylactorium* is made sponsor to some community : the great Moscow *prophylactorium* is sponsor to a collective farm near Moscow. Every now and then, therefore, groups of considerable size visit the *kolkhos* under their care with their own orchestra of wind instruments, their own dramatic performances, lectures, etc. The doctors who accompany them hold courses of lectures, all are welcomed and made much of, and if need be they help with the work ; and thus the " new path to life " grows ever more tangible and gives promise of a new future, a to-morrow that has yet begun with to-day.

That is what life is like in a Soviet Russian *prophylactorium*.

In the summer of 1931 I also had an opportunity to visit a sanatorium for venereally diseased women in the neighbourhood of Vienna ; here, too, the programme included the notions of " occupational therapy and welfare " and, as is stated, the institution is " not only described by foreign specialists and deputations as different from anything that they had seen before, but was actually recommended as an example to be imitated by the Hygiene Committee of the League of Nations ".

A comparison was very instructive, and at the first

glance, seen purely externally, it was hardly favourable to Moscow. For there the premises were generally old and ill adapted to the purpose ; the space was very, nay excessively, inadequate, and sometimes there was not the smallest comfort, whilst in Vienna there was a group of well-adapted magnificent buildings all surrounded by beautiful shady gardens and so many offices that you feel as if you were on a perfectly managed feudal estate instead of in a home for " fallen " girls.

From outside I could cast a glance into the roomy, perfectly designed kitchen, where dinner was just being prepared : such dishes of vegetables and tasty puddings are not served to you in Moscow anywhere in a whole year.

But as soon as you enter the institution, which is otherwise a model of equipment, you notice another kind of difference : in the Soviet Russian homes the walls greet you with strips of mottoes in gay confusion, instructive and full of meaning, with portraits of Lenin in his childhood and of other leaders ; on the tables you often see flowers, photographs, and gay ornaments, and, in spite of all simplicity, the whole atmosphere radiates happiness, snugness, and confidence ; whereas in Vienna the place is dominated by a symbolism remote from life in all its solemnity and severity. A crucifix commands the room, and you are received by pious sisters who make you feel at once how great a gulf must lie between them and the " sinners ".

And then the aspect of those " sinners " ! Nowhere is there a trace of that eager directness, of the wholesome gaiety animating their faces, which greets you in all Soviet Russian institutions of the kind and helps you to overlook all shortcomings. Here there are about 300 poor creatures hunted through life, scared, frightened, harried—here, too, by far the greater number are recruited from domestic servants—with restless, flickering glance, or already partially dulled. They are divided into three groups : one for juveniles and one for non-juveniles, that is " secret prostitutes " who have been arrested in police raids and found to be diseased or suspected of disease when examined by the police doctor. The third group consists of women placed under the control of the moral police and consequently regarded as irretrievably lost, and these are not even allowed to come in contact with the others. Each of these main divisions falls into two sub-divisions according to the disease from which the woman is suffering, and each sub-division into several groups of two to three dozen beds : " in order to separate the inmates in accordance with their moral qualities ".

In this home the patients receive the best of care, like that in a first-class sanatorium. For purposes of entertainment and pleasure there are " four entirely separate gardens, a theatre, and a library ". There are two large workshops to provide employment. Here, too, the women choose their own employment freely in accordance with their training and capacities, and, in order that the patients may receive practical benefit from labour as well as educational therapy, all work is paid on principle (to the amount of 75 per cent), so that they have the chance of saving money while they are in the home which will at least protect them from extreme distress for a short time after their discharge.

We see, therefore, there are here a considerable number of prerequisites for an educational influence upon " moral derelicts ", whereby, it is stated, in most cases it is actually possible " to call forth good resolutions and arouse the desire to abandon prostitution ".

But since, as the proverb has it, " the road to hell is paved with good resolutions," the question naturally arises whether the community does anything to translate these " resolutions " and " desires " into fact. And that brings us to the weak point of this model institution, which proves to be an idea not thought out to the end, a half measure, a still-born child, in a democratic society which is in fact a pseudo-democracy where women are in a far worse position than men economically, legally, socially, and legislatively—in short, in every respect— where abortion laws are still in force to which a hundred thousand women are sacrificed annually, and where the state wages war on prostitutes but not on prostitution.

For, as appears from a medical article about this sanatorium, the women stay there only as long as is necessary to cure them : " Their stay is never prolonged for welfare or similar reasons." And the article continues : " A stay of only several weeks in the institution is proved by experience, even in the case of juveniles, for whom after-care is obligatory (for adults it is voluntary) to be far too short." For a woman discharged from this institution as " cured ", but outcast from society and left workless even before the world crisis because she is unaccustomed to work and helpless, without any stay, any guidance, surrounded instead by the lures of a large city— for such a woman what remains then, but to return to the streets in spite of all her " good resolutions " ?

AT THE FIRST CONFERENCE OF FORMER PROSTITUTES, NOW WORKERS

LET me quote another example to show how far the success of the war on prostitution in Soviet Russia has gone and how new, newly awakened human beings, creative forces, constantly rise from the prostitutes' ranks, if only the requisite conditions are offered by means of unified organization ; I mean an undertaking which is little known even among the Soviet Russian public, because those who initiated it were far too modest and regarded it as something to be taken for granted.

When after several years the Moscow *prophylactoria* were in a position to look back upon a considerable number of discharged women who might be regarded as completely cured, of whom 1,127 were pursuing the most various trades and professions with success by 1932, several persons in leading positions decided to summon a conference of former workers in the Moscow *prophylactoria*, now in employment, in order to exchange ideas and experiences, to make reasonable wishes and complaints known, and to receive new suggestions.

Contrary to the usual custom on such occasions, when invitations are sent wholesale and therefore openly, they were sent this time in sealed envelopes, privately, addressed to the person in question by name, and in some cases the management was asked, also privately, to give the woman in question leave of absence for the particular purpose ; for in each factory only individual women were concerned.

On the afternoon of October 31st, 1931—out of doors the wind howled and the rain poured down as if there were to be another Flood—things looked festive in the fair-sized hall of the United Curative and Labour *Prophylactorium* for Women at No. 2 Myeshchanskaya (Petty Bourgeois Street, now renamed Grashdanskaya, Citizen Street). Long before the hour when the conference opened all the seats were occupied and endless queues were forming in the passages. But still crowds of fairly young, no longer young, and very young women were gathering and demanding admittance, disputing excitedly with the others in the high-pitched voices which are usual with Russian women on such occasions. There were also a few tall men with beard and moustache among the crowd ; as I heard afterwards, the registered husbands of the conference members who sat beside them.

A number of other women attracted notice by the enormous trumpets, polished bright, shimmering yellow and silver, that they were just tuning (a kettle-drum among them was especially noticeable) ; these were members of the brass band. And amongst the crowd one caught sight of bright scarlet specks : many a clever, intelligent face framed in a becoming red cap, the sign of a *komssomolka*. All round on the walls there were, of course, plenty of red strips bearing mottoes, all kinds of propaganda posters, and portraits of Lenin and Stalin ; whilst at the front of the stage, for the hall was also used for dramatic performances, a bust of Lenin more than life-size was placed before the red-covered chairman's table, and surrounded with red banners embroidered in gold, Soviet stars, and the hammer and sickle. And so the total impression, oral and ocular, which is always presented to the spectator on such occasions in Soviet Russia, was complete : colourful, gay, winning, and popular. Only the little children, otherwise never absent, had been left at home this time.

Almost 150 former prostitutes—in prerevolutionary Russia and to this day in all bourgeois countries the poorest of the poor, exposed irretrievably to certain ruin, to the profoundest misery and shame—had gathered in this their first conference : born anew, erect, workers, knowing exactly their place in the labour and life of the community, inspired by a new class consciousness, a social ardour in the performance of their duty, so that many of them had already rendered great services as *udarnitsa*, storm workers. Half a dozen of these *udarnitsas*, who had not infrequently won distinctions, were appointed on the committee, where they joined the representatives of the Moscow Soviet. The secretary of the party cell in the *prophylactorium* took the chair, and I, as a guest, was given a place on the platform.

A bell was rung and silence fell in the hall. After a short address of welcome by the chairman 300 eager eyes were fixed on Ssyemyon Markovich, the head doctor of the Moscow *prophylactoria*, Dr. Danishevskyi, who be-haves with marvellous tact and consideration towards these women, whom they trust and love entirely, and who now presented a report on the experience gathered in the course of years of after-care for the former inmates of the *prophylactoria*, now in employment.

The women tried to follow with attention, but as most of them lacked the power of concentration they showed frequent restlessness as he explained simply and clearly the material collected by the after-care sisters who are responsible for keeping watch on the discharged pupils of the *prophylactoria*. He divided the women into two groups. One comprised 87 women in employment, with 42 storm workers, 36 women who had undertaken some social work, 3 who had already been admitted to the party, and 6 in the *Komssomol* : these he called the " satisfactory " group. In the other, larger and " less satisfactory ", there were, indeed, also 43 per cent storm workers and 1 *komssomolka*, but only a small percentage were attending classes and some of them were given to drink.

Of 178 working women cited there were 139 " disci-

plined " ones, who had accepted an established order, and
10 per cent " undisciplined " ; 21 per cent earned up to
60 roubles a month, but the majority earned up to
80 roubles, and there were some who earned over 100
roubles a month. Only 138 of them were attending
classes (too small a percentage), 12 had left the factory
voluntarily, and 4 had to be dismissed for theft. Seventy
per cent of the women under consideration were about
twenty-five.

The conduct of some of the women workers, who
behaved well enough in the factory, was far from satisfactory at home ; they often held drinking bouts and took
presents from men. Without mentioning names, the
lecturer quoted a few specially bad cases. But this
exceedingly undesirable state of affairs, which must not be
allowed to spread, was mainly due to the utterly inadequate " collective " dwellings which often led to quarrels
and produced an atmosphere of irritation ; and it was to
be hoped that as *shilstroityelystvo* (house-building) proceeded they would be overcome.

Generally speaking, Dr. Danishevskyi continued, it
was nevertheless possible to say that the results already
attained exceeded all expectations, and that the shortcomings of the " less satisfactory " group would likewise
soon be overcome with goodwill, if good examples were
followed. Again without mentioning names, he selected
certain cases from the case papers before him. He then
pointed to the good number of storm workers, *komssomolkas*, and members admitted to the party, and to the
fact that besides some inevitable cases of women who were
dissatisfied with their new work, there were a great
number who were thoroughly satisfied and who, when
asked how they were getting on, had only one answer :
" Like a fish in water ! " He ended with the intimation
that a legal advisory centre had just been attached to the
prophylactorium and was always at the disposal of the
women.

The " discussion " which followed, and was, of course,
far less organized and objective than in other Soviet
Russian mass meetings, whether of women or otherwise,

took a very lively course, and was extremely personal in character.

First several women sent up their names who expressed indignation that there were working women who stole in the factories, behaved ill at home, and in addition were drinkers. " . . . The story that Dr. Danishevskyi has told," an exceedingly fiery *komssomolka*, wearing a little red cap on her energetic head, thundered out into the hall, " is very sad and most regrettable. It is a scandal that workers should thieve in the factory and they must be publicly stigmatized ! We women workers who enter the factory must do more than the others, we must prove our worth . . . we must become *udarnitsas* and undertake social duties ! "

It was mainly two questions that stirred the women to fever heat : the problem that affected them so deeply of dwelling-space, which called forth interruptions on all sides every time that it was mentioned : " I have no shelter still. When shall I get a room ? " And an *udarnitsa*, a candidate for admission to the party who earned 95 roubles a month and had been living for two years in much too small a room with seven other women, raised the complaint : " Why don't I get a room ? Because I say nothing ! And if I ask, they say : ' You're a candidate for admission to the party, what do you want with a room as well ? ' "

The second question that was discussed with passionate impetuosity, like everything else here, was whether one ought to conceal the knowledge in the factory that one had come from the *prophylactorium*.

Whilst reading his report Dr. Danishevskyi had touched upon this question and stated that most women made a secret of the fact that they had come from the *prophylactorium*, but that it was by no means true that all there had been on the streets, for there were many destitute among them, many who had got into trouble because of housing shortage, and that the views about venereal disease inherited from a former period must be done away with.

A puny brunette of about twenty-five, with short hair,

who now sent up her name to speak, told of another woman who "destroyed the reputation of her colleagues". " She's always and everywhere calling the others' attention to our having come from the *prophylactorium*. I'm not afraid of it myself ; I work in the factory, am a candidate for admission to the party, do social work, and make no secret of the fact that I was in the *prophylactorium*. But it's disagreeable to have her telling it all over the place and calling people's attention to it." A blonde with her cap pulled down over her forehead added : " *Tovarishchi*, I am working in the Tenth Factory, I was sent there from the *prophylactorium*. It has been said that people hurt us when they remind us that we come from the *prophylactorium*. That is not true, *Tovarishchi*, we need not be ashamed of it, only we ought to do more social work, because it is our duty to make ourselves better and to bear all the difficulties that come our way. On August 28th I was present at a *Tovarishcheskyi Ssud*, the proceedings of a comrades' court, and we all heard how the working woman was sentenced who had stolen material. . . . It is high time to have done with such things ; we must all become storm workers and remember what the *prophylactorium* has done for us. Long live the Soviet Government ! "

The above-mentioned *komssomolka* with the red *kossynka* of course gave her opinion on the subject with peculiar fervour : " . . . Once we have cast ourselves among the general mass of the workers, we must work in the proper spirit . . . and on no account conceal the fact that we were in the *prophylactorium*. For that is no shame. On the contrary, people pay far more attention to a working woman then, they take much more trouble on her behalf. And if she is insulted, there are plenty of party organizations to shut the mouths of those who pester the working women with unnecessary chatter. And you must not be afraid of your past. . . . Once we are discharged from the *prophylactorium*, we have settled accounts with the streets. I, too, came off the streets, but not a single workman in the factory has ever made me feel it, and I for my part do not make a secret of it.

Don't you make a secret of it either, *Tovarishchi* ; on the contrary, admit it frankly and you will be all the better treated, for people will say : she has suffered much. . . . And they will give you a *shilploshchady* all the sooner and generally show you more kindness. . . ."

After this speaker, who was much applauded, one of the husbands, a workman, sent up his name to speak. " No doubt it sometimes happens that people do not behave properly to the women in the factories. There have been such cases, and still are, but nobody has exposed them yet. If it happens again, however, just let us know ; we will come and point out what kind of an institution it is, and how we are struggling against destitution among women, and how we are abolishing the undesirable *byt*, the existence, the daily life, that we inherited from the war and from the Tsar. . . ."

The debate went on interminably, but the chairman spoke the last word ; he, too, was a workman, and likewise spoke words of encouragement to the women : ". . . Better conceal nothing, *Tovarishchi*, it is no disgrace, only a misfortune. . . . We all live in a proletarian state that the working class is building up ; the workers will understand you all right, and will come to your aid. . . ."

Meanwhile it was getting very late, and although a dramatic performance was on the programme and still to come—already one or two actors in costume were making their appearance behind the scenes—the customary resolution of the committee was unanimously passed asking me to tell the women assembled there something about the war against prostitution in bourgeois countries and especially in Vienna, whence I had come to Moscow.

The interest and attention of the audience were aroused once more. Everybody gathered closer together, the actors vanished into the darkness of the ante-rooms, the instruments already brought out to play the *Internationale* were set aside for the time being. I got up and gave the women a brief description of the difference, which is obvious to any objective, unprejudiced observer, stressed the medical and hygienic and other equipment, the advantages in the curative and labour institution near Vienna, but also pointed out how useless the whole work was that it accomplished in comparison with only a fraction of the achievements of the Soviet Russian *prophylactoria*, and closed with the wish that at the next conference I might find only a single group of working women, " satisfactory " through and through and in every respect.

After my speech I was surrounded by the women and flooded with all manner of possible and impossible questions : how many women were there in the Viennese *prophylactorium*, was it as difficult there to get an order for shoes, what were the conditions as regards *shilploshchady*, what was the percentage of illiterates and storm workers, what kind of a " co-operative " was it where I bought the stuff for my coat, was the " Paris Commune " anywhere near the Viennese, and so on. One woman handed me a letter, asking me to take good note of the contents :

. . . I can't keep silent. I must go on telling people how much the Soviet Government has done for us sick and destitute women. We come straight from the streets into well-warmed, light rooms, we receive medical treatment, and without having to stand in a queue we get ready cooked food.

When the cure is finished we are placed in factories and workshops as citizens with equal rights and accustomed to work. And then you might think the *prophylactorium* would trouble no more about us. But that is not the case. Many working women are found shelter when they are placed in factories. It is true that not all can be satisfied while our housing shortage is so serious. Still, the administration and our doctors do all they can.

Of myself I can only say : for seven months after I had entered the factory I stayed in the Home. Then I found a room. But I needed an official certificate and pressure from the administration. They were indefatigable in doing everything for me, and I secured my room. And am I the only one ? Not a bit of it !

And so I am grateful to the *prophylactorium*, the doctors, and the directors for their goodness to us. It really is very difficult to work with us. I, too, was impudent and undisciplined and gave myself and the whole staff plenty of nerve torment. But now I have entered a working life, I have my room—and I have to thank the *prophylactorium* for it all. Hereby I contribute forty roubles for a bond in the " Second Industrialization Loan " on behalf of the destitute.

Finally this resolution was proposed, not by the committee, but by the women themselves, and passed unanimously : " We instruct *Tovarishch* Halle to communicate our heartfelt sympathy and fraternal greetings to all destitute women living in Vienna whom the hard times have reduced to distress."

On March 10th, 1932, another conference of women workers in the Moscow *prophylactorium* was held, but this time I was not present. The head of the educational section of the *prophylactorium* wrote to me :

There was little trace in the second conference of the reserve and hesitation that still prevailed at the first. The members spoke in support of their opinions with remarkable clarity and assurance. Personal and material interests were less prominent than the general good, and hardly anything was heard of the eternal complaints about bad housing conditions. . . . This time, too, the speakers nearly all stressed the fact that the *prophylactoria* enriched the working family of the Soviet with persons of energy and ability, and that among the former inmates there were storm workers, " brigadiers ", chairwomen of occupational committees, and party members. . . .

The letter goes on :

The urge of the working women to take part in the cultural life of the Soviet Union increases daily. The time is long past when we had to resort to persuasion or wiles to incite the women, especially those who came straight from the streets, to educate themselves. It seems, therefore, that the whole life of the Soviet Union is a stimulus to study. I believe that in our circle of women of arrested development one of the most important functions of re-education must be to rouse the desire for culture. For as soon as a desire is felt to acquire knowledge it gradually grows to a passionate eagerness for learning. . . . When the storm workers and a few other women from the *prophylactorium* recently went on an expedition to the *Dnye-prostroy* in order to learn about the constructive work and activities of the *prophylactoria* in other towns, I had the opportunity of observing with satisfaction that my pupils had gained considerably in receptive capacity and interest in political, cultural, and economic questions. . . .

THE FINAL GOAL

AND now let us proceed to the last question, which some readers have perhaps asked themselves first of all : is there any serious prospect of abolishing prostitution in Soviet Russia at an early date ?   Let me attempt, with the help of certain facts and figures, to throw rather more light on that question.   Since there is no kind of system of supervision in Soviet Russia, no regulation, it must be admitted that it is somewhat difficult to estimate the number of prostitutes still remaining.   But without doubt the number is immensely reduced in comparison with that of pre-revolutionary Russia, and is being further reduced daily.   A census of prostitutes on the streets carried out by the Moscow Venereal Dispensaries (Vendispensaries) in collaboration with their " Commission for the Betterment of Labour and the Standard of Living " in 1928 in Moscow, with the aid of Workers' Brigades, showed that there were some 3,000 prostitutes, whilst they were estimated at 40,000 in St. Petersburg in 1913, as I have already stated, and at about 20,000 in Moscow.   Professor Bronner reaches the same conclusion indirectly, basing his estimate on the number of venereally diseased who were infected through prostitution, the chief source of the disease.   Thus it was ascertained of the urban population of Russia, for instance, that in 1914 56·9 per cent of all infectious venereal cases amongst men were solely due to prostitution.   But in the course of the four years from 1922 to 1925, according to the Vendispensaries, the percentage had fallen to 31·7 per cent for Moscow and for the frontier towns to 26 per cent.   Moreover, according to a statement of the First Moscow Vendispensary, the percentage of those who came there for treatment who had been infected by prostitutes was 19 in 1924, but in 1930 only 9·8.

Bronner records an even greater reduction in the number of cases of infection in the small towns of the frontier provinces : thus in Barnaul, in Western Siberia, where all the cases of venereal disease in the place received treatment in the one local vendispensary, there were still eighty-two persons infected by prostitutes in 1926, in 1928 thirteen, in 1929 only nine in all. Equally eloquent are the following figures of the First Moscow Vendispensary : of the students treated in 1924 at the age of twenty 21·6 per cent had resort to prostitution, whilst in 1930 it was only 2·8 per cent. In this connection, however, we must take into account that simultaneously with the diminution of prostitution in recent years there has been a change in the social composition of the student body ; young proletarians and peasants resort far less to prostitution than the young people of other social sections of the population, as a number of written questionnaires have shown.

The diminished number of cases of infection due to prostitution in the years 1929–30 tallies with the facts revealed in the 1931 census of street prostitutes in Moscow : it was found that there were exactly 400 prostitutes as compared with more than 3,000 in 1928. In Tula in the two years from 1928 to 1930 the number of prostitutes fell from 500 to 24.

Further, the statistics of the curative and labour *prophylactoria* support the view that prostitution is gradually disappearing ; in earlier years they were hardly able to deal with the numbers calling for their services, but since 1930 matters have progressed so far that of the five *prophylactoria* in Moscow four have recently been closed. Quite recently steps have been taken to carry out a project for a single combined *prophylactorium*, transformed into a " Curative and Labour Institute ", to be housed in a building specially erected for the purpose, where the work is not only to be extended but also carried on by totally new methods.

If we examine the reasons for the great reduction in

prostitution, just in the last year or so, it may doubtless be attributed first and foremost to the reduction of unemployment—and since 1930 its total disappearance—for it is assuredly unemployment that most frequently provides the motive driving a woman into prostitution. And now we find that both the inquiries conducted by the vendispensaries and the material collected by the militia point to the significant fact that, in spite of hundreds of thousands of unemployed women in previous years, only a very small percentage fell victims to prostitution, and those mainly untrained women out of touch with proletarian circles, so that to-day we cannot regard unemployment alone as a sufficient cause of prostitution. This fact is likewise confirmed by a much-debated anonymous inquiry by the vendispensary in the city of Kursk. This questionnaire was circulated in 1923 among unemployed women at the Labour Exchange there.

Bronner states that a thousand questionnaires were circulated and that they contained two questions, one as to the period of unemployment, the second whether prostitution was practised ; three-quarters were returned filled in, and they presented a most instructive picture. Eleven per cent of the unemployed women had never worked, whilst all the rest had been without employment for a considerable time : 27 per cent about six months, 19 per cent from six months to a year, 27 per cent from one to two years, and 16 per cent for more than two years. The second question, whether they practised prostitution, was answered by the vast majority with a simple " no ". Thirty answers said : " Not at present, but I can't be sure about the future." One woman wrote that she was beginning to think of it ; twenty-six others repudiated the possibility with horror : " I'd rather put a bullet through my head." " I'd rather starve." One woman said : " If I were capable of thinking of prostitution, I shouldn't have been a year and half on the books of the Labour Exchange." Another : " The Labour Exchange is no place for women who offer their bodies for sale." And, finally, one wrote : " There is no room for prostitution in a free country." Only fourteen or fifteen women felt themselves on the threshold of prostitution.

This inquiry, therefore, which is now nearly a decade past, points to the same conclusion as Professor Bronner's statement in the same article (" Once More the Question of the War against Prostitution ") that among several thousand unemployed female members of trade unions in the Kuban Black Sea district who were questioned in the same year, hardly one had been involved in prostitution : that is to say, even at that time the inclusion of the working woman in the trade union family and the growing class consciousness were exceedingly strong influences in the struggle against prostitution.

Since that time Soviet Russia, and especially Soviet Russian women, have advanced far. To give one example only : whereas on October 1st, 1923, there were only 2,394,000 employed women in the whole Soviet Union, their number subsequently rose to six million, and in 1932 a further million and a half women found employment in the factories, of which more elsewhere.

The inclusion of these masses of women in the economic and so also the social and political life of the country has been of immense educational value in other respects ; it means that they " re-qualify " ; unskilled housewives are trained afresh in factories to workers proud of their occupation ; it means also that they are made economically and legally the equals of men, so that they become active collaborators in the whole reconstruction of the national life. In the towns that alone amounts to a good *prophylactorium*, a barrier against prostitution.

Similar in its prophylactic influence is, of course, the increasing inclusion of women in the villages in the socialist organizations—in the *sovkhosi* or state farms and *kolkhosi* or collective farms. Indeed, the whole of Soviet Russian legislation as it affects women aims at destroying the foundations of prostitution systematically. That object is promoted by the far-reaching protection of women's labour, the prohibition to discharge single women with children, the equal treatment of illegitimate children, the legalization of abortion, and, in addition, countless institutions for the protection of mothers and children, homes for destitute and solitary women and mothers, women's advisory centres, and so on.

All these conditions, then, have produced an un-exampled cultural advance among women in Soviet Russia. And co-education in the schools, systematic training as workers, comradeship and social responsibility, together with the new sex code, produce, as we have seen, such a totally different type of youth, such wholly new relations between the sexes, that they, too, help to do away with the evil of prostitution. As soon as the demand ceases for venal love, which the new ethical code stigmatizes as vile, the supply vanishes.

In order that these preventive activities in the war against prostitution may be carried on the more inten-sively they are made to assume cultural and educational forms, series of lectures and debates in the clubs, the trade unions, the youth organizations, and the Red Army divisions, etc., with prostitution always as the central theme, how shameful and intolerable it is in a republic of workers. I must also mention the " social guardian-ship " which has been established for years, which includes among other things the duty of keeping watch over solitary and inexperienced women at the stations who have come from the provinces or the country, and seeing that they are cared for, find shelter, or perhaps are sent back home ; this work is valuable in its prophylactic effects, especially since the present increased demand for workers promotes the same object.

Recently the supervision of suspicious resorts was entrusted to the guardian sisters. The general public is likewise enlisted in the war against prostitution and venereal diseases : voluntary workers' brigades inspect the night shelters for women and unemployed domestic servants, tenements, and public lavatories, in short all the dark corners in which the so-called *podsabornaya*, street-corner prostitution, carries on its evil existence, and which are known to be the chief sources of venereal disease. These brigades often even undertake night duty in such places, so that they are in a sense under public control.

Further, legislative measures are being prepared to combat this variety of prostitution, which is closely connected with the housing shortage.

Moreover, since it was regarded as a weakness in the direct attack on prostitution through the *prophylactoria* that the women had to be already diseased before they could be admitted, steps have now been taken to establish *prophylactoria* for healthy women who are on the verge of prostitution. In general, prostitutes are divided into two groups at the present stage in the war on prostitution. The first consists of the so-called " parasitic " elements, formerly described as " labour deserters ", who do not feel able to do without a certain degree of luxury. The second consists of women with unhealthy minds. In so far as it is possible still to speak of remnants of prostitution in Soviet Russia (the number of girls on the streets in Moscow is now estimated at 700 at most), they are found almost exclusively in the luxurious hotels for foreigners. It is noteworthy that the idea seems to prevail in Russian circles that foreigners from capitalist countries cannot live without venal love. Nevertheless, serious steps have recently been taken in this matter too. New laws are to be introduced providing for compulsory labour or treatment in closed establishments for the remaining prostitutes, according as to whether they belong to the first or second groups. In this way the law secures the power of intervening where it is a question not of diseased but of work-shy or abnormal persons. For the rest, the view is held that prostitution is already disposed of in the Soviet Union and it is significant that the Russians, who really cannot in general be accused of unwillingness to enter into discussion, have hardly any interest for discussions on general questions about prostitution.

On the other hand there is a growing appeal to combat one of the saddest types of prostitution, that of children and juveniles, a matter that is closely bound up with the troubled problem of the *besprisorniye*, the destitute children. I will not discuss that problem fully here, especially as it is held to be almost solved ; not long ago it was still a burning question, much debated both as to its nature and the methods to be adopted for its solution, and presented pictorially in the film *On the Threshold of Life*. There are a number of institutions all over the Union whose aim it is to combat this prostitution of juveniles : the Society of Children's Friends, the Children's Commission of the V.T.S.I.K. (the All-Russian Central Executive Committee), and a network of children's homes, besides various educational institutions for juvenile prostitutes who are difficult to train. These institutions work on the same principles as the *prophylactoria* for adult prostitutes or the homes for destitute boys, but their scheme of work is greatly restricted by the age limit beyond which they do not keep girls. For the rest, " child prostitution " is naturally chiefly to be found in the capitals—in Moscow far more than in Leningrad— and that facilitates the work of combating it.

In this connection, indeed in connection with the whole problem of a radical attack on prostitution, those who are well acquainted with the whole question call with increasing urgency for an attack upon the demand. A new law now under consideration makes the consumer of prostitution liable to a considerable fine, and under certain circumstances to imprisonment, and not merely to moral reprobation, as was the case in the " Judicial Proceedings concerning a Prostitute " ; he is regarded as the protagonist of an anti-social view of women and as one who is capable of exploiting their defenceless position.

" Without abolishing the demand the abolition of prostitution is unthinkable ; they are two parts of a whole " ; " Prostitution degrades woman, the demand for it degrades man " ; " There is no excuse for the consumer of prostitution "—these are the latest mottoes. This particular problem is more and more frequently debated in public discussions, in meetings of working men and women, and brought before the young people through educational activities. A similar attitude is already to be seen in the appeal issued by the Central Soviet for Combating Prostitution to its branch organizations in the summer of 1928 :

THE ABOLITION OF PROSTITUTION

In a workers' state which bases the reconstruction of life upon the repudiation of every form of exploitation, we still find such exploitation in its most negative form : the exploitation of the human body. Such exploiters deserve to be publicly exposed. . . . Practical experience has shown how useful it is to raise this question in meetings of workers and students and to pass appropriate resolutions. The names of those who violate these regulations must be published in the wall newspapers. The names of those consumers of prostitution who are found when centres of vice are raided must be published in the local newspapers.

Professional organizations are enlisted in the war against the *potrebityely*, the customer of prostitution, and the Central Committee of the Communist party uses its influence over party members for the same purpose, accusing the client of prostitution of unproletarian conduct. All the measures adopted against the *potrebityely* are to be applied within the framework of the cultural Five Years' Plan.

Since people have been considering the problem of the clientèle of prostitution, the question of its composition has naturally arisen. In view of the free and easy relations between the sexes which prevails in the Union, it is not immediately manifest to what circles the men belong who still resort to prostitution, with the exception of foreigners and travellers. At any rate they include a considerable number of men who have come from the provinces, have not much to do, want to try their fortune in the city, and have not yet made friends. Likewise the connection between alcohol and prostitution, which exists everywhere, is of especial importance in Russia, where the people have been addicted to alcoholic drink for centuries, and this creates considerable difficulty in the work of the *prophylactoria*.

The war on the centres of vice, which have greatly decreased in number both in the principal cities and in the provinces, is being continued vigorously. Several were suppressed as late as 1931. Those which are set up anew do not survive long, a few months at most, for the housing shortage in the large towns means that there are always neighbours who inform the police. The family Turkish baths, so popular in pre-revolutionary Russia, where prostitution flourished, have been closed on that account. No less successful is the struggle against procuring, which, as we know, renders the culprit liable, under Clause 171, to imprisonment for not less than three years and total or partial confiscation of his property. A procurer, known in Russian as *kot* (tom-cat)—perhaps referring to the proverb about the cat prowling round the hot broth—is sent to administrative exile.

It cannot be denied that there are various difficulties and obstacles which obstruct the abolition of prostitution, besides those already mentioned, but they are of a more or less general nature. For instance, there is prostitution carried on as a part-time occupation, which has recently spread ; this means that the favour of a working woman or employee can be bought for a pair of stockings or shoes or a theatre ticket, thanks chiefly to the present shortage of clothing. The numerous foreign specialists now employed in the Soviet Union, whose influence on prostitution I have already mentioned, contribute their full measure of guilt for this form of feminine venality. Unquestionably some of the foreigners who are entering the Union in large numbers from all parts of the world have a demoralizing influence in this respect. Some say that one of the first words they learn is *spaty*, to sleep in a special sense. The mere attraction of novelty makes them irresistible to a certain number of women of weak character. But not infrequently serious unions result. Prostitution as a part-time occupation is combated by raising the cultural level of women in general, but in particular by propaganda among working women, who are made to realize that this method of adding to one's earnings is contemptible.

Far more serious, because it cannot be so speedily remedied, although much is being done to cure it, is another evil, the evil of all evils : the shortage of *shil-ploshchady*, of housing space, which, as we have already seen, was the subject of bitter complaints by the members of the first conference of former workers in the *prophy-lactoria* as one of the sorest troubles in women's lives, and not infrequently as the sole cause of their relapse. The perpetual consequences almost amount to a menace. The few remaining prostitutes, unless they are members of a more well-to-do class who have a house of their own and a definite clientèle that pays well, are obliged in nine cases out of ten to carry on their " labour " in the boulevards, in railway carriages or trucks, in dark corners of the stations, and in the entrances to better-class houses which they call *paradniki* in their jargon, latterly even in taxis, literally, therefore, on the streets, which are their sole shelter because they have no abode. But it must be understood that these are the remnants of prostitution and conditions due less to the nature of things than to the prevailing housing shortage.

Taking it all in all, therefore, it may be said that it will certainly be some little time before the various measures, preventive and direct, adopted in the war on prostitution succeed in exterminating it altogether. But the greater part of the road to that final goal has already been covered, as every objective observer must admit. Prostitution in Soviet Russia already presents a totally different aspect, and its final abolition, which is part of the programme for the realization of socialism, is no longer Utopian, but belongs to the immediate future.

CASE PAPER

for the Pupils of the Moscow Curative and Labour *Prophylactorium*, People's Commissariat of Public Health.

1. Family name, Christian name, Patronymic ?
2. Age ?
3. Are the parents living ? Father ? Mother ? Orphan ?
4. When did the father, the mother die, and of what ?
5. What education has she had ? At home ? In some other family ? To what age ?
6. Did she grow up in a peasant family ? A worker's family ? A civil servant's, tradesman's, industrialist's, handicraftsman's, or intelligentsia family ?
7. Place of birth : Government, town, county, parish, village ?
8. How long has she been in Moscow ?
9. From what part did she come to Moscow ?
10. Address in Moscow before she entered the *Prophylactorium* ?

11. Living conditions before she entered the *Prophylactorium*: a dwelling of several rooms ? How large the superficial area ? If a single room, how large ? A corner of a room ? A bed ? Did she spend the nights at the night shelter ? Had she no shelter ? If a room of her own, had she a bed to herself, or shared with someone else ? Is the room light, dry, warm, damp, dark, cold, in a cellar ? Has it electric light ? Or oil lamps, or nothing ?

12. Education : when did she first begin lessons ? How long did her education continue ? Is she illiterate ? Can she read or write, or read and write ? Has she attended a secondary school, or a university ? Did she pass the leaving examination ?

13. Has she learned a trade ? What ?

14. What was her occupation before the revolution ? Was she a working woman, a staff employee, or a student ? Did she live with her parents ? With her husband ?

15. After the October revolution, or during the period preceding her adoption of prostitution, was she a working woman, a staff employee, a student ? Did she live with her parents, with friends, with her husband ? Was she unemployed ? How long ? Had she registered at the Labour Exchange ? Is she a member of a trade union ? Which ?

16. Family situation : Spinster, married, divorced, widow ? Does she live with her husband, has she a lover, does she live alone ?

17. When did she become independent ?

18. On what is she living at present ? From her earnings in the *Prophylactorium* ? From relief ? Given by whom ?

19. Are there convictions against her ? For what offence ?

20. At what age did she commit the offence ? Where did she undergo the penalty ? Was it imprisonment ? For how many years, months ? How long is it since the penalty ? Years, months, weeks, days ?

Heredity Taints

Relatives : died of old age, alcohol, tuberculosis, syphilis, mental disease, and other causes.

1. Father.
2. Mother.
3. Brother.
4. Sister.
5. . . . .
6. . . . .

THE ABOLITION OF PROSTITUTION

CHILDHOOD

1. Did she wet her bed at the age of seven?
2. At a later age?
3. Was she a sleep-walker (somnambulist)?
4. At what age did she go to school?
5. How did she do at school: well, badly, medium?
6. Did she ever witness sexual intercourse as a child?
7. Did she see examples of prostitution as a child?

SEXUAL LIFE

1. When did she begin to menstruate?
2. At what intervals does menstruation occur?
3. Is menstruation vigorous, slight, medium? Is it accompanied by pain?
4. How many days does it continue?
5. At what age did she begin to experience the sex impulse?
6. Does she practise masturbation? How often?
7. At what age did she first have sexual intercourse? With whom? With her husband, her fiancé, an acquaintance, or a person she met by chance?
8. Did her first sexual intercourse cause violent emotion? Disgust?
9. How often does she have sexual intercourse at present?
10. How strong is the sexual impulse: augmented or weak?
11. Her attitude towards the sexual act: does it give her satisfaction, is she indifferent, or does she feel repulsion?
12. Is the sexual act preceded by taking cocaine, alcohol, or other intoxicants?
13. Has she a lover whom she maintains?
14. Does she practise types of perversion: Sapphism, Sadism, Masochism, and so forth?
15. Has she been pregnant? How often?
16. What did she do to check pregnancy?
17. If she has undergone operations for abortion, how often?
18. Has she children? How many? Where are they being brought up?
19. Did she love her children?
20. Does she want to have children? If not, why?
21. Is she fond of children in general?
22. Does she like attracting men?
23. When did she first prostitute herself? At what age? With whom? Was he her lover, employer, or a chance acquaintance? What was his social position: worker,

peasant, staff employee, soldier, student, in the navy?
Where?

24. Under what circumstances and for what reasons did she
resort to prostitution: unhappy love, sexual desire, in
consequence of trickery, procuring, force, hunger, unemployment, sickness, unmarried motherhood, distress, compulsion? In what condition: sober, drunk, drugged?
25. How often does she practise copulation: per day, week,
month?
26. With adults, juveniles, elderly persons?
27. Her attitude towards venal love: is she ashamed of her
occupation, is she indifferent, does she practise it without
emotion as a trade?
28. Has anyone else in her family practised prostitution?
Mother, sister, other relative?
29. How much does she receive each time? How much does
she earn per month?
30. Is prostitution her principal source of income, or subsidiary?
31. Has she infected anyone with venereal disease? How
often? Knowingly?
32. Is she herself afraid of the infection?

RELATION TO ALCOHOL AND INTOXICANTS

1. Does she take alcohol? At what age did she begin?
2. How often: daily, occasionally, continuously?
3. Does she get drunk? Is she easily intoxicated?
4. How does she behave when drunk: is she merry, sad, unconscious, quarrelsome, or does she go to sleep?
5. Does she misuse cocaine?
6. Does she smoke? When did she begin?

OTHER TASTES AND INTERESTS

1. Does she like fine clothes?
2. Does she like going to the theatre? To the cinema?
3. Does she like spending the nights in company? At
festivities?
4. Is she fond of reading? What kind of books?
5. Does she like sweet things?
6. On what does she chiefly spend her money?
7. Does she save or does she readily spend her money?
8. Does she dislike work in general? Does she dislike her
present occupation in the *Prophylactorium*?
9. Does she soon get tired of her surroundings? Does she
want frequent change?

THE ABOLITION OF PROSTITUTION

TEMPERAMENT

1. What is her prevailing mood : sad, gay, indifferent to everything ?
2. Does she live without anxiety or thought for the morrow (thoughtless) ?
3. Does she take life hardly ? Is she anxious about her health, about her material prosperity ? About her family ?
4. Is she attached to anyone : to relatives, friends ?
5. Does her mood easily change ?
6. Is she easily influenced by her situation ? Discouraged by failure ? Pleased at success ?
7. Is she sometimes out of humour for no reason ? With accesses of fear or malice ?
8. Is she fond of day-dreaming ?
9. Has she attempted suicide ?
10. Is she sensitive to other people's troubles ?
11. What is her attitude towards her fellow-creatures : hostile, indifferent ?
12. Has she helped anybody, materially or morally ?

VENEREAL AND WOMEN'S DISEASES

1. Has she been previously infected with syphilis, chancroid, or gonorrhœa ?
2. Has she had women's diseases ?

INTELLECTUAL CONDITION

1. Manner of capacity to express herself ?
2. Does she give the impression of a mentally retarded person ?

BEHAVIOUR

1. Is she affected, coquettish, does she strike attitudes ? Is she simple in her manner, clumsy or graceful in her movements ?

SOJOURN IN THE *PROPHYLACTORIUM*

1. How long has she been in the *prophylactorium* ?
2. In which workshop is she employed ?
3. Is she satisfied with the work, the rooms, the food ?
4. What complaints does she make about the *prophylactorium*, and what innovations does she think necessary ?
5. Can she live on what she earns in the *prophylactorium* ? If not, what resources has she in addition ?
6. What sort of a life does she want in the future ?

266

WOMAN TAKES POSSESSION OF HER NEW REALM

> Without the millions of women we cannot realize the dictatorship of the proletariat and constructive communism. We must, therefore, seek a way to them, we must search out and attempt many things in order to find it.
>
> —LENIN.

> The Soviet Union is the first state in the world in which the government authorities and the whole public is consciously working at the solution of the women's question. The liberation of women can only be the concern of the women themselves. Only then will they enjoy, with Faust, the supreme happiness of standing " on free soil with a free people ".
>
> —CLARA ZETKIN.

EVER since Lenin the social politicians of the new Russia have been reproaching the democracies in bourgeois countries with treating the women's question in a manner—torn away from the social complex of which it forms a part—that cannot lead to a solution. To solve a problem is to make an end of it, and woman, they say, can only be emancipated with all mankind, the women's question can only be solved and made an end of together with the social question. Without equal rights for all mankind, not only political but also social and economic, without a social revolution, the true equality of women is a mere figment of the imagination. The only country that has already been through its social revolution is also the only one where the women's question is really solved, because there emancipation has been realized, so that it no longer exists as a special problem. " There is no women's question with us," it is said. " But we have in our country problems such as that of women in the state administration, in literature and art, in industry, in the form of problems how we shall make the most rational use of the influx of new and vital forces created by the revolution." We will now try to gain a clear idea of the scope and nature of these facts.

First and foremost it must be stated that the equal rights of women in the Soviet Union have not remained a mere catchword, a means of agitation. Already there is no field in the social and political, the cultural and economic, life of the country, in which women are not working to the utmost of their power. The social revolution of the past fifteen years has placed the millions of women in the front ranks of the struggle for economic reconstruction and the cultural revolution of town and country, and for the new way of life. The tempestuous onward rush of history has created and is still creating ever new conditions which favour the complete liberation of women from " domestic slavery ", their enrolment among the leaders of the state and the country's intellectual life, their equality with men in the social process of production.

There are two factors which particularly strike us when we consider this process of growth, so significant not only for Russian history but for the whole history of mankind, two factors which cast a clear light upon it : the part played by Russian men in the liberation of women, and the price which women were able to pay, and are still paying daily, for that liberation, which was also self-liberation. I have already shown in a general way that Russian intellectuals have always regarded women as comrades, friends, and colleagues, and their cause—alike in life and literature—as their own. But what we must further bear in mind is that Russian women collaborating in the creation of a new era have, as a result of their whole historical development, a store of vigour, untapped energy, vitality, and delight in creative work which actually gives them a certain advantage over their male comrades in the struggle and has, perhaps, stamped the character of the present period in Russian history and determined its colour more than anything else. Doubtless psychological and ideological opposites come into conflict, especially in the country, in the villages, here more than in any other department of life. The law of inertia still proves its great strength and there are many prejudices to be overcome. But all these obstructions and complications are yielding more and more and are compensated by the boundless readiness for sacrifice and the eager determination, the pure, honest enthusiasm, with which the women are now devoting themselves to their new tasks ; in their ranks there is far less opportunism, far less self-interested conformity, than in those of the men. And nobody who now sees them at their work, at the many posts where the revolution has placed them, can still doubt that something unprecedented has been achieved in a short time, that here the world is actually being " created by human hands ", that its construction would be unthinkable without the concentrated drive of millions of women, and that women, with their far-reaching civilizing influence, must and will stamp this new world with a character of their own, and give it a new inspiration. This finds expression in the clear-cut statement, told me by Krupskaya, with which a large number of women unanimously answered the question how they liked work : " We don't want to live in idleness ! " And the finest thing which I myself heard from the lips of a proletarian woman official in Moscow in this connection, and should like to preface as a motto to the following observations on the part played by women in building up the life of Soviet Russia, was the phrase : " We are on fire ! "

IN THE STATE AND IN POLITICS

IF we want to have a true picture of the degree in which Soviet Russian women participate in the administration of the Soviet state, it is primarily important to know that gifted women have access even to the highest posts, and that the cook of yesterday may rule to-day, and in some cases is actually ruling. But of still greater, indeed of decisive importance, is the fact that genuine efforts are made in the Soviet Union to draw the mass of women into participation in political life and to rouse and foster interest in state affairs in all sections of the feminine population as well as among men. In accordance with the socialist ideal of merging the state ultimately in the community, the Soviet Russian state is constructed throughout so as to serve that ideal; it is like a pyramid, with the working citizens, regardless of sex, as its broad base.

The lowest plane in women's practical collaboration in administration and politics consists of the delegate meetings, dating back to 1919. The women delegates, who number more than a million to-day, are elected in towns and industrial centres by the women factory workers and in the country by the peasant women, so that on the average there is one special *delegatka* for every five to twenty-five factory workers, and one for not more than every fifty village women.

The activities of these delegates, which may be briefly described as educational, a road to social work, cover all fields of public life. For example, it is mainly thanks to their efforts that the Soviet state's provision for the protection of mothers and children is already known and taken advantage of in all sections of the population. The delegates also do good work, chiefly in the country, in establishing children's crèches, combating infant mortality, and improving sanitary conditions in town and country. They affiliate to various particular organizations, especially the Advisory Centres, and concern themselves with the welfare and troubles of their constituents, reporting to them from time to time in public meetings. Their activities have also great cultural and economic significance: they arrange classes, establish reading circles, combat both actual and political illiteracy, inebriacy, and all the prejudices of an outworn manner of life, amongst which they count religious beliefs, incite the zeal of the mass of women for social work, and so prepare the way to the new *byt*. Especially in the Soviet East these women have carried out work among the national minorities of marked historical significance.

In all the industrial areas the women delegates promote increased production by means of rationalization and competitions and vigorous *ssamokritika*, self-criticism ; whilst in the country they take steps to establish new communes, to introduce progressive methods of cattle breeding and arable cultivation, to garner the corn, to send " red consignments " to Moscow, to attain the prescribed quantities, in short, to carry through the Five Years' Plan.

But all these extensive cultural and economic activities are designed, in addition to their practical purpose, to educate the delegates and their constituents politically, as already mentioned. For the hundreds of thousands of factory and village delegates form the powerful tie between the working women and the Communist party, whose watchwords they make known among the masses. In order to unify this labour the women delegates have their own journal, *Delegatka*, and hold national conferences. Almost all the women of proletarian origin who fill a responsible post in the state administration have been through the school of the delegate meetings, where they received their political education ; indeed, the road to the Soviet Government and to the party is necessarily through these meetings. A letter in the journal *Krestyanka* (The Peasant Woman) of February, 1931, describes the career of a peasant delegate, and is typical of thousands of similar letters addressed to the editor :

> I can say that my life has been one hard struggle to learn to read and write and to fit myself for social work. I was married very young, when I was eighteen, and I became a member of a very God-fearing family. Nothing good came to me in my life. Only the grumbling of the old people, subjection to the will of my husband, my mother-in-law, and my father-in-law, who wanted to force my life into their ways—that is my experience of marriage.
>
> Although my husband was chairman of the village Soviet, he never once came to my assistance. And so I lived on as an illiterate and was ignorant of everything but housework and the care of the cattle, the washing, and the children. My husband was ashamed of my illiteracy, and took me neither to the meetings nor the discussions ; he did not even let me go to the cele-

bration of International Women's Day on the 8th of March. On the contrary, he said: " They'll manage without you. You're too dirty and stupid. It's just about enough for you to look after the cow."

I cried a lot that day. But then a *kolkhos* of twelve farms were started in our district. We were almost the first to join. And in the *kolkhos* a reading hut was set up where I learned a great deal and was shown the way to social activities.

And so it wasn't long before I was elected to the *Politschool* as a woman delegate, and to the soviet of the reading room. And many, many things have since become clear to me and have drawn me to the party.

I sent in a petition to the party and worked unceasingly in public activities. And so people began to come to me for advice and information, and the whole village began to behave quite differently towards me. They began to have some respect for me and have long ago given up making fun of me.

I have now been a candidate for admission to the party for two months.

S. LOBANOVA of the *Kolkhos* " Stalin ".

Thousands more in the Soviet Union, chiefly peasant women, have had to carry on a heroic struggle for years against their husbands, a struggle which is not yet over and which has cost some their lives.

In previous conferences the discussion of this question occupied considerable time, for there were complaints from all sides that the peasants simply would not accept " petticoat authority ". The line of argument was always the same: " It's simply out of the question for a *baba* to govern us." " Under no circumstances will we obey a *baba*." Or: " If the woman had a husband who gave her a good beating, she wouldn't carry on like that." " I'll give you a good hiding if you're always running off to meetings," the husband shouts at his wife, Marya the Bolshevik, in a story called after her by Nyevyerov, the poet of the new peasant woman; for the husband says that " since the Bolsheviks came with their freedom and put her up to all kinds of suspicions, life with her is unbearable. She speaks in meetings. Doesn't want any more children. ' I've had enough of it,' she dares to say. A disgrace for her husband."

How often—not only in literature, but in real life—
the result has been comic as well as tragic situations.
For instance, at the Seventh Conference of the Soviets
in Moscow in 1921, just as the proposal was to be considered to include a clause in the resolution on the inclusion of peasant women in the Soviets, the excited voice
of an indignant peasant delegate made itself heard and,
as it was impossible to suppress him, he had to be allowed
to speak out of his turn. A sturdy peasant, no longer
very young, crossed the hall of the Great Theatre where
the meeting was being held with hurried steps, leapt
on to the platform, and declared as he thumped the table
with his fist: " I just won't stand having my wife in
the Soviet. I have eight children. What should she
do in the Soviet ? "

All the efforts from the platform to calm the delegate
were in vain. Obviously applauded by a section of the
conference members, he demanded that the clause about
the inclusion of women should not be introduced in the
resolution.

In 1927 there was a similar scene at the Thirteenth
Conference of the Soviets when a group of delegates
discussed the question of admitting a peasant woman,
the chairman of a village soviet, to the W.T.S.I.K. The
husband of the peasant woman, who was present at the
conference, and also did social work in the village, rose
and approached the women delegates, declaring:
" There'll be nothing else to do, I shall have to divorce
my *baba*." When asked in amazement for what reason,
he answered: " How can I help it ? How could I
' teach my wife a lesson ' in case of need, if she is the
actual embodiment of the Government ? "

When one of the women delegates suggested that his
objection should be publicly discussed he was enraged:
" Do you want to make me a general butt ? How can
I oppose the election of women to the W.T.S.I.K. ?
People will abuse me immediately as a serf-holder,
although I do social work. I shan't be able to show my
face in the village."

These two examples are instructive, for they mark the

change going on in peasant minds. Whereas the one peasant in 1921 did not shrink from opposing the proposal to include women in the Soviets in the public conference, another peasant six years later—although he had not yet renounced his right to " teach his wife a lesson "—nevertheless felt it to be a disgrace and thought that he would be decried as a serf-holder if he publicly opposed the advancement of women to governing positions. He had not the courage to expose himself in that way.

And now we understand not only the letter quoted above but also the story of a woman delegate at the last Soviet Conference in which she describes how the men in the village mocked at her at first : " Your humble servants, Commissar in petticoats ! How are you, little Domna ? I suppose there's going to be a decree soon that the *babas* and the *mushiks* are to have the children turn and turn about ? " And now they are very well satisfied with her, address her politely by her name and patronymic, and life goes on normally. In the towns men's behaviour to women is better. But there are conflicts there as well, and in this connection it is worth mentioning the propaganda films which exercise a considerable educational influence, urging the men not to obstruct the social and political activities of their wives. One of these films, dealing with an obstreperous husband—it was entitled *The Trial must Proceed* and concluded with the sentence : " It is now for proletarian public opinion to speak "—was being shown daily in Stalingrad in the autumn of 1931 when I was there, and all the performances were always sold out. And it was there that I heard the extremely popular four-lined verse in which the Soviet Russian wife addresses her husband :

> Like it or not, I do not care,
>   Your wife's no addlepate,
> Lay finger on me, if you dare,
>   And I'll be a delegate.

The outcome of the delegates' activities, who, as we have just seen, were formerly regarded with suspicion by the country population and not infrequently suffered severe maltreatment, is shown in the growth of political activity among women, which may be measured by the increase in the participation in the elections to the soviets. Whereas in 1929 it amounted in the towns of Soviet Russia to rather less than 50 per cent, it had risen to over 75 per cent in 1931, and even in 1929 56·5 per cent of the women not in employment, the " proletarian housewives ", cast their votes. Even more striking are the figures of participation of peasant women in the soviet elections, for they have more than doubled in the last four years.

Meanwhile the women of Soviet Russia are making increasing use of the passive as well as the active franchise. The number and influence of women in administrative and governing bodies are growing from year to year, although it was precisely in this matter that the strongest opposition on the part of the men had to be overcome, especially in the country. Thus there are in the village soviets to-day at any rate 21 per cent women, and in the towns they constitute more than a quarter of the members. It is not uncommon to find women workers or members of a collective farm in leading positions in the village soviet or executive committee. There are in the Soviet Union to-day nearly 5,000 chairwomen of town and village soviets in all, whilst the number of women working in the various soviet departments is calculated to be over 500,000. At the Fifteenth All-Russian Soviet Conference nearly a quarter (23·2 per cent) of the delegates were women.

There are also, of course, a considerable number of women organized in the party, and even their place in the central government organs is not insignificant. Thus in 1931 there were 89 women in the Central Executive Committee of the U.S.S.R. and 137 in that of the R.S.F.S.R. Likewise there is hardly a single state institution where you do not find women in responsible positions, whilst in certain People's Commissariats former working and peasant women are members of the committees and commissions. But in the interest of truth it must be stated that the percentage of women precisely in the key positions is still relatively small and the last decisive step to complete their participation in government authority has still to be taken : hitherto there is no woman Commissary for the whole Union.

The part played by women in the Executive and the Judiciary, as well as in the governing and administrative organs, is notable. Although they are no longer to be found in the ranks of the army, and the Red women soldiers of the civil war now belong to history, a very important rôle is assigned to them in preparations for national defence. Future commanders of the Red Army are trained in the military colleges, and there are several women on the General Staff of the army. There is also a woman captain of a man-of-war.

In the *Ossoafiakhim* founded in 1927, the Society for Aircraft and Gas Defence, they constitute the majority of the millions of paying members. The aims of this society include preparation for a war of defence and the instruction of the population in factories, *kolkhosi*, and *sovkhosi* on the subject of modern armaments and defence in case of hostile attack. Consequently the women organized in the *Ossoafiakhim* have formed a special section to carry on propaganda among workers and peasants. They can also join defence detachments or undergo training in other departments of war service, such as field telegraphy and the field telephone service, but especially of course in ambulance service in the field and behind the lines. Women membership of the militia is an institution almost as old as the revolution itself.

Finally we must remember women's collaboration in the administration of justice in Soviet Russia. It is impossible now to conceive of a People's Court in the new Russia without it. It can almost be said that there is a smack of womanliness, of civilizing motherliness, throughout the whole judicial system. The experience of years justifies the expectation that in future increasing use will be made of women's collaboration precisely in this field.

I spent much time in the Moscow People's Courts,

especially in the *Proletarskyi Rayon*, where a particularly
healthy atmosphere prevails, inspired by the spirit of the
industrial workers, in contrast with certain other districts
which are inhabited more by the *déclassés*. The Court
troyka consists of one judge who has won his position
by previous service as an assessor, and two assessors ;
all three are workers, usually two women and one man ;
on more than one occasion I have been amazed at the
frequency with which one of these women makes a
suggestion in a spirit of pure human fellowship to an
accused person, and almost always successfully. Indeed,
the educational influence of the women judges not infrequently extends beyond the actual sphere of their responsibilities. Thus on one occasion I was present when
a case was being tried where the defendant actually
appeared in the morning in a slightly tipsy condition ;
he was an assistant in a baker's shop who had sold a
loaf to a relative without taking the money. The woman
judge spoke to him as one does to a little child whom
one admonishes gently : " You've been drinking already
to-day ? " " Only a very little." " How much ? "
" Honestly, *Tovarishch* Judge, only half a glass." " Why,
how can you appear before the court drunk ? I mustn't
listen at all to what you have to say. I might be imprisoned if I did. That means that I must judge your
case without hearing your statement. Sit down and
don't speak a word. How can you be so lacking in
respect for the Soviet power and the People's Court ?
It's a positive insult ! " Among the public—there are
always a number of housewives and other unconcerned
persons listening to the cases—tittering might be heard ;
the man sat down with bowed head, thoroughly ashamed
of himself, and the case proceeded.

Most of the disputes that come before the courts in
Moscow and throughout the Soviet Union arise from
housing disputes. But alimony suits make up a considerable proportion of the cases in Soviet Russian courts,
since many men, as already stated, try to evade their
paternal duty of supporting their children, in spite of
the hopelessness of the attempt.

Fear of the burdensome duties of fatherhood is so great that there was a time when the youths in some villages walked on the other side of the road from the girls, and people said : " If you cross over, you'll have to pay alimony." And a jest current among Soviet Russian men illustrates—in rather an exaggerated form —the severity with which alimony is accorded. It is like this : two friends meet. " How are you getting on ? " " Badly." " Why ? " " Because I've got to pay a third of my salary for a child." " But you've still got two-thirds." " Not a bit of it ; I've got two more children, and each costs a third." " But what are you living on, then ? " " On the third that my wife gets for a child from another man." Of course the women judges show no more consideration for those who try to evade their responsibilities than their male colleagues— and in any case Soviet Russian law is severe towards them. And on one occasion, to the delight of all the women present and for the instruction of the masculine public, a young woman judge asked the following awk- ward question of a father who had appealed for a reduc- tion of the sum he had to pay for the child's maintenance on the plea that he had leave of absence in order to recuperate and wanted to marry an unemployed woman : " Do you imagine that it is possible to support a child on fifteen roubles ? " (He had paid thirty hitherto.) " You yourself want to recuperate and to marry an unemployed woman, and think such a sum enough for your child— you, a Soviet father ? " The verdict was, of course, that the alimony was certainly not to be reduced.

Here is the most amusing incident that I saw in a Moscow People's Court : a case was just coming on in which a woman wanted to eject her divorced husband from their home, partly because he got drunk and was always making a racket and beating her, but partly be- cause of his refusal to pay the sum due for the mainten- ance of the child ; the man's case was, therefore, hope- less from the outset. But as ill-luck would have it the whole *troyka* in the court consisted of women on this occasion. The husband, who had already entered the

WOMEN JUDGES HEARING A CASE IN MOSCOW

[face p. 279

court without misgiving, was seized with such terror at the sight that he sprang up with the words : " Nothing but *babas*, then I'd better let it be ! " and made off.

Not lacking in interest were the things that Yemel-yanova, a Moscow woman judge of twenty-nine, told me both about her own life-story and about the experience gathered during years of work in the courts, as we sat over a cup of tea in her modest home ; she is a splendid woman and I was filled with genuine admiration both for the great objectivity with which she conducted her cases and the thoroughly ethical spirit in which she weighed all the factors for and against. She was a tailor's daughter and first saw the light in a county town in the Government of Nishnyi Novgorod, in a family where there had been sixteen children, nine of whom are still living. At the age of twelve she was obliged to take a post as *nyanyka*, children's nurse. From four-teen to sixteen she was in a sawmill, and she has been a member of the party since 1918. Her parents were sectaries, and when her father saw her one day with a *komssomolets* he gave his daughter such a merciless thrashing that she was confined to her bed for a week.

After that Yemelyanova left her native town—it was at the time of the civil war—and went to Siberia, where she joined the army and, since she grasped everything quickly, she was soon appointed commander of a unit whose task it was to combat banditry. She was only nineteen. But she had 250 Red soldiers under her com-mand, and not one of these men—she specially stressed this point—ever offered her the slightest insult as a woman. " A woman may have a disintegrating effect on the army, but she may exercise a wholly beneficial influence. And my mind was full of enthusiasm and the cause. . . ."

She was wounded in the breast and had to retire from the theatre of war. From 1920 to 1922 she acted as instructor in a women's organization, but at the same time she took to writing, and during those years several short stories of hers appeared in *Siberian Fire*, the same journal in which Lydia Sseyfullina's first literary efforts appeared. In 1922 she was ordered to attend a short course in the Department of Justice at Leningrad. In 1923 she married—" a great event "—and returned for a short time to her native town where everything had completely changed in the interval. Her grown-up brothers were already communists, a younger brother was a *komssomolets*, and the youngest of all a Pioneer. Her father had broken away from the sect ; he was a member of a co-operative and scolded his little son when he neglected his duty in the Pioneer band. His former acquaintances now envied him and people always said : " You're well off, all your children are communists."

Later she worked for a year in Tula as an examining judge. And now she was in her third year as a People's Judge in Moscow. I also made the acquaintance of her husband, a communist and a divisional chief in the G.P.U., who, although he was a good and energetic worker, had not been summoned to such responsible work till six years later than his wife.

With two little sons and a family—Yemelyanova concluded her biography—it was certainly not easy for a woman to carry on a profession which made heavy demands on her conscience. But her mother-in-law, whose five sons were also party members, helped her as much as possible in the house.

In her profession, Yemelyanova continued her story after a pause, she had much to do with alimony suits, and it was hardly believable what virtuosity some men showed in their efforts to avoid acknowledging a child. Formerly she had worked for a long time in the textile districts, where there were always a great many women and very few men, and consequently many tragedies— in addition to the frequent spectacle of some derelict man with a wife who was a *krassavitsa*, beautiful and healthy, " as red as blood and as white as milk."

" And so one grows up and grows old . . ." the plucky, warm-hearted woman concluded the evening which will always remain stamped on my memory ; and she fell silent.

Besides the People's Judges there are plenty of scholarly

women jurists in Soviet Russia. There are some whose work is mainly theoretical, following a regular course of study, whilst others, such as examining judges and public prosecutors, have passed through a short, special, limited training for their profession, like Yemelyanova. I have to thank one of these public prosecutors, who was detailed for the task by her chief in the *Narkomyust*, that I was able for some days to get into touch with the system of People's Courts in Moscow with all the problems, law-suits, and persons connected with it, which were of great interest to me, and was even able to get a peep behind the scenes of life.

Let me also tell something of this woman, Gubina, whom in Western Europe one would have taken, to judge by her clothes and her whole appearance, for a poor nursemaid, certainly for anything rather than a government official. When in 1929 the process began of permeating the machinery of government with workers, and specially able persons were being promoted in large numbers from below to higher responsible posts—a process which has now slackened—she was appointed to a position in the *Narkomyust*; she was then twenty-three and had hitherto been a compositor in a printing press. " Just as Lenin said of every cook," she told me, " so I was commanded straight from labour to a governing post." At first she had to work under an instructor. Purely theoretical work. But practice followed immediately, and now she knows her department well and is devoted to her duties, and even in that short time I was thoroughly convinced that she took them exceedingly seriously.

Gubina had previously attended the evening courses at the University of the Red Chair, and had undertaken a great deal of social work in addition to her purely professional duties, so that she hardly left herself three hours to sleep at night and in consequence contracted tuberculosis. Of course she was already married to a worker when I made her acquaintance two years ago in Moscow, and equally of course she was not registered. " For it really does nothing to consolidate matters." She had a

child a year and a half old, but no dwelling ; the whole
family of three lived in a passage room at her husband's
parents. And as she was therefore unable to have a
nurse, the mother-in-law generally looked after the child
when its parents were absent. If the mother had to get
up in the night to suckle the child, the father washed
the napkins during the day, as soon as he could make
time. In this way they shared the care of the child and
the work involved.

In Soviet Russia, as I have said, the question of
women's participation in public life is treated as a mass
problem of drawing wider and wider sections of the
female population into politics and the administration.
The fact that there are individual women of great ability
in high posts is regarded as a matter of no significance,
something certainly due to women's position in Soviet
Russia, but based upon purely personal capacity. Nevertheless, it is by no means without interest to us to know
what the leading women in Soviet Russia look like seen
at close quarters. Let me give some idea with the help
of a few examples.

Nadyeshda Konstantinovna Krupskaya is already
known to us as the companion of Lenin's life and struggle.
In spite of her sixty-two years, she is still a deputy
Commissary in the People's Commissariat of Education,
and unwearying in her activity as a writer, speaker, and
revolutionary.

After Lenin's death, when people began to talk of
erecting his memorial, Krupskaya wrote :

> *Tovarishchi,* working men and women, peasant men and
> women, I have a great favour to ask of you : do not let your
> sorrow for Ilyich degenerate into a purely external veneration
> of his personality. Do not erect monuments to him, do not
> build great palaces in his honour, and do not arrange great
> celebrations in his memory—he cared very little for all that
> during his lifetime, he felt it as something burdensome. Think
> how much poverty and disorder there still is in our country.
> If you want to pay honour to the name of Vladimir Ilyich,
> establish crèches, kindergartens, homes, schools, libraries,
> itinerant dispensaries, hospitals, homes for the disabled, and

the like, and—most important of all—let us translate his teaching into concrete reality.

Millions of workers throughout the land venerate Nadyeshda Konstantinovna. From all parts of the Union working and peasant women turn to her for advice and help in purely personal troubles, and yet more in their public difficulties of a wholly social nature. "How I should like to go to Moscow to see Krupskaya again," you often hear women in the provinces say. Or: "We must tell Nadyeshda Konstantinovna that. We must ask that of her." And Krupskaya is always distressed because it is physically impossible for her to answer all the letters addressed to her, to speak at as many meetings and write as many articles as she is asked.

And with all this Nadyeshda Konstantinovna is not in the least "famous" or "great", but entirely the same simple, homely, unselfish woman, accessible to everybody, that she was always in the hard times of her "subterranean" existence. When you enter her office in the *Narkompross*, the People's Commissariat of Education, a slightly bent woman of medium height in a rather worn black cotton dress rises from the writing-table to welcome the visitor. Her smooth hair is combed back plainly, her eyes—in consequence of an illness—are somewhat protuberant, and radiate kindness, understanding, I might almost say practical wisdom, so that you are compelled to drop your own, at once touched and abashed.

When she begins to speak and tells you about her work, about the children in the homes who all call her "mother", and about the grown-up people for whom she has now been turned from a teacher of the people to a national teacher and national leader, a kind of national mother, then everything that she says is so warm-hearted, so inspired, that you would like to listen for hours, if you did not know how precious her minutes are. . . .

You leave this room where the air has been sanctified by so much human sympathy in a mood of thankfulness and reflection.

I made the acquaintance of Ssmidovich in the women's section of the V.T.S.I.K. in Moscow, of which she is the president : a characteristically Russian head, beautiful, clever, radiating motherly kindness. She, too, is greatly venerated in Soviet Russia, and is of a type akin to Krupskaya, with whom she lives in the Kremlin and is close friends ; it is the gradually disappearing type of Russian revolutionary woman of the older generation, the Lenin Guard. Of a similar type is Yakovleva, formerly Lunacharskyi's deputy in the *Narkompross*, now People's Commissary of Finance of the R.S.F.S.R. She told me that mostly women work in her department, and that they often prove far better workers than the men. Here, too, therefore, the atmosphere is by no means quite clear of the often cited " assault upon men by the women ".

Nyurina makes an impression of great womanliness combined with great ability and purposeful determination ; she was formerly the assistant of the Public Prosecutor of the Republic, and now the only woman member—together with seven men—of the Board of the *Narkomyust* and head organizer of the administration of instruction. Like all these women, she is an admirable writer and speaker. In former years she was occupied besides among working women, and she still occasionally writes on the subject. She is, moreover, one of the group of women coming from the intelligentsia —one could add various names to the list : Moyrova, Rosmirovich, and others—who, with the exception of the ambassadress Kollontay who is permanently abroad, lived and worked in foreign countries in former years and have some idea of Western Europe, though one that is somewhat out of date.

The *vydvishenki*, women mainly of proletarian origin, leaders of the succeeding generation, the *Ssmyena*, who have been promoted to responsible posts, are, of course, quite another type. Of most of them one can say almost the same as has been said of the young people in the *komssomol* : they were born into a new era. For even if they are older, they have hardly any knowledge of

284

WOMEN IN THE SOVIET NAVY

[face p. 284

MILITIA WOMEN OF THE MOSCOW STREETS

yesterday, for it is only since the revolution that they have awakened to real life ; they know nothing beyond the frontiers of their own country, are burdened by no traditions, no possibilities of comparison, no inner conflicts in their past, and not even by an excess of culture, and they build the present and the future of the state, free from impediments, conscious of their goal, and with a strong sense of responsibility. They are the new, class-conscious, proletarian women of Soviet Russia, with both feet firmly planted, whose aspect and nature and appearance is, indeed, not wholly transfigured in every detail, yet more or less complete in the essential features.

I came across two of the best and most attractive representatives of this new type in Leningrad. One of them, Bogdanova, filling the responsible post of a secretary of the *Oblispolkom*, the Executive Committee for the whole district of Leningrad, is the daughter of a washerwoman whose husband deserted her. "It's a good thing that my mother taught me to read and write," she said by way of opening the conversation with me. When she was still a child Bogdanova was a nursemaid in a strange family at the age of ten, in a strange town, Pskov, and came from thence to a cigarette factory in Leningrad where she worked for some years. She has been in the party since 1919 and has filled the most various posts in succession until in 1924 she became deputy manager of a textile mill and four years later herself " Red Manager ". From the factory " Red Lighthouse " she entered the Leningrad Soviet and thence—at the age of about thirty-five—was appointed to her present post.

I sat opposite her at her neat and tidy writing-table with a small table beside it on which three telephones stood, all of which rang together from time to time. The wall was adorned with a portrait of Lenin and the room looked very pleasant. " Of course I am learning a great deal now," Bogdanova told me, " *politeconomy, politgeography.*" She looked at me, smiled like a child, and added : " But my favourite subject is German."

And then she told me about her work, about her activities among the women in the Leningrad factories, the courses for Red managers, and about the new " kitchen factories ", about the " learned " nursemaids in the villages, and much more besides. I listened to her ; she spoke calmly, quietly, confidently, and had a very pleasant, deep voice. I looked at her ; she was very simply dressed all in black and did not, of course, wear any ornaments at all, but she looked nice, perfectly womanly, and had beautiful hands and well-cared-for nails. Just as I was preparing to go a bell rang—this time only one telephone. Bogdanova's voice assumed a gentler, more eager note : " Dearest, is that you ? It's Shaposhnikova," she said, turning to me. " She's expecting you." I took leave of her and noted as I left : that is quite a different type of *vydvishenka* than any I have met in Moscow yet.

I was now doubly curious to see Shaposhnikova. A woman who had risen from the ranks, secretary of the trades council in the Lenin district—the only woman in such a position in the Soviet Union—and candidate for the committee of the T.S.I.K. of the Union—there, too, the only woman. What type would she be ? What would she be like ?

First I was told her biography quite briefly. She was thirty-six. Until the revolution she was a textile worker and illiterate. She had been a member of the party since 1917. Had taken part in the civil war. Had been in a responsible position since 1922. In 1925 she completed her course in the Workers' Faculty and was also studying political economy. This very good-looking woman also sat at a table with three telephones. She, too, was very clever and objective, grasped everything directly, and in my presence, because it happened to come so, she conducted a meeting with fifteen men whom she had summoned ; she was fully mistress of the situation and discussed urgent and important questions with them ; they all addressed one another with the familiar singular pronoun.

Then, when we were alone at last, she turned smiling to me who had heard the whole discussion : " You see although I have the fair complexion of the north, am *ssyeveryanka*, yet I am hot-blooded. We are all young and hot-blooded now, because everything is new among us and you must grasp things quickly and be adaptable, and be constantly agitating."

And then she told me how she had not begun to learn till she was twenty-seven and held a scholarship at the Workers' Faculty on which she could just live. She, too, spoke enthusiastically of her work, of the vigorously developed proletarian self-criticism, and added in the same voice : " There is a flame burning in us all. We are constantly in a state of magnetism, and we ourselves hardly notice now how democracy is being created among us and is establishing itself with creative force."

" Are we advancing culturally ? " After a short pause she asked the question herself. " I often think about that and ask myself how it is with myself. Then I look at my old photograph that I found somewhere a short time ago : a woman in a velvet or plush jacket wearing a bead necklace and with waved hair—a regular doll. I can't help being ashamed every time I look at it. And then, formerly when I strolled along the streets and saw some iron railings, they were nothing but iron railings. But now I know that they come from Rastrelli. Or when I went to the theatre it was only the plot that interested me. But now I pay attention to the artistic form, now I know who Beethoven and Verdi were—so you see we have advanced culturally."

Shaposhnikova's hours of labour, like those of all men and women who occupy responsible posts in the Soviet Union, are really unlimited. She works from nine o'clock in the morning often till one o'clock at night, has generally no time for middle-day dinner, and not infrequently must speak at several meetings on one evening, so that often she does not see her husband, who is also a responsible worker, for days. She has no children and says that she can work all the better. But she has one passion : gymnastics, which she does with zeal early in the morning before she goes to her office ; as president of the Society for *Physculture* she conducts vigorous propaganda in favour of gymnastics.

As I learned afterwards, for a time women were promoted more energetically in Leningrad than elsewhere, which may have some connection with the fact that the proletariat there has the oldest revolutionary tradition in Russia and has always set the tone. But I saw evidence not only among high officials but also in the lower ranks —among women tram conductors and simple working women—that the women in this town are incomparably more womanly and pay far more attention to their appearance ; perhaps the explanation is that in the eighteenth century Leningrad was the royal residence, built almost entirely by foreign architects, and has always been smarter, more orderly and European, whilst the sprawling Little Mother Moscow, which even in earlier days absorbed a vast mass of unwashed provincials like a sponge, could hardly compete with the elegant city on the Neva in the matter of culture.

But what the women of Leningrad have in common with those of Moscow and with the leading women of the larger and smaller provincial towns, whether they go with or without a kerchief over their heads—as, for instance, the vice-chairman of the Soviet of the textile centre Ivanovo - Vosnyessyensk—what all these social workers have in common, wherever they may be, is the fact that their own individual concerns are subordinated to the cause. That they all regard themselves only as instruments of a great idea, that they carry on their work under the constant control of public opinion in the wider and narrower sense, that each feels responsible for all and all for each, and that all personal ambition, everything personal, pales and shrinks into the background before the immense power of this sense of responsibility. It is the resolute will to foster a new anonymity, which is still more noticeable among Soviet Russian women than among the men.

Once only I came across a woman in Moscow who seemed to me to be an exception to this rule. Whereas everyone else showed great readiness to assist me in my work, she refused me all information on the subject of her work, and that in a repellent manner. And this after people had replied to similar doubts which I myself had expressed : "We are not in Western Europe here. When a matter of cultural importance is in question, everything personal must give way." This woman, of whom I heard later that she is the daughter-in-law of a German woman communist leader who has rendered valuable service, seems nevertheless to have been infected with "Western European" habits.

But what I have said is confirmed by the fact that among hundreds of women in public life of the most various types with whom I came in contact in the Soviet Union in recent years I only came across a single case of this kind.

Let me repeat it then : Soviet Russian women in public life regard themselves simply as tools in the service of the community, and have already proved themselves wholly worthy of the political emancipation which no women in any other country have obtained in the same measure ; and their participation in the public life of the Soviet Union represents a new chapter in the history of womanhood.

IN INTELLECTUAL LIFE

"It is impossible to build up a socialist society in an illiterate country." Such was Lenin's motto which is the starting-point of the vast cultural work that is being carried on to-day in the Soviet Union.

In October, 1917, when Russia entered upon the latest phase of its history, it was still the country with the most illiterates in comparison with all other European states ; not even one in ten persons could read and write. A truly heroic struggle was necessary against the most disgraceful heritage of Tsarism, ignorance, and in this struggle, now approaching a victorious end, an important part fell to women in Soviet Russia, both passively and actively. Whereas in 1907 there were 13 per cent illiterates among the women even in the towns, they number to-day, together with the male illiterates, only about twelve million, all of whom, except three million, are over thirty-five and live for the most part in remote villages. In the last four years alone over fifty million Russian men and women have learned to read and write. *Likbes*, the liquidation of illiteracy, which is directed by a woman in the Moscow district, assumed an almost tempestuous mass character at this period, and it was crowned with success : to-day there are hardly any illiterates in the towns, and during 1932 no less than 1,100,000 " soldiers of culture " were mobilized for the campaign.

Every day you hear instances of the way in which illiteracy is being liquidated in individual cases—always with the active co-operation of the women or by their initiative—and also what it meant to the women in the country to take the first step in the path of learning, often at an advanced age. At a conference in the Moscow Palace of Labour a working woman from the Ural province stated : " I live in the village of Kotovka, about six miles from the mines. The village is a remote, gloomy hole. We have no schools yet, and almost all the women are illiterate. A teacher was sent to us, certainly, but she did not stay long. Then we agreed at the meeting that we must all learn and get hold of a good teacher. I made a list of all the illiterate women ; there were seventy in all. We demanded a new teacher and now we are all learning, we who did not know before what the liquidation of illiteracy meant." And another peasant woman of sixty-two recounted : " Don't think that I am too old. It's true I'm past sixty-two, but the fifty years that I lived under the Tsar don't count, for then I could neither read nor write. But now I even write for the papers." And so there are to-day many former illiterates in responsible positions, and a few who have risen from illiteracy to be doctors, agronomists, and engineers. Altogether the passion of the Russian masses for learning is unprecedented. The whole people have been seized by a perfectly ravenous appetite for knowledge, and it is not without reason that Russia is constantly compared with a gigantic school—doubtless it is the biggest school-room in the world. Wherever you look round—in the railway, in the trams, in the stations, in the public eating-houses and tea-rooms, or on the benches in the boulevards and parks, wherever people have half an hour's leisure, to say nothing of the clubs and Red Corners—you see people, and often more women than men, deep in some book, or at least spelling out words. As if they were one and all in the world for no other purpose but to learn, and especially to learn reading and writing.

In this vastest of all educational institutions the women are often the best pupils. For here, too, they are generally in the foremost ranks, fill the lecture- and class-rooms, are proved to read more than men in general, and are altogether " infected " with the zeal to learn. " We all learn, whether we are big or little. Ignorant young people are exempted from work and we force them to learn," a woman from a mining locality said at a conference in Moscow. In a village in the Government of Nishnyi Novgorod, as was reported not long ago in Soviet Russian papers, a housewife and her domestic help signed an agreement that is by no means unusual in the Union, in which each undertook to devote an hour and a half a day to study.

An incident in Leningrad described to me by eye-witnesses there : ninety young working women begged earnestly of the *Fabkom*, the factory committee, to employ them only in the mornings so that in the evening they might attend classes and learn. Or another scene which I witnessed in a tobacco factory in Rostov on the Don: a working woman of about twenty-five burst into tears before the head of the *Kultprop* (cultural propaganda) section because she was told that the class in which she wanted to enrol was already more than full. " If I'm not admitted, I shall die, and I might be a lot of use to the state as an inventor," she protested with tears.

Here, too, then, Lenin's legacy, which is hammered into you at every step in Soviet Russia, is full of life and vigour : " We must learn in the first place, and learn in the second place, and learn in the third place—and then see to it that learning does not remain a dead letter with us or a modern phrase, but becomes flesh of our flesh and bone of our bone, and really is transformed into a fundamental part of the new *byt*." To-day Lenin would be satisfied with his pupils. Universal compulsory education has been introduced and the whole life of the nation is borne along upon an elemental urge to learn. In the universities, technical schools, and workers' faculties the number of students has increased on the average 45 per cent in the year 1932 alone, and if we also take the primary schools into account and the secondary schools with a seven- and nine-year course (*ssyemiletka* and *dyevyatiletka*), as well as the *likbes* schools, which, indeed, are steadily losing pupils and will disappear altogether with the liquidation of illiteracy, then the network of organizations for popular instruction embraced more than fifty-seven million eager pupils, and if we include the factory schools, nearly fifty-nine millions in all.

As regards the participation of women, their percentage in the technical colleges and factory schools has risen considerably. Women were attracted in masses into factory work and the consequence was that the number of girls among the pupils in factory and works schools had risen to nearly 50 per cent, as compared with 28 per cent in 1927. And it is the same in the universities and workers' faculties : in 1930 27·6 per cent women were admitted, whilst in the following year it was already 40·9 per cent. In the medical colleges there are 75 per cent women, in the Teachers' Academies 51 per cent, and in the rest of the university faculties 39·3 per cent. In the workers' faculties there are 18·1 per cent women, and 67 per cent among the teachers in the schools of the first and second grades.

Of course the number of students is far below that of persons engaged in study. In addition to the children and adults embraced by an educational system which is almost entirely free, we must count the members of the innumerable classes affiliated to the immense network of party instruction, the most various workers' courses, special courses for Red leaders and factory managers, besides postal courses to help those who are educating themselves. According to calculations made in 1932 there would be at the end of that year eighty million persons engaged in study in the Soviet Union, so that on the average there would be *one learner for every two inhabitants*, and the sum provided by the state for educational purposes had to be raised to 5,845 million roubles as compared with 4,126 million in the previous year. The number of those enrolling in the classes—mostly women—is so great that as a rule no more names can be entered within an hour or two of the announcement of a class.

The postal tuition, already mentioned, is a Soviet Russian speciality. It includes all manner of subjects, mainly technical, and has its headquarters in Moscow. Those who enrol from all parts of the country—and they also are mainly women—receive all the books and other requirements free of cost and send in their work to the appropriate institute, where it is corrected, classified, and sent back to the students with the necessary instructions for further work. The courses of postal tuition embrace all grades from elementary to university. But in other respects likewise there is the closest possible connection between study and practical life, not only through the institution of factory study—the future engineer, hydraulic or mechanical, and chemist do practical work in the factory like everybody else—but also through the widespread custom of " sponsorship " : almost every factory is " sponsor " to some school or university, which, in turn, is " sponsor " to some other community.

It is a matter of course that the Russian school system still presents considerable defects and drawbacks as well as great advantages. In particular it is very one-sided and has been popularized on the American model. For instance, although German is compulsory in all the schools, it is difficult to avoid the impression that Russian education has only the training of technicians in view. But it is impossible to judge finally, since the first Soviet generation of scientists, doctors, professors, agronomists, etc., has barely entered the field. There are comparatively few of these among women, but their zeal for learning justifies increasing hopes. In thirty scientific institutions for the training of those who wished to enter such professions there were already 25 per cent women. (Moreover, there are even now numerous inventors in the factories, simple working women who widen their practical experience by independent study and think out small innovations which are nevertheless not infrequently valuable in perfecting a process and increasing productivity.) And among research workers there is a growing number of women.

Besides the zeal for learning which positively possesses the population of the Union at the present time, the universal interest in books, in everything printed, may be regarded as a passion simply for reading, a reading epidemic. Within a few days of publication, almost before you get a sight of them, all books and pamphlets (these latter are especially popular) have run through immense editions. And if you want to buy something in one of the many, many bookshops—nowhere else are they so numerous—you must often take your place in a queue in the morning. Immense sums are spent in stimulating the love of reading still further. Wherever you go, wherever you sit or stand, at every turning, from every ceiling and wall, from bands with mottoes stretched across the street, in all colours and generally in gigantic letters, these words strike your eye : " Books will teach you to conquer " ; " Books are a mighty weapon in the struggle for the Five Years' Plan " ; " No Communism without knowledge " ; and so on. In every factory, in every public office, wherever there are so much as a couple of dozen people, you find a book kiosk, a Red Corner, a reading room, a library, and it is sure to flaunt the inscription : " Not a working man or woman outside the library ! " And if it is attached to a works of any size, as, for instance, the *Traktorstroy* at Stalingrad, all the newspapers and journals of the Union will be available there. Besides, the country is covered with a network of itinerant libraries. And, as if that were not enough, the *Komssomol* has quite recently collected ten million " books for the villages " most of which—that, too, is significant—now contain a request to the readers to communicate their view of the work in question to the State Publications Department, together with their age and occupation.

The unparalleled interest of the whole population, but especially of the newly awakened women, in the printed word applies, of course, not only to books but to the press. But the extension of the Soviet press is seen most clearly in the rapid increase in the number of women's journals, of which there are already more than twenty.

The editorial departments of the three leading Soviet Russian women's journals, *Rabotnitsa* (The Working Woman), *Krestyanka* (The Peasant Woman), and *Delegatka* (The Delegate), all with an immense circulation— *Rabotnitsa* alone has a circulation of a quarter of a million —receive correspondence from all parts of the Soviet Union every day. Working women, peasant women, delegates, housewives, servant maids, and all other kinds of women workers, old and young, town and village dwellers, those who could write a little in former days, and those who have only learned with difficulty since the revolution, all pour out their hearts. In these letters you sometimes come across the most marvellous things, showing the intensive growth, the inner force, the marked individuality, and the power of originality of the new woman in Russia. In recent years the great masses of Soviet Russian women, yet more than the men, have been seized with a real rage for writing as well as for learning and reading.

Even women who cannot yet write do " write " : they dictate their letters to those who have already learned the art of writing, and it is precisely these communications that the journals particularly like to publish. For in each of these journals, as well as in many newspapers, there is a special column for *rabkorki* and *ssyelkorki*, women correspondents of the workers and peasantry, who already number tens of thousands.

In this way the masses are drawn into active co-operation in everything that is done, and already their voices may be heard on all sides. Where necessary, answers and advice are given or help is provided, and just as the whole structure of the Soviet Union is a collective product, in which great and small collaborate, so it is with the journals and newspapers.

Not infrequently these working and peasant women correspondents, whose number and attainments are growing daily, send in poems, little stories, sketches, and tales. And these somewhat primitive works of art are also often printed, the embryo authoresses given support where possible, and encouraged to continue their efforts.

> *Tovarishchi, rabkorki*, and readers, send in your verses to the editor of *Rabotnitsa* [is the standing appeal on the back page of the journal]. Your poems will be read from time to time in the circle of our working women correspondents. Those authoresses whose poems cannot be printed will receive full answers by post. Some of your poems will appear in the literary surveys. Send your letters unstamped.

In this way a new type of folk poetry is springing up in Soviet Russia ; in a techniquized, Americanized, materialized milieu, bristling with realism, speed, figures, and schemes for the future, it is linked in a sense to an ancient tradition which has not quite died out even to-day in some parts of northern Russia. And yet more : these antitheses are so close together—the new epic of the Five Years' Plan and the old *bylinas* or epics—that not very long ago, since the revolution, a living piece of that past suddenly emerged in Moscow, in the heart of the Soviet state. I mean the native Russian story-teller and poetess of *bylinas*, epics, and fairy-tales sprung from the people, *Babushka* (Grandmother) Marya Krivopolyenova, whose very life-story sounds like a myth.

She was discovered in the neighbourhood of Archangel in 1915 at the age of seventy-two—a beggar-woman tramping from village to village, and half reciting, half singing her traditional, unique poems to the people for a bit of bread. In that strange and magic district in the far north of Russia, therefore, where nature, the

MARYA KRIVOPOLYENOVA
Poetess and Reciter of Folk Epics

[face p. 296

landscape, and the people's lives are blended in almost incredible unity and beauty. In that district where the days know no end for weeks at a time, because no night separates them ; where you see the fantastically gay-coloured domes of the wooden churches rising on the banks of the broad, gleaming rivers, sometimes close together like mushrooms, sometimes springing from the ground like slender firs ; where there are ancient forests, grey and dark and sombre, in whose solitude and silence you imagine undiscovered worlds of music. . . .

In those parts the Russian people have been racially pure and free from time immemorial, have never known serfdom, and there a race still survives in whom love of the spoken word and of everything beautiful and sublime has always been keen and vital.

Marya Krivopolyenova, a piece of her native landscape become flesh, word, and music, an old woman of the forest, was brought to Petrograd in the middle of the world war and set on a platform and, although she had hardly three teeth in her mouth, she captured the hearts of thousands in a flash by her fire and incomparable art, and was eulogized in the press in long articles. At the end of three months she returned home, her material needs provided for.

After the October revolution of 1917, in 1921 *Babushka* Krivopolyenova was invited by Lunacharskyi, at that time People's Commissar of Education, to come to Moscow. She was already seventy-eight, but she appeared there, and again in Leningrad and a number of other towns, in a new and totally changed world, before a totally new audience—besides dozens of times in all manner of learned and literary societies, and almost a hundred times before students ; and again she celebrated triumphs. Then she finally retired.

Marya Krivopolyenova died a few years ago—one of those miraculous beings which only the inexhaustible, nearly virgin soil of Russia can produce, a woman whose art formed a link, in spite of all, between two apparently unbridgeable worlds. But the race to which she belonged still lives in Russia, and to-day she survives in one Alyonushka Novikova-Vashintsova. But this *babushka* shall speak for herself :

I was born in 1860 in the Moscow Government. My mother was a messenger in the service of my lady who owned the estate. My father was a locksmith. He taught himself to read and write and wanted to teach me. But my mother scolded him for it : what was he thinking of, she said ; to put the Lord knew what in the girl's head and make sport for the devil. From the beginning of the world there had never been such a thing as girls' learning. So I failed to learn to read. From the age of twelve I was employed as a spinner, a pious slave of God, the slave of my own life. At twenty I married a peasant in the village of Gavrikovo and became the slave of my husband. I had ten children, of whom I only raised five, and a wretched life : my husband was always brawling and I prayed. The Tsar's war scattered my children throughout the world—some went to the war, others God knows where. When I was fifty-three I left my husband and lived as a day labourer.

The Tsar's war enveloped us all like a terrible, black cloud. I was fifty-six. I worked as an attendant in a hospital in Kiev for spotted typhus and wounded soldiers. And as I was forced to listen to the groans and curses of the mutilated men, how they cursed the war and God and the Tsar, I realized : there is no God. And when I was sixty I turned with all my heart to Bolshevism.

In 1923, when I was working with the porters in the Moscow Customs Office, I was elected as delegate in the *Shenotdyel*, the women's group, at a meeting of my fellow-workers.

Then I trembled at my age and my semi-illiteracy. But the Soviet Government opened the door wide and let in light and knowledge. And then I began to regain my youth. I enrolled in a *rabkor* circle. A few of my half-illiterate notes were published in the central journal. At the beginning of 1924 I was superannuated.

Now that I had no occupation I read the journal *Delegatka* and reflected on a little picture in it : a woman who is a worker is regarded as a human being in the Soviet State, and when her time comes she lies in a light maternity ward. But in our old *byt* a *baba* was considered unclean in such a case, like an animal. It hurt me so much that the tears came into my eyes. And then the wish was kindled in me to write something about the old *byt*.

298

But where was I to begin ?   How was I to put pen to paper ?
I didn't know how to. . . .

So I bought a pencil, beat my brains, even cried a little, and
the desire only grew stronger.   It went on like that for a good
time.   But in the end I did write down what I wanted to say
under the title : " What Memories came to me when I read the
Delegatka."

In the journal it turned out that my contribution was the best.
Then I wrote on a big sheet of paper : " The Old *Byt*."   It was
all printed, to the last word, and given the new title of " Bitter
Sorrow, Woman's Sorrow."

From that moment I was positively infected with the rage for
writing.   Now, I thought, I must learn something more.   I
bought a little book, a grammar, and enrolled in the library so
as to be able to get books.   And so I began to study, quite
alone, in my little room : so as to be able to read and write
better.   Besides my stories in the women's journals several
little books of mine were published by *Gossisdat*, the State
Publications Department, between 1924 and 1928.

And so I sometimes look at these little books of mine and can
hardly believe that it is I who wrote them.   I turn over my
papers and notes : oh, yes, those are my scribblings, my simple
little books, without words of wisdom, but yet able to teach
something to a few illiterate women.

Ever since I began to write I had cherished the idea of writing
a big book about our women, beginning at birth and carrying it
on to the present day.   There was paper on the table.   I held
a pencil in my hand.   My life in the village and the factory
passed before me in memory as a long, long, narrow way, a
path through the thorny tangle of the hateful old *byt* in all its
darkness, with all the insults and blows, the bitter woman's lot
of tears and humiliation. . . .   Impatiently and stubbornly I
wrote, or, more correctly, I learned to write, the story of
Marinka's Life.   To the best of my ability I have now
learned literary wisdom, and my first big book came out at
the end of 1930.

In 1933, on March 8th, on International Women's Day, I
shall be seventy-three.   But thanks to the Soviet Government
my youth is renewed and I have the spirit of a *komssomoltsa*.
The end of my life is not yet in sight, and so I hope to leave the
third part of *Marinka's Life* as a memorial for the young generation who are building up the shining future.

My old age is fair and bright.   And I shall die the happiest of old women, guided all along my literary path by a woman, my comrade and friend Ludmilla. But I write this because I want to prove how untrue all the things said about women in the Tsarist days were. For there is no undertaking, no difficulty that a woman cannot master, even in her declining days, if only she is resolute and determined. . . .

When *Marinka's Life* by Alyonushka Novikova appeared, M. Gorykyi wrote of his " youngest " colleague : " A hard task for her, but a remarkable fact in our astonishing Soviet actuality. . . . We have millions more such *babas* as Novikova-Vashintsova, and for them an example like hers may give the impetus to start on a new road, the road of freedom."

But Novikova's book, like everything that she writes, is far more than a mere " remarkable fact in Soviet actuality ". This *baba's* style is so colourful, so fresh and picturesque, her character sketches are so lifelike and clearly outlined, her descriptions so truly felt and experienced, the thoughts expressed so independent and original, that we enjoy these artless stories as if they were extracts from the old Russian *bylinas*, epics, ballads, folk-songs, fairy-stories, proverbs, and aphorisms—in short, all the wisdom of the child-like Russian nation with its rare art of expression, which we may admire just as much in its living form now as before the revolution. And we ask in spite of ourselves : what manner of people is this whose language is so full of nuances, always flexible, finding its way to our hearts, expressive, melodious, delicate without being nerveless, and at the same time lofty, inspired by true feeling—a language, it is true, much better suited for epic and lyric poetry than for drama. Whence this rich diversity ? Perhaps because the territory inhabited by the Russian nation, Eurasia, embraces the vast treasures of two continents, geographically, racially, historically, their landscape and their culture, their human types and their art, and therefore also their speech.

We can point to Lydia Sseyfullina as the truest and finest symbol of this union of East and West in Russian literature ; among the authoresses of the new Russia she holds the first place unchallenged. She was born in 1889 and was of Tatar origin on her father's side (in Arabic Sseyf-ullah means the Sword of God). While still a child she was made acquainted with the wealth and beauty of the Russian language by her Russianized father, who was a priest and loved Russian literature ardently, but also by her mother, grandmother, and *nyanya*, who, although they could not read or write, nevertheless made her familiar with the world and speech of Russian fairy-lore, drawing upon the wealth of their own oneness with the people and their native soil. When at the age of six she wrote a letter to the Tsaritsa begging her to ease the life of her sick father—from whom she together with her sister was parted—and so likewise her own, her father began to dream that his daughter might some day be an authoress. When she was nine the little girl really did begin to write a novel, and in the Russo-Kirgiz preparatory school which she attended in a town in the Orenburg Government she experienced her first literary mortification : the teacher refused to believe that she had herself written a composition that she gave in. She passed the secondary school leaving examination in 1906 and worked for a time, now as an actress, now as a teacher, and finally, after the revolution, as a librarian in Siberia. After several of her shorter stories and articles had been published in the local press from 1919 onwards, her story *Four Chapters* appeared in the journal *Siberian Fire* in 1922, and that was the beginning of her literary career properly speaking. There followed in 1923—still in Siberia—the first volume of her stories ; then *Rotten Manure*, *Virinyeya*, *The Peasant Legend of Lenin*, *The Breakers of the Peace*, in short, the six volumes of her works, some of which have been translated into other languages. I have already quoted a few extracts from her latest, still unpublished book, *Drifting with the Current*.

What is it, then, which distinguishes Sseyfullina from a number of women writers, not only abroad, but also in Russia, making her something unique like a rock, a piece of nature ?

To this question the well-known Soviet Russian literary critic Voronskyi answers :

Sseyfullina belongs as a writer wholly to the post-revolutionary period : both in the date at which she began her literary activity and in its substance, character, and tendency. Her stories are of the peasantry, of the intelligentsia, and of children during the revolution. Especially of the earliest phase of the October revolution, of '17 in Siberia and the Orenburg steppes, and of '18 and '19. . . . Sseyfullina's Siberia comes home to us. Its winters and storms remind us of our own, and its peasants are very like those of Ryasany and Tambov. It is the familiar village : the old, wooden Russia, the land of the Russians with coarse cloth and meal-bread and sheepskin. . . . The centre of it all is the village and the town at the time of the decisive October victories and the outbreak of the civil war. And the village is shown from within, in the days when its poverty came into violent clash with property, in the days when things traditional were being destroyed, in the first thaw of spring. The ice is hardly broken. The stream is just beginning to move and already the current is sweeping everything along.

The peasants who set the tone in the village—the soldiers back from the front and the soldiers' wives—are an integral part of it and of the land, the fields, flesh of their flesh ; there they were born and there they will die. But it is no longer the old, half-blind, oppressed, priest-ridden village, where people took off their caps to the *uryadnik*, the country constable, as soon as they saw him in the distance, but the new, rebel village, intoxicated with the first flush of the revolution, a village that has risen and felt its great strength. . . .

Sseyfullina as the painter of a milieu depicts not the village pure and simple, not the Siberian and Orenburg *mushik*, but village poverty. That is what is most important in her art. Her Ssofrons and Artamons are not only alive, truthful, and convincing, but are brought home to the reader with rare ability and unparalleled power. They literally belong to us, one is closely akin to them. It is as if she herself sprang from these families. And it seems to me that when the time comes— and it will come soon—when our villages really begin to produce authoresses and artists in their cottages who have not first been sent to school in the towns, they will write like Sseyfullina, who has penetrated the village with the eyes of a simple village woman, a sister or daughter of these Artamons. . . ."

One of the best things that Sseyfullina has written is
her novel *Virinyeya*, which was received with enthusiasm
in Soviet Russia and afterwards dramatized, and has had
long runs on the stage in foreign countries—in Paris and
elsewhere. Virinyeya is a type of Russian village woman
hitherto unknown to Russian literature, new and uncommon, utterly unlike the earlier traditional *baba*, outcast, patient, and pitiful. What characterizes her is her
protest against everything with which as a woman she
has most to do and from which she has most to suffer :
against the petrified form of the family, the relations
between the sexes, and especially against the hypocrisy
which is inevitable so long as the old way of life continues.

Virinyeya grew up somewhere between town and
village, she could read and write and observe keenly, and
she knew what to think of the " respectable " life of the
ruling class and their talk. It was hard for her to find
her true path, but she found it together with the Bolshevik Pavel, who had returned from the front to his
native village. She shared with him his new, restless
life, shared his thoughts and feelings, and was killed by
the Whites whilst fighting her way to her child, " like a
she-wolf to her cub."

> The figure of Virinyeya [Voronskyi continues] is altogether
> new, unique, grandly conceived, and enthralling because of her
> vital force. The mighty, powerful calls of the instinctive life
> which fill her soul present her to us as a strong, resonant
> character ; she is defiant, self-willed, obstinate . . . frank to
> the point of rudeness and yet womanly, for she must love, bear
> children, and work. . . . Virinyeya is a new type of woman in
> Russia that has only become possible in our era, and points to a
> vast growth of personality in working humanity, especially in
> village women. . . . Whole generations of our intelligentsia
> formed their ideal of a beloved woman from Tolstoy's Natasha
> or Turgenyev's women, and sought such a woman in real life.
> The Virinyeyas have now taken that place in the life of the
> present youthful generation.

Lydia Sseyfullina's style is remarkably colourful,
concise, pregnant, pure, and graphic, and quite untranslatable, springing from the depths of the Russian language

and the Russian national soul, and can be understood only in that light. Like Tolstoy, to whom she is often compared, she loves the Russian countryside and Russian life with all its fresh odour of hay and earth and stable, but Tolstoy's passivity, his non-resistance, is utterly alien to her, she hates all fig-leaves, and, like her own Virinyeya, burns in protest against everything shallow, conventional, and characteristic of the intelligentsia. From the purely political point of view she belongs in Soviet Russia to those who conform to things as they are, who " drift with the current ". But it must be clear to any impartial observer that there is far more of the genuine, true, revolutionary spirit in the mirror which she holds up by her art to the tendencies of her age than in those who are so over-zealous and over-loud in condemning outward conformity in Soviet Russia that one not infrequently finds it difficult to throw off the suspicion that they themselves are by far the most dangerous of those who conform from interested motives.

Another distinguished Soviet Russian poetess is Marietta Shaginyan, who began her literary career before the October revolution and whose work belonged at that time altogether to the world of Russian symbolism—her book of poems, *Orientalia*, as well as a number of tales, short stories, and novels. Shaginyan, who is a seeker and a great admirer of Goethe, afterwards wrote her *Journey to Weimar*, in which she extols the idea of personality. She continued unrestingly groping her way, seeking, and has been following quite a new path since the revolution ; one of her latest books, *Hydraulic Power Station*, which was greeted with great applause in Soviet Russia, is a politico-philosophical novel in which she depicts the struggle between the new and the old which permeates the whole of Russian life and is transforming it from the bottom. The hero of the novel is an intellectual, but is not made to confront the worker in the earlier relation of instructor, rather he is one who, in the process of re-building life, is able to learn something himself from the enthusiastic builders. This hero embodies the authoress's own life history ; she has chiefly " the Soviet press and the land of the Soviets " to thank for her " self-discovery, her realization of her own ego ", as she herself declares.

Whereas Marietta Shaginyan has found her own path in recent years and is relearning to-day not only figuratively but literally, going to school daily to the " Marxian courses " and depicting with delight the intellectual rejuvenation that she is experiencing, her former comrade Olga Forsch (her best-known novel is entitled *Clothed in Stone*) is a little bit out of the main stream in Soviet Russia to-day.

The proletarian authoress Anna Karavayeva is heart and soul in the party ; her answer to a questionnaire addressed to Soviet Russian writers, asking how the October revolution has affected their work, was as follows: " The influence of October on me personally ? Is there much to say about it ? If there had been no October revolution, I should not have become an authoress. . . ." Her novel, *The Factory in the Forest*, which is known abroad also, treats the subject of the rebuilding of a derelict factory in a deserted village and its effect on the social aspect of the village, and the mutual influence of town and country.

" Half-way between the old and the new," as it is said, stands the gifted popular poetess, Vera Inber, who was writing nothing but modern lyrics in 1912, but since 1922 has written humorous prose as well : short stories in which she tries to describe the new life in Russia, to capture the new *byt* in lyric narrative, most vividly and wittily. Inber tells in her autobiographical tale *The Place in the Sun* of the mental difficulties that she had to overcome before she could transform herself from a good, middle-class intellectual to a conscious collaborator in the new régime. She made up her mind when she had the opportunity of seeing at close quarters the " cultural hunger " of the Russian masses. She describes feelingly how a sailor who had heard that she was stoking her stove with books because of the shortage of wood forbade her " to burn Alexander Pushkin, Nikolay Gogol, and Mikhail Lermontov ", for they " belonged to the people ". She also tells how it was once suggested to her to flee

abroad, and the man who made the suggestion argued :
" It is not my fault that the breakdown has come just in
my generation, which is bleeding to death in consequence.
I don't want to be a wound." She answered : " Rather
a wound than an abscess." These and similar experiences, outwardly insignificant but really of deep import,
determined her to take her " place in the sun ".

It remains to say that at the present time in Soviet
Russia, when not only is interest keen in all contemporary,
social, and cultural questions in the theatre, the cinema,
and the lecture room, but also all the problems of love,
marriage, the family, and the education of children are
passionately and widely discussed, a kind of personal
narrative literature has sprung up, sometimes even in
metrical form, something in the nature of diaries, modest
and restricted in scope. Its aim is to keep pace with
the times, the " Bolshevik tempo ", and to present only
such problems. The writers who have been drawn into
this movement, or, more correctly, into the Five Years'
Plan, and " attached " to the most various factories and
works as *ocherkisti*, story-tellers and poets of the heroes
and heroines of labour, of the Storm Brigades, of competition, of the *Gigants* in industry and agriculture, have
not fulfilled nearly all the expectations cherished of them.
Clearly, commissions cannot take the place of inspiration.
And so at the present time, when the *Pyatiletka* is in
any case at an end, this attempt has been given up and
poets make way once more for publicists and journalists,
amongst whom there are also a number of distinguished
women : S. Richter, W. Asarkh, and others.

This is the place to mention Larissa Reissner, already
briefly referred to as a chronicler of the civil war, who
died in 1928 when she was barely thirty-three and is
venerated as a saint by the young generation in Soviet
Russia ; she was one of the most brilliant of women
journalists in Soviet Russia, brilliant at once as a revolutionary, personality, and woman, a journalist who might
rather be counted among the poets.

She was only twenty-two [writes Karl Radek about her in the
foreword to the two-volume Russian edition of her works] when

the death-hour of bourgeois Russia struck. Yet it was not granted to her to witness the tenth year of the revolution in whose ranks she had fought bravely, whose battles she depicted as they can only be depicted by one in whose soul a great poet is united with a great warrior.

In a number of articles and books, in the whole literary remains of Larissa Reissner, there is only a single theme : the October revolution.

She was born in Lublin in 1895, where her father was professor in the Agricultural College. In her veins flowed the Baltic blood of her father and the Polish blood of her mother : the heritage of an ancient German family of stern jurists mingled with the fire of the passionate Poles.

Larissa Reissner grew up in Germany and France, where her father went to study and where he later stayed as a political emigrant. . . . The girl made the acquaintance of Bebel and Liebknecht and always retained a warm affection for Germany.

After the revolution of 1905 her parents returned to Russia, to St. Petersburg.

From the first moment of the February revolution Larissa Reissner was active in workers' clubs. She was also a collaborator in Gorykyi's paper, *New Life*. In the months directly after the October revolution she was engaged in taking over and cataloguing art treasures in museums.

But when the struggles began against the counter-revolution Larissa Reissner joined the party and went to the Czecho-Slovak front. She worked at Ssviyashsk, where the Red Army was actually forged in fighting the Czechs, and took part in the actions of the Volga fleet.

During the campaign she loved the sailors with a warm, brotherly love because of their simplicity and bravery and great humanity. Nobody ever dreamed that she was not only a comrade in arms at the front but also the wife of the fleet admiral, of Raskolnikov, at that time Commissary of the Naval Staff in Moscow, whom she had married in 1918.

In 1920 she went to Afghanistan, where her husband was ambassador, and spent two years at the court of an oriental despot. There she studied Marxist literature seriously, studied English imperialism and the history of the struggle for liberation in the neighbouring country of India, wrote her book *Afghanistan*, and was transformed from a Russian revolutionary to a soldier in the international army. In 1923 she returned to Soviet Russia, went to Dresden to work there, came to Hamburg during the rising, wrote her *Hamburg at the Barricades* and also *Coal, Iron, and Living Men,* and from thenceforward a new period began in Larissa Reissner's literary work.

And here is an extract from a hitherto unpublished letter of Larissa Reissner's to Lydia Sseyfullina, whose intimate friend she was ; at that time the poetess was just moving to Leningrad with her husband, to the " Scholars' House ", and Larissa urged her to return to Moscow ; this is a passage particularly in which she expresses her view about art, and it holds good just as much in Soviet Russia to-day :

. . . It is a long time since I wrote to you—and what right have I to arise and lament now that you have gone ? But it is not that. It is in Moscow that art is created, and in general that spider's web without which a person cannot live. Pityer (St. Petersburg) is a city of reflexes. You—in the Scholars' House ! In the midst of those people who are sick of mental malaria, soured and embittered, people whose sun has long ago set. Only a narrow strip of Polar light is still visible in their sky. And you—there ! However well you are and however sturdy Valerian Pavlovich's (the author Pravdukhin, Ssyefullina's husband) fists, it is death there, you mustn't be there. . . . Do get away soon !

Besides : Moscow is Asia, something like a bazaar in Samarkand. But you must sit there at your booth, you mustn't leave it. At the moment you are being attacked here. It was settled long ago, before your last book appeared, so that there can, of course, be no question of a justification. But all the people that are good for most in this desolate town are talking of you and thinking of you, as they should. Perhaps that is why the tiny handful of dirty reviewers are throwing so much mud at your name, because the great mass of the people have acknowledged your right to write as you choose. If you succeed, well and good. If you do not, that is your affair. That is just the privilege of such highly gifted people as you. You win that right at one stroke—once for all. And afterwards nobody can rob you of it. You won't be angry with me, will you ? I should like to beg one thing of you. Write something altogether bad, something nonsensical, topsy-turvy. You have to do that, else you can't advance a step. And let these brutes just swallow it. People like that must be given a good bang on the head, so that they may not dare to touch what an artist wins at so great a price : the price of his creative independence, the right either to roll in the gutter or to walk on the roof. . . .

And so we can understand how Larissa Reissner's mother, also a highly gifted woman, ended a letter to Lydia Sseyfullina when she was utterly broken by her daughter's early death : " . . . I kiss and embrace you, as I did her. For you, like her, are on fire with the grace of the elemental power. . . ."

It is hard to make any final statement about the position of women in the *plastic and pictorial arts* at the moment, although the world crisis in art, like the economic world crisis, is less keenly felt in the land of the Soviets. It is first necessary to build dwelling-houses, " kitchen factories ", eating-houses, children's crèches, homes, schools, hospitals, and so on. It is first necessary to be able to dress properly, to wash, have enough to eat, sleep one's fill, and recuperate, and then the decorative will follow. Nevertheless, the new complete cultural Five Years' Plan is concerned principally with such things, and Soviet Russian painters, sculptors, and graphic artists are not in distress. In so far as they are not occupied in schools of art and academies, the state gives them a variety of commissions. There is an immense deal of building going on in Soviet Russia, nothing but building : by native architects and by whole staffs of foreigners. And so the painters are called upon frequently to paint gigantic pictures, frescoes (the dream of every painter!) and panels for public buildings and institutions, " palaces of labour," workers' clubs, homes, etc., whilst the Soviet Russian poster, which is still in process of development, likewise makes great demands on the powers of the artist. The sculptors can embellish public squares, vast cultural parks, and socialist towns more than adequately, and carve statues of popular revolutionary leaders. Besides that the museums buy a great many modern works of art. Graphic artists have a wide field not only in the

309

highly developed art of book illustration and in newspapers and journals, but particularly in the children's
books—Soviet Russia's are the loveliest and most instructive that there are—which are decorated by men
artists, and even more by women. Men and women
artists are also called upon to collaborate in all the cinemas
and theatres, as well as in the planning of street proces-
sions, mass demonstrations, mass festivals, and mass
celebrations. I will only mention in passing that plastic
and pictorial art, like music, in Soviet Russia is almost
entirely lacking in the new form that will be an adequate
expression of the new substance—for that the time has
been too short—and the Russians can hardly be said ever
to have possessed plastic art of their own worth speaking
of ; that is a question that should be treated in quite a
different connection.

It is worth observing that the new line along which
women are developing in Soviet Russia, and which has
produced a certain masculinity in them, may be traced
just now in plastic art in the disproportionate number
of women, in Moscow for instance, who have taken up
sculpture, which after all involves a considerable physical
effort when it is necessary to work alone with large blocks
of solid material. Another circumstance is interesting to
note, which may be repeatedly observed in museums,
exhibitions of sculpture, and in all manner of private
studios (in Moscow the sculptors have formed a separate
organization and exhibit their work apart from the
painters) : whereas the men sculptors produce figures,
groups, busts, statues, and statuettes that are life-size at
most and frequently much smaller and possess a certain
charm, works which have an unmistakable kinship with
antique sculpture and for which, therefore, white marble
is greatly preferred in so far as it can be obtained, the
women principally exhibit work more than life-size and
incomparably robuster and more forceful. The consequence is that people talk in Soviet Russia of " assault
by women " not only in statecraft and politics, but also
in art, and chiefly in plastic art.

Besides the recognized women sculptors, Mukhina,

Lebedyova, and others, whose art, however, rather belongs to the past, it is chiefly Beatrissa Ssandomirskaya who has struck out independently, left the old tradition, and turned to the most beautiful native material, wood. From this wood, from birch, oak, and lime, Ssandomirskaya hews her peasant men and women ; and she works exactly in the same skilful way as that in which Russian peasants in the north formerly built not only the most perfect wooden churches, " dwelling-houses of God ", but also their own dwelling-houses, and produced the richest wood carving—with nothing but an axe in their hands, without making any sketch beforehand, straight from the tree-trunk. She draws her " boors "—as unfriendly critics call them—from the heart of the tree, from the innermost being of a material that has grown in her native soil, brings them to life, and only helps them, so to speak, to acquire that expressive, simple, laconic form because of which they seem, without any additional embellishment, without technical skill, to be works of nature, of organic growth, not to be repeated, speaking with the voice of an inspiration that comes from within.

At the age of fourteen Beatrissa Ssandomirskaya already attracted attention in St. Petersburg, and her *Styenyka Rasin* and peasant busts have often been exhibited with success abroad ; even in America people realized significantly enough from her work that " the plastic art of Soviet Russian women far outstrips that of the men in expressiveness, vigour, imagination, and colour " ; but like her own *Oktyabryonok*, she is herself as an artist a child of the October revolution. When in the summer of 1918 Lenin gave a commission for fifty monuments, in plaster of Paris in the first instance, for the Moscow squares, in the form of a competition to celebrate the first anniversary of the October revolution, and when half were put into the hands of fully qualified sculptors and the other half into those of young art students in the schools, Ssandomirskaya, who was still a student, asked to be entrusted with the monument of Robespierre—three monuments were planned for the revolutionaries Robespierre, Marat, and Danton. People warned her : " Who knows whether the revolution will survive till next year ; it would be safer, then, not to choose a revolutionary subject and to take the poet Kolytsov or Shevchenko." But it was useless to advise her against it, Ssandomirskaya insisted on taking Robespierre and delivered her statue in three months ; it was set up in the Alexander Garden by the wall of the Kremlin and really was blown up a week later by the Whites. But Ssandomirskaya won a prize for her work and used it to go to Turkistan, where she spent eighteen months and learned a great deal from the natives.

When she returned to Moscow she resumed her work, " wholly absorbed," to quote her own words, " in the revolution and the task of finding a new and adequate form for the new themes demanding expression." She produced a number of works, all in wood, including her really magnificent *Mother*, more than life-size and pulsing with warm life. It was no longer that Mother of God whose cult had flourished in old-time Russia as nowhere else, from the cathedral of the Moscow Kremlin where the Tsars were crowned to the smallest peasant's hut—a being remote from the world, denying the world, other-worldly, utterly immaterial, living only in the idea and the spirit —but the new-time Russian peasant mother, earthbound and still somewhat rude, both sturdy legs firmly planted in the soil and clearly not yet emancipated from the soil, the *Mother Black-Earth* who, promising victory and carrying her child in her arms, covers her blooming, exuberantly healthy, and beautiful nakedness with nothing at all but a *kossynka*, the *komssomolka's* head kerchief. This figure, a symbol not only of the new woman in Soviet Russia, but of the whole " Little Mother " Russia, watered by " Little Mother " Volga, deserved to be set up in a place of honour in the midst of " Little Mother " Moscow.

A certain note of masculinity strikes us in the work of the Soviet Russian women painters—Bebutova, Myelnikova, Kulagina, and Syernova—as well as in that of the women sculptors, and at the same time a permeation

MOTHER BLACK EARTH
Wood Carving by B. Ssandomirskaya

[face p. 312

with the new revolutionary subjects which is even more noticeable, perhaps because of their direct contact with the new *byt* (in posters, theatres, and illustrations). It would be difficult to imagine outside Soviet Russia that women painters should perpetually prefer such subjects for their pictures as " Women embroidering Banners ", " *Ssyelmashstroy* " (works for making agricultural machinery), " Building ", " In the Factory ", " Rifle-range ", and the like. But their other, womanly qualities find expression the more in decorating the children's books which I have already mentioned.

It is unnecessary to discuss the Russian theatre, for many people who have not been in the land of the Soviets are familiar with it, partly through their own eyes, partly because so much has been written about it. It is known that the Soviet Russian theatre, and indeed the theatre in general, has always been something wholly personal, profoundly serious and profoundly ethical, for the Russian public, a " moral institution ", a " school of human conduct ". It is known that there are nearly three dozen theatres in Moscow, and yet no sign of a theatrical crisis, and that every evening they are all sold out, some, indeed, weeks in advance, so that you often have to stand or run round for hours in order to get into any theatre at all. It is known, too, how close is the contact between the public and the stage, how strong the bond between them, and that the stage is often transposed into the auditorium. And lastly it is known that the Soviet Russian theatre is primarily a communal affair, in which all who collaborate —from the first to the last, so that there can hardly be said to be any who is last—regard their work as a kind of priestly calling, so that they study and play their great and minor parts with equal ardour, an equal devotion, sense of responsibility, and perfection. Consequently there are no stars in the Soviet Russian theatre and no *prima donnas*. Nay, more : as the new Russian plays contain as a rule few women's parts and no specifically feminine, erotic problems, no tension and conflicts between the sexes, but deal primarily with purely social, political, and economic questions, women as such, as

313

actresses, do not occupy anything approaching the place
in the Russian theatre that has been accorded to them in
civic life. In modern plays there are simply no " elegant
ladies " on the stage, unless perhaps as a caricature of
the *burshuyka*, the bourgeois woman. And whether they
are beautiful or not is for the most part of small account :
an actress need not excite, and allure, and carry away
anybody as a woman. For the stage, too, as a mirror
of life, is wholly swept clear of eroticism, mechanized,
made objective ; it sets itself quite other aims, lofty and
universally human. And the overwhelming impression
produced by the Russian theatre upon everybody is due
to its unsurpassed power of presentation still more than
to the splendour of its æsthetic form and the depth of its
purely ethical achievement. For the time being there
is no room here for sex or for a struggle between the
sexes. Here all are struggling together—on the stage as
in real life : to build a new world. And so in the new
Russian theatre there are no " tragic actresses " and no
actresses who are distinguished as stars : the serious
acting, which is here reckoned as life, knows nothing of
rival players, but only of collaborators in the play.

Whilst speaking of the theatre it is also worth mentioning that there are a number of women stage managers
in Soviet Russia, the best known being Natalya Ssats,
the admirable founder and manager of the first Moscow
children's theatre. There are various similar children's
theatres now in the Union, and they, too, bear eloquent
witness in their own way to the fact that the " century of
the child " has dawned in the land of the Soviets.

What has been said of actresses in the theatre is equally
true of film actresses. It would be vain to search among
them for Soviet Russian stars, and if you tried to find
the " heroine " of Eisenstein's film, *General Line*, which
has been presented with great success beyond the
frontiers of the Soviet state, you would find yourself
straight in the cowshed of a village in the Ryasany
Government : for Marfa Lapkina, who has been regarded
and admired as the central figure in the film, is nowise
a professional actress but a simple peasant woman

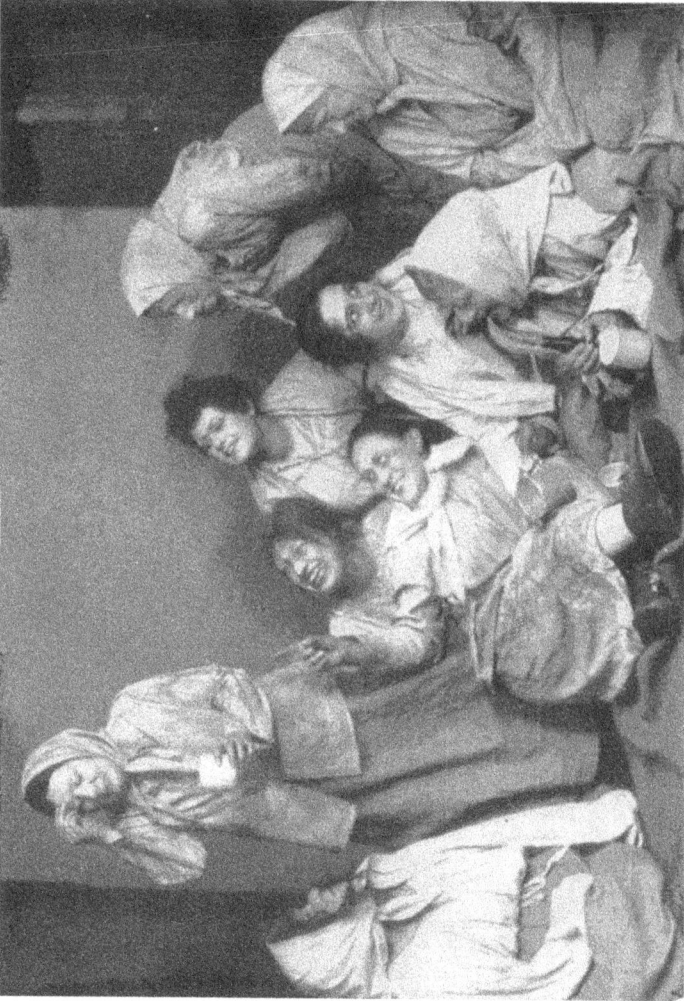

A GROUP OF PLAYERS AT THE MOSCOW ART THEATRE.
A Scene from *Resurrection*, after L. Tolstoy

[*face p.* 314

THE PEASANT WOMAN, MARFA LAPKINA
Principal Actress in Eisenstein's Film, *General Line*

[*face p.* 315

who has been working in the fields since her ninth year.

Eisenstein had first searched in vain among the actresses of Soviet Russia for someone suitable to represent the character : the attempt always failed because actresses could neither plough nor guide tractors nor milk cows. He hunted up thousands of peasant women in all imaginable villages for the purpose—the women were summoned by ringing the bells and carefully inspected to see if they would do ; but for several months nobody suitable was to be found. Eisenstein filmed all the workers in *sovkhosi*, making the women appear with their backs to the public, and one day, when he was almost in despair, he chanced to notice the back of the agricultural labourer Marfa Lapkina on one of these reels, and knew at once that she was the right one for his purpose. Marfa, who had never yet been present at a cinema performance, refused at first to leave her home. The money that was offered her induced her to consent, and she took her little son and set out on her travels with the film company. It was a far road. And the very first photographs showed that Marfa had no difficulty in fulfilling all the requirements of the cinema ; not only did she take well and make good pictures, but she could follow the slightest hint of the stage manager, and understood in no time what was wanted of her. She required only very few rehearsals. She herself was of opinion that these rehearsals only confused her. And really, if she was told briefly what she had to do, everything went well immediately.

When the film was finished and Marfa Lapkina was offered a post in a film factory, she refused and returned to her village, and it is very doubtful whether she will ever show her face in a studio again : it is lucky for the women stars of the cinema that this *baba* cares so little for world-wide fame.

And now the question arises : is this peasant woman Marfa, who possesses a true, native talent, a rare exception among the women of the Russian villages ? We can now answer with an assured No. For Marfa Lapkina is a

chip of exactly the same block as *Babushka* Marya Krivopolyenova, whom we already know, as Alyonushka
Novikova-Vashintsova, and as the millions of yet unknown, nameless village women who are now waking
from profound slumber, from pitchy night, are slowly
stretching their stiff limbs, trying to open their half-
closed eyes, to stand on their own feet, who are beginning
to walk and to grow into a new way of life. Into a new
era which not only comes to mould them, but receives
from them and their hitherto latent powers a new rich
note, a new wealth of colour, and, in spite of all the
process of Americanization, the stamp of the typically
Russian folk character.

IN PRODUCTION

ONE of the most emphatic demands of the October
revolution was that women should be given their place
in the process of production, and during the fifteen years
since the Soviets assumed power hardly anything has
been written or said about the economic development
of the new Russia without reference to the significance
of the expanding growth of women's labour. That in
itself is no speciality of Soviet Russia : in all countries
the rise of industrial production has gone hand in hand
with the growing participation of women in the manufacture of goods, so that even in Soviet Russia it need
not be regarded as other than the natural accompaniment
of the process of industrialization which set in at such
a tempestuous pace after the revolution. The craze for
figures that has seized the whole population of Soviet
Russia in recent years nowise alters the fact that women's
entry into economic life would be conceivable even without the revolution. What is unique, then, is not the
mere fact but, on the one hand, the unparalleled speed
and extent and, on the other, the circumstance that the
forces of economic progress, working according to a
natural law, are being consciously guided in the Union
according to plan, that an occurrence independent of
human agency is being subjected here, too, to the will
of the human community. It is only when regarded in

this light that the growing participation of women in the economic construction of the Soviet state can be considered as an historical innovation.

The resolve to regulate consciously according to plan a process which otherwise takes place more or less independently of the common will finds expression in the measures adopted to protect women's labour and working women. Hardly anywhere are such efforts made as in the Soviet Union to take the physiological peculiarities of the female organism into account in connection with employment, to show respect through the law for women's work as mothers, as described in the chapter on the problem of " Mother and Child ". The extension of women's labour here must not and cannot injure either the working woman herself or her offspring. Besides leave of absence for childbirth and legal provisions for the protection of mothers suckling their children, there is a general prohibition to employ women at work that is too much for their physical strength. Women under eighteen and over fifty are freed from the compulsion to work. And in particular the Soviet Union is the only country in which the unequal payment of men and women has ceased—which, as is well known, is one of the principal inducements to employ women in capitalist states : it is work that is paid for here, not sex.

And so factory work, which women in other countries, as formerly in pre-revolutionary Russia, only accept unwillingly under pressure of economic distress, appears to the great mass of women in the Soviet Union as their natural calling. The high-speed construction of recent years and the appearance of great new centres of industry brought about an influx of working women into the factories which exceeds all expectations, and latterly the calculations of the Five Years' Plan. Women's work is expanding in all branches of industry. In 1931 about six million women were occupied in productive labour in the Soviet Union, double the number in the middle of 1930, and 1932 augmented that number by a further million and a half. That means that *one-third of the whole labour force of the Soviet Union consists of women*. In quite a number of the factories, known in the Union as " female factories ", the number of women employed is out of all proportion to the men. In these factories with a majority of women the *troyka*, which is responsible for all the work as well as for the feeding of the workers, generally consists of two women and only one man.

A detailed survey of the branches of industry in which women are more or less numerously represented is unnecessary here, the more so because it would only amount to an enumeration of almost all. I will only mention that the number of women workers is largest —after agriculture—in the cotton industry, in transport, in the ready-made clothing trade, and in communal concerns. Of course women carry on a number of trades that have hitherto been regarded as unsuited to them : for instance, a great many are employed in the coal mines. There are everywhere to-day women builders, women station-masters, women conductors, and so on. In Ssamara, for instance, all the tramway workers are women. And as " storm workers " they themselves carry out all repairs and other mechanics' jobs on their " storm coaches ".

As one would expect, as the number of employed women increases so does their participation in the work of the trade unions, in which 4,500,000 of them are now organized. Among 773 executive members of the trade unions there were already 104 women in 1931 ; similarly they filled about 20 per cent of the places in works' councils and other productive committees. And the vigorous share of industrial women workers in social activities is evident from the circumstance that in many branches of industry—engineering, mining, and the coal industry—the number of women who fill public official positions is greater than that of men.

Yet it is not only the quantitative increase in women's work which marks the position of women in Soviet industry, but to a far greater degree its qualitative development. The whole Soviet Union is covered by a single network of courses on technical subjects, agricultural science, and pedagogy, accessible to all, and in these the women improve their qualifications and prepare themselves for the Workers' Faculties and technical colleges : the pupils in the factory apprentices' schools, where skilled labour is chiefly trained, consisted as early as 1931 of 47 per cent girls ; and in addition there are opportunities for the working women to requalify in the factories themselves. The question was particularly under discussion in 1931 when the influx of women into the factories was increasing. When the conveyor system was introduced into the Charkov tractor works letters were printed in *Pravda* from various experienced works' managers emphasizing the greater aptitude of women workers, even for delicate processes. The People's Commissariat of Labour was instructed to determine a number of branches of industry in which skilled women workers could be employed. And so once more wide prospects were opened out to Soviet Russian women which could hardly have been dreamt of before the revolution. The trade of fitter, of electrician, of engine-tender in mines, of die-sinker, of turner, and a number of other special metal trades, as well as highly skilled work in the chemical, textile, and foodstuffs industries, were opened to them.

An increasing number of women are, therefore, employed on skilled labour to-day. In the great " Hammer and Sickle " Works in Moscow there are nearly 60 per cent women ; in the steel wire-works, where at the end of 1928 there were no women employed, there are already 31 per cent. In the new Russia there are airwomen, women veterinary surgeons, railway engineers, and tractor drivers. And if you ask Soviet Russian girls what occupation they want to take up later, the answer is generally : civil engineer, constructing motor roads and bridges and sinking mines, mechanical engineer, architect, agricultural scientist, chemist, or hydraulic engineer. These are wishes which may easily be fulfilled in Soviet Russia to-day. For the career, too, of women employed in the factory lies by way of skilled work to engineer and thence to works manager. Any working woman may gradually reach the position of master, assistant manager, and manager. In 1931 there were already eighteen women managers in the Soviet Union. In one such factory with a woman manager, the tobacco works " Rosa Luxemburg " in Rostov on the Don, I heard that all the responsible posts there were likewise occupied by women. In this factory—which, by the way, publishes its own paper, *The Voice of the Bench*— when I visited it in the autumn of 1931, the number of women employed had fallen considerably, to 50 per cent of the total, because the most capable skilled workers were sent to other factories from time to time in order to increase production. It is common to find women as departmental managers, and even for the *Dnyeprostroy*, the country's gigantic dam, a woman is directing engineer.

In Moscow and Leningrad, too, women are placed at the head of several factories as managers or deputy managers, for the most part former employees who had worked ten years or longer in the factory in question. Until recently the men in these professions were very sceptical on the subject. How often one heard : " We will wait and see how the ' manager in petticoats ' turns out." But she has since turned out very well indeed, and to-day most of the doubters are converted.

It is hardly necessary to explain at length that this immense growth of women's work, and the practice of seemingly quite unwomanly occupations, has changed the character and mentality of Soviet Russian women in town and country considerably. And the fact that the average type of Russian woman has undergone a change which is only approximately described by saying that she has acquired male characteristics is linked first and foremost with the problem which rose to transient importance even in Western states during the world war in consequence of the shortage of men, but, as we have seen, is due to other causes in Russia and of growing actuality. It is involved in that remoulding of life that I propose to deal with in the next chapter, and which is causing the " housewife " to die out. The factory —and employment in general—has long ceased to be

WOMAN MASON ENGAGED IN THE BUILDING OF ENGINE WORKS
in the Ural Province

[face p. 320

WOMEN WORKERS ON A SOVIET PLANTATION

[face p. 321

felt as a painful necessity in Soviet Russia, as in other
countries, or sometimes as a means of passing the time ;
it is a lifework and the aim of existence. " Whereas in
Tsarist days," writes M. Denissova, " women thought
themselves lucky if they could occupy themselves with
housework and only escape taking up the factory work
that made havoc of their lives, at the present time women
regard productive work that is of service to the community
as the essential aim of their existence."

Here, too, then, we see how the growing participation
of women in productive work is producing a new type
of woman, whose incarnation—the representative woman
of the new Russia—is the young tractor driver, just as
the tractor is the symbol of industrialization, of socialist
construction.

As the modern Russian sketch writers have attempted
to capture this type, I will quote a sketch of such a
tractor driver from Gorykyi's journal *Our Achievements* :

. . . Polinka had come to the commune from Moscow. As
rudder-wheel she has brought the firm determination that on no
account shall her sex prevent her from carrying out her duties.
She wears a blue blouse and a *kepka* is cocked on her sparse,
bobbed, lustreless hair, to which a pair of motoring spectacles
is attached. Polinka is very tall, has square shoulders, hard
hands, and hairy lower arms like a man's. It is only above her
elbows that Polinka begins to be a woman, so strong and firm
are her hands. In her Red Army coat she looks like a boy, and
the angularity of her movements is, perhaps, only mitigated by
the unconscious remembrance that she is a woman and that it
is her duty to be a woman. Maybe she represents precisely the
type of woman born on the steppes, where women have always
had the right to do men's work so that it fails to astonish even the
most insipid of novelists.

The gang had gone to the field the day before and all day long
the tractors had been at work ; the hot breakfast—millet with
milk—was brought by a Red Army field kitchen in the ninth
hour. . . . Whilst Polinka was waiting for the meal I sat down
beside her outside the tent : " And what of your young life ? "
I asked by way of opening the conversation. She took off her
cap and her tousled, colourless hair stood on end. She told me
that she had studied in Moscow, had been employed there in an

engineering works, and had passed through a course for tractor drivers. Then she came here, to the steppes, where she meant to die, for the whole Union was her home. This was the right place for her, and here she would stay, unless she were transferred somewhere where she was more urgently needed.

" And your home ? Your husband ? Or your child, if you have one ? " I interposed.

" That is of no account," she said, and I felt that it would prove a barren subject of discourse. I knew that she had a husband, who had just driven to the station to fetch firewood, and would doubtless return to the commune, but who would not once come out to her in the field in all the succeeding days. . . .

The shift was relieved. The night was black and solemn and the ploughed triangle spread like a carpet of damp sand beneath the scanty light of the stars.

Cautiously, with clattering blades, the tractor slid from the grass down to the ploughed strip of land, and only then did Polinka's really responsible work begin. For she was not an ordinary tractor driver, such as any boy could become to-morrow who mounts the tractor to-day. She had to keep a straight line and would draw the furrow between two guiding posts that the agricultural experts had set up, almost as straight as a line drawn on paper with a ruler. And the others would follow with their tractors in that line. Perhaps this sense of straightness was so strongly marked in Polinka because she had the commander's furrow between her eyebrows.

The black tractor that ploughed the virgin steppe seemed to me like a ship steered by a mechanic's hand, like the flagship of a squadron leading the boys' clattering tractors into the struggle. And so I gradually grasped how it was that I had never once heard Polinka called a *baba* in the commune.

THE FIVE YEARS' PLAN AND WOMEN

AT the present time, when the *Pyatiletka*, the Five Years' Plan, is finished and the second Five Years' Plan is ready in the form of a cultural *Pyatiletka*, it is not necessary to tell a Western European reader much about the epoch-making attempt to build up industry organized according to plan on a gigantic scale. The time is long past when people thought the Five Years' Plan was an " engineering romance " of a nation with a tendency to unrealist day-dreaming ; rather it has

WOMAN MECHANIC REPAIRING A TRACTOR

[face p. 322

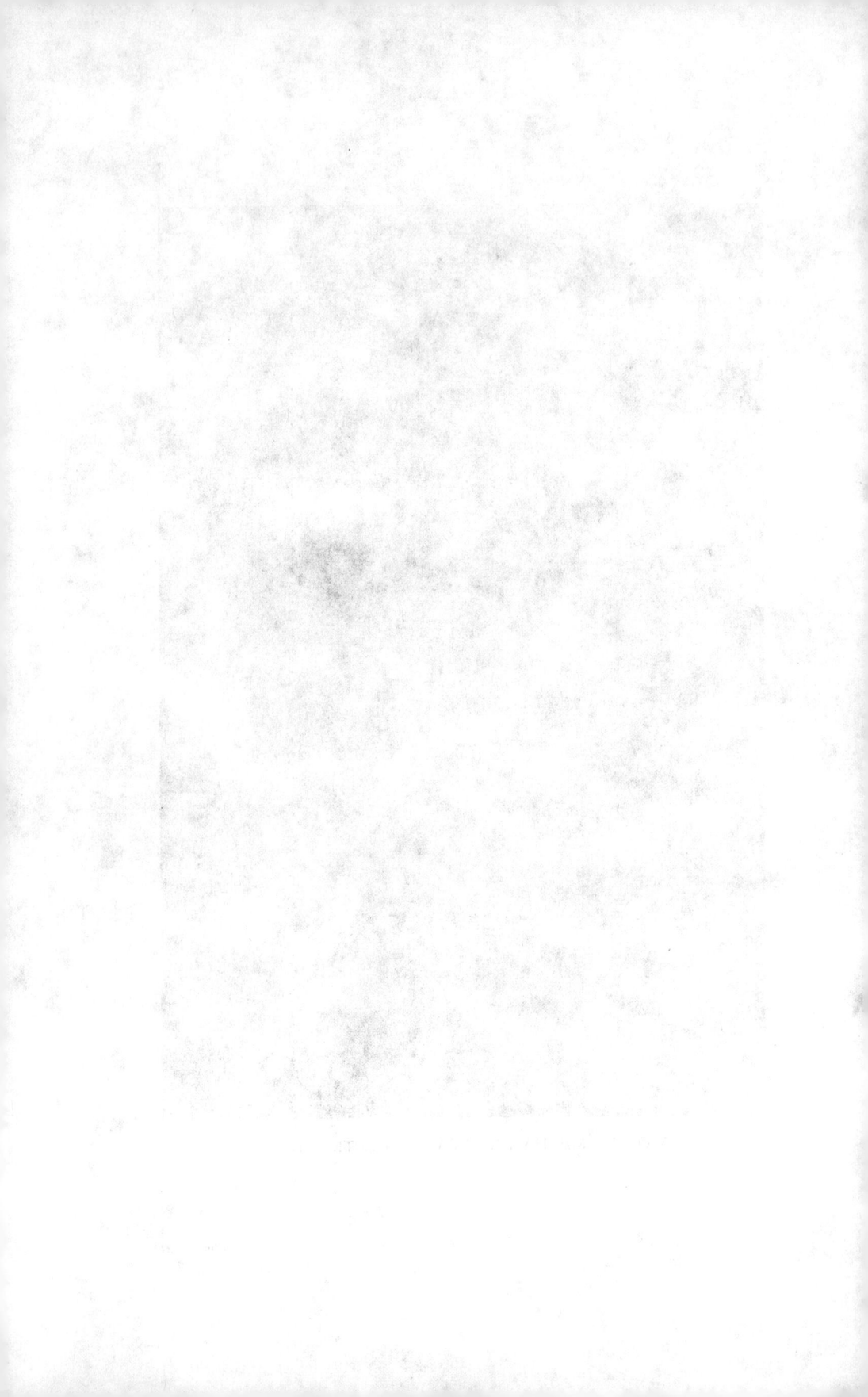

proved a living epic of labour. Where not long ago deserted steppes and uncultivated woods and fields stretched, gigantic works now rise aloft, monuments of man's constructive will, full of promise for the future.

The Five Years' Plan was like a tempest : it was the outcome not of wage labour but of the fire of battle and stimulating images of the future which made even the present glow. The driving power for the immense demands which the Plan made on every individual sprang from nerves made tense day after day by intoxicating figures and an emotion which never fails to grip a people receptive of everything on a grand scale : they accepted the superhuman sacrifices and privations required of them with a true heroism which it is difficult for Western Europeans to understand. It is rare in the new Russia to meet a person who is not in a certain sense a martyr of the Five Years' Plan and does not show signs of overwork and overtiredness. But life in Soviet Russia is a permanent state of war, it demands the day-to-day exertion of all one's strength, and the exhausted body is restored by perpetually renewed enthusiasm.

In this heroic struggle women, who are accorded equality in state, industry, and intellectual life, were called upon to play an equally responsible part. It is universally recognized that women have contributed at least as much as men, and perhaps even more, to the fulfilment of the grandiose Plan. Indeed, they have actually proved to be the pillars of the Plan, for reasons that are in part specifically Russian and in part general : they do not drink, do not shirk any work, do not swindle, are even more capable of enthusiasm than the men, and not least, it is said of them that they know how to handle the machines, those precious possessions of the state, more carefully than the men, against whom serious accusations are made in precisely this connection.

The Five Years' Plan, which has enriched the Russian language with a quantity of newly coined technical terms, almost all derived from war, has produced new forms of labour organization. Thus the true pillars of the Five

Years' Plan are the " battalions ", the storm workers, in whose ranks there are, significantly enough, more women than men. Whilst about half the men belong to storm brigades, no less than 60 per cent of the women are *udarnitsas*, and some little time ago *Pravda* wrote that these women storm workers often attained a speed which the men failed to reach. But what the women accomplished in the service of the Plan in almost all the factories in the country exceeded the boldest expectations. In most large works the women storm workers are in the majority, as, for instance, in the Putilov Works, famous in the history of the revolution, where 1,600 of the 2,500 women workers are enrolled in storm brigades. In Magnitogorsk it was the women storm workers who first showed all the rest how working speed could be stimulated and accelerated. And in the Rostov tobacco factory, a fully rationalized concern in which the shifts follow one another in unbroken succession, the unparalleled skill of the women workers amazed me ; they did not turn their heads, did not even raise their eyes from their work, and carried out their tasks with the precision of machines.

Of course it took some years before women attained such perfect skill in industrial labour. To quote an example :

In 1928 the Leningrad tractor works, the Red Putilovets, needed new hands ; instead of 3,000 tractors, as hitherto, they were to produce 12,000 tractors in the second year of the *Pyatiletka* ; hitherto they had employed no women. But there were not enough male workers at the Labour Exchange, and so a number of women were sent to the factory.

The management of the tractor section was indignant and exclaimed : why are they sent ? What are we to do with them ? Surely everybody knows that a woman can be neither a locksmith nor a turner nor a cutter of cog-wheels. But the Labour Exchange continued doggedly to send women and the tractor section had to make the best of it.

And now a dogged struggle began in the workshops in which the newly engaged women workers fought for their rights and for recognition. The first women's brigade was organized.

It consisted of eight women, two of whom were Party members. This brigade was headed by the working woman Ssyemyonova. Much depended upon the victory or defeat of this women's brigade, especially the recognition of women as equal fellow workers. The members thought it over. Every day there was a bitter struggle for the quality and quantity of their output.

It was not long before results appeared. Thanks to the women's careful and conscientious work the brigade managed to get rid entirely of the waste which generally occurs through the fault of the worker. Moreover, no member of the brigade absented herself from work without being able to offer a serious reason.

The brigade celebrated the first victory on the long and difficult road on which the storm workers had set forth. The second victory : no more waste through the fault of the workers ; further, no more absences without a serious reason ; likewise no late-comers. The struggle proceeded. The women workers captured one bench after another, section after section.

At the present time there are women there engaged in every kind of work. They are even employed in places where a few years ago no woman was to be seen, where nobody had thought of employing a woman. Everywhere—at the benches, by the cranes, in the casting shops—the women workers have won their spurs. And in quality their work is no worse than the men's.

There are five women storm workers at the costly imported benches in the cog-wheel cutting shop, where highly skilled and accurate work is done under the foreman Andrey. And what does the foreman say about them ?

" I have no complaint to make either of the quality or the quantity of the women's work. And as regards workshop discipline, the conscious attitude towards the work and the plant, the women workers are much better than the men. The women stick deliberately to their work and are very careful with the plant. And one characteristic circumstance deserves mention : it never happens that an instrument is damaged through the fault of a woman worker." (*Yelykovich* and *Shileyko, Women Storm Workers.*)

Efforts are made to stimulate the pleasure and delight in productive work among the storm workers, and especially the women, by rewards and honours. In addition to the various orders, which are granted fairly freely—in *Traktorstroy* in Stalingrad a woman was the

first to receive the Order of the Red Labour Banner—
bonuses are often distributed. These take the shape
of useful articles, books and clothing, which are specially
welcome to the recipients in a country suffering for the
time being from a shortage of manufactured goods.
Even more popular than bonuses for storm work are the
so-called storm workers' books, which entitle the holder
to obtain wares of which not nearly enough are produced
to meet the demand. When 263 of the storm workers
employed in the mechanical section of the above-
mentioned works in Stalingrad—they are 48 per cent
of the total number of employed women—were suddenly
rewarded with such books, the event was celebrated
as a fresh triumph of women's work. In two cases
several hundred storm workers, including about 30
per cent women, were granted a trip to Western Europe
on board a Soviet steamer as a reward for the performance of storm work. The distinction was all the greater
since it is exceedingly rare for Soviet Russian workers
to see foreign lands—which they regard as something
almost fabulous—with their own eyes. No wonder
that the journals and newspapers went on for months
publishing the reports and stories of these foreign travellers, which were sometimes very interesting, but
sometimes exceedingly naïve and comical.

The zeal of the male and female storm workers is
kindled by the honour which they enjoy before Soviet
Russian public opinion even more than by rewards:
for they are set up as the type of the new, socialist
humanity, and made much of. And we can hardly
doubt that the type really is something quite new when
we read the following poems, written by women storm
workers, and then think of women's lyric poetry in
Western Europe:

THE SONG OF THE WOMEN STORM WORKERS

Oh, no, we will not stay nor pause,
Class-conscious we, and strong;
The burning force of Russia's cause
Welds all our hearts in one.

WOMAN STORM WORKER FROM A *KOLKHOS*

Be firm, thou heart of steel,
  My heart, with ardour swell;
We needs must haste,
We needs must haste,
  To rest now were not well.

Malignants who would injure us,
  In hell's deep jaws we'll throw.
See the stream of molten steel,
  Its red and fiery glow.

    Grow, industry, prosper and grow,
      'Tis our will, our delight.
    Magnitogorsk shall be cast up
      By hearts of dynamite.

The ore for centuries long hid
  Now stirs beneath the mould,
And train on train
Is brought to gain
  Its precious freight, black gold.

    Oh, no, we will not stay nor pause,
      Class-conscious we, and strong;
    The burning force of Russia's cause
      Welds all our hearts in one.
                    TATYANA KORETSKAYA.

STORM TRUCKS

Signal-boxes, semaphores, and rails,
  Rhythmically wheels are rolling still. . . .
And the engine draws behind the long
  Chain of waggons crawling up the hill.

Iron comes from the Urals;
  The Don gives black coal to us;
Timber and planks are sent from the North,
  Oil from the Caucasus.

The lights are gleaming forth like flames,
  The whistle's a joyful call;
Tractors and tanks we know there'll be,
  And factory benches and all.
                    V. SHAPOSHNIKOVA.

The hero-worship of storm workers of both sexes in the party assumes forms which recall the manner in which sporting champions or film favourites are honoured in other countries. There is hardly a factory in Soviet

Russia in which the outer hall or courtyard is not embellished with a portrait gallery of the " heroes and heroines " of the day. In order that all may have their turn, the pictures are frequently changed, and even more has been done : just as in Berlin there is a " Siegesallee ", so the famous " Park of Culture and Recreation " in Moscow has its *Udarnik* Walk, bordered on either side with busts—of small artistic merit, it is true—of distinguished men and women storm workers. The press, too, is readily at the service of this successful propaganda. And the Marxist Karl Radek argues as follows that such a cult of heroes is compatible with socialist theory, which more or less denies the significance of personality :

> Neither Marx nor Lenin held that the masses are composed of identical individuals. History was not to them the struggle of an unarticulated, anonymous mass. So long as the human race survives it will constitute an advance guard that will struggle to solve the problems posed by history. There have been and still are heroes, but their heroism is the expression of mass endeavour ; their heroism can lead to victory only if it becomes mass heroism, if it raises the masses to its own level. (*Moscow Review* of August 16th, 1931.)

What encourages willingness to pledge everything for the Five Years' Plan even more than the institution of workers' Storm Brigades is socialist competition : the spirit of sporting rivalry is transferred to the field of industry. As almost invariably when it is a question of a watchword introduced into practical life, we have here a mass phenomenon which has captured the whole of Soviet Russian production. The Russian motto is : Enthusiasm plus organization. And Stalin spoke on the subject at the Sixteenth Conference of the All-Russian Communist party : " What is most important in competition is that it changes a man's attitude towards work fundamentally, and raises it from the heavy, oppressive burden, for which it has hitherto counted, to an affair of honour, of glory, of heroism. There is nothing similar in capitalist countries and can be nothing, for there the supreme good fortune to which everyone

aspires is to possess a private income, to live on divi-
dends, and to escape from work, which is regarded as
something despicable. But with us in Soviet Russia,
on the contrary, the only aspiration which is publicly
approved is to be a hero of competition, surrounded by
the halo of the reverence of millions of workers."

There is competition between the separate departments of a factory and between whole factories. We
gather from statistics the zeal with which the Russian
women enter into it : of the women employed in the
metallurgical industry in 1931, 44 per cent took part
in competitions, 54 per cent of those in chemical works,
57 per cent of those in the textile mills, and 59 per cent
of those in the paper industry. Since then the per-
centages have risen further among the women. But
in the same measure they are turning away from love,
and in the textile district of Ivanovo-Vosnyessyensk,
where there are more than 60 per cent women among
the workers, there is a four-lined verse which the young
men sing to the accompaniment of the accordion, a verse
which gives humorous expression to their resignation :

> Caresses ? Once upon a day,
> But now she's careless of my woe.
> " So long," she says in her rough way,
> " The competition, I must go."

The women's journals have a permanent column for
appeals to enter competitions and announcements of
their result. When you look in the most widely read
journal of that type, the *Rabotnitsa*, and see this column
headed " Appeal to Storm Women throughout the
Union ", you are strangely affected : here storm women
workers answer the appeal of the female storm battalions
in Magnitogorsk ; they engage to improve the quality
of their work, to redouble their efforts for the organization of cultural institutions, and to train for better
and more skilled work. There storm brigades state
with satisfaction that they have proved their mettle in
the battle of labour. Again, working women complain
that their factory is insufficiently rationalized. Now

women miners promise that they will throw themselves into the task of catching up the arrears which are unfortunately increasing, and will deliver the " black gold " in the quantities required by the Plan. And now factories announce that they are about to take on a large number of women workers and so promote the drawing of women into the process of production. Now ruthless war is declared on shirking. And now ways and means are pointed out and slackers swept into the whirlpool of tempestuous production.

Let me give an example to show how a competition is carried on within a factory. In the Leningrad factory *Leninka* a red banner is instituted to reward the department which shows the best results in the coming month. For four whole weeks the factory is in a fever. In the entrance to the workshops movable diagrams are shown with all the symbols customary in competitions : an aeroplane for record achievements in the shortest time, and beside it, symbolizing decreasing speed, a motor-car, a train, a tortoise, and a crab. The diagrams show the position in the competition from day to day. At the end of the month it is carefully ascertained which department has produced the best results, including the degree of participation in political and social work. And since two departments have ultimately produced equally good results, a general factory meeting has to be summoned to decide which of the two is to receive the prize, the red banner.

Interesting, too, are the individual competitions—which perhaps go rather too far—which are not infrequently between women and men, and even between husband and wife. Socialist competition penetrates the home and sweeps along the few who refuse to keep the pace of the times. A wife whose husband and son are working in the factory, who belong to storm brigades and are constantly entering for competitions, cannot bear to remain at her domestic hearth ; she begins to listen, to follow what goes on outside the four walls of her kitchen, and she steps in. In Stalingrad brigades were formed of 500 housewives to control victualling

330

and the communal food supply. In the Don Basin housewives and girls determined to work once in five days in the mines and to hand over their wages for the erection of an engineering college. They drew up an appeal to all workers' wives, and from the next day only children remained in the settlement and one woman in every five houses to look after them. And indeed it was no trifling labour which these women performed on that one day : they loaded two goods trains with coal, brought so much mine-timber that it lasted for a fortnight, and oiled a number of lorries. But even that did not satisfy them. They chose a storm group from among their number and made them promise to learn the work in the ore-sorting department and to get to understand the machines within a fortnight, so that the men might work in the pit and yield their places in the sorting department to the women.

The Soviet press recently reported one of the most comical cases, a competition between a housewife and her husband in Bashkirs. The woman's challenge was as follows :

" In order to expedite the speed of construction in the fifth year of the *Pyatiletka*, I, Anichkova, challenge my husband, Konstantin Anichkov, to a socialist competition and accept the following obligations :

" I will be economical with our earnings and only buy the most necessary articles. I will not spend a single copek on superfluous things like scent, powder, etc.

" On no account will I tolerate my husband shirking his work in the factory and will combat drunkenness at home by all means in my power.

" I will devote the utmost attention to bringing up our children in the spirit of communism, will do away with the habit of missing party and delegate meetings without serious reason, and will see to it that other housewives also attend such meetings.

" I will enforce hundred per cent fulfilment of all obligations imposed by the Party and the Delegate Headquarters and bring my husband to the *Politschool* and the Party meetings."

The husband announced his acceptance of his wife's challenge in the following words :

" I accept the challenge of my wife to a socialist competition. I undertake to carry out all the points and add on my own account :

" I will not keep a single copek at home, but will put all money into the savings bank.

" On the issue of the ' Five Years' Plan in Four Years ' loan I will exchange all bonds in my possession for that and will in addition subscribe a sum equal to my income for one and a half months.

" I will take an active part in the work of the organizations for social work such as *Ossoafiakhim*, *Mopr*, The Red Assistance, etc., and if these bodies have no branches here, I will organize them.

" I will subscribe to the journals *Red Bashkirs*, *Besboshnik* and *The Atheist*, and for the children *Mursilka*, till the end of the year.

" K. ANICHKOV."

(From *Rabotnitsa*, January, 1931.)

There are also other forms of competition within the family. But what is probably most remarkable is the cases of competition between parents and children—a thing that would be wholly incomprehensible outside Russia. I have before me a draft agreement written by an eleven-year-old schoolgirl with her own hand from a place in the neighbourhood of Moscow ; here is its characteristic wording :

SOCIALIST AGREEMENT

I —— a worker in the —— factory, conclude an agreement with my $\begin{Bmatrix} \text{daughter,} \\ \text{son} \end{Bmatrix}$ the Pioneer —— in which I undertake till the conclusion of the *Pyatiletka* to collaborate in the closest possible manner with my factory, and I join the storm brigade " Fourth Year of the *Pyatiletka* ".

I, a young Pioneer, sign this agreement and promise that I will not have unsatisfactory marks in any subject, will never be late for school, never play truant, will attend Pioneer instruction diligently, and not fail to pass on from any group. I bring this agreement to the knowledge of the school soviet and the Pioneer troop.

332

FIVE YEARS' PLAN AND WOMEN

We can tell how powerfully the current of socialist competition carries people along from the fact that it has gradually flooded the villages, which in other respects are still backward. A report which appeared in *Pravda* on March 8th, 1932, which I quote in abbreviated form, illustrates vividly how such a competition between husband and wife in a southern cotton *kolkhos* is carried on :

Vassyka is in a bad humour. His wife has exposed him in an unheard-of manner before the whole village, has made him the laughing-stock of all the peasants. The damned *baba* has had the impudence to insert a notice in the commune wall news-paper in which he is represented as an incurable slacker and loafer. According to former customs, he ought to give his wife a good beating. But now the times have changed. Still, he will not put up with the insult, and the next evening he goes to the editor of the wall newspaper with the following announce-ment, asking that it may be published :

" My wife has challenged me to a competition. Yesterday she gathered thirty-six kilograms of cotton. But I have gathered fifty-two kilograms to-day, and I pledge myself to increase the amount to sixty in the next few days. And I call upon you, *Tovarishch* Editor, to publish the following appeal to all the men in the *kolkhos* of the New Lighthouse in my name : Men, do not stay at home, do not listen to the *kulak* fable telling you that the gathering of cotton is women's work. All, without exception, follow my example."

This letter was discussed in all the *kolkhos* meetings, and the women took the offensive against their husbands, brothers, and neighbours who had shirked hitherto. It was a battle without much noise. A new weapon had appeared in the village, known as competition, the press, publicity. And the new village woman, the *kolkhos* woman, the woman storm worker, adopted that weapon.

But in a neighbouring village the shirkers summoned a meet-ing, which resulted in the following letter appearing in the local newspaper : Hitherto we have been shirkers, but in future we shall give the *kulaks* little cause for satisfaction. From this day we declare that we are non-shirkers, are storm workers, and will follow the example of the men and women who have been working at storm workers' speed on the cotton planta-tion.

333

Where storm work and competitions have failed to penetrate, the Five Years' Plan has brought about a radical change in the way of life and attitude of mind of the villages by means of the *collectivization* so much debated in Western Europe. A considerable proportion of the individual peasant holdings were transformed into component parts of a communal system of agriculture, into *kolkhosi*, and that at a pace which had later to be checked ; and many expectations have been fulfilled, and even exceeded, by results, since the Communist party issued its pregnant watchword : " Eyes on the village ! " In spite of certain relapses the villages, collectivized to a considerable degree, have accustomed themselves to the new way of life in a relatively short time, and absurd ideas such as were possible only a few years ago, at the beginning of the process of collectivization, now belong to the realm of fable. Thus when collectivization was first initiated in a village in the Ryasany Government, the women assembled weeping and lamenting in the market-place and begged that their plaits might not be cut off. They could not survive such disgrace and threatened therefore to appeal to Moscow with a petition.

The steadily growing participation of the peasant women in the committees for mutual assistance in the villages and in the agricultural co-operatives is a sign of the strengthening of social feeling among the rural population ; where agriculture has not yet been collectivized these co-operatives serve the very important purpose of uniting the scattered farms and meeting the needs of the workers. And a simple instance with which the writer Panfyerov, one of those who knows most of the subject, illustrated the position to me, shows how the changed circumstances are transforming the whole manner of life of the peasantry : A peasant owned a house, a cow, a pig, and a bit of land. He meant his son to marry. Of course his father looked out for a wife for him who also possessed a strip of land, chests, cows, and pigs. But now he no longer needs land, or a cow, or a pig. He neither has anything himself nor seeks it for his son, who has no need of it. All these restrictions vanish—and so the son can marry the girl he likes. The old people no longer even oppose him.

Assuredly the part played by women in the collectivization of agriculture and in the life of the *kolkhosi* is also important, and of no less account than in all the other fields of material and intellectual production. In the management of the *kolkhosi* they are often called upon to direct, and if the requirements of the Five Years' Plan in basic production, which are frequently pitched high, can just be satisfied, it is not seldom due to the enthusiastic collaboration of the *kolkhosnitsa*. The woman president of a *kolkhos* in the Don Basin, where there are 70 per cent women and the deputy president is also a woman, answered my question about her life in the *kolkhos* as follows : " Of course it is easier now than in individual farming before collectivization. It is true that we work from early morning till evening and in case of need into the night, because we have to deliver three times as much grain to the state as formerly. All the same, we don't leave the work to anyone else. We work conscientiously. And we are better nourished now. And dress ourselves and our children better. Judge for yourself if our lives are not easier. Formerly the *kolkhos* women were hampered by their children, but now twenty-seven crèches, besides schools and wash-houses, have been set up in the settlements on the steppes and so the *kolkhos* women have been liberated for productive work, so that at the present time there are 120 women beside 147 men occupying responsible posts in the *kolkhos*."

It is well known that one weak point in the process of collectivization is the shortage of cows, rendered really serious by acts of sabotage by large-scale farmers who were too hastily forced into *kolkhosi*. Here, too, the women often stepped in in the interests of the state and the Plan. Thus the milkmaids of a dairy *kolkhos* in Novodyerevyankovo relate in the journal *Krestyanka* how in the previous September they saved their stock of cattle from destruction. When the place was socialized the small peasants' cows were brought with those of the large-scale farmers together to one farm, and nobody troubled about them any more. At the instigation of the party cell the former milkmaids and the poor peasant women of the place took charge of the half-starved beasts, organized themselves, and within six months had created a flourishing model dairy farm in which the number of milch cows had been doubled and not only the quantity but also the quality of the produce had been considerably improved.

In a general way, indeed, it is no more possible to speak of a marked type of *kolkhos* woman than it is to pass final judgment on collectivization. It is just in the country that the old and the new come into collision with elemental force, and it is doubtless hard for some peasant women to adapt themselves to the new conditions in the villages. But the authorities do everything to facilitate the transition for them and to raise and strengthen their self-confidence. And Ssergey Tretyakov, in a meeting of the *kolkhos* to which he is attached as a writer, cried to them : " Do not creep into hiding, *kolkhosnitsa*. Hold your head high. Look proudly before you. You are the centre of observation from all quarters of the earth. You are far more famous in the world now than all the Shalyapins. People admire you and learn from your example." At which the *babas* nudged one another and giggled, saying : " Sh-sh, they're looking at us from America."

The figurative statement of *Babushka* Lukerya, an old *kolkhos* woman from the commune " Lenin's Spark " (Kursk Government), in *Isvestya* of May 8th, 1932, explaining why the transition period in the *kolkhos* is often so hard for the women, is moving and very Russian :

> The new life is born in struggle. The village, like a woman, gives birth in pain. A delivery is always painful. And that is why the women are so full of lamentations. Before the child actually comes, they always scream louder and louder. But hardly has it appeared when devotion springs up, fervent mother-love, anxious care, and the impulse to guard the young from all enemies and all evil in the world.

But the real heroine of collectivized agriculture is the woman tractor driver, of whom we have already given a sketch. Although she works in the country, she is essentially an industrial worker, a champion of the Five Years' Plan and the new *byt* in the village, whose assimilation to the town raises her to a type of historic significance. Moreover, it is generally said in her praise that she outdoes the men in working capacity and enterprise. When in the autumn of 1931 field work was proceeding too slowly in several remote *kolkhosi* in the Urals, 300 women from the *sovkhos* Gigant in the south, under the leadership of ten delegated women tractor drivers, went there and established a new *kolkhos*, organized storm brigades and competitions, fired hundreds of peasant men and women by their example, very quickly caught up with the arrears, and cultivated vast tracts of virgin soil. Soviet Russian mythology has made this enterprise its own, and it has become part of the history of the Five Years' Plan under the name of the " Great Campaign ", remembered with fervent gratitude.

And when you hear people sing and speak of this campaign of the women tractor drivers on their " steel chargers " in the Urals, and of similar achievements of the women in the Five Years' Plan, you really do seem to be listening to the tempestuous roll of a yet unwritten epic, the epic of the new Russian woman. . . .

I have a vision of builders at their unceasing work. . . . We
have to create a new world and a new humanity and new forms
of human relations. . . . The land is labouring day and night.
All are working, nobody enjoys the privilege of idleness.
Altogether, we have done away with idlers. . . .

—PILNYAK.

THE preceding chapter dealt with the question
how Soviet Russian women are taking possession of the new realm which the revolution
has created for them. But little was said in detail of
that realm, as it appears at the present time in Russian
history. This final chapter will make good what was
there intentionally omitted.

Everything which we describe as ways of life among
mankind, as human relations and conditions, whether
they are regulated by law or merely by customs, traditions, and habit, is summed up to-day in the Russian
language in the now stereotyped word *byt*, derived
etymologically from the verb *byty*, to be. The expression is untranslatable in its richly laden brevity, containing an objective and a subjective aspect which inter-
penetrate and blend dialectically ; it comprises the whole
surrounding world in which man is placed as well as his
attitude towards it. And when the theorists of present-
day Russia never weary of emphasizing that every *byt*
is economic, conditioned by productive forces and the
state of production, then they are stressing, in addition
to the materialist conception of history which Marx,
when he originated it, differentiated sharply from the
characteristically bourgeois milieu theory, a factor which
it is essential to understand, if we are to approach the
meaning of *byt*. In a country where the new economic
order is in process of construction with such intensive

338

vehemence the milieu is not fixed, not established once for all ; it is in a state of flux. And so man, together with his attitude of mind, cannot be the finished product of his surroundings, but changes with them every day, *at the same time as and just because he changes them every day*.

Thus it is the Russian view that industrialization, the kernel of the Soviet plan of construction, is calculated to produce a fundamentally new milieu in the country and so to remould the subjective aspect of the *byt* altogether, the relation of man to his human surroundings. The new manner of life, the socialist *byt*, is to be the product of the new economic conditions in process of growth. Or, in other words, the new *byt* is the sum total of all aspects of life that are not directly economic in a society which conducts production on a socialist basis but which has not reached its final goal. And so desires hasten in advance of facts even in the Soviet state, truth conceived comes earlier than truth realized, although people work for its realization with vigour and a clear vision of the goal.

Whilst the question of the new *byt* is perpetually under discussion, in speech and writing, and people almost abuse the word by its too frequent utterance, it is well understood that all this talk is rather about something to come in the future than anything already existent. The new *byt* is only the measure by which the present may and ought to be estimated, and, as with the socialist economic order, only certain factors have yet been realized, although they are factors of increasing force. We can already discern these factors plainly in the most universal forms of social life, especially in the mutual relations of the sexes, in love, marriage, and the family. But even there we still find for the most part the old and the new side by side, outworn elements and others which are forcing their way into being. And no less frequently than they welcome certain phenomena as elements of the new *byt*, people condemn others as products and remnants of the old, or, as the Soviet Russian catchword is, as " eruptions of the past ". When people

339

note such facts they add a current phrase in jest, which may be translated more or less as : " And it was for that that we stood on the barricades ? ! " On the other hand, much that puts itself forward as something new, yet is immature, is designated as a " grimace of the new *byt* ", as " growing pains ".

At any rate, people are exerting all their powers, making every effort, to shorten the birth-pangs of the new *byt*, and that not only in the relations of men and women, which we have already considered at length so that there is no occasion to enter into the subject again here, but also in those other aspects of social life which are known as culture, civilization, manners, and with which we will begin the discussion of the new *byt* in the sense here indicated.

OLD AND NEW

U.S.S.R.—the Union of Socialist Soviet Republics— that is an area of about eight million square miles. More than six times Western Europe, sixty times Germany, and more than 160 times England, one-sixth of the land surface of the earth. The most southerly part of Russia lies nearer to the equator than the most southerly part of Italy. The differences in climate, topography, flora, and fauna are so great that in the south oranges ripen, whilst in the province of Yakutsk for the chief part of the summer the soil only thaws to a depth of one foot at most.

And such contrasts as there are in nature there are also in the peoples who inhabit this wide area, the Russian continental plain : according to the ethnographical map of the Moscow Academy of Science there are thirty-two different peoples in Siberia alone.

The Russian people were cradled in the open, amidst steppes and forests, on the banks of great rivers, between the Islamite and Christian East, with Byzantium to the south and the Germans and Latins to the west. In that peaceful, vast, and tranquil countryside, the immense stretches of plain and the infinite curves of the landscape, bounded only by the horizon, give rise to a unique sense

340

of life and of worship and confer the power of large-minded vision and feeling. That, no doubt, is the source of the *shirokaya natura*, the broad character, of the Russians, and the epic quality of Russian literature.

The Russian type of humanity, Russian history, the Russian world, are products of the same extremes which characterize Russian topography and the Russian climate. Whilst Moscow, the heart of the country, still represents in every fibre a fragment of deepest, wildest Asia, the clumsy, unwashed, scantily clothed, barefooted giant is given a Western European hat by the Petrograd of Peter the Great.

And now, when all barriers have been overthrown, when north and south, yesterday and to-morrow, upper and lower, west and east, are mingled in confusion, the extremes are elbowing one another still more closely.

Every town in the Union of any size has its " Revolution Square ", its Lenin monument, its Twenty-fifth of October Street—at each end of the street and in every large square a church towers aloft. Frequently either a garage or a cinema or even an anti-religious museum is housed in the church, and standing before the ikons there exhibited, stripped of their former pomp, you may easily come upon a peasant who is crossing himself zealously, automatically, without thinking. Is he not, in fact, one of those peasants who will cry on their death-bed with the famous character in Sseyfullina's story (*Rotten Manure*) : " Lord God, Little Father, graciously receive the soul of the Bolshevik Artamon."

Ivanovo-Vosnyessyensk is the Manchester of the Soviet Union. About six years ago, the last time but one that I went there on the way to the " Russian Lombardy ", the ancient " Vladimir Ssusdal ", there was nothing to be seen all around but forests, forests, forests. To-day the forests have disappeared and instead of the trees you see factories, factories, textile mills making mixed fabrics, and workers' settlements. But through the clearings which have been made by the cutting of timber the ancient church towers and domes look in

341

amazement from left and right on this unaccustomed frenzy of popular activity.

In Stalingrad there is a large, beautiful park, a people's Prater on the Volga. In the evening none but young people walk there, to the sound of music. All couples, the future of the country. Hardly anyone over twenty. Overflowing with vigour, laughing, gay, untroubled by problems : all work, however hard, is a mere bagatelle to them, a pleasure. But outside the gate of this Paradise —a man who has been mercilessly driven from the Garden of Eden, and now, as one of the old régime, can be only a spectator of life, and is happy if happy youth buys a bunch of flowers from him.

In *Traktorstroy* at Stalingrad 100 tractors are produced daily, and in the " kitchen factory " there some 120,000 dishes are served daily. The people have their meals at white - clothed, flower - decked tables. Those who serve the meals are dressed entirely in white. There is a kitchen for milk dishes and one for special diets. But people still frequently spit on the floor.

Twenty thousand workers are housed in smart new settlements near the giant factory. The 250 American specialists, most of whom have brought their wives with them, live in a special settlement of their own and have their own canteen. Sixty interpreters are allotted to them during their hours of work. But in the town, at the post-office, where the first thing you notice at the entrance is a stand with books and newspapers that fills half the room, the girl behind the counter asks me, when I wish to send a telegram to Vienna, whether there is a post-office there.

In *Traktorstroy* they are building day and night, hammering, and building again. Socialist competition. Storm brigades. Red labour banners. Red corners. Workers' clubs. Children's crèches. Wall newspapers. Libraries, reading-rooms, all the newspapers in the Union. Portrait galleries of the heroes and heroines of labour : intelligent, clever, tense, earnest proletarian heads. A totally new world, a new consciousness, a new sentiment and therewith a new ethical system—all sprung up overnight. Not a few of these people are strict teetotallers. And close by, in the dirty, dusty town, where there is no vegetation but all the more malaria, in the old market-place and in all the side alleys, often literally wallowing in the gutter—utterly derelict human beings, unrecognizable, no longer to be attributed to any particular class, beings whose faces are bloated and purple with drink, and in such numbers as if all the drunkards of old-time Russia had made a *rendezvous* of the place.

In the harbour of Nishnyi Novgorod : twenty steve-dores, posted symmetrically, are pulling at an immensely thick rope. They have to load a steamer with a whole mountain of oil-barrels as big as houses. They pull in jerks, pausing but little. And each time when there is to be a renewed pull one of them, the leading singer, strikes up a peculiar melody, melancholy and rhythmic-ally monotonous. The others join in a second later. A strong tug, a shove—and the barrel moves on a bit : work that has not yet been mechanized here. And so these stevedores pull at their old rope quite unthink-ingly and sing their old Volga songs, as if they were the " Volga boatmen " whom Ryepin depicted. But to-day they can all read and write, they have learned *polit-gramota*, the political ABC, most of them are storm workers, many enter for competitions, and thus they perform their part in building the life of the country anew.

The Volga steamer plying from Yarosslavl to Astra-khan, in ten days according to the time-table, but in reality generally a fortnight or more, is packed. On the upper deck, down below, on the middle decks, and most of all on the lowest deck of all. At every stopping-place there are terrific battles between those who are disem-barking and those who are coming on board. But more people always embark than land. And always with countless bundles in their hands, on their backs, on their heads, with boxes and trunks and bags. Some of the men push forwards with enormously long chests, as big as houses, in which anyone might live, spreading devasta-

343

tion as if they were simply two-legged tanks. Everybody shouts and swears and curses, elbows one another and spits. Children cry, dogs whine and bark, but the young people crack jokes as if nothing were happening. And what a medley it is that floods into this moderate-sized steamer, *To the Memory of Mirkin*, a sailor revolutionary (there are some of these steamers called *Griboyedov, Pyotr Chaykovskyi, Paris Commune, W. G. Korolenko*, etc.). Great Russian peasants, long-bearded and long-haired with patriarchal heads—wearing sheepskins in the hottest summer weather—and peasant women with good-natured, broad, childish faces, often enveloped in bright-coloured kerchiefs. Yellowish-brown Kirgizes with keen eyes, Tatars with gold-embroidered little caps and close-fitting garments, black or coloured. Kalmuks with slit eyes, expectant mothers surrounded by a flock of children. *Komssomoltsi*. Warlike Caucasian figures wearing tall fur caps, with glittering cartridge-pouches across their breasts and slender sabres in their belts. Tousled gipsies in high spirits with gleaming white teeth. Red Army soldiers, former members of the well-to-do classes, and Volga Germans who—although they have been settled in Russia for generations—often do not know a word of Russian, although their German is also incomprehensible. A constant flow of new people, an endless flow, people of all races, all tribes and degrees of civilization, a very migration of the peoples. . . . Where are they going as a matter of fact ? Why are they here, for what purpose ? Hardly any of the inhabitants of this Noah's ark could tell you their destination and the object of their journey. But there is no need of that. They want to try their luck somewhere else. Little Mother Russia is spacious, the Tsar is deposed, and somewhere there will be a place where one can lay one's weary head.

Somewhere, but hardly on the lower decks of the steamer. For there it is unbearable, even to these much-tried people, so well accustomed to bearing things. Not only because near the engine-room it is terribly hot in the height of summer, and not only because such a glaring light burns there day and night that it dazzles

you all the time—one might get used to that if need be
—but chiefly because hundreds of people are " accom-
modated " in a very moderate space, at least four times
as many as there is really room for. And so all these
passengers lie and sit and stand about day and night,
side by side, one on the top of the other, one above
another—men, women, children, the aged, young and
old—without being able to stir a step. Some leave and
others come. Women are delivered, children fall into
the water and are picked out again, sometimes one of
them has a fit. . . . But the salesman in the obligatory
book and newspaper tent, which is replenished at every
halt and stands like a fortress with its motto strips, its
banners, and its portraits of the leaders in the midst of
the surging waves and people, cannot satisfy the demand.
And the highly cultured Red commander, my cabin
neighbour, who was once a prisoner in Austria, talks with
me about German literature, whilst Little Mother Volga,
broad and darkly gleaming, who has seen so much in
her long life, and the burning August sun, smile with
kindly superiority upon all the many contradictions
which are yet the essence of things here.

The " Scholars' House " in Leningrad is in the finest
part of the Neva embankment, next to the Tsar's Winter
Palace, in the famous palace of the former Grand Duke
Vladimir Alexandrovich, the uncle of the last Romanov
on the throne. Of course it is not very suitable for its
purpose. Hundreds sleep on hard little iron camp-beds
in vast, high rooms with extravagantly rich decorations
in marble and gold, yet almost impossible to heat. In
the morning you have to push your way and stand in
a queue to get access to the water-closet which is also
the only lavatory for at least three dozen of the inhabitants. In a splendid dining-hall wainscoted entirely
with rare woods, at costly tables and beneath heavy
crystal and bronze chandeliers, very weak tea is served
without sugar, millet porridge, and cucumber salad, and
only every other day something like meat pasties or
actually meat.

In the former boudoir of the Grand Duchess, marvel-

345

lously furnished in pale pink, breathing the fragrance of
the most delicate rococo, of a vanished age, the excellent
Lukerya Bogdanova now sits, the head of the economic
department of the Home. But previously she had stood
for four decades at four benches in a textile mill of the
Moscow district. Although she was illiterate, she had
rendered valuable service to the party ever since 1903
(distributing proclamations and the like among the
women workers), and in 1930, at the age of fifty-two,
she was nominated a " heroine of labour " and superannuated. For two years she has now filled her new
post, talks much and picturesquely, likes the sound of
her own voice, and repeats constantly, as if she were
referring to Christ : " *Tovarishch* Lenin is gone, but his
teaching still lives on earth ; we shall never forget it.
And just as he strove, so we must follow in his footsteps.
Anyone who swerves is past help. But I, I should like
to live to see it all! Especially union in a common
association with the working women abroad, for Germany is such a country for culture. *Nichevo*, we shall
live to see it all."

But the greatest contrasts are to be found in Moscow
—indeed, nothing else is to be expected—in the city
which has always gathered all the conflicting elements
of the country, as if in a spectrum. Petrograd, the Tsar's
capital with the gilded towers of the Admiralty building
which you almost always see before you, with its absolutely straight streets, was the city of decorative elegance,
of self-absorbed baroque and classicism, and, with its
touch of the Western European spirit, it struck one as
objective and reserved, like a straight line. But little
Mother Moscow, broad-hipped and white-stoned, on the
other hand, with her " forty times forty " churches, has
always been vital, gay, native, like many a village *baba* ;
it was itself an immense village, but full of character—
in the eighteenth century it was largely built of wood—
a gate to Asia : incalculable, always warm-hearted,
hospitable, and sometimes glowing like a dream.

A great deal of this Moscow still survives. But to-
day its symbolism is much more striking. How fantastic

is merely the contrast of Red Square with its dominating
background of the colourful and picturesque richly
silhouetted lines of the Basilius Cathedral, the old
Kremlin walls with their countless towers and turrets,
gay and variegated in form, and behind the masses of
gilded domes, large and small, of venerable cathedrals,
crowding and peeping over with childish curiosity, the
long, outstretched neck of Ivan Velikyi whose voice is
foremost here, and in the middle of Red Square, attracting more than anything else the eyes of all the world in
these days, the Lenin Mausoleum, solemn, severe, grand,
built of dark red granite. The contrasts are particularly
striking on days when the Square is enlivened by some
great parade : on the first of May, the seventh of November—the anniversary of the revolution—or on January
22nd, the day of Lenin's death. On these occasions,
when hundreds of thousands—Red Army soldiers, in-
fantry, cavalry, artillery, the navy, working men and
women, hundreds of organizations—the *Komssomol*, the
school-children, delegates from all parts of the country
—in short, the whole Soviet Russian world with its bands,
its red flags, its workers' banners, and other emblems,
march smartly past the leader's grave in endless files,
and high in the sky beautifully disposed squadrons " of
heavenly birds created by human hands ", as they are
called among the people, circle above, then the orphaned
monuments of Tsarism become part of the Bolshevik
order, the old and the new blend in a picture of such
symbolic strength and unity that, whatever one's views
may be in general, one cannot escape its power. But
late in the night, when all is still and the Red Square is
veiled in darkness, the red flag waves above the Kremlin,
illuminated from below and much more clearly visible
than by day—waves over all the Russia of yesterday and
burns heavenwards like a fiery signal.

There is no town in the world to-day where the pulse
of life beats so continuously—nowhere is life carried
along so powerfully by an inner dynamic force, an in-
visible motor of many thousand horse-power, as in the
Red capital. Wherever you go or linger, everywhere

347

you receive the impression that all Moscow is on its legs
from early morning till late into the night. And that
really is the case. A little before six working men and
women who have been on night-shifts are already going
home, and others hasten to the factories. But this city,
which already numbers nearly three million inhabitants,
has as yet no underground railway. Yet since everybody
is either a manual worker or a staff employee and is
occupied out of the home, at that hour people are already
beginning to stand in queues and elbow their way to
trams and buses, to be pushed forwards and thumped
and shouted at and bellowed at—a process which makes
even the shortest trip in Moscow a real torment, beyond
the scope of Western European imagination. The
drivers and conductors are almost all women. At eight
o'clock and even earlier—for who knows how long you
will have to wait for the tram or bus, and if you are at
all late at your work it is noted—the second lot appear
at the halts, hurrying to public offices, institutions, commissariats, shops, schools, etc. That goes on till ten or
eleven. But meantime the housewives have set out to
do their shopping; from one to two some of the children are returning from school, and towards three the
return flow of the masses begins and continues till
evening, until the time when people set out for clubs,
lectures, meetings, and evening classes, to the theatre
and cinema. That goes on till two or three in the night.
Even between three and six in the morning the streets
of Moscow are seldom quite empty. But all day long
a vast crowd is ceaselessly moving about the town; in
the oldest, but always gay-coloured, quarters the most
modern buildings now appear at every step, and fortun-
ately people have begun latterly to abandon the dismal
colouring of these buildings.

At first sight these crowds in the streets of Moscow
strike you as poverty-stricken, down and out, and grey.
There is still a shortage of clothes. For that reason you
recognize the foreigner, man or woman, at once by hat
and coat and shoes. Nevertheless, the picture is gay
coloured, and contrasts perpetually strike you. At one

moment a huge motor-lorry flashes past—you hardly have time to realize its presence—crammed with young Red Army soldiers, standing and looking cheerfully about them, their heads ensconced in grey helmets; and directly behind it a derelict *isvoschik* with a half-starved little horse and the customary absurd little cab, loaded, however, with a great, big sofa or even a cupboard with two doors. Then a curious vehicle with a long box passes along the road and behind it a handful of people hurry, obviously anxious to attract as little attention as possible. That to-day—at one time it was a great event —is a funeral among the former well-to-do classes in Moscow; not in life alone, but also in death, they want to avoid notice as much as possible.

But in other cases, too, death in Soviet Russia to-day is nowise a stirring mystery; rather, like everything that occurs, it is a purely practical affair which people have no time to consider more fully, and an obstruction and hindrance to the continuous programme of work which cannot unfortunately be overcome as yet. Soviet Russian youth, drunk with life, feeling death as something even more alien than is generally the case with the youth of other countries, refusing, moreover, to recognize other problems, is somewhat perplexed on this point. Once in the Tverskaya in Moscow I saw a Red funeral procession pass by—quite a young *komssomolka* covered with red flowers lay in an open red coffin in a red hearse drawn by horses with red trappings, and beside it marched a troop of *komssomolkas* in uniform with hands raised for the *komssomolts* salute (Always prepared !), whilst a band of wind instruments played by *komssomoltsi* accompanied the whole with the strains of the *Internationale*. It was, indeed, a solemn sight, grave and beautiful, but it might almost as well have been part of any political mass procession.

How often you can witness the following scene through the lower window of a shop in Moscow or workshop or minor public office, late in the afternoon, after work : some fifteen or twenty persons, men and women, sit about in a room on chairs, benches, or tables ; their

faces are tired, they have long been ready to go home.
A man stands in the middle of the room and speaks.
Of those who are present some are only half listening,
others are obviously attending with difficulty, whilst others
again are constantly throwing notes to the speaker. But
the man gesticulates, turns his head to left and right,
and goes on speaking without caring for the interruptions. It is often impossible to wait for the end of his
speech. But when he has done another is sure to come,
and so it goes on, not infrequently for hours. It is a
meeting after work : perhaps they are practising *ssamokritika*, self-criticism, to which there are no bounds, but
perhaps it is the preliminary of a *chistka*, a cleansing,
later to be carried out in the party cell and sparing nobody.
But at any rate speeches are made in meetings all over
Russia not only in the afternoon but yet more in the
evening, and even in the morning, and no one may absent
himself.

The first thing that I struck in Stalingrad upon my
arrival at the hotel at nine in the morning was a meeting
of the waitresses employed there. And in Moscow at
every hour of the day and night, even on the telephone,
you may hear a propaganda speech in support of the
Five Years' Plan or something else that is being broad-
cast in the streets by means of a loud speaker. The
Russians, whether men or women, are born speakers,
rhetoricians, and their love of talking is so great that on
such occasions time generally stands still even to-day,
and the old, familiar Russian *ssyeychass* (directly) or
podoshditye (wait a minute) may still be heard through
the "Bolshevik tempo", for it still survives. Just as
the ingrained love of official acts continues to delay the
eradication of bureaucracy.

The street is drawn into politics in Moscow in other
ways, too. In all the windows of the countless bookshops you see displayed, besides the portraits and busts
of international as well as Russian revolutionary leaders,
principally books on questions of the day or books on
technical or politico-literary subjects. In all public
places, in buildings, institutes, tramcars, and wherever

350

opportunity offers, there are serried rows of advertisements, posters, and appeals containing admonitions,
mottoes, declarations, and watchwords of a general
political character, and yet more on practical questions.
And in addition in the busier parts of the town mottoes
in gigantic letters are stretched across the streets on
broad bands, the same or something similar repeated
every few hundred yards. And since all these magnificent educational advertisements, which are constantly
changing, are always brilliant, colourful, impressive, and
striking, as if designed for children, they lend a peculiar
gay and cheerful aspect to the town. One understands
how it comes about that the comparison with an immense
kindergarten occurs to certain foreigners, not only in
Moscow but all over the Soviet Union, especially when
they see the universal passion for learning—a kindergarten where the pupils' interest has to be perpetually
kindled and kept alive. And in very truth : are they
not all children, all the men and women of the people
who stand for hours at the shop windows wherever there
is something glittering, painted, gay-coloured—especially
old curiosity shops, and picture and jewel shops—
admiring, analysing every detail, never weary of gazing
at the things ? Where else could it happen that a little
before two o'clock in the morning a woman carrying a
child should stop me before the window of an old
curiosity shop and ask me what a particular bird represented on a plate painted with animal figures ? And if
we add that dance and music, song and games, are vital
to this intensely artistic people, that they cannot do
without them even in the midst of all the mechanization,
then we realize that there is no real cause for anxiety
lest the Five Years' Plan and the process of mechanization might eradicate the childlike folk element in them,
their native genius and closeness to nature.

And what finally strikes one in the Moscow streets is
the numerous women who are barely distinguishable
from men in garb and demeanour, besides the many
expectant mothers already mentioned. One often sees
elderly, simple women of the people smoking, hardly

ever fat women ; and likewise the numerous women
students from the East and the remotest parts of Siberia,
mostly *komssomolkas* who also wear the red *kossynkas*,
help to make up the general aspect of the city. Many
women wear men's *kepkas* instead of hats.

Each time that I have returned from Soviet Russia I
am asked on all sides : what do people wear in Russia ?
I might answer in the words of the actress Goncharova
in Olesha's play *List of Benefits*, of whom the same question is asked by a White dress-maker in Paris : " In the
evening they wear morning dress." " And what material
is fashionable ? " " Steel, I think." " And what do
people wear in the theatre ? " " Felt shoes." " What,
a dress-coat and felt shoes ? " " No, you see no dress-
coats." " Why ? Because they don't care for dress-
coats ? " " No, because they do care for the theatre."

It is true that a well-known and otherwise very clever
German authoress gives quite a different account of
Moscow ; she observed the Soviet Russian women a
short time ago from the vantage ground of diplomatic
society, chiefly, no doubt, at the dinners and suppers at
the foreign embassies, and noticed that what they chiefly
lack is lip-stick, scent, and lace-trimmed underclothing.
But she is wrong : lip-stick and scent are by no means
among the wares of which there is a shortage in Soviet
Russia ; there is plenty to be had, so that the demand
cannot be so very large. And the fact that a " little bust-
supporter of curtain net " made as great an impression
upon her and told her more than " Red Square with
the hundreds who are always waiting at Lenin's monument " proves that her trip to Moscow was a regrettable
error.

Of course the Soviet Russian woman has not altogether
lost her pleasure in dress. For all their proletarian
subject-matter, the women's journals have a regular
section devoted to cutting out dresses, in addition to full
reports on economic questions, the Five Years' Plan, and
competitions. But a simple style is approved. Ornaments are taboo. Nevertheless, the time is already past
when it was a disgrace for a *komssomolka* to pay atten-

tion to her appearance. All that is required is an avoidance of excessive interest that might degenerate into coquettery and feminine affectation. Mehnert, in his admirable book on *Youth in Soviet Russia*, writes on this question, which was pretty much under discussion among the young people for a time :

> If a girl has waved hair, if she is painted and powdered and prettily dressed, some call after her : " Philistine behaving like the petty bourgeoisie ! " Indeed, she may be expelled from the *Komssomol*. But if she pays no attention to her appearance and goes about just as she happens to be, then she may find that others, who regard untidiness and plainness as unworthy of the proletariat, may regard her as a Philistine and petty bourgeois and apply the very same words to her. There was a general sense of uncertainty, nobody wanted to be a Philistine and petty bourgeois, but nobody was quite sure how to demean herself.

It is still regarded as unproletarian and petty bourgeois to think much of one's outward appearance, and in this respect, likewise, there are naturally " eruptions from the past ". For instance you may often hear in a tram, when women are disputing excitedly : " Because you've put on a hat, you think you belong to the intelligentsia." " I've only put on the hat because it's cheaper ; a kerchief costs sixty roubles and a hat only sixteen." Dandyism among men is in still worse odour. Cravats tied in a bow, called *babochkas*, butterflies, are regarded by the people much as a monocle is in Western Europe.

But a lament over *komssomol* manners in a semi-official paper proves that conditions have changed considerably, even in the *Komssomol*, nay, have swung over to the opposite extreme since the time when all thought devoted to dress was condemned. It is stated there that young Leningrad *komssomoltsi* refuse to recognize their female contemporaries in the theatre or cinema if they are not well enough dressed, and declare the next day in the workshop that they did not see them. (Ssmirnov, *The Komssomol and the Girls*.)

Naturally there are endeavours in the land of planned industry to solve the question of dress on a scientific and mathematical basis, and to attack the " wretched fashion psychosis " by producing a uniform dress which is to combine economy, practicability, and simplicity, although in fact there is little to be seen of the fashion psychosis now. For nearly two years there has been an institute in Moscow known as *Nishi* (abbreviation for Scientific Institute for the Clothing Industry) in which expert research is conducted into the question of occupational clothing. The principal, Mashurina, is herself an artist and works with a whole staff of highly trained assistants, besides well-known historians of art in an advisory capacity. She says : " Dress is a reflection of the economic and social structure of society. The form of our garments ought to express the character of the industrial age. In Soviet Russia to-day it demands simplicity, plainness, and a close fit. In particular dress must be suited to a person's occupation, and yet the æsthetic effect, for instance the colours, must not be overlooked ; in the country, perhaps, they may be a little reminiscent of the former national costume."

Models are produced of dresses for various occupations, and the thing is done so thoroughly that the special requirements of a particular kind of work are scientifically studied on the spot, motions are observed, and times measured. Already it has been worked out in essential outline how a tractor driver, a milkmaid, or a *kolkhos* woman can be most conveniently dressed. Most interesting is probably the intention of introducing a standardized dress of which the separate parts, sleeves, front, and the like, can be changed and replaced at any time. This standardized garment is also to have the advantage that on various occasions it can be partly turned inside out and worn differently, having a coloured (red) lining. There are already finished designs of this *byt* dress too. Its entire form, its colour and cut, are to express the technical practicality which characterizes the new *byt* in other directions as well.

What has been said of the streets and of dress applies also to the other aspects of civilization. There, too, the old and the new blend, there, too, people pride them-

PATTERNS OF THE SOVIET UNIFORM DRESS

(*Byt* Costume)

selves on the evolution of new forms of human intercourse, whilst on the other hand old customs and abuses
still prove exceedingly vigorous. For there is often a
lack of competent educators for the systematic guidance
of many who have recently worked their way up, plenty
of whom have never heard of things that are taught to
the children as something to be taken as a matter of
course. Thus, for instance, the semi-official publication
of Ssmirnov already quoted, which aimed at calling attention to the negative aspect of the situation and so finding remedies, says of the Girls' Homes in Leningrad,
principally occupied by the former inmates of the foundling homes (badly neglected, as we know, in Tsarist
Russia) :

> The beds are not aired and the most elementary requirements
> of hygiene are absent, and that not only in the matter of accom-
> modation. The girls themselves tell of their dirty ways, and
> say that there are days, when they have overslept, when they do
> not wash at all, or at least not with soap. Teeth are only
> cleaned when they are going to the theatre or to some social
> function.

And this nice story appeared recently in the journal
The Proletarian Cadre :

> Nastya Pranina is a student in her third semester. She
> decides to wash her feet before going to bed. She fetches a
> bucket of hot water, sits down on her bed, and plunges her feet
> in. But she has mislaid her flannel, so she takes her tooth-
> brush and uses it to rub her feet above, underneath, and
> between the toes. Then Nastya goes to the washstand, washes
> herself, and cleans her teeth with the same toothbrush. And
> yet Nastya is one of the best champions of hygiene in the new
> *byt*.

There are other abuses, too, that have not yet disappeared : cursing and swearing, rough manners, the lack
of polish in society of which Olearius complained in the
seventeenth century, and which are found in close com-
bination with the utmost readiness to oblige, kindliness,
humanity, hospitality, and unselfishness. For instance,

in every tram in Moscow six seats are reserved for expectant mothers ; purely theoretically a fine gesture of reverence for motherhood or even weakness. But how often it happens that these seats are only applied to their intended purpose after a dispute. And it is unthinkable that a boy should ever dream of letting an old woman loaded with bundles go in front of him in the rush for the tram, or should give up his place to her in the car. In general, one often feels the lack of consideration for others, and much as one approves the equality of the sexes, one cannot avoid the impression that in some cases the diminution of courtesy towards women is carried out altogether too thoroughly.

On the other hand, the effect of using the familiar second person singular among party members, even when speaking to those in authority, a custom which therefore obtains throughout the ranks of the young people in the *Komssomol*, is very good. The address with name and patronymic, formerly customary in Russia, is likely to grow gradually less frequent. In general the forms of speech in social intercourse have been greatly simplified. (For a time even shaking hands was out of favour.) You never hear " Mr.", " Mrs.", and " Miss " now, but only " Citizen " or " *Tovarishch* ". And if somebody uses the expression " gentry " from habit, he receives the stereotyped rebuke : " There are no gentry nowadays. All the *gospoda* lie at the bottom of the Black Sea." Thus Russian habits of speech are making a clean sweep of countless ancient and venerable traditions, a unique process of development when one thinks, say, of the Western European languages which continue, particularly in modes of address, to drag the débris of the Middle Ages along with them (" Monsieur ", " Signore ", and " Senor " are derived from " senior ", the title of the feudal lord). For the rest, it may be observed in this connection that the Russian language is becoming more practical ; on the one hand it is being enriched by a number of technical terms in consequence of recent developments, but on the other hand is being coarsened by the commercial abbreviations, contractions of initial letters, and a variety of new forms which frequently are alike ugly and a violation of the spirit of the Russian language in their sound.

People have abandoned willy-nilly one Russian abuse which Olearius censures, the vice of gluttony, particularly the excessive consumption of meat, and there are numerous meatless, " vegetarian " restaurants in the Soviet Russian towns to-day. Here, in accordance with the new *byt*, the guests are urgently advised to wash their hands before sitting down to table—only at present there is no place to wash, to say nothing of soap, which is always rare and expensive. It is an open question how far in a general way the shortage of soap as well as other necessities of civilization is responsible for defects in physical culture, hygiene, and cleanliness. Even sport, *physculture*, whilst so much is spent on its advocacy, cannot be developed as much as is desired for want of such essentials as footballs, croquet balls, bats, skis, and the like.

Moreover, the isolation from foreign countries checks the advance of civilization. Most Russians have no standard by which they can estimate and compare Russian and foreign customs objectively. Side by side the tendency already mentioned to overestimate Western European culture, you frequently find an underestimation bordering on complete ignorance of everything that really is European culture. You also sometimes meet people who are proud beyond all measure of achievements which have long been taken as a matter of course in Western Europe. I should not like to say that the whole burning enthusiasm for technical science falls under this head. But in Leningrad a woman official called my attention in her office to the automatic telephone dial and she was visibly disappointed when I told her that such appliances were quite common in the West ; she disputed their existence even in America.

Taking it all in all, the externals of life, which we sum up under the name civilization, are by no means satisfactory at present, any more than the housing conditions which fall in the same category and which we shall consider

357

later. Except for the situation of a minute section of
the population, they never were in Russia. The difference is that to-day people have recognized these defects
clearly and are combating them vigorously and setting
out systematically to create the material conditions of a
kultura which is now being preached on all sides, for
which a demand has been roused and now exists beyond
all doubt. The cultural Five Years' Plan has the express
object of raising the standard of life of the masses in
Soviet Russia without delay. I will close with the words
of A. Lunacharskyi :

> The class-conscious worker in our country has proved his
> willingness for self-sacrifice. But we cannot proceed on a basis
> of enthusiasm and hope alone. Working energy demands good
> food, good housing conditions, in a word, hygiene, aiming to
> reach the standard dictated by normal human physiology at the
> earliest possible moment. . . . It would be a mistake to post-
> pone all the joy of life to a time after victory and to leave no
> delights for the present days of hard struggle for the future.
> (" The Cultural Achievements of the Soviet Union," *The New
> Russia*, May–June, 1932.)

THE SOCIALIZATION OF LIFE

ONE of the weakest spots in Soviet Russian reconstruction
is the housing question, or rather the miserable housing
conditions. Building activities cannot meet the need
and are out of all proportion to the growth of population
in the towns, largely because of the constant influx from
the country, especially into Moscow. But even the
newly built houses leave much room for improvement,
although they enjoy the advantages of many modern
inventions in domestic architecture. Only the workers'
settlements—often on American models—put up in
certain towns foreshadow in some measure the socialist
towns of the future. Let me give a picture of how people
live in Soviet Russia, even in new houses, by an extract
from a clever novel by Pantyeleymon Romanov, *Three
Pair of Silk Stockings* :

> . . . The immense house . . . was impressive because of its
> imposing façade. Each of the five storeys had pretty little

balconies with parapets carved like leafy tendrils, so that they looked like baskets of flowers. The whole front of the house was freshly painted bright pink, on the pavement were receptacles for cigarette-ends, and in the evening there were lights in all the windows of all five storeys. In the spacious hall, embellished with mirrors, quantities of perambulators were crowded ; on the wall hung a black-board with the names of the tenants, and beside it was a fly-blown sheet of paper bearing these words :

" Citizens, save your energies, use the lift ! "

On the door of the lift was a similar sheet, also bearing plentiful traces of flies, with the laconic statement :

" Lift not working."

After the house had been renovated it had been taken into use, but by the next day it would not work. A large group of tenants in high spirits had wanted to find out whether it would not take a heavier load than was indicated on the little notice inside. In consequence the tenants were now obliged to climb the stairs on foot, and in the evening they had to feel their way, knocking against one another in the darkness and frightening one another, for the electric bulb had been stolen from the staircase light. But the bulb was always stolen, although it was protected by wire netting and placed at a dizzy height. The management had long accepted the situation and finally abandoned the convenience of a staircase light, whilst the tenants refused to buy one at their own expense.

There was a card outside every door with a long list of tenants, and beside each name a number saying how many times the bell must be rung for the tenant in question.

The door-bells generally passed through three stages. At first you saw a newly varnished wooden disk with a white button in the middle. Then the disk and button disappeared and all that was left was the circular wooden base with two little copper plates. Then the wooden base likewise disappeared and the two ends of wire stuck out. In order to ring you connected the two ends of wire, and when they, too, disappeared you just belaboured the door with your fists. But you forgot to keep to the right number of blows, which caused ceaseless noise in the flat.

. . . The house was occupied partly by members of the educated class, partly by proletarians. The latter were blest with numerous children, whereas the educated occupants owned innumerable dogs.

. . . On the back stairs you were greeted by an atmosphere of smoke and cooking odours, as you are by steam on entering a bathroom. On each landing, opposite the open kitchen door, stood wooden boxes and dustbins crammed with all manner of kitchen waste : cucumber peel, egg-shells, and melon rind. Some of the receptacles were already overflowing and the garbage collected round about on the floor, and even on the steps where the children, in spite of the narrow space, had improvised a game of football with a melon rind. Dirty, bedraggled cats also added to the dirt and disorder.

The flat in which Kisslyakov lived was occupied by ten families consisting of twenty-seven persons in all.

The long passage, with doors on both sides, was packed with trunks, baskets, and cupboards. The consequence was that it was always dark, and when the tenants wanted to go from the kitchen or lavatory to their rooms they knocked against all the corners, bruised their foreheads, hurt their knees, and appropriately cursed those who stored their goods here, although their own rubbish took up considerable space too, and in the darkness it was impossible to know whether you had knocked against your own property or someone else's. Quite unlike the front of the house, the flat gave the impression of a furniture shop or pawnshop where everything had been piled up after an auction. . . .

The lavatory was in a little lobby outside the kitchen, and it was perpetually in use. In use in the morning, in use at midday, in use in the evening.

" Who the devil's sitting there again ! " stormed someone, desperate and infuriated, who had come several times in vain from his room to the lavatory. The constant occupation of the room was partly due to the fact that it contained the bath as well as the water-closet.

The tenants of the flat were as various, their occupations and social position as manifold, as if they had taken refuge there during a flood and everybody had established himself just where he happened to find himself in his haste. There were about two-thirds educated people and one-third proletarians. The latter were represented by two locksmiths and their families and a company of masons who always left a long white trail from the door of their room to the lavatory. . . .

This description, which is as plastic as it is true to life and full of characteristic detail, needs little supplement. Nowhere, perhaps, do the contrasts between the new and the old appear so crude, so glaring, as in the Soviet Russian house and home. Most startling is the contradiction between the cultural claims, which are intentionally pitched high, and the quite disproportionate means of realization. It is very characteristic of the Russians that articles of daily convenience when once broken, as appears from this description of Romanov's, should never be repaired and should therefore be regarded as simply non-existent. For the most part Russians have no idea of considerate treatment of the things about them, much less love for them, and things are seldom used, but rather used up. It is doubtless natural that no domestic culture in the Western European sense can arise under such circumstances, especially during the present housing shortage. And things are worst in the domestic offices. Particularly the water-closets in the trains and hotels, at the stations, and on the steamers, are in such an impossible, unhygienic state as nothing could surpass. The notice " Ladies " on the door of one such closet in the supposedly elegant Hotel Orient in Tiflis struck one as mockery. On the other hand there was an admonition in another hotel in Rostov on the Don : " Citizens, the attendants are human beings like yourselves. Behave decently and see that it is not necessary to clean up after you."

In the dwelling-rooms, too, it is not easy for the occupants to maintain cleanliness and order even with the best will in the world, for they are mostly overcrowded. In the interior of the houses the old and marked Russian sense of colour and delight in colour produce negative results at present : Red tawdriness dominates both in the bad-coloured reproductions with which the walls are covered and in the small statuary which ornaments the rooms— not excepting the Lenin bust—and which is in appallingly bad taste. It is a worthy counterpart to various commonplace films and novels of foreign origin which, strangely enough, are very popular in Soviet Russia. Anything more petty bourgeois than the domestic arrangements of many a loyal, enthusiastic revolutionary can hardly be imagined, and one often asks oneself in amazement how such antitheses can be united. For doubtless the deeply felt letters of Rosa Luxemburg from prison, if they were to appear anonymously to-day, would be branded as petty bourgeois and impossible by the very people who display so much tolerance of this shoddy Philistinism on their four walls.

It is true that the authorities are not blind to the fact that the present housing conditions are nowise favourable to the development and invigoration of the new *byt*. One propaganda pamphlet says :

> We have thrown off much of the old *byt*, but we are still in part captives of former habits and traditions. The worker knows from daily experience how deep a gulf still parts the tempo of industry from the other aspects of life which still persist. Thus his daily existence is, so to speak, rent in two. Part of the day he spends in the factory where he co-operates actively in social life and is carried away by enthusiasm in productive work. But when he comes home from work he is caught in the grip of the most conservative, dreary, individualist surroundings.

In the Soviet Russian home it is just the past that asserts itself vigorously. It is not only in the country that you find the old-fashioned, piled-up Russian beds, but frequently in the towns too. They have not been abolished even in the women's hostel of the " Red Rosa " factory (Rosa Luxemburg) in Moscow. And in spite of all the attacks on religion, the old, glowing ikons have not by any means all disappeared—those unique expressions, regarded from a purely artistic point of view, of the Russian soul, the Russian character, the Russian people. Once when I paid a visit to a well-known communist woman who is obliged to live with her husband's parents, I was not a little astonished to see her baby's cradle placed beneath the ikon wall. The mother explained the position in this way : her parents-in-law were people of the old school who would not give up their religion, nor even the visits of the reverend priest. There is a silent understanding between the old and young people not to interfere with one another in any way. Only the old grandmother frets secretly because her little grandchild has not been christened, and every time she lulls it to sleep she sings : " Light of my eyes, flower of my life, if only you were christened." Of course the child's parents overhear these lullabies with their timid allusions. The arrangement continues that the little thing is to grow up unbaptized but beneath the ikons. For the rest, it was born in the fourteenth year of the revolution—that is the communist era—and is called Electrifikatsia. But at the time the parents hesitated for a long time whether they should not call it Agita, Lenina, or Kommuna, for these and like names are in vogue in party circles in Soviet Russia to-day, and there is a well-known four-lined verse :

> Our lives now follow a new way,
> The past's burst like a mine ;
> The name we give our sons is May,
> Our daughters Octobrine.

The discomfort of the overcrowded houses has produced a mass flight from the home which is definitely encouraged just because of the intended collectivization, one of the most essential conditions of the new *byt*. But the Russian mentality itself, with its strongly social tendency, shows a far less marked need for solitude than is the case with Westerners. " I and my wife have only one room," a fellow-traveller told me on the steamer on which I journeyed down the Volga ; " we live there, and if anybody is comfortable with us and we do not disturb him, he may remain. We don't mind." The social life of which pre-revolutionary Russia made so much has practically ceased in consequence of the double shortage of time and room, although Russian hospitality would probably revive immediately if circumstances permitted. But as it is people pay one another visits less and less. And a remark made by the hero of one of Gladkov's novels is exceedingly characteristic :

In the course of our exhausting work we do not observe people ; we estimate them simply and solely as they fulfil definite functions. . . . During the whole period of my work

363

in the Industrial Office, that is, for five years, I never once visited my colleagues and do not know what their interests are and what their needs. Personal ties are broken and vanish from our lives. And our lives—are the permanent influence of the process of labour.

For people who are not so entirely absorbed in their work the problem of the flight from domesticity is rather more difficult. There are few cafés in Soviet Russia where one can pass the time, and still fewer bars and taverns, whilst all the brilliance and allurements of the street have disappeared. So people go to meetings, to the theatre and the cinema, and especially to the clubs whose number, already large, is growing daily, and whose formation is encouraged because they are regarded as nurseries of the new *byt*. At the present time there is hardly a single factory or co-operative in Soviet Russia that has not its own club, or at least its own Red Corner with newspapers and journals. Theatrical performances, concerts, and lectures are held in the clubs, and chess, draughts, or billiards are played ; people use the reading-room and library and get into conversation.

Thus the whole trend points in one direction and must end with something which is included in the programme of the socialization of life as a whole, but which may also be described as the disintegration of private life. Without the absorption of the individual in the mass, without the breaking down of barriers which separate him from the community, the new *byt* is unthinkable. But it is for the housewife, shut in within the circle of her domestic duties, that it is hardest to surmount those barriers. The solution of the question whether the new way of life is possible depends, therefore, upon the question how far women can be brought outside the house and fitted into the great process of socialization. And that brings us to a problem that is connected with the subject of women's share in production, which we have already discussed. Lenin in his day pointed out the importance and urgency of this task, and ever since it has been repeatedly emphasized that the liberation of women from domestic slavery is supremely important,

364

not only to the economic development of the country, so that millions of hands may be gained for labour, but also from the political point of view because " the domestic *milieu* dulls a woman's wits ". In spite of all endeavours to represent women's activities in the household and in bringing up the children as equal to productive labour and nowise beneath the dignity of a man, people are never weary of stressing that such labour must vanish, as being unnecessary and out of date, when the feeding and education of children have been sufficiently socialized. In a rationalized life domestic work, which cannot be rationalized, has forfeited its right to existence, according to Soviet Russian opinion.

" Women's domestic life is a daily sacrifice amidst a thousand insignificant trifles," said Lenin on one occasion. And the statisticians, too, are at hand to state numerically the loss to the communal economy through the female labour used up in domestic activities. It is noted as a lamentable fact that, according to their calculations, there are still about eight million housewives whose co-operation is lost to industrial construction. According to the figures of the Workers' and Peasants' Survey for Soviet Russia, thirty-six million labour hours are wasted daily in the Union in this way, whilst the same results could be obtained by factory production with only six million labour hours. Thus the centralization of food supply would involve a saving of thirty million hours daily, that is the liberation of four million hands for work.

But in addition to the hours passed by the Soviet Russian housewife in the kitchen we must reckon that aggravation of her difficulties which wastes no less of her time and which Western Europe experienced only in war-time : standing in queues. A housewife who has been infected by the example of the statisticians writes in *Rabotnitsa* :

> One million seven hundred thousand housewives are to be drawn into productive labour this year. But will they at the same time be freed from the kitchen and the fetters of house-work ? No. That will not happen till they themselves take the matter energetically in hand. Only think ! Of those

365

seventeen hundred thousand women each one stands in a queue every day for not less than two hours. That makes three million four hundred thousand labour hours per day, which means as much as a factory with two thousand women workers working eight months without interruption.

There is certainly no lack of understanding on the part of influential theorists of the exploitation of which women are victims in housework. It is a commonplace that the wife and mother who works in the home has the longest hours of anyone in Soviet Russia ; her working day is at least five hours longer than that of the factory hands. But for the time practice flies in the face of theory, and even in the case of gainfully employed women the double labour still continues : a working woman who comes home tired in the evening often has to make good what she has neglected in her house during the day, and has not nearly enough time for so much as half the rest she needs. That is even true of the days when she does not go to the factory, which are so fully occupied with washing, mending, sewing, and all manner of domestic duties that it is common to read anecdotes and jokes like this in the comic papers : A mother stands at the washtub and answers her child, who begs her to take him for a walk : " What are you thinking of ! Why, it's my day out to-day." Here, too, then, we must console ourselves for the present with the thought that matters will improve in time.

At any rate people have already recognized that the new socialist *byt* can no more be built up with untrained women, lacking interest in the great questions of the day and imprisoned within the narrow bounds of the home, than—to repeat the well-known saying—socialism can with illiterates. " The saucepan is the enemy of the party cell ", and " Away from pots and pans ! " is the general cry, and a witty aphorism declares that : " The separation of the kitchen and marriage is an event of yet greater historical importance than the separation of church and state." We have already seen that many millions of Russian woman have trodden the road " from kitchen to factory bench " since the October revolution, especially in the last year or so. And although on one occasion seventeen housewives from Ulyanovsk, Lenin's native town, complained in the women's journal *Rabotnitsa* that " even now, in the fifteenth year of the revolution, they still remained ignorant in their kitchens ", on another occasion a liberated housewife proclaimed her satisfaction in this four-lined verse :

> My kerchief all of lace
> A rosy border has.
> A wife I was and made the soup,
> Now I am in the women's group.

Meanwhile, it appears more and more frequently that even housework and the kitchen are not islands isolated from life, and more and more frequently housewives become " active ", as the saying goes in Soviet Russia, without taking final leave of their kitchens, that is they undertake some political activity or even take their place in production. The latter occurs particularly when defects in the local food supply have to be remedied by the organized co-operation of all the housewives, when they are elected delegates, or when *ssubotniki*, afternoons of voluntary work, are arranged. Thus the " proletarian housewives " in a mining administration in the Urals formed a storm brigade in order to make up arrears ; in Stalingrad 500 housewives formed similar brigades to organize supplies and provisioning, and in a number of localities declared their readiness to work on certain days of the week without pay in a neighbouring factory or *kolkhos* " so that we may no longer sit idle at home and chew sunflower seeds ".

Where the link between kitchen and production is, at all events, already close, there can be no doubt—in spite of the slow development which cannot keep pace with the tempestuous will—that the evolution towards a socialization of the kitchen and at the same time towards a really new *byt* is already in progress. And the process is considerably hastened by the purely external difficulties in conducting a separate household, among which I have already mentioned the necessity of standing in queues. For it must be admitted that it is anything but a pleasure to be a housewife in Soviet Russia. There is shortage of practically everything and there is little hope of relief by engaging a domestic servant, known in Soviet Russia as a household worker, quite apart from the fact that it is a stroke of luck to secure one at all. The reason is in particular that the tendency " away from the pots and pans " has taken possession of domestic workers as well as others. It is natural that since the inauguration of the Five Years' Plan all former domestic servants should endeavour to " requalify ", that they want to be tractor drivers, mechanics, and chauffeurs—and succeed, too. A case even occurred in Ivanovo-Vosnyessyensk in which hundreds of domestic servants streamed to the factory, which compelled the skilled women workers employed there to return to their households. That was a bad exchange, and so it became necessary to require the domestic servants who were clamouring for admission to the factory to prove that their mistresses could dispense with them.

In general the post of domestic servant provides a transition, usually of very short duration, for the girls who come from the village to the town. I will give the story of one such country girl which may be taken as typical in a certain sense, although as a rule it is not love of a man but love of independence and gainful employment that puts an abrupt end to a girl's career as domestic servant.

Pasha came from the remotest parts of the Ryasany Government. When I made her acquaintance in the winter of 1930 in the house of friends in Moscow with whom I live there she was nineteen and had quite recently arrived from her village home. She wore tall felt boots and a sheepskin and her kerchief enveloped her head so closely that all you could see of her face was the cheek-bones and two grey slit eyes. She washed very little, and even when she went to bed she kept on most of her clothes. Pasha had never been in a town before ; she was afraid to ride in a tram—without horse or locomotive—refused to turn on the electric light because it was an invention of the devil, and when the telephone bell rang she ran screaming out of the room. But she had already learned to read and write and seemed to be naturally very intelligent.

Four months later the first metamorphosis had taken place. The felt boots, sheepskin, and kerchief had disappeared. Pasha wore a simple cotton dress that she had made very skilfully herself and laced boots ; her dark, rough hair was cut quite short, and a head had become visible, very clever and energetic if not exactly pretty, set with a fairly obstinate mien upon a strong, well-moulded body.

By day Pasha read a great deal, just whatever she came upon, but among the rest Pushkin, Korolenko, and Gorykyi ; she did not work much and was great friends with six-year-old Garrik. In the evening she put on a red *kossynka* and always had a number of engagements : she had to go either to one or two district meetings or to the household inspection. That is : she had been made delegate of a group of domestic workers, and so she visited some of the many flats in the house co-operative in which our flat was situated to ascertain whether the domestic servants were kept at work by the housewives after nine o'clock. If she found any of her colleagues at work at that hour, and if the colleague told her in the mistress's presence that she had undertaken the work voluntarily, she stood with arms akimbo and said with a meaning glance at the " exploiter " : " We know that kind of voluntary work ! " and departed full of her new class consciousness.

But if my friend, her mistress, herself wanted to go out in the evening sometimes, she always had to inquire what Pasha had arranged to do, for Garrik could not be left alone in the flat, and his mother had, of course, to subordinate her plans entirely to Pasha's. For : " Pasha has to play a part in the government, so that it is clear that she has precedence on all occasions." Yet it was impossible to dismiss her, for then she could have pointed out that she was homeless and have demanded to remain in the flat. So that nothing would have been gained.

Six months later, when I returned to Moscow, a new and wholly unexpected change had come over Pasha. The red *kossynka*, her position as delegate, and her whole political interest had been laid aside, for a man had entered Pasha's life for the first time. She now wore her hair thick and wavy, her dresses were elegantly cut and generally pink, she had dainty shoes and manicured hands, she made up and used lipstick, and her dream was to possess a " *crême* "-*de-Chine* dress.

She was now wholly a devoted, loving woman, read mainly melodramatic novels, and went to all the shoddy foreign films. And when my friend, her mistress, appeared in the tiny kitchen to make herself tea she was always greeted with this spectacle : on the bed covered with a patchwork quilt, fully dressed and in tall boots —nearly always slightly tipsy—" he " lay, the unique, the incomparable. But at the foot of the bed sat Pasha looking as if she had just come out of a bandbox, a book in her hand. As soon as she saw my friend come in, the girl glanced past her as if she were empty air. The position was exceedingly uncomfortable for the mistress, and at that period Garrik had often to be put to bed without his customary semolina pudding.

It was more impossible than ever to think of dismissing Pasha, for it was to be feared that now she would demand that her friend should also remain in the flat.

Eight months passed, and again I was with my Moscow friends. I asked after Pasha, whom I missed, and was told : shortly after I went away last time she announced that she was not going to continue as a domestic worker but would be working in a factory henceforth, and she wanted to occupy, together with her Ivan, the little room that my friends always gave me during my stay in Moscow as their guest. On the plea that no foreigners were allowed to live permanently in a house belonging to the co-operative, the pair appealed to the court, but they lost their case. So Pasha departed willy-nilly with Vanyka, whom she had meantime herself recognized as a scoundrel and drunkard, as if nothing had happened, and lived wretchedly with the man whom yet she could not leave ; she was much aged and emaciated, and had already twice undergone the operation for abortion and once attempted suicide.

And since then a real tragedy seems to have occurred. Only a few weeks after she left she turned up to see her former mistress and ask her advice in difficult circumstances. Her husband had brought another woman to the little room where they lived together and had declared to Pasha that it depended on her behaviour henceforth whether he would stay with her or with the second woman. She had come to find out what " clever people " would think about such a situation. Yuliya Mironovna answered that in such a case it was very difficult to advise a third person, that everybody must decide for themselves, and that she would on no account consent to such an arrangement. Pasha went away and six weeks later she returned triumphantly as victor : she had stayed and her rival had been obliged to withdraw. It was only unfortunate that " he " was quite incorrigible and regularly spent not only his own wages, but all that she earned in the factory, on drink and pleasure.

Then a few weeks later, when last I saw her, she was taciturn and pale and moved like a shadow, and there were various blue marks on her face. She had come to take a final farewell of the family, but chiefly of Garrik, her most faithful friend. For she had resolved to return to her village, and the way in which she spoke of it augured no good. Perhaps she has since found some third way in spite of everything.

But the socialization of the household and the liberation of women from cooking does not solve the problem of feeding without the socialization of the kitchen. Something is being done in that direction, though not nearly enough. In place of the small communal kitchens which formed the majority till recently, they are now building canteens for large numbers worked by machinery —" kitchen factories " and so-called Food Supply Works. During 1931 the number of undertakings providing for the feeding of the public in the Soviet Union was in-

creased more than fivefold and their capacity sixteenfold.
Since the end of 1932 70 per cent of the workers and
50 per cent of their dependants are fed by socialized
canteens which employ over half a million workers. Like
the clubs, these institutions for communal feeding contribute not a little to the abolition of private life and the
development of the new *byt*. Still more is this achieved
through the *Communes*, which are the true pillars of
the new *byt*, as is seen from the circumstance that they
are called *Byt* Communes. Not infrequently they are
formed from single households on the basis of some
such proposals as that made by a woman to the editor
of a women's journal :

> There are 100 flats in our block. In each flat a kitchen and
> a kitchen stove. At each stove two or three housewives cook
> in from four to six pans. If you reckon that each housewife
> needs two hours to prepare dinner, it makes 600 hours, 85 full
> working days, passed solely at the cooking stove on one single
> day. If the housewives of only twelve flats would combine,
> and two or three of them cook in turn, then each would only
> have a turn every four or five days and could rest on the others.
> If one housewife alone would do the shopping for all twelve
> flats, it would mean that the other eleven would be saved stand-
> ing in queues for at least two hours per day. Moreover, the
> queues would be reduced to a twelfth of their present size and
> this would mean in practice the abolition of standing in queues.
> I, therefore, vote for the *Byt* Commune.

For the rest, inquiries in the Moscow *Byt* Communes
have shown that they owe their origin to the most various
causes. In addition to lack of house room and anxiety
to secure better nourishment, previous residence in
educational and convalescent homes and the consequent
habits have contributed to encourage the foundation of
these communes. But as a rule it is a question of
" enthusiasts whose primary aim is the creation of new
human relations, often not quite grasped by themselves ".
(Naystat, etc., *Youth Communes*.)

Be that as it may, there are already in Soviet Russia
hundreds of factory communes which often develop after
a short period to true residential and *byt* communes by

establishing more and more of the prerequisites of a communal life, such as kitchens, crèches, and laundries. And there is vigorous propaganda to get every *Komssomol* and party cell to encourage its members to found communes.

The communes, which are regarded as " the highest form of organization of the new *byt* yet known ", are not, moreover, without precedents in Russia's historical past. Thus in the last decades before the world war agricultural communes had sprung up in various places on the basis of Tolstoy's doctrine of simplicity. At the end of the 'seventies of the last century the writer Sslyeptsov tried to set up the labour and residential communes already known to us in St. Petersburg, but they only survived a few months, for they immediately attracted the attention of the police. Besides this, Russian revolutionaries in exile or as emigrants often founded small communes of a provisional character which, however, were closely akin to those of to-day both in their internal organization and their manner of life. In this connection, moreover, the theorists of present-day Russia admit historical continuity—an exception to their usual practice.

And now : life as it is lived in the new residential communes is novel and strange not only to Western Europeans, who may almost be said to have the principle of personality as the supreme happiness in their blood, but also for the majority of Russians who do not belong to them. A community prevails in everyday life, and especially in the youth communes a sense of solidarity, which might be said to amount to a new family feeling. Although most of the communes have recently abandoned the practice of having the members put their whole income into the communal fund, and therewith the so-called *uravnilovka*, equalization, has actually been given up, the collective character is nevertheless preserved, for everything else remains common property. Each commune keeps a day-book in which all the members enter their thoughts, experiences, and opinions, in short, all their joys and sorrows. Many of these day-books throw an interesting light on the way in which the property sense gradually fades and dies out in these germ-cells of the future, whose rules include a demand for the " eradication of all bourgeois habits ". Here, for example, is an extract from such a day-book :

> I have brought my electric kettle with me to the commune, but they use it carelessly. Why did I bring it ?

But even whilst he writes this member notices that his entry is a product of property psychology. He crosses out the sentence and adds penitently :

> I ? . . . Mine ? . . . Brrr. . . . The old régime ! . . . In our place the clock on the wall is broken. . . . In our place people use the sewing-machine carelessly. In our place the electric saucepan has been allowed to burn by cooking potatoes in it. All " eruptions of the past ". Slaves formerly ruined the tools that were entrusted to them like that. But it mustn't happen in a commune. Here we must handle common property carefully.

The care often taken by the community of comrades who are in trouble or ill is touching :

> Manya has to put up with unpleasantness at her work. She is quite depressed. We have already discussed the unpleasantness. Now she is cheerful again.
>
> SSONYA.

> There seems to be a misunderstanding about Yanya : he has not been admitted to the V.U.S., the University. We shall raise the matter for discussion on Friday. If he has been justly refused admission, we must note the fact that he has not passed the examination. But if he has been unjustly treated, we shall do our best for him, take up his case, and see what can be done.
>
> KOLYA.

> It is very pleasant to be ill in the commune. No hospital is to be compared with it. In the morning hardly anybody is there. Quiet. Those who are on duty attend on you. But that is as it should be. Members of a commune must be helpful. Everybody does what he can to help the sick member and to say something kind and affectionate to him.

374

If anyone feels ill, I would advise him to go to this best of all sanatoriums in the Union. He will be completely restored within three days here.

BORIS.

And another member adds this last entry in the day-book :

The present task of the commune is to obtain a bed in a sanatorium for Boris for two months. When Motya was convalescent we were all very much concerned about her. Once we caught her scrubbing the floor ; we rushed at her and stopped her and strictly forbade her to do it. We went away and looked through the window to see if she wasn't doing it all the same. She is like a sister to us. Sister, did I say ? She is far more. I don't know a bit how to express it. A dear member of the commune. And what delight we have in all these cares. It makes another being of you. It is as if a light shone within you. And so we look at one another and do not believe our eyes. Is it possible to live like that ? Yes, we do live like that.

(GRIGOROVICH, *Thus we live*.)

One gets the impression that a new family feeling is here developing, only comparable with that which else-where people have for their parental home. And this is confirmed by the letters of members who are absent or have for any reason left the commune. They are always addressed to the whole community and in a style which people elsewhere only use in writing to their nearest and dearest. And sometimes former members send money to the commune family. Thus in the collective day-book of the Moscow commune on the Varvarka there is an entry about a sum of 180 roubles which Irina earned by chance on her summer holiday and immediately sent to the commune. The members were annoyed and said that Irina ought to have used the money for better food and recuperation. But secretly they rejoiced at this " strengthening " of the " spiritual bond ".

After reading such instances we are no longer surprised that new ties come into being in these " factories for the remaking of the human soul ". But the real question

375

for us concerns the position of women in the communes, already to a certain degree in the new *byt*, that is to say, and the relations between women and men. On these two questions the members themselves shall speak :

" With us," state the members of the Moscow factory commune " Amo ", " women are, in the first place, freed from the ancient yoke. Secondly we enable them to devote their whole energies to the service of production. Liberation from the numerous insignificant trifles of daily life, and economic liberty—are these not a true liberation ? In the commune the very expression ' housewife ' is unknown. Among us there can only be domestic experts, cooks and cleaners, with a working day precisely regulated, or productive factory workers. There is no third alternative. One of our members recently married a ' born wife ' : she had never learned anything nor worked in a factory. We procured a place in a factory for her and put her to her apprenticeship. She was transformed from a ' better half ' to a complete, independent human being."

In the youth communes the boys and girls undertake the daily duty turn and turn about and in some of the other communes, too, you see men doing the household work together with the women.

In Soviet Russia people regard the commune as the model not only of the future family, but also of the future relation between the sexes, arising from the new *byt* and at the same time its prerequisite condition. On this point we read :

The commune repudiates vigorously every sort of sexual indiscipline, nor does it tolerate lascivious talk. If you ask them what form the relation between the sexes takes in a youth commune, the young members reply : " We all live together, and are witnesses of the life of the other half of our community. That has on the one hand a sobering effect, on the other it simplifies mutual relations. There have, of course, been cases in which purely comradely relations changed." It is a matter of course that the commune cannot reeducate all its members immediately. For most of them do not join as children, but as adults. If the boys in the commune respect

376

the views of their comrades and refuse to tolerate a frivolous, uncomradely approach to the girls, they have a way out by removing their love from the commune. . . .

The question of marriage seems undoubtedly to have been solved rightly in the communes in principle. Isolated cases of extremism, the demand that married pairs should live apart or that men and women should share rooms, rarely occur and are generally vigorously repudiated by the whole commune. Marriage and children, it is occasionally said, must on no account undermine the common economic foundation of the commune. This principle is of great importance in its influence on the creation of the new family. The economic foundation of the former bourgeois family is already sufficiently undermined, and with the further entrance of women into productive and social life the process will proceed farther. The new *byt*, like the new family, will be able to grow up only when all the necessary economic conditions are fulfilled. For that reason it is not yet time to consider a complete reconstruction of life on a socialist basis. . . . We begin by building up the fundamental conditions of a socialized life : the commune is the model of the future socialist *byt*. But even now marriage in a commune is different from marriage elsewhere. For it anticipates the marriage of a socialist society in that the economic tie has ceased to play a part in the mutual relations of husband and wife. The same applies to the question of the children, although the communes have little experience in this matter at present. During their early years the communes did not desire children for material reasons. But now there are a considerable number of commune children. (Naystat, etc., *Youth Communes*.)

One thing, then, is established : In the communes, each one of which is a little world of its own in wholly changed surroundings, what is really new in the new *byt* is visibly taking form. And it is precisely personal relations, the relations of man and woman, besides the position of women within the community, which unquestionably bear a wholly new stamp to-day in the communes. Only the future can, of course, show whether this really is an evolutionary process which moves along the line of progress and will continue uninterrupted.

THE NEW *BYT*

IN THE ARTYUKHINA WOMEN'S COMMUNE

" The hen is a bird and woman a human being."

IN the previous section I have given a brief account of the communes and the position of women in the factory, residential, and *byt* communes. But there are also communes in Soviet Russia where not only housing and meals but also work, production, has been socialized, that is to say producers' and consumers' co-operatives of a wholly new type. This type is of the more interest to us here because one of the co-operatives in question is known throughout the Union as the " Women's Commune " because it had no men at first and still has few.

When in the autumn of 1930 I heard in Moscow of this almost legendary commune " somewhere in the Northern Caucasus, in the neighbourhood of Rostov on the Don ", I wanted to go there at once in order to make the acquaintance of what was described as a unique co-operative. But winter was approaching and everybody advised me against undertaking the nowise easy journey at that season.

For nearly a year I was on tenterhooks about this " matriarchal state " on which I could obtain no information even from the officials of the many agricultural authorities in Moscow, except what I read in the minutes of the meetings of the Women's Section of the V.T.S.I.K. which were kindly placed at my disposal. You see Russia is very large and the enterprise was then very new.

It was not till I was in Rostov on the Don in the summer of 1931 and made inquiries about this women's settlement that I learned one thing at least, that the Artyukhina Women's Commune was quite near the town of Ssalsk and could be reached from Rostov in eight or nine hours ; but even there nobody could tell me any details.

Ssalsk, right in the midst of the genuine South Russian steppes—not the steppes which so many brand-new Western European travellers in Russia see even before they cross the Polish frontier—is a pleasant, thoroughly civilized, typically Russian, former county town with a population predominantly Cossack. And when one beautiful, burning August afternoon I made my appearance at the office of the local *Isspolkom* (Executive Committee) with my papers and letters of introduction and wishes, my arrival was immediately announced to the Women's Commune by telephone and I was told that the carriage would come to fetch me in an hour's time. Meanwhile a small, clean room was allotted to me in the only hotel in the place and, so as to waste no time, I decided to take a short walk, for I wanted to see the town.

The first thing which struck me as quite familiar at a street corner was what you see everywhere in Moscow, in Leningrad, and everywhere in the Union : a kiosk crammed with newspapers, journals, and the usual portraits of the leaders. Of course people read *Pravda* and *Isvestiya* in Ssalsk, too. But here they also read the Rostov *Molot* (The Hammer), and it is a matter of course that the town should have at least one paper of its own. I was struck in Ssalsk, as I had been previously in Rostov and was later in Tiflis and all over the Caucasus, with the prevalence of white still worn not only by women but also by men in the streets—a good old Russian custom which, however, has now almost died out in the large industrial cities. The red *kossynkas* with the white dresses of the Cossack women are exceedingly becoming ; most of them have fine figures, and a remarkably large number are very fair-skinned with black hair and intensely blue eyes ; you also come across a great many men of this type in the Northern Caucasus ; they are a handsome breed. There is not much vegetation in Ssalsk and these patches of colour, like walking poppies in a cornfield, are a really refreshing sight. M. Sholokhov's novel, *The Tranquil Don* (translated into German), has made the Cossack women known : a passionate race who have preserved their own character with irrepressible determination and stubborn vigour in spite of centuries of oppression ; whose life has been radically transformed by war and revolution and the " de-Cossackizing "—the taming of their fierce menfolk.

The Commune is called after the leader of the *Shenotdyel*, the women's section of the Party Central Committee, Artyukhina Commune. A little over a mile from the town, it is situated on the steep bank of the little River Yegorlyk, a tributary of the Don. You see its scattered white houses before you pass over the atrociously made raft bridge which is already half sunk in the water and which you cross literally at the risk of your life.

On the spot where the Commune stands to-day—in close proximity to the famous *sovkhos* Gigant—there was only a bare hill five years ago and near it a so-called " machine co-operative " which did, indeed, comprise seven farms, but possessed not a single machine. At the end of the winter of 1929, at a time when the question of collectivization was particularly burning in Russia, some hundred solitary women from the surrounding villages of Ssalsk county, weary of day labour on other people's farms, united, with their children, at the instigation of the woman labourer Ssorokina, and resolved to found a *kolkhos* of their own with the support of the competent village soviet, which allotted a piece of land to them ; they were for the most part day labourers themselves, quite poor peasant women, mothers and widows of Red party members, and there were among them a number of Cossacks and " Khokhlushki ", Ukrainians of mixed origin. On May 1st, 1929, therefore, the Artyukhina Commune was officially established. The most important share capital that the women brought was their strong, horny hands, and in addition they managed to collect about 5,000 roubles. The seven families already settled there, whom the Commune members joined at first, soon left, for they did not want to have anything to do with women alone, who, moreover, gave their *kolkhos* a woman's name.

The women who remained and had for the most part camped in the open till then, established themselves in the now empty barns and cowshed. Ssorokina, as chairwoman of the Commune, engaged two capable labourers, and the life of the Commune members, hard enough at first, began with a tractor, two camels, three harvesters, and four yoke of oxen. Not only must 350 hectares (about 865 acres) of land and 12 hectares (about 30 acres) of vegetable fields be cultivated on the naked, sun-baked steppe, but many thousand bricks had to be baked so that a more solid shelter might be built for the winter. Credit was granted to the women and they worked untiringly day and night in order to bring together what was needed for their enterprise, bit by bit, stone by stone. Some of the women could not stand the hard work over a long period and left the *kolkhos*. But to make up, five of the families who had left at first returned in the autumn. From the outset the settlement had been intended as a purely women's commune, and a practical example for the training of women *kolkhos* workers. But in the time of general collectivization the women were obliged to abandon their exclusiveness, and so in the autumn of 1929 there were eighteen men among the 168 mouths in the Commune.

In addition to the wearing, purely material struggle which the brave women in the newly founded " women's or widows' *kolkhos* " had to carry on, there was another war that they had to wage on many fronts—against slander, hostility, suspicion, against the various monstrous reports that were zealously spread abroad in the neighbourhood about the unprecedented undertaking of the *babas* ; and that was a hard struggle. The proletarian writer Merslyakov has caught the general atmosphere very vividly in a hitherto unpublished sketch :

Round about they were unsleeping. Certain people had detected a mortal enemy in the rising *kolkhos*, and sinister rumours glided like snakes through the neighbouring villages.
" Have you heard ? "
" What ? "
" What ? About the row in the *kolkhos*."
" Well, now ! "
" And how they went for one another ! How they knocked one another about ! It was something awful. Their first chairwoman, Ssorokina, had all her hair torn out, and such bruises under her eyes that she won't get rid of inside a year. And after the row half the *kolkhos* made off."

The women who met Ssorokina afterwards always glanced at her furtively, but they could see nothing of the bruises and were greatly astonished: "What things they invent, the brutes!"

But the sinister rumours gathered volume every day. "In the Commune your children are taken away and converted to the anti-christian religion. The marks of Satan are stamped on them." Over a radius of seven versts at least the peasants steered clear of the women's *kolkhos*.

"And the mean things they spread abroad about us," *Tovarishch* Mogila recounted, one of Ssorokina's two helpers, and illustrated his remark by this very amusing story: "I had to go to the village of Yegorlyk about thirty versts from here, to buy horses. Whilst I was looking round in the market I saw a lot of *babas* and *mushiks* standing round a cart. And in their midst was a dignified, white-haired old man who was telling something about our *kolkhos*. I must go and listen to that, I thought. So I elbowed through the crowd and got close to the old man; I listened and could hardly believe my ears.

"'It's not a *kolkhos* at all, but a real thieves' den, a nest of crime, God forgive me!' said the little old fellow, smacking his toothless lips. 'They all sleep together under a coverlet seventy yards long, and the women are common property. If a man lies down at one end in the evening, he gets up the next morning at the other. Such sin! . . .'

"'Chatter away, chatter away,' I thought to myself; 'I'll hear first what's coming.'

"But when the old man saw that after his talk the peasants all stood with wide-open mouths and the *babas* crossed themselves and said their prayers, he naturally poured more oil on the flames: 'The eldest man they've got there, his surname is Mogila, and he's got twelve wives at a time. . . .'

"Then I could stand it no longer and I asked the old fellow: 'And have you ever seen this Mogila, Grandad?' 'How could I help having seen him, my boy? I've seen him at least five times. A great, clumsy chap. He's got a phiz like a sieve, and his eyes fairly jump about in his head.' 'And would you recognize him, this Mogila, if you met him?'

"'Should I recognize him? By God, I could recognize him half a mile off.'

"'Really?'

"'I swear it! By the holy ikons! Else may I be glued to the spot.' The old man took off his cap and began to cross himself zealously.

"'What a story-teller you are, Grandad. I'm Mogila my-self.' And I fetched my identification papers out of my pocket and showed them to the peasants.

"'What a scandal, Grandad, why do you lie so wickedly, you old wretch?' the peasants now all shouted at him. And he stood there and stared goggled-eyed, and just snorted and could find no answer.

"'It's true,' he burst out at last, 'I haven't seen him with my own eyes, but a man from our village, a regular serious, rich, respected man, not just anyone, he was there. . . .'

"But this time the peasants laughed and so did the *babas* who had shed tears before over his stories. And the old man disappeared into the crowd. . . .''

Marussya, the fair-haired, bobbed secretary of the Commune, who looked like a boy in her dark blue, high-necked, Russian *kossovorotka*, received me together with the secretary of the party cell in the absence of the present President of the Commune, Chebotaryova (Ssorokina is engaged elsewhere at the time), who had gone to Moscow. "At the present time," she said, "our commune comprises 678 mouths. Of these 424 are females and 254 males. They include 225 able-bodied women and 110 able-bodied men, and the remainder are children and old people. We have 2,800 hectares (nearly 7,000 acres) of arable land, 67 hectares (about 185 acres) of vegetable fields, 3 hectares (between 7 and 8 acres) of orchard, and some 600 head of beasts—more than 100 horses, 80 milch cows, 270 sheep, over a hundred pigs, 12 camels, and 18 oxen—and 5 tractors."

I learned further that the whole work of the Commune was divided among five brigades, each under its own committee of control, each with its own party cell, its own wall newspaper in which here, as everywhere, all events are commented on, frequently in a polemical and at the same time political style, and each with its own village correspondent. There is one field work brigade, one for animal breeding, one for vegetable growing, and one central handicraft brigade which carries out tractor repairs, locksmith's and blacksmith's work, saddlery, carpentry, shoemaking, and tailoring. There is further a mill and a special brickyard. The Commune's fundamental speciality is chicken breeding at the present time. And they breed exclusively snow-white Leghorns which are housed all over the estate in fifteen large henhouses ; they have a stock of 60,000 birds and each group resembles a great, white, moving island in the wide steppe. Two-thirds are usually delivered to the state in the autumn and one-third kept for the winter. In 1932, according to the Five Years' Plan, sixty more henhouses were built, and in 1933 the American incubators are to turn out some 150,000 chickens and two million eggs. There are some 10,000 cocks, of no less handsome and magnificent breed, to fertilize the hens.

When I asked how the Commune members, women and men, got on together, *Tovarishch* Ssyerekov, the secretary of the party cell, grinned broadly and answered : " We feel like a single family, and that's all there is to say about it." The Commune has a simple, cleanly dwelling-house for married couples, in which space is allotted according to numbers, and two more dwelling-houses for 120 single persons each, men and women separately. Besides that there is, of course, a common kitchen run by women, a bakery, and laundry, and a vapour bath, all worked by electricity. Meals are taken in a common dining-room, and on the first evening after my arrival, when I was invited to take my meals in the Commune for the period of my stay in Ssalsk, there were bowls piled sky-high with *vareniki*, a pudding of flour and sour milk, and poured over it cream so thick that you could almost cut it with a knife. As dessert juicy, deep red water melons were handed round, and instead of a serviette I was given one of the Russian peasant cloths richly embroidered with cross-stitch and bordered with *ajourée* and hand-made lace that used to be hung round the ikons, and that ought only to be kept in museums now.

Every member of the Commune is still working for three, often without even observing the days of rest, so that every minute is precious and the midday meal is hurried and much less plentiful : some kind of soup and a few slices of melon with bread. There is very seldom

384

CHICKEN YARD IN THE WOMEN'S COMMUNE

meat. The children eat apart from the adults, who limit themselves so as to let the children have more ; these latter are given only the best, most wholesome food and look very merry and well fed. Some of the members eat their food at the place where they work, and the rest, for whom there is not room enough at the long tables set with benches, have their meals in two or three shifts : men and women, old and young, all together, and the prevailing mood is at once gay and serious.

They talk of the work accomplished and what has still to be done, of the silo tower that they have just built, the pride of the Commune, where the fodder for the cattle is stored in winter, of the new club, the dwelling-house for 500 persons, and the big cowshed that is just about to be begun. They grumble at the herdsman through whose carelessness a camel has been lost on the steppes. They talk of the " Comrades' Court " where Stepan yesterday received a public reprimand because he had absolutely ruined some part of a machine. And again and again the women tell me with pleasure of all the mockery and scorn that they had to put up with from their neighbours at first, who spat in at their windows and shouted the most impossible abuse at them, and how everybody made fun of them : " A chicken farm ? Whatever do you do with chickens ? " And how that department has proved the most lucrative, and how greatly the authority of the Commune has increased in a short period, how the other *kolkhosi* get their experts from it, and that the latest proverb about the new women's *kolkhos*, in contrast to the earlier one, now runs : " The hen is a bird and woman a human being."

Illiteracy has been wholly eradicated from the Commune, where a fairly vigorous cultural life obtains. Thus there are several courses for semi-illiterates, for advanced students, and a special *kolkhos* school for women conducted by women with a three years' course, theoretical and practical, to train managers and organizers for the most varied branches of agriculture in the *kolkhosi*. Specially zealous pupils have passed through this course in two years. Of course there is a Red Corner in the

Commune with newspapers and journals, and as the women's demand for books is constantly increasing there are plans for a reading-room. By day everybody works, but in the evening, more particularly on winter evenings, people study in the Commune, study and study again ; with great perseverance and tenacity.

In the light and airy women's common-room, in which the clean beds stood in rows, a good-humoured peasant woman of about forty, whom I found bending over books and papers after her hard day's work, said to me : " It is only since we have begun to study that we have really begun to live at all." And I shall never forget another spectacle in this Commune which I saw the next day. When I started with Marussya on a long walk over the fields and meadows, through gardens and workshops and all the henhouses, which are miles apart, and came at last to the last isolated section, at the extreme end of the Commune, I found a Cossack woman, no longer quite young, sitting right among the chickens and watching over them, barefoot, a kerchief over her head ; she had an open exercise book and spelling book and in the intervals of her work she was trying to read and write, pencil in hand. And Fenya, the young milkmaid, told me : " I was twelve years in the service of a rich peasant and never learned a letter. I couldn't even distinguish a ten-copek piece from a fiver. And now . . ." Fenya flushed all over her face, plucked at her kerchief, glanced at me half furtively out of her clear eyes, and then said in a low voice : " Now I have sent something to the newspaper in Rostov, but it hasn't been published yet, and I haven't had an answer yet. . . ."

How many such Fenyas are there here, all working, learning, and becoming daily more conscious of their humanity ? . . . " The women are moving now," said Krupskaya once at a women's conference.

Besides its schools for adults the Artyukhina Commune has also a children's crèche for about fifty children, among whom there are already twenty " born members of the Commune ", whilst their number, as I was told with a certain pride, is likely shortly to be increased " by another

386

eight head ". There is a children's playground, too, for
about fifty children ; both institutions are under trained
management.

The Commune feeds and clothes all the children as well
as all the adults, and the parents can choose whether they
will leave their children altogether in the crèche or have
them sometimes at home : in any case, therefore, they
are no burden.

Of course the Commune has a wireless, and until it
can afford a cinema of its own the cinema from the town
comes out to it twice a week across the river. Until a
short time ago, I was told, the Commune had had its own
wind orchestra of twenty-seven women, which gave all the
inmates immense pleasure. The principal player, too,
was a woman. But one day her husband, a Red Army
soldier, came home and fetched his Masha, and the whole
orchestra had to be given up. Now there is only a band
of balalaikas, guitars, and mandolins, beside the inevitable
accordions. The young people, all in the *Komssomol*,
dance and sing a great deal of course ; they get up a
variety of plays and " living newspapers ", study, work,
and are attracted to one another. " There are no divorces
at all," the lively young Marussya assured me, throwing
back her vigorous head in a characteristic way. " But
plenty of marriages." There have even been cases when
girls have had to leave the Commune because of their
marriage : " If she likes a boy in the town, let her marry
him ! She even gets a day off out of her turn for the
purpose." But in the past year six couples in the
Commune itself have married.

A few days after my arrival the women in the Commune
invited me to be present at a meeting of the party cell.
I found various of my new acquaintances gathered round
a table in a medium-sized room in which there were not
enough seats for the three or four dozen who had turned
up, so that some had to sit on small footstools or even on
the floor. Here, too, old and young sat together, and
once more I was struck with what I had already noticed
on several occasions in this commune : the remarkably
pleasant manner, at once comradely and courteously

obliging, of the men's intercourse with the women and the
young people's with the old—how they offered them their
seats and were helpful where the occasion required, etc.
This can only be due to the educative and civilizing
influence of women.

Decisions were taken upon the admission of several
new members to the party, including the absent President
of the Commune, Chebotaryova. *Tovarishch* Ssyerekov
conducted the proceedings and his representative read
briefly the facts and careers of the candidates, after which
the question for and against was put. As only members
were being proposed who were thoroughly known to those
present, there was little opposition. " A good girl ; what
need to discuss her," said a woman benevolently. And
when one woman ventured to hint that Chebotaryova's
Cossack origin could not be regarded as unquestionably
proletarian, she received the emphatic answer : " It does
not matter to us in the least whether her grandmother
possibly sat in a shop ; what matters to us is that she is a
first-rate worker and a brilliant manager."

It is hardly necessary to mention that the Artyukhina
Commune is included in the Five Years' Plan, and that
not only do all the brigades, sub-sections, and groups
compete at storm speed and at the same time support one
another's work to the best of their ability, but also groups
of a dozen compete, and even the single henhouses. In
reply to the appeal of the " Lenin Way " *Kolkhos* (Lower
Volga district) in *Pravda* to join in socialist competition,
the Women's Commune published the following answer
in *Molot* on April 26th, 1930, rather less than a year after
its establishment, that is :

Tovarishchi, men and women of the " Lenin Way " *Kolkhos* !
In your appeal you write that you have been through a great
struggle for the *kolkhos* ; you write of your achievements and
shortcomings, and beg all *kolkhos* members in the Soviet Union
to tell you about their work. We respond to your appeal and
give you our Commune answer.

In May of last year we founded an agricultural co-operative
" Ssalsk ". But in the same year, in December, we adopted the
statutes of a commune and gave it the name of the head of the

women's section of the Party Central Committee, Artyukhina. Our co-operative consisted almost entirely of women labourers and very poor peasant women.

The Commune had to suffer many evils. The population made fun of it because it was a women's commune. All manner of ugly rumours were spread abroad about us, and everybody said that nothing would come of a " baba commune ". So life was not easy at the beginning. We had no dwelling, and 178 women members were housed in a shed together with the cows. Although we suffered great want and our enemies abused us violently, we did not give in.

Here are some of the basic achievements of our farm. These show you what our village co-operative owned in 1928-9 and what we now own in the Commune. In those days we comprised 78 mouths, and in 1929-30 there were 626 mouths among the Commune members. Of these 165 were men, 204 women, 257 juveniles and children. Ninety-six labourers' families live in the Commune, 70 quite poor peasant families and 40 peasant families of medium poverty.

There follows a detailed account of the stock and the cultivated area; then the statement proceeds:

In order to carry out the spring work at storm speed we entered into a socialist competition with the Commune " Idea " and the Commune " Lenin's Bequest ", and have kept to it fully by means of establishing storm brigades. All the women in the Commune gave up their free days and there was no holiday at Easter. . . .

We have planted 500 fruit trees and 38,000 mulberry bushes for silkworm breeding. During seed-time we set up a " culture brigade " which took all the cultural work of the steppe in charge. . . .

Three of our women are attending agricultural colleges. One is studying the mechanics of the cinema trade, and a few are attending other courses. More than twenty women students are attending our courses on poultry breeding.

The President of our Commune is a woman, and there are women directors of each agricultural department except the arable department. We also employ three workmen from the town, who are very helpful to us. We thank the working class for helping our communes and *kolkhosi* through its best representatives.

In summer we work a ten hours' day, in winter eight hours,

389

reduced to six for those who are studying. According to the group to which they are attached, members receive advances for clothing and other purchases, whilst board and lodging are the charge of the Commune. Old people and children are supported altogether by the Commune.

Only six families have left us in the course of the year, being unable to accustom themselves to collectivism in work and in our way of living.

Our Commune was the first in the whole Ssalsk district to finish sowing. As a reward we received a tractor.

Tovarishchi, now we have responded to the appeal of the *kolkhos* men and women of " Lenin's Way ", and we, in turn, call upon all the communes and *kolkhosi* of the Northern Caucasus to respond to the appeal of the *kolkhos* " Lenin's Way " and of our Artyukhina Commune, and to join in the socialist appeal for the spring sowing, for the organization of the work in the *kolkhosi* and communes, and for the harvest.

On the day which I had fixed for my departure I was told that Chebotaryova, the President of the Artyukhina Commune, had returned from Moscow and awaited me in the Board Room. I was kindly welcomed by a strong, tall, dark-haired woman of middle age, dressed in black, with a clever, energetic face and lively blue eyes that were still quite youthful ; she began at once to give me information, as if she must somehow make up to me for the days of her absence.

" Our women have now taken their fate into their own hands," she stressed in our talk ; " they have their special plan for each single day. They are building up their lives and know exactly what they want, and everything that you have seen in our Commune is solely the result of hard work, perseverance, and strict organization. The climate here is mild and healthy and we work all the year round without a break. But such words as ' salary ', ' earnings ', or ' payment ' are not in use among us. The managing committee of the Commune consists of seven persons, five of whom are women. There has been no single case of a woman complaining about a man, of a man refusing her his help, or of the smallest dissension. Everybody keeps watch at his post, gives of his best, and is fully conscious of his responsibility to the community, and it is astonishing how greatly the women's influence has raised the moral tone—and there is a positive scramble among them to reach their goal : in spite of the proximity of the town and the various temptations involved, drunkenness has been wholly abolished in the Commune. You never hear a contemptuous word, and the older members, the ' veterans of the kolkhos ' (they include several women who broke ice on the river and carried it away for a whole winter in order to procure the necessary resources for the Commune), are specially respected and honoured by the younger ones. It is true that we are very cautious in our attitude towards new members, and hundreds of requests for admission are regularly refused for lack of housing accommodation.''

Finally I was told that the Women's Commune, which is to be decorated with the Lenin Order, is already so popular that in 1930 alone it was visited by about 8,000 persons, including a number of foreigners—Americans, Germans, Mongols, and negroes—and that on October 1st, 1930, a conference of women *kolkhos* workers attended by nearly 300 women delegates of the Ssalsk district was held there ; various lectures were given and experiences exchanged. Shortly afterwards the great trek of peasant women to inspect the Artyukhina Commune began, and one day 400 mountaineer women turned up from the Caucasus who first asked to see the coverlet seventy yards long under which, as they had heard, all the members slept. These women, too, evinced no small surprise when they heard that this was a myth. But when they were shown everything in the Commune in detail they were filled with enthusiasm and would have liked to stay.

It was evening when I took leave of Chebotaryova, of Marussya, Ssyerekov, and the whole Artyukhina Commune and stepped out into the now familiar large court-yard which was tinged with a faint rosy hue by the last rays of the setting sun. A gigantic cart piled sky-high with fresh, fragrant hay was just driving in. A group of milkmaids were coming with their milking pails from their cows, which graze day and night out in the fields. The chickens were already gone to roost and on one side, near the kitchen garden, some two dozen young women members were preparing whole mountains of cabbage for to-morrow's midday dinner. The air was clear and bright, a little aromatic, with already a touch of autumn in it. The steppes extended beyond the reach of the eye. The world ended with the horizon, and from somewhere I heard happy, young, care-free laughter mingled with the rattle of a tractor steaming in the distance, whilst from another side sounded a melancholy song, an ancient melody. . . .

One last look from the other side of the little Yegorlyk, and the Soviet Russian, really existent and not Utopian, " Island of the Great Mothers ", where already the first lights were lit, was lost in the darkness of the night. . . .

Late that same night I took the train back to Rostov on the Don. I was lucky : a whole seat was free and I promptly lay down to sleep. Towards morning I was hesitatingly waked by a deep, kindly voice. I opened my eyes. The ticket-collector was standing before me in a faultless uniform with a metal watch-chain and a signal whistle peeping out of the breast pocket ; he smiled good-humouredly and asked for my ticket, and I observed with surprise that he had a red *kossynka* on his head and was consequently not a man but a woman ticket-collector, with whom, of course, I immediately got into conversation. The train was almost at the station, but this Cossack woman, Marya Petrovna Barysh, pleased at my interest, hurriedly and willingly told me her typical life story : she was fifty-one and lived in the town of Ssalsk. In 1919 she lost her husband and was left alone and without means of support with her three children. In former days there would hardly have been anything for her to do but to go begging. But now the first thing which she, hitherto an illiterate, did was to learn to read and write, which immediately made her " ten years younger ". The children were soon placed in various institutions where they also learned some things. She herself took a position in the railway service and had been able to save so much in the course of years that even without the

batyka, father, she had been able to secure a little house.
" And now," she said, her whole face beaming, " one of
my daughters is an agricultural expert, another is working
in a co-operative, and the third is secretary of the party
cell. I, too, am a member of the party and work for it
three times a week. But my chief occupation is study.
For what I already know is not nearly enough for me.
Marry again ? Oh, no ! Nothing would induce me to
submit to the yoke again. It's delightful to live like this.
I'm studying with the help of the postal courses now and
trying to educate myself further by every means in my
power. What am I studying ? Party science and
geography and chemistry. When I read anything about
chemistry I want to know more and more about it.
And now I know what Darwinism is ! But till I was
forty-nine I knew nothing about it and thought God had
created man. But I'm just as much interested in the
history of Rome in the fourth century. . . . I'd like to
read everything and know everything. . . . And I get
younger every year. . . ."

I think Barysh could have gone on for ever telling me
of her rejuvenation through re-learning, just as I should
have liked to listen for hours to her talk. For whilst she
spoke I thought not only of her personal history, but
linked it up with the countless other life stories of many
millions of Russian women, told by word of mouth,
written, and yet more still unknown to me. And when
the train stopped at Rostov and I shook the dear woman's
hand heartily her development to a human being became
a symbol to me for the development to human beings of
the feminine half of something approaching a continent.

CONCLUDING REMARKS

IT is the habit of authors to conclude their books with a survey of the future. If I wished to follow that custom, I should have to answer not only the question whither Russian womanhood is driving, but at the same time what issue is decreed to the world-shaking historical events of which Russia is to-day the scene. But I feel myself no more called upon to answer that question than capable of doing so.

As I have endeavoured to keep the book free from contentious matter, as far as possible, I will now discuss two errors common abroad with regard to the position of Russian women. The first has its origin in the rumours spread abroad by former anti-Bolshevik propaganda about the socialization of women, but it frequently reappears in a new form as the statement that Soviet Russian women are more the slaves of promiscuity than their sisters in other countries. It is unnecessary to go further into this subject, for my whole book is a refutation of all such myths, which are for the most part not even meant seriously.

More interesting is the other hypothesis, that sees the first steps towards a matriarchate, or even the dawn of an epoch of female domination, in the increase of power of Russian women, which is, indeed, unique in history. And it is true that since the female population of the Soviet Union, borne along by a tremendous wave of historical evolution, began to take possession of their new realm, they constitute the great reservoir of humanity and energy upon which the revolution can draw and rejuvenate itself. Women influence the whole of life and help to mould its new forms by their determining action, for nothing is done without them—much less in opposition to them—and mother and child occupy not only a

394

TURKOMAN MOTHER WITH HER CHILD

[face p. 394

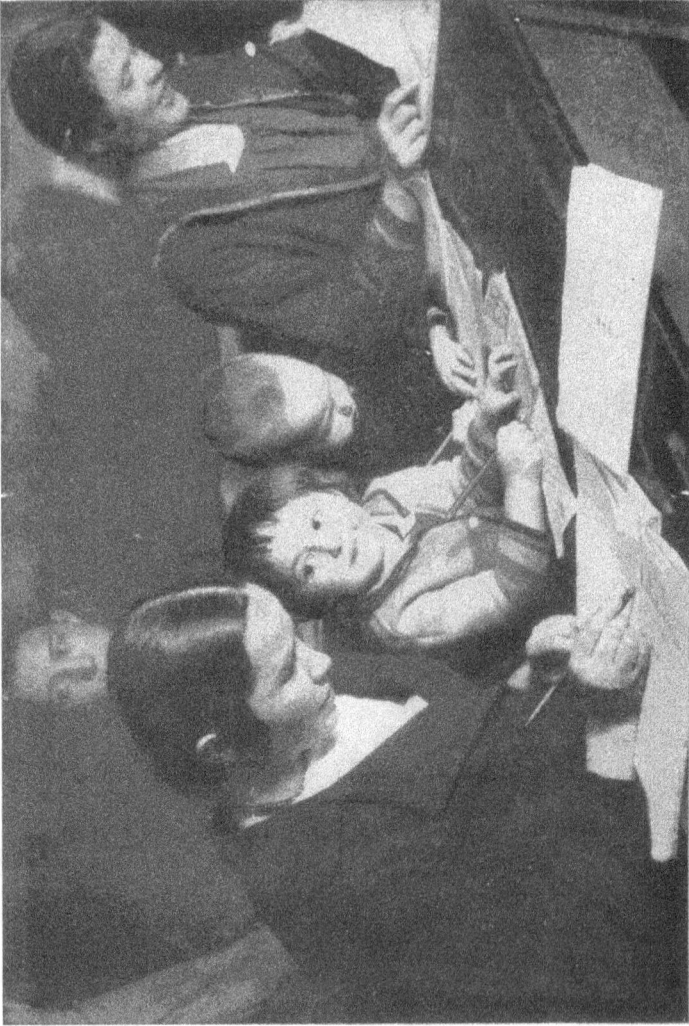

TARTAR WOMEN LEARN TO WRITE TOGETHER WITH THEIR CHILDREN

prominent but a central position in public interest. And in the Union itself the immense energy with which the women there have established themselves in the positions made accessible to them by the October revolution has given rise to the complaint of which we have heard of an " assault by the women ".

In spite of all this we should not be justified in speaking of a matriarchate in any such sense as that in which Keyserling ascribes it to the United States of North America. In the Soviet Union there are no such distinctions of rank in the sphere of *being* which there, thanks to the " principle of polarization ", are supposed to secure for the women a position of power and domination over the men, who are judged merely by their achievement. In Russia, on the contrary, a hierarchy of achievement rules, moulding the whole of life on one consistent principle, estimating the worth of every person, whether man or woman, according to his or her achievements, and achievements according to their social value. This hierarchy includes women, not only because motherhood and the upbringing of children are valued as achievements of great social value, but also because the women are being drawn into productive work in all fields, and it depends solely upon their own ability and energy what rank they rise to in a hierarchy built solely upon achievement. But where both sexes are judged by a single, common standard, the domination of one over the other is unthinkable as a permanency, however the prejudices of the past may retain their influence in particular cases.

Moreover, it is a mistake to seek only patriarchal elements in the past precisely of the Russian people, as Count Keyserling again does, regarding Bolshevism as the typical product of a patriarchal nation *par excellence*. On the contrary, so far are we from failing to find traces of the matriarchate in the historical development of the Russian people, that it is still possible to point to lingering signs of it in Christian Russia, as I have done in this book.

Taking it all in all, it is just as arbitrary to speak of an evolving " dictatorship of women, supplanting the dictatorship of the proletariat ", as of the unbroken development of the patriarchate still proceeding. Rather we must be content with the truth. And that is that in the land of the Soviets—in sharp contrast, it is true, to the one-sided masculine civilization of the West—something new in history has arisen, a society based upon the absolutely equal rights of the sexes, and in process of developing ever richer and more varied forms. A relapse into patriarchal and masculine rule would only be conceivable, if it were possible that some day women might fail to play their part within a hierarchy that is impartial in the matter of sex. The only question based upon realities which could be raised would be as to that possibility. In a certain sense my book is simply a negative answer, supported by facts.

What positive elements the book contains the reader must judge. I myself regard it as a report upon the momentary position of an experiment of world-wide historical significance: the experiment, tried for the first time in human history, of according to both sexes the same right to mould our life.

BIBLIOGRAPHY

WOMEN IN ANCIENT RUSSIA

BACHOFEN, J. J., *Mutterrecht und Urreligion.* A. Kröner Verlag, Leipzig, 1927.

DOBRYAKOV, A., *Russkaya shenshchina v domongolyskyi period* (Russian Women in the Pre-Mongolian Period). St. Petersburg, 1864.

Domostroy. Edition of the earliest transcription with an Introduction by I. Sabyelin (in the *Chtyeniya Obshchestva istorii*). Moscow, 1882.

HERBERSTEIN, SIGMUND, FREIHERR ZU, *Moscovia.* Verlag der philosophischen Akademie, Erlangen, 1926.

KOSTOMAROV, N. I., *Ocherk domashnyey shisni i nravov velikorusskavo naroda v 16–17 vyeke* (Sketch of the domestic Life and Customs of the Great Russians in the sixteenth-seventeenth century). Collected Works, Vol. 8, St. Petersburg, 1906.

KOTOSHIKHIN, G., *O Rossii v tsarstvovaniye Alexyeya Mikhaylovicha* (Concerning Russia under the Rule of the Tsar Alexyey Mikhaylovich). Published by the Archæological Commission, St. Petersburg, 1884.

KOVALYOV, K. N., *Istoricheskoye rasvitiye byta shenshchiny, braka i ssyemyi* (Historical Development of Women's Life, of Marriage and the Family). Compilation edited by Prof. S. Wolfson, Prometyey, Moscow, 1931.

OLEARIUS, ADAM, *Vermehrte Moskovitische und Persianische Reisebeschreibung.* Schleswig, 1656. (English: *The Voyages and Travels of the Ambassadors sent by Frederick Duke of Holstein to the Great Duke of Muscovy, and the King of Persia* . . . Faithfully rendered into English by John Davies of Kidwelly. For John Starkey and Thomas Basset, London, 1669.)

POKROVSKYI, M., *Russkaya istoriya ss drevnyeyshikh vremyon.* Leningrad, 1924. (English: *History of Russia from the earliest Times to the Rise of Commercial Capitalism.* Martin Lawrence, 1931.)

— *Ocherk istorii russkoy kultury* (Brief History of Russian Culture). Moscow, 1915.

397

BIBLIOGRAPHY

SABYELIN, I., *Domashnyi byt russkikh tsarits v XVI i XVII stoletii* (Domestic Customs of the Russian Tsaritsas in the Sixteenth and Seventeenth Centuries). Moscow, 1901.

SHASHKOV, S. S., *Istoriya russkoy shenshchiny* (History of Russian Women). Collected Works, Vol. I, Part 2, St. Petersburg, 1898.

SHCHAPOV, *Mirossosertsaniye, myssly, trud i shenshchina v istorii russkavo obshchestva* (Philosophy of Life, Thought, Work, and Woman in the History of Russian Society). In the journal *Otyechestvenniye Sapiski*, Nos. 5, 6, Moscow, 1874.

SEIFERT, J. L., *Die Weltrevolutionäre*. Amalthea Verlag, Vienna, 1930.

CHUDINOV, A. N., *Ocherk istorii russkoy shenshchiny v possledovatyelynom rasvitii literaturnykh tipov* (Historical Sketch of Russian Womanhood in the developing Sequence of literary Types). St. Petersburg, 1889.

THE DAWN OF A NEW AGE

AMFITEATROV, A., *Shenshchina v obshchestvennykh dvisheniyakh v Rossii* (Women in the Social Movement in Russia). Geneva, Selbstverlag, 1905. (Also in the journal *Vssyemirnyi Vyestnik*, 1906, No. 9.)

— *Die Frau* (In *Russen über Russland*, edited by I. Melnik). Literarische Anstalt Rütten und Loening, Frankfurt a/M, 1906.

BESSMERTNY, M., *Geschichte der Frauenbewegung in Russland* (In *Geschichte der Frauenbewegung in den Kulturländern*, Vol. I, edited by Helene Lange and Gertrude Bäumer). Berlin, 1901.

CUSTINE, MARQUIS DE, *La Russie en 1839*. Paris. (English: *The Empire of the Czar or observations on the social, political and religious state and prospects of Russia made during a journey through that Empire*. London, 1843.)

KECHEJI-SHAPOVALOV, *Shenskoye dvisheniye v Rossii i sagranitsey* (The Women's Movement in Russia and Abroad). St. Petersburg, 1902.

KOVALYOV, K. N., *Istoricheskoye rasvitiye byta shenshchiny, braka i ssyemyi* (Historical Development of Women's Life, of Marriage and the Family). Compilation edited by Prof. S. Wolfson, Prometyey, Moscow, 1931.

MILOVIDOVA, E., *Shenskyi vopross i shenskoye dvisheniye* (The Women's Question and the Women's Movement). Anthology edited and prefaced by Clara Zetkin. Gossisdat, Moscow-Leningrad, 1929.

BIBLIOGRAPHY

PEKARSKYI, L., *Nauka i literatura v Rossii pri Petre Velikom* (Learning and Literature in Russia under Peter the Great). St. Petersburg, 1862.

POKROVSKYI, M., *Russkaya istoriya ss drevnyeyshikh vremyon.* Leningrad, 1924. (English : *History of Russia from the earliest Times to the Rise of Commercial Capitalism.* Martin Lawrence, 1931.)

ROSSOLOVSKAYA, V., *Rabotnitsa i krestyanka v khudoshestvennoy literature* (Working and Peasant Women in Belles Lettres). Gossisdat, Moscow-Leningrad, 1930.

SABYELIN, I., *Domashnyi byt russkikh tsarits v XVI i XVII stoletii* (Domestic Customs of the Russian Tsaritsas in the Sixteenth and Seventeenth Centuries). Moscow, 1901.

STRASSER, NADYA, *Die Russin.* S. Fischer Verlag, Berlin, 1917.

VOLKONSKAYA, M. N., PRINCESS, *Sapisski* (Memoirs). St. Petersburg, 1906. Translated from the French.

ZEDERBAUM, S., *Shenshchina v russkom revolutionnom dvishenii* (Women in the Russian Revolutionary Movement). Leningrad, 1927.

WOMEN IN PRE-REVOLUTIONARY RUSSIA

AMFITEATROV, A., *Shenshchina v obshchestvennykh dvisheniyakh v Rossii* (Women in the Social Movement in Russia). Geneva, Selbstverlag, 1905. (Also in the journal *Vssyemirnyi Vyestnik*, 1906, No. 9.)

— *Die Frau* (In *Russen über Russland*, edited by I. Melnik). Literarische Anstalt Rütten und Loening, Frankfurt a/M, 1906.

FIGNER, VERA, *Sapyechatlyennyi trud* (English : *Memoirs of a Revolutionist.* Martin Lawrence, 1929).

KOLLONTAY, A., *Istoriya dvisheniya rabotnitsy v Rossii* (History of the Women Workers' Movement in Russia).

KOVALYOV, K. N., *Istoricheskoye rasvitiye byta shenshchiny, braka i ssyemyi* (Historical Development of Women's Life, of Marriage and the Family). Compilation edited by Prof. S. Wolfson, Prometyey, Moscow, 1931.

KRUPSKAYA, N., *Vospominaniya* (Memoirs). Gossisdat, Moscow-Leningrad, 1926.

MILOVIDOVA, E., *Shenskyi vopross i shenskoye dvisheniye* (The Women's Question and the Women's Movement). Anthology edited and prefaced by Clara Zetkin. Gossisdat, Moscow-Leningrad, 1929.

Na shenskoy katorge (In the Women's *Katorga*). Compilation edited and prefaced by Vera Figner. Moscow, 1930.

399

BIBLIOGRAPHY

POKROVSKYI, M., *Russkaya istoriya ss drevnyeyshikh vremyon.* Leningrad, 1924. (English : *History of Russia from the earliest Times to the Rise of Commercial Capitalism.* Martin Lawrence, 1931.)

ROSSOLOVSKAYA, V., *Rabotnitsa i krestyanka v khudoshestvennoy literature* (Working and Peasant Women in Belles Lettres). Gossisdat, Moscow-Leningrad, 1930.

SASSULICH, VERA, *Vospominaniya* (Memoirs). Moscow, 1931.

STRASSER, NADYA, *Die Russin.* S. Fischer Verlag, Berlin, 1917.

TROTSKI, LEO, *History of the Russian Revolution.* Gollancz, 1932.

ZEDERBAUM, S., *Shenshchina v russkom revolutionnom dvishenii* (Women in the Russian Revolutionary Movement). Leningrad, 1927.

THE OCTOBER REVOLUTION OF 1917 AND THE LIBERATION OF WOMEN

BOGAT, A., *Shenshchiny-boytsy krassnoy armii* (Women as Soldiers in the Red Army). Moscow-Leningrad, 1930.

FREUND, DR. H., *Das Zivilrecht in der Sowjetunion.* Bensheimer, Mannheim, 1927.

GOIKHBARG, PROF. A. G., *Brachnoye, ssyemeynoye i opekunskoye pravo sovyetskikh respublik* (The Law of Marriage, the Family, and Wardship in the Soviet Republics). Gossisdat, 1920.

NYURINA, F., *Shenshchina v borybe sa novoye obshchestvo* (Woman in the Struggle for the new Society). Proletaryi, Charkov, 1930.

ROSSOLOVSKAYA, V., *Rabotnitsa i krestyanka v khudoshestvennoy literature* (Working and Peasant Women in Belles Lettres). Gossisdat, Moscow-Leningrad, 1930.

ZETKIN, CLARA, *Erinnerungen an Lenin.* Verlag für Literatur und Politik, Vienna-Berlin, 1929. (English : *Reminiscences of Lenin.* Modern Books, London, 1929.)

THE NEW SEXUAL ETHICAL CODE AND THEORY

Brak i ssyemya (Marriage and the Family). Compilation : Essays and Facts. Molodaya Gvardiya, Moscow-Leningrad, 1926.

FREUND, DR. H., *Das Zivilrecht in der Sowjetunion.* Bensheimer, Mannheim, 1927.

GOIKHBARG, PROF. A. G., *Ssravnityelynoye ssyemeynoye pravo* (Comparative Family Law). Moscow, 1927.

KOLLONTAY, A. M., *Lyubovy tryokh pokolenyi* (Love in Three Generations).

BIBLIOGRAPHY

ROMANOV, P., *Bes cheryomukhi.* Nyedra, Moscow, 1930. (English : *Without Cherry Blossom and Other Stories.* Ernest Benn, 1930.)

SALKIND, PROF. A. B., *Polovoy vopross v ussloviyakh sovyetskoy obshchestvennosti* (The Sex Question and Soviet Russian Public Opinion). Leningrad, 1926.

— *Revolutsiya i molodyosh* (The Revolution and Youth). Moscow, 1925.

SMITH, J., *Woman in Soviet Russia.* Vanguard Press, New York, 1928.

ZETKIN, CLARA, *Erinnerungen an Lenin.* Verlag für Literatur und Politik, Vienna-Berlin, 1929. (English: *Reminiscences of Lenin.* Modern Books, London, 1929.)

MOTHER AND CHILD

BOGAT, A., *Okhrana matyerinstva i mladyenchestva* (The Protection of Mothers and Children). Medgis, Moscow-Leningrad, 1931.

FEDER, E. A., *Ssotsialisticheskaya rekonstruktsiya byta i okhrana matyerinstva i mladyenchestva* (The Socialist Reconstruction of Life and the Protection of Mothers and Children). Gossmedisdat, 1931.

GOIKHBARG, PROF. A. G., *Ssravnityelynoye ssyemeynoye pravo* (Comparative Family Law). Moscow, 1927.

HALLE, PROF. FELIX, *Geschlechtsleben und Strafrecht.* Mopr Verlag, Berlin, 1931.

LEBEDYOVA, DR. VERA, *Proydyenniye etapy* (Past Phases). Moscow, 1927.

— *Ueber die soziale Fürsorge auf dem Gebiete des Mutterschafts- und Säuglingsschutzes.* Die Neue Generation, Berlin, 1928.

MILOVIDOVA, E., *Shenskyi vopross i shenskoye dvisheniye* (The Women's Question and the Women's Movement). Anthology, edited and prefaced by Clara Zetkin. Gossisdat, Moscow-Leningrad, 1929.

Okhrana matyerinstva i mladyenchestva (The Protection of Mothers and Children). Compilation edited by Perel and Lyubimov. Narkompross R.S.F.S.R., 1932.

RUBEN-WOLFF, DR. MED. M., *Der russische Nachwuchs.* In the journal *Die Neue Generation*, Berlin, 1927.

SSMIDOVICH, S., *O novom kodekssye sakonov o brake i ssyemye* (On the new Legal Code of Marriage and the Family). In the journal *Kommunistka*, I, Moscow, 1926.

SSYEMASHKO, N., *Die Grundtendenzen des Mutter- und Säuglingsschutzes.* In the journal *Die Neue Generation*, Berlin, 1928.

BIBLIOGRAPHY

Love, Marriage, and the Family

BOGDANOV, N., *Pervaya dyevushka* (The First Lass).

GLADKOV, F., *Pyanoye ssolntse* (The Drunken Sun).

— *Tsement* (Cement).

KOVALYOV, K. N., *Istoricheskoye rasvitiye byta shenshchiny, braka i ssyemyi* (Historical Development of Women's Life, of Marriage and the Family). Compilation edited by Prof. S. Wolfson, Prometyey, Moscow, 1931.

LASS, D. I., *Ssovremyennoye studenchestvo* (The Student of To-day). Molodaya Gvardiya, Moscow, 1928.

LINDSEY AND EVANS, *The Companionate Marriage*. Brentano, 1928.

NYEMILOV, A. V., *Biologicheskaya tragediya shenshchiny* (The Biological Tragedy of Woman).

PLATOSHKIN, M., *V doroge* (On the Road). Molodaya Gvardiya, Moscow.

SSEYFULLINA, L., *Virinyeya*.

SSMIRNOV, A., *Komssomol i dyevushki* (The *Komssomol* and the Girls). Priboy, Moscow, 1930.

STÖCKER, H., *Die Ehe als psychologisches Problem*. In the journal *Neue Generation*, October, 1929.

SSYEMYONOV, S., *Natalya Tarpova*. Molodaya Gvardiya, Moscow, 1930.

WOLFSON, PROF. S., *Brak i ssyemya v ikh istoricheskom rasvitii* (Marriage and the Family in their Historical Development). Prometyey, Moscow, 1931.

ZETKIN, CLARA, *Erinnerungen an Lenin*. Verlag für Literatur und Politik, Vienna-Berlin, 1929. (English: *Reminiscences of Lenin*. Modern Books, London, 1929.)

Towards the Abolition of Prostitution

BRONNER, PROF. V. M., *Boryba ss prostitutsiyey v R.S.F.S.R.* (The Struggle against Prostitution in the R.S.F.S.R.). Second Supplement to the Russian edition of Prof. A. Flexer's *Die Prostitution in Europa*. Moscow, 1926.

— *Prostitutsiya i puti k yeyo likvidatsii* (Prostitution and the Methods of abolishing it). Gossmedisdat, Moscow-Leningrad, 1931.

— *Prostitutsiya v Rossii do 1917 goda* (Prostitution in Russia up to 1917). Moscow, 1927.

GELYMANN, *Polovaya shisny ssovremyennoy molodyoshi* (The Sexual Life of the Youth of To-day). Moscow-Leningrad, 1923.

BIBLIOGRAPHY

HALLE, PROF. FELIX, *Geschlechtsleben und Strafrecht*. Mopr Verlag, Berlin, 1931.

OBOSNYENKO, *Podnadsornaya prostitutsiya St. Peterburga* (Regulated Prostitution in St. Petersburg). St. Petersburg, 1896.

POTALAK, P. V., *K trudovoy shisni* (Towards a Working Life). From the practice of the Institute for Labour Training for Female Juveniles. Moscow-Leningrad, 1931.

LASS, D. I., *Po puti k likvidatsii prostitutsii* (On the Road to the Abolition of Prostitution).

PASHITNOV, K. A., *Poloshenïye rabochevo klassa v Rossii* (The Situation of the Working Class in Russia). St. Petersburg, 1906.

STÜRMER, K. L., *Prostitutsiya v gorodakh* (Prostitution in the Towns). Report to a Conference of the Medical Department, St. Petersburg, 1897. (*Trudy*, Proceedings of the Conference, I.)

UCHEVATOV, A., *Is byta prostitutok nashikh dnyey* (From the Lives of Present-day Prostitutes). In the journal *Pravo i shisny*, 1928, I.

YANSHUL, PROF. I. I., Factory Inspector for the Moscow District: *Otchot sa 1885 god* (Report for the Year 1885). St. Petersburg, 1886.

YELISTRATOV, PROF. A., *Prostitutsiya v Rossii do revolutsii 1917 goda* (Prostitution in Russia before the Revolution of 1917). Supplement to the Russian edition of Prof. Flexer's *Die Prostitution in Europa*. Moscow, 1926.

WOMAN TAKES POSSESSION OF HER NEW REALM

ARTYUKHINA, A. V., *Na novom etape* (In a New Phase). Gossisdat 1930.

--- *Nakas delegatkam* (Instruction to the Delegates). Gossisdat, Moscow-Leningrad, 1928.

— *Delegatka na borybu sa kadry* (Delegates in the Struggle for the Cadres). Gossisdat, 1930.

BERESOVSKAYA, S., *Trudyashchiyessya shenshchiny—v ssotsialisticheskoye stroityelystvo* (Working Women—in Socialist Construction). Moscow, 1931.

DENISSOVA, M., *Die Frau im Betrieb* (In the journal *Sowjetkultur im Aufbau*, V.O.K.S., Moscow, 1932, No. 2/3).

DMITRIYEVA, S., *Die Frau in der Industrie* (V.O.K.S. organ of the Society for Cultural Relations with Foreign Countries, Moscow, 1932, No. 2).

G. A., *Traktoristki* (Women Tractor Drivers). In the journal

BIBLIOGRAPHY

Nashi dostisheniya, edited by M. Gorykyi, Moscow, March, 1931.

KOLLONTAY, A., *Trud shenshchiny v evolutsii khosyaystva* (Women's Work in the Development of Industry). Gossisdat, Moscow-Leningrad, 1923.

KRUPSKAYA, N. K., *O rabotye ssredi shenshchin* (Work among Women). Gossisdat, 1926.

MARSHEVA, B., *Shenskyi trud v 1931 godu* (Women's Work in 1931). In the journal *Voprossy truda*, Moscow, 1931, No. 1.

MELYNIKOV, A., *Shenshchina i oborona* (Woman and Defence). Sakkniga, 1930.

NOVIKOVA-VASHINTSOVA, Y., *O ssyebye* (About Herself). In the journal *Nashi dostisheniya*, edited by M. Gorykyi, Moscow, March, 1931.

NYURINA, F., *Trudyashchiyessya shenshchiny v oboronye S.S.S.R.* (Working Women in the Defence of the U.S.S.R.). Gossisdat, 1927.

— *Shenshchina v borybe sa novoye obshchestvo* (Woman in the Struggle for the New Society). Proletaryi, Charkov, 1930.

OSAROVSKAYA, O. E., *Marya Dmitriyevna Krivopolyenova, Babushkiny stariny* (Grandmother's Old Tales). Leningrad.

REISSNER, LARISSA, *Collected Works*, with an Introduction by Karl Radek. Gossidat, 1928.

SIBIRYAK, S., *Vom Kochtopf zur Werkbank*. Verlagsgenossenschaft ausländischer Arbeiter in der U.d.S.S.R., Moscow, 1932.

SSATS, N., AND ROSANOV, S., *Teatr dlya dyetyey* (Children's Theatres). Leningrad, 1925.

SSEYFULLINA, LYDIA, Monograph on (Critical Series). Moscow, 1928.

SSMIDOVICH, S., *Shenshchina v sovyetakh* (Women in the Soviets). In the journal *Vlasty sovyetov*, 1931, No. 7.

TRETYAKOV, S., *Vysov* (Challenge). *Kolkhos* Sketches *Federatsiya*. Moscow, 1930.

YELYKOVICH, K., AND SHILEYKO, A., *Udarnitsy* (Women Storm Workers). Ogis, Moscow, 1931.

THE NEW *BYT*

GRIGOROVICH, A., *Shivyom* (We Live). *Byt* Communes, Isdatyelystvo, V.T.S.P.S., Moscow, 1930.

KEYSERLING, COUNT HERMANN, *Amerika, der Aufgang einer neuen Welt*. Deutsche Verlagsanstalt, Stuttgart-Berlin, 1930.

BIBLIOGRAPHY

KOSHANYI, P., *Bes pyechnykh gorshkov* (Without Cooking Pots). Gossisdat, Moscow-Leningrad, 1927.

MEHNERT, K., *Die Jugend in Sowjetrussland*. S. Fischer Verlag, Berlin, 1932.

NAYSTAT, A., RYVKIN, I., SSOSSNOVIK, I., *Kommuny molodyoshi* (Youth Communes). Molodaya Gvardiya, Moscow, 1931.

ROMANOV, P., *Tovarishch Kisslyakov*. (Referred to in the text under the title of the German translation, *Three Pair of Silk Stockings*.)

INDEX

INDEX

Kolkhosi, 155, 157, 161, 162, 241, 256, 272, 276, 333, 334, 335, 336, 337, 354, 380, 381, 382, 385, 388, 389, 390, 391
Kollontay, Alexandra, 83, 89, 109, 110, 116, 121, 122, 123, 124, 149, 169, 284
Korolenko, 344, 369
Kotoshikhin, 11
Kovalyov, 202, 215
Krassnopyorov, 215
Krivopolyenova, Marya (poetess), 296, 297, 316
Krupskaya, Nadyeshda, 81, 82, 83, 87, 167, 216, 269, 282, 283, 284, 386
Krylenko (Public Prosecutor), 120
Kurskyi (People's Commissary of Justice), 117, 125

Lapkina, Marfa (film actress), 314, 315
Lebedyova, Dr. Vera, 137, 149
Lenin, Vladimir Ilyich, 81, 82, 83, 87, 93–8, 104, 105, 106, 112–16, 117, 145, 149, 150, 161, 165, 166, 174, 179, 205, 218, 219, 239, 245, 267, 281, 285, 289, 291, 292, 301, 311, 328, 346, 347, 361, 364, 365, 367
Lenintsi (Lenin Boys), 166
Lermontov, 30, 305
Likbes (liquidation of illiteracy), 290, 292
Lindsey, 201, 204
Lomonossov, 23
Lukerya, Babushka, 336
Lunacharskyi, 284, 297, 358
Luxemburg, Rosa, 103, 362

Marx, Marxism, 68, 75, 76, 77, 78, 79, 81, 103, 112, 113, 194, 305, 307, 328, 339
Mashurina (dress expert), 354
Matriarchate, 3, 4, 394, 395
Mayakovskyi, W. (author), 192
Mehnert, K., 353
Mendyeleva, Professor, 151

Merslyakov (author), 381
Monomachos, Prince Vladimir, 8
Morosova, 19

Narodnaya Volya (People's Freedom), 54, 59, 60, 61, 78, 81
Narodniki, 40, 68, 77, 78
Narodovoltsi, 68, 77, 78, 79
Naystat, 372, 377
Nestor, Chronicle of, 3
New Economic Policy, 108, 174, 224, 225
Nicholas I, 28, 30, 46, 48, 74, 221
Nicholas II, 88
Norinskyi, 80
Novikova-Vashintsova, Alyon-ushka (poetess), 297, 300, 316
Nyekrassov, 30, 31, 34, 35, 55
Nyemilov, Professor, 194, 195
Nyevyerov (poet), 272
Nyurina (in Ministry of Justice), 95, 284

Okhrmatmlad (Protection of Motherhood and Childhood), 150, 155, 159
Olearius, Adam, 14, 15, 16, 19, 355, 357
Olesha, Y. (dramatist), 178, 352
Olga, Princess, 5, 21
Ossoafiakhim (Society for Aircraft and Gas Defence), 276

Panfyerov (author), 334
Pekarskyi, 22
Perovskaya, Ssofya, 41, 56, 57, 58, 59, 65
Peter the Great, 14, 21, 22, 23, 25, 26
Pilnyak, 338
Platoshkin (novelist), 209
Plekhanov, 75, 76, 77
Pokrovskyi, 3, 48, 75
Possadnitsa, Marfa, 9
Pushkin, 26, 28, 238, 305, 369
Pyatiletka. See Five Years' Plan

Radek, Karl, 306, 328
Raskol schism, 19

For Product Safety Concerns and Information please contact our EU
representative GPSR@taylorandfrancis.com
Taylor & Francis Verlag GmbH, Kaufingerstraße 24, 80331 München, Germany